Social Problems

Social Problems

*A Christian Understanding
and Response*

Jack O. Balswick
and
J. Kenneth Morland

BAKER BOOK HOUSE
Grand Rapids, Michigan 49516

Copyright © 1990 by Baker Books
a division of Baker Book House Company
P.O. Box 6287, Grand Rapids, MI 49516-6287

Second printing, August 1994

Printed in the United States of America

Library of Congress Cataloging-in-Publication Data

Balswick, Jack O.
   Social problems : a Christian understanding and response / Jack O. Balswick and
J. Kenneth Morland.
         p.   cm.
   Includes bibliographical references and index.
   ISBN 0-8010-0979-0
   1. Social problems.   2. Sociology, Christian.   3. United States—Social conditions—
1980–   4. Church and social problems—United States.   I. Morland, J. Kenneth (John
Kenneth)   II. Title.
HN28.B35   1990
361.1—dc20   90-42128
                                                                                          CIP

Contents

Illustrations

Figures

Tables

Preface

The purpose of this book is to present a scientifically informed understanding of social problems and to suggest appropriate Christian responses. We have attempted to combine academic research and theory with a biblically based perspective on contemporary society and its structures.

The book is divided into three parts. Part One, "Introduction: *Social Problems, Sociological Analysis, and Christianity*," begins by defining the term *social problem* (chap. 1). We then examine the subject matter, methodology, and basic focuses of sociological analysis (chap. 2). Having presented this background material, we will lay a foundation on which to develop a Christian approach to social problems (chap. 3). We will see how theological beliefs have influenced responses to social problems in the past, and we will formulate a biblical understanding of social relationships and social structures. Part One concludes by presenting the five questions we will use as a guide in analyzing specific social problems: What is the evidence and nature of the concern? What are the dimensions of the problem? What are some of the explanations of the problem? What programs for prevention and treatment are being used to ameliorate the problem? and What should be done from a Christian perspective?

Part Two, "Analyses of Selected Social Problems," consists of in-depth examinations of eleven major social problems. While we have not exhausted the list of social problems that could have been analyzed, we do believe that the topics we have selected are among those generating the greatest concern in contemporary society. The primary focus in our analysis is upon social problems in the United States. However, because many social problems know no national boundaries—we are thinking, for example, of environmental quality, poverty and world hunger, and maintaining peace in a nuclear age—some chapters have a worldwide perspective.

In Part Three we suggest paths which might be taken by Christians who want to become seriously involved in efforts to effect social change.

The strategies outlined here are broader and more comprehensive than the suggestions in Part Two as to how best to approach particular social problems.

Although most of our graduate training has been in the field of sociology, Ken has a bachelor of divinity degree in social ethics from Yale Divinity School, while Jack has postdoctoral seminary training in theological and biblical studies. While we are academic sociologists, having spent a total of sixty-five years in writing and teaching at the college, university, and seminary levels, both of us have been actively involved in efforts to change society. We have struggled to integrate our academic knowledge of social problems with our understanding of Scripture.

We have agonized over the extent to which the Christian church in our society has divided itself by emphasizing either the personal gospel or the social gospel. Like many Christians, we too have struggled to find a balance between faith and works—between witnessing to the personal regenerating power of the gospel and actively endeavoring to change evil, unjust, dehumanizing social structures. It is our hope that this book might be a guide, a road map as it were, for other Christians who are also struggling to be faithful to the total Christian message in a complex society straining to make it through the twentieth century.

For their assistance and encouragement at various stages of our research and writing, we would like to thank Sandy Bennett, Nathan Brooks, Ruth Ann Edwards, John Good, and Leslie Nation. We have also greatly appreciated the enthusiasm and diligent work of our editors Allan Fisher, Jim Weaver, and Ray Wiersma of Baker Book House, and cartoonist Ron Wheeler. Finally, we have found a constant source of support and encouragement in our wives Judy and Margaret.

Part 1

Introduction

Social Problems, Sociological Analysis, and Christianity

1

A Definition of Social Problems

It was the best of times, it was the worst of times, it was the age of wisdom, it was the age of foolishness, it was the epoch of belief, it was the epoch of incredulity, it was the season of Light, it was the season of Darkness, it was the spring of hope, it was the winter of despair.

Dickens, *A Tale of Two Cities*

It is the best of times! Life is great! We have never had it so good! Most of us, after a restful sleep on a cushiony mattress in our extrawide bed, wake up to a melodious tune from our clock radio. We tumble out of bed, take a hot shower to become fully awake, proceed to dress after deciding which of our closetful of clothes to wear, and then continue on to the kitchen where we decide what to eat from our well-stocked shelves. As we sit down to eat breakfast, we begin to reflect on our good fortune. All of our basic human needs are met—shelter, food, clothing. Moreover, we possess a whole host of labor-saving devices which operate at the mere push of a button—a stove, microwave oven, vacuum cleaner, dishwasher, garbage disposal, washer and dryer. In fact, many of our mechanical devices are self-operating. We use automatic timers to wake us up and to water our lawn, and we are even lullabied to sleep by a radio which will shut off by itself.

As we begin to eat, we turn on the television set and open the morning newspaper to find out what has been happening in the world while we have been asleep. We discover that the news has not changed much in general, only in the specifics—another attempted hijacking, rumors of a radiation leak at a nuclear-power plant, the shooting of a husband by his wife, a report that the fish caught in a particular bay are unsafe to eat because of pollution, and the likelihood of a smog alert. In suppressing the urge to go back to sleep to the sound of soothing music, we begin to think that this is indeed the worst of times.

What Charles Dickens thought to be true of late-eighteenth-century England is also true of the United States at the close of the twentieth century. Good arguments can be set forth in support of the notion that the present era is both the best of times and the worst of times. On the one hand, we are reaping the benefits of the technological revolution as well as just beginning to realize the even greater luxuries that computers will undoubtedly bestow upon us. From a technological point of view, our potential standard of living would seem to be unlimited. On the other hand, many of these technological advances appear to be mixed blessings, inasmuch as they have helped to spawn such societal maladies as industrial pollution and nuclear war. Moreover, there is evidence which suggests that the most advanced countries are the very ones experiencing the worst problems with alcoholism, drug abuse, mental illness, motherhood without marriage, divorce, runaway children, alienation, juvenile delinquency, adult crime, and neglect of the elderly. At the same time, we continue to be confronted with racial discrimination and prejudice, poverty, and world hunger—conditions that have plagued humankind throughout much of its history. Although there may be much about life in present-day America that has never been better, our society is still faced with a multitude of social ills.

In addition to these diverse problems, the sheer complexity of social life with its multiple layers of organization makes it impossible for the average person to even begin to understand the causes, to say nothing of the cures, of these problems. In response, most of us simply adopt a posture of noninvolvement. And for those Christians who do become socially involved, the results are often disappointing—an attempt to help a drug addict fails, an effort to aid an unmarried pregnant teenager is undone by a second pregnancy one year later, an endeavor to rid one's neighborhood of a theater showing X-rated movies is dismissed in a court of law.

Because of these disappointing results, much of our so-called social action becomes narcissistic, that is, simply an attempt to better our own lives. We attend seminars in an effort to make our marriages happier, to become better parents, to develop better relational skills or a more integrated sense of our selfhood. This self-centered orientation is reflected in the vast number of self-help books available in virtually every Christian bookstore.

Our purpose in writing this book is not to heap guilt upon Christians, many of whom already feel guilty and frustrated about their lack of meaningful social involvement. Rather, we wish to help Christians understand the causes of social problems as well as to give them direction and inspiration which will in turn enable them to engage in much-needed social action. This task can be accomplished only by seeing the roles of sociology and Christianity as being complementary to one another. That is, while sociology can provide us with an understanding of the causes of social problems and the probable effectiveness of proposed remedies, a Christian framework is needed to provide the foundational theological truths that will help us to identify morally objectionable social situations and to decide what should be done about them.

An Overview of Our Approach

Most approaches to social problems can be classified as either *exhortative* or *analytical*. The exhortative approach stresses the urgency of dealing with particular situations and advocates specific solutions. This is the approach of business, labor, religious organizations, conservationists, and racial groups. For example, the National Council of Churches, the Sierra Club, the National Association for the Advancement of Colored People, and the National Rifle Association promote actions designed to implement their partisan views.

The analytical approach, on the other hand, does not involve itself in promoting specific social-action programs; rather, it concentrates on understanding the problems. Such a methodology seeks to determine all pertinent facts, including the points of view of different groups, and to analyze these facts in as unbiased a manner as possible.

We do not believe that the exhortative and analytical approaches are mutually exclusive; rather, they are complementary to one another. In our analysis of each of the social problems to be discussed in this book, we will utilize the sociological perspective to gain an understanding of the problem. In addition, we will be employing a Christian perspective when we advocate a specific form of social action. Without the sound foundation that sociology can give, Christian interpretations of social conditions may well be erroneous. Conversely, without Christian interpretations, sound sociological understanding will be quite sterile. That is, it will be sterile unless it is infused with a sense of values which can give guidance in determining (1) which situations warrant being defined as a social problem; (2) what the desired end is to be; and (3) which of the various means to reach that end are morally justifiable.

For example, a sense of values rooted in Christianity can help us answer these three fundamental questions regarding the nagging issue of poverty. First of all, on what basis can instances of poverty be classified as a social problem? Is the criterion to be used only that of material deprivation; or does poverty also include psychological, spiritual, and moral dimensions? To what extent is poverty a culturally relative concept—especially in light of the fact that the average poor person in the

United States would, on the basis of income, belong to the middle class in any country of the Two-Thirds World? (Throughout this book we will refer to economically poor countries as the "Two-Thirds World," a more inclusive term than "Third World.")

Second, if the goal is to end poverty, what should this goal entail? Is poverty, as a social problem, eliminated when minimal levels of food, clothing, and shelter are available to all persons? Or is poverty eliminated when every person is a member of a household with a car, a color television, and access to full-time employment? Should we be more concerned about poverty in our country than in other countries?

Third, which of the many potential means for the elimination of poverty are morally justified? For instance, Karl Marx's ideas of a utopian state of communism were developed in part as an answer to poverty. Now regardless of whether or not this ideal state would work, is it morally justified? Or again, our country might give minimal levels of food, clothing, and shelter to persons in need. Is this morally acceptable? Finally, one of the main factors contributing to poverty in developing countries is a runaway growth in population. Reducing such growth would undoubtedly do much to alleviate global poverty. Methods of population reduction might include forced sterilization, contraception, abortion, and infanticide, each of which would be technically effective. But are these methods ethically justified?

Our approach to understanding and dealing with social problems will be an integrative one involving the utilization of social-science research and theory as well as biblical insights. In taking a Christian approach, we will indicate areas where society needs to be better sensitized by Christian values in the judgments which it makes. Also, we will discuss the role of Christians, both as individuals and as part of the body of Christ, to be salt and light to a needy world.

What Is a Social Problem?

We began this chapter by suggesting that the present can be viewed as a time of both unlimited potential and unparalleled danger. But though the modern setting is unique, social problems are certainly not new. The term *social problem* can be used to refer to a wide range of concerns—crime, poverty, water pollution, racial prejudice, and divorce, which, on the surface at least, appear to be unrelated. Yet in all of these situations there are similarities that cause them to be categorized as social problems. First, they are *problems* in the sense that they are troublesome and therefore demand a solution. Second, they are *social* in that they are causes for concern among members of a group who agree that they need to work together to improve the situation. Formally defined, *a social problem is any situation which the members of a group consider to be undesirable and which they think should be remedied by cooperative action.*

Figure 1

Structure of a Social Problem

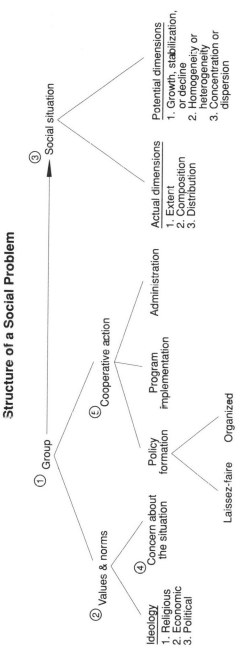

Figure 1 is a visual representation of the structure of a social problem. There are five elements involved here. First is the group itself. Now an issue that concerns only the members of a particular family, church, or community might conceivably be designated a social problem. It is usual, however, for the group to be a society or nation. Accordingly, we will deal only with situations considered to be undesirable by the people of the United States as a whole.

Second, there are values which are held by the group and serve as a basis for their judging a particular situation to be a social problem. (For a discussion of the major values of American society see pp. 28–34.) Values are based on and emerge out of the beliefs held by a group. Taken together, these beliefs constitute ideology.

The main ideologies in any culture are usually religious, economic, and political. In most societies, including ours, religious ideology is the most important element in the formation of societal values. Similarly, it is from a religious group's theology (explicit or implicit) that its norms emerge. In the Soviet Union, by contrast, the economic ideology is the most important, although some suggest that even here the beliefs in communism function more as a religion than an economic system. As we consider social problems in the United States, we should ask ourselves where we too as a people are allowing our values and norms to be established more by our economic and political ideology than by our Christian beliefs.

Although the values of the American populace as a whole have determined what we will present as social problems, we will nevertheless state when we think closer adherence to Christian ideology would yield an alternative assessment. We believe that all of the social problems which will be analyzed in this book deserve to be so defined on the basis of both general American values and Christian ideology. However, we will also suggest possible societal blind spots such as attitudes toward materialism, exploitation of the powerless, abortion, and dehumanization—conditions which Americans as a whole may not view as being social problems, but which Christians do so regard.

The third element is the situation, any aspect of group life that is considered undesirable by certain members of the group. An example is the estrangement and alienation of many workers in modern society. The situation includes the circumstances of the individuals most directly affected, for example, victims of discrimination because of race or gender, individuals suffering from drug addiction, and those in poverty. The situation also includes the effects of these estrangements and undesirable circumstances on others, for instance, the family of the drug addict, those from whom the addict steals to support his habit, and society itself, which loses the addict's potential contribution. If the situation causes concern to the group and calls for remedy, it is classified as a social problem.

Concerns may exist regarding both the actual and the potential dimensions of the situation. Thus, much of the present discussion pertaining to environmental issues is directed toward the destruction which will occur if current societal practices are allowed to continue. Assessment of the actual situation includes data on its extent, composition, and distribution. The potential dimensions of a situation include whether it will grow, stabilize, or decline, whether it will be homogeneous or heterogeneous, and whether it will be concentrated or dispersed.

Fourth is the judgment by the members of the group that a social problem does indeed exist. According to our definition, if the members of a particular group are concerned about the situation, it is a social problem; if they are not concerned, it is not a social problem.

In order to be true to God's will, the church must attempt at times to prick the conscience of the American people to sensitize them with regard to a particular situation. Past examples of this sort of activity include the church's stance on such issues as child labor, slavery, racial discrimination, and abortion.

The question might be raised, How many members of a group must be disturbed for a situation to be labeled a social problem? Our definition does not intend to imply that all members of a group must be concerned. Rather, what is meant is that the greater the number of persons who are concerned, the more readily will the situation be viewed as a social problem.

Figure 2 will help us at this point to see that there is a continuum between social issues and social problems. When public opinion toward a social situation is evenly split, we have a social issue. A current example is the matter of smoking in public places, since the American people appear to be rather divided on this question. Fearing that public opinion may be turning against smoking in public places, the tobacco industry is currently campaigning for tolerance of smokers. Abortion is found in the center of the continuum because the public has been increasingly concerned, though there is still a vocal portion of the population who

Figure 2
A Continuum of Public Opinion toward Social Situations

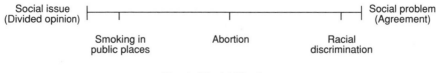

Social issue (Divided opinion) |———————————————————————————| Social problem (Agreement)

Smoking in public places   Abortion   Racial discrimination

Types of Social Situations

argue for abortion as a legitimate means of birth control. An example of almost total agreement on the undesirability of a social situation is racial discrimination. Although racial prejudice continues to exist, numerous federal laws have been passed in the last thirty years in an effort to eradicate discrimination.

Another question to be raised is, How intense or deep must a concern be before a situation may be called a social problem? While the answer to this query does not lend itself to mathematical precision, it is correct to say that an issue which is a subject of concern for relatively few persons is not properly labeled a social problem even if those individuals happen to be passionate and morally correct. However, many such situations develop into what may be categorized as social problems when a mere handful of people are able to persuade others of the harmfulness of a particular societal practice. It was in precisely this manner that child labor and slavery came to be regarded as social problems.

In order to determine the extent and intensity of concern about social situations, one must systematically observe what people say disturbs them. This can be done through nationwide public-opinion polls and more-limited polls conducted by religious groups, businesses, political organizations, newspapers, and magazines as well as television and radio stations. An accurate perspective can also be derived by analyzing the content of newspapers, magazines, television, radio, and movies, all of which reflect public opinion to a certain degree. In addition, government hearings, proposed legislation, and newly formed interest groups also serve as relatively reliable indicators of those social issues which concern the American public at any given time.

The fifth element in the structure of a social problem is the group's belief that the undesirable situation cannot be effectively dealt with on an individual or piecemeal basis, but instead needs the input of all of the group members. Once the group judges a social situation to be undesirable, it will begin to take cooperative action in an attempt to ameliorate the situation. The first cooperative action which the group needs to take is policy formation. This step involves drawing up appropriate goals and agreeing on the means to fight the social problem. As an example, the stated goal in the case of drug abuse could be merely to contain the problem, to reduce it, or to eliminate the problem completely. Although few Americans believe that the problem can be entirely eliminated, as a society we have very little difficulty holding this up as an ideal goal while we make reduction of the problem our actual goal.

Agreeing on the means of reducing drug abuse is still another matter. One of the hindrances to effectively combating any problem in a society as diverse as our own is that there exist a myriad number of perceptions as to how that problem should be resolved. Thus, there are some today who argue that the problem of drug abuse in America could be eliminated by legalizing certain narcotics, while others believe that the problem would be most effectively handled if those who deal in drugs were imprisoned for life or even put to death. From this it is clear that social ills sometimes fail to be resolved not because of a lack of agreement pertaining to the undesirability of the situation, but because of the group's inability to reach a consensus on goals and means at the policy-formation stage.

Policy formation can be either laissez-faire or highly organized. It is usually somewhere between these two extremes, with a laissez-faire approach taken during the early phase and increased organization seen in the later phase. A case in point is the reaction to gender discrimination: various factions within the women's movement have in recent years attempted to unite in order to form a joint policy against sexism.

The second stage in cooperative action is program implementation—setting in motion the policy formulated during the first stage. The group commits itself to a course of action which it believes will achieve its goal.

The third stage of cooperative action involves the administration of the program—establishing and maintaining structures which will alleviate the social ill. The human resources available must be organized so that everyone is striving to achieve the same end via the same means. Only in this way does the project have any chance of succeeding.

Because a large proportion of the population has a very low degree of commitment to combating any given social problem, it is crucial that there be a consensus among those who are highly concerned. This consensus must be of two types: (1) a technical consensus among the experts who design the problem-solving programs, and (2) a consensus on values—all highly concerned persons must agree on the desirability and legitimacy of each step of the problem-solving process.

Efforts which are designed to resolve social problems often begin as informal experimental programs, but are eventually transformed into a part of governmental bureaucracy. In fact, many municipal, state, and federal agencies began in just this manner. Having achieved this status, the problem-solving effort becomes institutionalized.

Once a program becomes institutionalized, there are vested interest groups which argue for continuation of the program in its present form. Unfortunately, many of these programs, which were originally intended to help solve a problem, actually contribute to that very problem. We have in view programs which perpetuate dependency rather than empower the victims of social problems. We urge the reader to carefully consider whether each of the social programs described in the following pages empowers its clients or encourages dependency.

The Relativity of Social Problems

Since the existence of a social problem is determined by the members of a particular society, it can be expected that what are defined as social problems will likely vary from society to society and, over a period of time, vary within the same society. The relativity of what are considered to be problems in any given society should sensitize the Christian community to its important task of critically examining existing conditions in light of the enduring truth of Scripture. In addition, the church must continually engage in a process of critical self-examination lest it be so shaped by secular values and beliefs that it renders itself incapable of being the leavening influence which God intends it to be in a fallen and hurting world.

Illustrations that social problems do vary over time and within the same society abound. For instance, at the turn of this century, great concern was shown for the problem of child labor, and plans were proposed for its elimination. Today, though, concern is rarely expressed about this social condition since it has been virtually eliminated. Comparatively new social problems in the United States include the pollution of our air and water, the redefinition of sex roles, and the care of the elderly. On the other hand, some social problems in America, such as juvenile delinquency and adult crime, have persisted over a long period of time, while drug abuse is the object of greater concern today than it was in the past. It is clear, then, that as societal conditions change, so do our conceptions of what constitute social problems.

The variation of social problems among cultures is a reflection of different views regarding what is desirable and what undesirable. Thus, when Americans assume that the lack of freedom of expression and mobility in totalitarian societies should be considered social problems, they may be making an ethnocentric judgment that is not shared by the citizens of those societies. On the other hand, when those who live in communistic countries define as a social ill the American penchant to criticize the government, they may also be expressing an ethnocentric bias, since such behavior is readily accepted in this country.

There is a significant implication here. According to our definition of a social problem, those living outside the bounds of our society cannot determine what social problems exist within our culture. Individuals who attempt to define the problems of another culture are merely expressing their own prejudices. What are we to say, then, about the clear teaching of Scripture that the church must unceasingly critique those abuses which it sees being committed anywhere in the world? We must recognize that every culture's prerogative of defining its own social problems in no way negates the church's obligation to speak prophetically. If the Old Testament teaches us anything at all, it is that God's prophets continually rebuked those sinful beliefs and practices which they observed both within Israel and outside of her borders.

Earlier we mentioned the church's speaking out on such issues as slavery and child labor. Currently, certain segments of the church are attempting to speak prophetically about such issues as abortion, pornography, the nuclear-arms buildup, drug abuse, poverty, pollution, and racial prejudice. Different segments of the church are speaking about different issues. Thus, while the conservative wing of Christianity is addressing such issues as abortion, pornography, and drug abuse, the more liberal wing is relatively silent on these subjects. It has chosen to focus instead on the nuclear-arms buildup, poverty, and racial discrimination—issues on which the conservative branch is noticeably silent. Tragically, the church universal is here seen to have involved itself in a

DO YOU THINK THIS IS WHAT THE APOSTLE PAUL MEANT WHEN HE SAID THAT THE BODY OF CHRIST IS A UNIT MADE UP OF MANY PARTS?

contradiction by condemning abortion and, at the same time, affirming the construction of weaponry capable of inflicting massive damage.

Perhaps it is too much to expect that a community as diverse as the church universal can reach a consensus on social issues. Each member of the body of Christ should be concerned, however, when the church as a whole is working against itself. The apostle Paul states in 1 Corinthians 12:24–26: "But God has combined the various parts of the body, giving special honour to the humbler parts, so that there might be no sense of division in the body, but that all its organs might feel the same concern for one another. If one organ suffers, they all suffer together. If one flourishes, they all rejoice together" (NEB). Since another theme of 1 Corinthians 12 is that God gives different gifts to different parts of the body, it is permissible for different parts of the church to focus their attention upon different social situations. This does not mean, however, that the body should be working against itself, as seems to be the case today. All segments of the church must exhibit a consistent social concern and involvement!

Topics for Review, Reflection, and Discussion

1. Is it really necessary to study social problems before attempting to do something about them?

2. Distinguish between the exhortative and analytical approaches to social problems. Do you agree that the two can be integrated into a single approach?

3. Make a list of situations that society as a whole regards as social issues, but the Christian community considers social problems. Are there situations that one segment of the Christian community identifies as social issues, and another segment views as problems?

4. Give examples of situations that in the past were considered social problems, but are no longer so regarded. Give examples of situations that, though they are considered social problems today, were not so regarded in the past. Why the change?

5. Are there areas in which the church should be taking a more prophetic role in sensitizing the public to the immorality of certain social situations?

2

Sociological Analysis

The major purpose of our sociological analysis is to increase understanding of social problems. The analyses presented in this book have a fourfold focus: (1) the nature of the concern; (2) the dimensions of the problem; (3) explanations of the problem; and (4) proposed solutions. Before discussing these four steps of analysis, however, we need to look at the subject matter and method of sociology.

The Subject Matter

Sociology can be defined, in brief, as the scientific study of human groups. Human groups, then, are the subject matter of sociology, and scientific investigation is its method. It is the task of sociology to seek for and to formulate the principles or laws that underlie the way human groups develop, are held together, carry on their existence, and change. Such an approach assumes that human groups, like the physical world, are subject to the laws of nature. In other words, it assumes regularity in the structure and function of human groups.

By human group is meant two or more persons bound together by an interdependent function and a common set of norms, values, and goals. Groups may be comparatively small, for example, a family, a teenage gang, or a bridge club. They may be comparatively large, for instance, a political party, a community, or a nation. They may exist over a long period of time, as the Roman Catholic Church; or they may be of short duration, as an ad hoc committee.

A human group is to be distinguished from a social category, by which is meant a classification on the basis of some socially significant characteristic held in common. We may put persons into categories on the basis of age or race or sex or occupation. These categories are not "human groups" by our definition, for the persons included in them do not necessarily depend on one another for the performance of some function, nor do they necessarily share common norms, values, and goals. Thus, "medical doctor" is a social category comprising all those who are engaged in this profession. On the other hand, the American Medical Association is an example of what we are here defining as a human group. True, it is composed of medical doctors, but all members of the association have different tasks to perform to keep the organization operating, and they share certain norms, values, and goals in the process.

This focus on the human group does not mean that sociology considers the individual to be unimportant. Indeed, it is generally accepted by sociologists that it is only for purposes of analysis that the group can actually be considered apart from the individual. Although sociologists do not focus on the individual, they, either explicitly or implicitly, accept certain assumptions about the basic nature of human beings. The foremost of these assumptions is that individuals are social beings who develop elaborate language systems by which they create and transmit culture. As Christian sociologists, we in addition assume that every individual is created in the image of God, but exists as a distorted image of God. More specifically, we assume that the individual is (1) free in part to behave creatively and spontaneously; (2) self-conscious and capable of choosing goals; (3) capable of doing evil as well as good; and (4) responsible for his or her own behavior.

To affirm these aspects of human nature is not to say that individuals are not also products of human groups. The basic contention of sociologists is that the behavior of individuals cannot be fully understood apart from the groups to which they belong. We agree with French sociologist Emile Durkheim's claim that society is a reality sui generis with a nature of its own. For while men's and women's actions in society are to a large extent determined by certain basic universal human qualities, society is neither shaped nor limited by these qualities.

All groups are composed of individuals, and all individuals belong to groups. On the basis of the sociological and Christian assumptions about being human which we have mentioned, we submit the following proposals:

1. Human groups are capable of creating symbolic meaning and thus their own view of reality.
2. Human groups are not the sole producer of reality and of human nature. Individuals and human groups maintain a dialectical relationship: human groups are a human product, but nevertheless an independent reality; and human beings are social products, but not exclusively so.

3. Human groups are free to distort reality. Christians understand that human groups do so because they exist in a state of separation or alienation from the God who created reality.
4. Human groups are partially motivated by selfish interests.
5. They justify their selfish behavior on the basis of their definitions of reality. Humans are not only capable of selfish activities, but they are also capable of defining reality in such a distorted way that they do not interpret their selfish behavior as selfish.
6. Human groups are a source of nurturance, identity, and support, as well as of hostility, tension, and conflict.

The Method

When we define sociology as the scientific study of human groups, we are making certain claims. Empirical investigation is relied upon as the means of uncovering the nature of human groups. By "empirical" we mean actual observation and measurement as opposed to armchair speculation. Consider what this signifies for a study of whether a disproportionately high number of juvenile delinquents come from broken homes. The question might be answered by logical deduction: children from broken families have a home life less favorable than do children from unbroken families; they have less supervision, are more likely to get into trouble, and therefore become delinquent. But the sociologist would insist on firsthand investigations of the backgrounds of delinquent and nondelinquent children to see if, in actuality, a significantly higher proportion of children from broken homes become delinquents. No matter how reasonable a generalization might appear, it cannot be accepted by the sociologist without substantiation by empirical research. This is not to say that sociological insights cannot be obtained through novels or poetry or journalistic writings. Rather, it is to assert that while such insights can provide starting points for empirical research, they cannot take the place of that research.

Having the goal of objectivity is not sufficient in itself to guarantee objectivity. Therefore sociologists have devised ways of checking and improving the validity, reliability, and precision of the measures used in research. A measure is valid to the degree that it is true; that is, a measure of what is actually present. A measure is reliable to the extent that it is consistent, meaning that it will always measure in the same way. Finally, a measure is precise to the extent that it quantifies all results in terms of the same standard unit of measurement.

The scientific method also has its limitations. There are certain types of questions with which sociology cannot deal. It cannot answer questions which are not susceptible to empirical observations and the checking of those observations by others. Thus, it cannot deal with religious and philosophical questions: What is the meaning of life? What is the good society? What is morally right, and what is morally wrong? What action should be taken in a given situation? What sociologists can do is find out how members of a group define the meaning of life, the good society, moral right, and moral wrong. They can, through investigation and within limitations, point out the consequences of certain kinds of actions. The knowledge gained through such sociological inquiry can help people come to conclusions about these questions, even though sociological data cannot give answers per se.

The method of sociology restricts not only the types of questions with which it can deal. It also restricts the kinds of answers it can give. For example, sociology states what is in fact true of human groups, and not what ought to be true of them. Its answers are stated in terms of probabilities rather than absolutes. A sociologist cannot declare with absolute certainty, but only with probability, that a particular relationship exists between social phenomena. A sociologist cannot predict that class mobility (i.e., movement from one social class to another) in America will increase regardless of the situation. The most one can do is to state the conditions under which the rate of class mobility is likely to change. The sociologist might say, for example, that if educational and occupational opportunities are opened more equally to all Americans, then it is likely that class mobility will increase.

The point is that sociology, as the science of human groups, cannot tell a society what it ought or ought not to do. Nor can it make absolute statements about the nature of human groups or unconditionally predict their future. What it attempts to do, through the scientific method, is to increase knowledge and understanding of human groups. It is, however, our contention that such knowledge and understanding can be practically applied, something which we will attempt in this book.

The Fourfold Focus of Sociological Analysis

The Nature of the Concern: Violation of a National Value

In defining a social problem as a situation which members of the society think is undesirable, we imply that a value judgment is being made. Thus, one way to determine the nature of the concern about a particular situation is to infer which of the values shared by the society are being violated. As our first step, then, we need to ascertain what the basic values shared by Americans are.

A value is anything to which worth is ascribed. Values may include objects, character traits, actions, beliefs, and goals that are considered to be desirable for the individual and for the society. Studies of American society, although conducted in different ways and over a considerable period of time, have generally agreed that there are values that appear and reappear in judgments made by Americans (DuBois 1955; Gillin 1955, Kluckhohn 1970; Williams 1970; Cochran 1985). While these studies have found that not all Americans agree with all of the values, that some are of greater importance than others, that some are in conflict, and that they vary to some degree by region and ethnic background, yet, taken together, they are one way to summarize what is characteristically American. We shall discuss ten of the major values reported by research.

Inherent worth of the individual

Basic to much of American life is belief in the importance and worth of every human being. This belief stands in contrast to the viewpoint in nations with centralized governments, where society is paramount and the individual secondary. Of course, Americans believe that the society and groups within it are important and must be maintained—not, however, at the expense of the individual. The family and the school emphasize that every child is an individual, different from all others, and is to be treated as such. In a political democracy every citizen can participate through voting and expressing opinions to elected representatives. Government is said to exist to serve the individual, not vice versa. In marriage the happiness of the individuals is stressed, and there is an increase in the number of marriages being dissolved because one or both of the partners are unhappy. Finally, the Jewish and Christian faiths insist that every person is a child of God and therefore of infinite worth. This belief in the inherent worth of the individual lies at the heart of the concern over almost every social problem with which we will deal, for in most cases it is unequal treatment of certain categories of individuals and barriers to individual fulfilment that lead members of the society to view the situation as undesirable and needing to be remedied.

Freedom of the individual

Freedom is closely related to the worth of the individual. Since persons are valuable in themselves, they should not be unduly frustrated or directed by others; rather, they should be allowed to express themselves in terms of their own individuality. They should have freedom in determining how much schooling is desirable, selecting an occupation, choosing a marriage partner, espousing a religious faith, voting for political candidates, protesting the conduct of public affairs, joining with others in a peaceful way to oppose or support various causes. These individual freedoms are often cited as basic to the American way of life and contrasted with the control of citizens by totalitarian states.

There is, of course, a recognition of the limitation on individual freedom. A distinction is made between liberty and license. It has also been argued that the recent emergence of a hyperindividualism unchecked by altruistic constraints can endanger social unity and cause problems to arise (Bellah et al. 1985). Within these limitations, however, individual liberty is of critical importance to Americans, and its denial results in expressions of concern.

Equality in treatment and opportunity

Following from and reinforcing the inherent worth of and freedom for each individual is belief in equal treatment of all. If everyone is of inherent worth as a person, each individual is, in effect, equal in value to everyone else and should be treated in the same way as others, with the same opportunity for development. Furthermore, freedom of expression means little unless there is an opportunity for expression. This conviction of equality is at the heart of political democracy, which gives every citizen opportunity to vote and to hold office. All Americans, regardless of social standing, are supposed to be equal before the law and to have an equal chance for a fair trial when they are accused of breaking a law. Public education gives all children, regardless of their background, the opportunity to attend school. Religion in America stresses the equality of all before God, and many religious organizations proclaim the equal chance of all to secure salvation. For the most part, husband and wife are thought of as equal partners in the marriage relationship, and children are (ideally) treated without favoritism.

This idea of equality does not, however, carry with it a belief that all persons are equal in natural endowment. There are individual differences; and if all have equal opportunities, then it may be assumed that those who have the greatest ability and work hardest will be the most successful. Therefore, inequality in wealth and position is acceptable as long as the opportunity to advance is the same for all. When such opportunity is denied, there is cause for concern.

Hard work

Americans believe that hard work is desirable and necessary for achievement. This belief in mastery and control through effort has been termed "effort-optimism" by some writers (DuBois 1955). The optimism characteristic of Americans is founded on the reality of hard work and ingenuity. While individuals may be accorded freedom and equality of opportunity, they can be sure of success only if they apply themselves sufficiently. Promotion in one's occupation comes through exertion and cooperation with those with whom one works. Good grades can be attained if one studies long and hard enough. Electing a political candidate may require more than casting one's vote. It may also require persuading one's friends to vote, distributing literature, and actively promoting the candidate in other ways. One's marriage can succeed if one works at it. Americans even work hard at recreation as they seek to improve their golf, bridge, tennis, or dancing in the belief that sufficient practice can bring about near perfection in almost any endeavor. A slogan of America's bicentennial celebration was, "The spirit of achievement is the spirit of America." And achievement is possible only through effort and persistence. This theme is expressed in concerns about social problems in two ways. (1) The continuance of a social problem over a long period of time is attributed to our failure to give it sufficient time and attention. (2) It is generally held that individuals and groups manifesting undesirable behavior—alcoholism, delinquency, alienation, racial prejudice—have not tried hard enough or are not sufficiently motivated to eliminate such behavior.

Practicality

Americans place a high value on the practical. There is emphasis on the application of knowledge in engineering and technology. We can see this theme operating in business and industry, where the employee who is highly productive is given special rewards. Schooling must be useful if it is to be worthwhile; that is, it should enable the graduate to get a better job, a larger income, a higher social status than the nongraduate can attain. Political leaders should have their feet on the ground and avoid unrealistic goals. Religious affiliation can provide not only spiritual nourishment, but also a chance to develop friendships and business contacts which will contribute to one's social status and economic success. Even recreation can be useful by providing relaxation so one can work more enthusiastically and become healthier physically and mentally. Practicality is also a theme in our concern about social problems—we wonder whether proposed solutions are bringing about the desired results. If welfare or educational programs do not work in a clearly demonstrable way, they are considered impractical and abandoned. Certain forms of behavior that are considered problems are discouraged by demonstrating that they are not useful for the individual or the society and should therefore be eliminated.

Efficiency

Efficiency refers to getting something done with a minimal expenditure of time and energy. Like practicality, efficiency is heavily emphasized in economic life, where practical application of technique has increasingly resulted in greater productivity in a shorter time and with less human effort. It is significant that the concept of scientific management developed in this country, as did time and motion studies that try to discover the most efficient way to utilize worker effort. It is also significant that "businesslike" is virtually synonymous with "efficient." Increased speed in transportation is another indication of the emphasis on efficiency, for increased speed saves time, money, and human energy. Efficiency is stressed in many other areas of American life. A household should be run efficiently, that is, on schedule, with a minimum of confusion and wasted effort. Educational institutions should be so organized that personnel and equipment are put to full use. Church meetings should start and end on time, and the economic affairs of the church should be run in a businesslike manner. Lawmakers should use their time and energies wisely and effectively in order not to waste the taxpayers' money. Leisure time should not be thrown away, but put to wise use. We shall find that one reason Americans are concerned about alienation, substance abuse, racial and sexual discrimination, and crime is that they result in inefficiency and wastefulness, as well as harm the individuals involved.

Improvement

Students of values in American society generally agree that Americans believe in the possibility and desirability of improvement. This is a theme that has appeared frequently in advertising: "Ford has a better idea"; "At Shell we try to make things better"; "At General Electric progress is our most important product." Innovations that reduce the amount of labor and time consumed in production are hailed not only because they promote efficiency, but also because they provide a better life for the individual. Americans expect continued improvement in the treatment and prevention of illness. Americans also hope for improvement in the education of their children, in forecasts about the economic future, in the safety record of travel by air and automobile. Concern is expressed if social problems persist—if there is no reduction, for example, in juvenile delinquency, poverty, alienation, racial discrimination, alcoholism, and divorce.

Competition

Competitiveness permeates American society. It begins early in life, when children are compared with their brothers, sisters, and the neighbors' children. In school, competition is formalized in the grading system and in intramural and interscholastic sports. Sports are based on intense competition in which defeating the opponent is all-important. Courtship is frequently a form of competition in which one seeks to win a potential mate away from one's rivals. Religious organizations often compete to attract newcomers in the community, and rival denominations strive to outdo one another in gaining members. Government representatives are chosen in competitive elections, and it is felt that the party out of power should help to keep the party in power alert by continuing a loyal opposition after the election is over. Finally, competition is at the heart of the capitalistic system; business organizations strive to outdo rivals in the production and sale of goods.

To say that Americans value competition does not imply a devaluation of cooperation, however. It is necessary to remember that cooperation is required before controlled competition can take place. Thus, the participants in a game must cooperate in following the rules, or they cannot compete and chaos results. While attracting customers, increasing profits, making good grades, and the like are important, the means used must be fair. Crime, the use of illegal drugs by athletes, cheating, and discrimination against others on the basis of race, ethnicity, sex, or creed are all violations of the rules that govern fair competition. Such actions therefore cause great concern among Americans.

Material well-being

Our discussion to this point has implied that an overall goal of the American way of life is greater material comfort. While hard work, efficiency, and practicality are good in themselves, they are also prized because they lead to an improved standard of living. The American economy is geared toward providing better goods and services to the consumer, including improved home appliances, automobiles, air-conditioning units, and recreational equipment. In fact, more-advanced models of these items are produced almost every year.

It was pointed out earlier that one of the reasons for getting an education is to make more money than one might otherwise. This, in turn, can bring more material comforts. In the area of religion, churches seek to have better buildings and equipment; these material objects can become a symbol of their success. Political parties are judged, in part, on whether they have brought material prosperity to the country; and the federal government has conducted a war on poverty. One reason Americans express pride in their way of life is that it has provided one of the highest standards of living in the world. On the other hand, concern is expressed that too many Americans live in poverty, with inadequate food, clothing, and housing. Racial discrimination, alcoholism, and the use of illegal drugs can contribute to an increase in poverty and are therefore condemned.

Physical and mental well-being

Some students of American values subsume physical and mental well-being under the inherent worth of the individual. At the same time, there is justification for listing it separately, for it is much emphasized in American life, and a lack of good health lies at the root of many of the concerns about social conditions. One indication of the importance of well-being is the large number of voluntary organizations that raise funds to conduct research and enhance the treatment of those afflicted with mental illness, cancer, heart problems, muscular dystrophy, and other diseases. Religious groups have established hospitals both in America and overseas, attesting to the importance they place on physical well-being. Schools teach physical and mental hygiene, and teachers are instructed how to handle the emotional and physical problems of pupils in a sound way. Government bodies have helped local communities build hospitals for the physically and mentally ill, and they have also provided research grants in these areas. Recreational pursuits are often justified on the ground that they help to ease tension and consequently improve physical and mental well-being. That Americans treasure well-being is evident in their concerns about the care of the elderly, inadequate medical treatment for the poor, the debilitating effects of alcoholism and drug addiction, and the pollution of the environment.

These, then, are some of the values which, according to scholars, are generally accepted by Americans. We are aware that they represent ideals, that they can be interpreted in more than one way, that some of them can be in conflict at times, and that there are countercurrents in American culture which challenge them. At the same time we are convinced that social problems in the United States cannot be understood without some knowledge of these values which underlie expressions of concern about and the urge to remedy undesirable situations.

The Dimensions of the Problem

The second part of sociological analysis is to present facts about each of the problems. A fact can be defined as an empirically verifiable statement about observable phenomena. Facts, as we shall use the term, are not based upon logical deductions or suppositions, but upon careful observation which can be directly verified.

In order to assure the objectivity of the data we report as facts, we shall present research in which the measures used have reasonably high validity, reliability, and precision. We shall depend heavily upon recent major research, including data from the *Statistical Abstract of the United States*, prepared from continuous surveys by the Census Bureau. We need to add that the factual data we present reflect operational definitions of the behavior or the situation being studied. An operational definition specifies the way the phenomenon is being measured. Thus the facts we present about juvenile delinquency reflect (and are limited by) the methods the government utilized to measure the problem. We cannot include every violation of the law by juveniles, because there is no way to know about every violation. By contrast, a conceptual definition of juvenile delinquency is all-inclusive. This is the kind of definition that can be found in a dictionary or glossary of terms. The operational definition is a way of measuring the concept, and it must always be derived from the conceptual definition. Both definitions are essential for conducting research. Accordingly, when we present data about alienation, alcoholism, illegal drug use, divorce, racial discrimination, poverty, and other social problems, we shall let the reader know how the data were gathered. Students of social problems should continually ask how the phenomena being dealt with were conceptualized and how they were measured; in other words, they should be aware of the conceptual and operational definitions.

The facts about a specific problem serve at least two purposes in sociological analysis. First, they inform us of the extent of the problem. They let us know how widespread the problem is, how many persons are directly affected by it, and whether the problem is increasing or decreasing in severity. Second, facts are necessary in order to develop explanations of the problem. While facts in and of themselves do not explain the presence of a problem, they are necessary before theories can be developed. The cause or causes of a social problem can be determined only by relating the facts about it to one another in a logical way.

The types of facts on which we shall concentrate are the characteristics of those directly involved and the areas in which the problem is found. We shall see if there are significant variations by age, sex, race, ethnic background, income, occupation, education, physiological makeup, personality traits, attitudes, and geographical setting. At times we shall find conflicting data or gaps in the data. We hope that such conflicts and gaps will be neither surprising nor discouraging. Science is an ongoing process; and far more research needs to be done, especially in the area of social problems. We are dealing with exceedingly complex phenomena for which research funds are sharply limited. Perhaps our readers will take time to look for additional facts and even to conduct research themselves.

Explanations of the Problem

The next step in sociological analysis is to bring the facts together in such a way as to explain the problem. Unlike some sociologists who attempt to attribute all social problems to a single cause (social change, or power conflict, or social disorganization), we shall deal with the causation of each problem separately. We shall also exercise great caution in stating causes, trying to avoid the glib generalizations and oversimplifications frequently found in the popular media. Scientific analysis shows that social problems are highly complex, and that they are not readily or easily explained.

As we examine the facts about a specific problem, we will attempt to formulate a theory. A theory performs three basic functions. First, it brings different facts together. And the more facts brought together by the theory, the more adequate the theory is. Second, theory provides an explanation by relating these facts in a logical way. And the more logical the correlation of facts, the more adequate the theory. Third, theory makes prediction possible. And the more accurate the prediction, the more adequate the theory. Notice that we have characterized a theory in terms of its adequacy, not in terms of whether it is right or wrong. Some theories are more adequate than others because they cover more data, are more logical, and predict more accurately. At the same time, all theories have certain limitations and are not to be considered the final word on a subject. They require continual testing to ensure maximum adequacy; they might even be displaced if a more adequate theory is developed.

Many scientific theories encounter problems. Consider, for example, the theory of organic evolution. It purports to explain the similarities and differences in organic forms past and present. It brings together myriad facts about both extinct and living animals and attempts to relate these facts in a logical way. The result is a three-part explanation of the emergence of new species: (1) variation in genetic makeup; (2) natural selection or increased chances of survival for those animals whose genetic traits are most adaptable to the habitat; and (3) the transmission of these traits to more and more offspring until a new species emerges. Major problems with this theory are the absence of transitional forms in the fossil record and the inability to explain major transformations, for example, from cold-blooded to warm-blooded animals. These problems challenge researchers to test and refine the theory further.

Note that a theory is not a fact and cannot become a fact, for theory and fact are separate, discrete concepts. Facts can be observed directly, while theories must be inferred from facts. While facts can describe, they cannot explain. Theories offer explanations of the relationships among facts. They are vitally important in increasing understanding and, in the case of social problems, developing effective action to ameliorate those problems.

The establishment of causation through a logical correlation of facts is so important that it requires further elaboration. In each of our chapters on social problems we shall have occasion to consider the ways in which cause and effect are established in the various theories presented. Before one factor can be considered the cause of another factor, three questions must be answered affirmatively. First, does the cause precede the effect? This might seem so obvious that it does not need to be mentioned. Yet if two variables occur together it is often automatically assumed that one is causing the other. In such cases there is a failure to establish that the variable assumed to be the cause preceded the variable assumed to be the effect. We shall frequently be asking the question, "Which came first?" when we find two variables coexisting; for example, particular personality traits and delinquent acts, use of illegal drugs and low income, racial discrimination and prejudice. Second, whenever the cause appears, does the effect also appear? Third, have other factors that might be bringing about the effect been controlled?

If these three questions are answered positively, we must ask further whether the variable that has been established as the cause is a necessary condition, a sufficient condition, or a contributory condition. A condition is necessary if the effect cannot occur without it. It is clear, for example, that the consuming of alcohol is a necessary condition for alcoholism to develop. The consuming of alcohol, however, is not a sufficient condition for the development of alcoholism, since the majority of people who drink do not become alcoholics. In addition there are several factors which make it more likely that alcoholism will develop. Among them are genetic inheritance, metabolic rate, certain personality traits, the individual's attitude toward drinking, and social ambivalence. These factors are neither necessary nor sufficient conditions but, rather, contributors to the development of alcoholism. One of the reasons for pointing out the differences is that some persons erroneously assume that a cause must be both a necessary and sufficient condition. In actuality, the type of cause with which we most frequently deal as we study highly complex, multifaceted social problems is the contributory condition.

Another task with which we shall be faced is to make clear where we are assuming the cause is located, whether it is within the individual or outside the individual (i.e., in the social structure and its norms). This distinction relates to the three types of theory with which we shall deal: physiological, psychological, and sociocultural. These three types of theories deal with different types of facts.

Returning to the example of alcoholism, we find that sociocultural theories are called upon to account for differences in the rates of alcoholism among various American Indian tribes, between Orthodox Jews and Irish Catholics, and between men and women. In each of these cases, we assume the cause is outside the individual and is to be found in social norms, expectations, and attitudes toward drinking. Sociocultural theories, then, are designed to handle differences in the rates of alcoholism among social categories; but they cannot explain why certain individuals in those categories become alcoholics while others do not. For this physiological and psychological theories are needed. In physiological theories the focus is the individual's genetic or biochemical makeup. In psychological theories the focus is personality traits, the individual's attitude toward drinking, and the way the individual has learned to use alcohol.

It is our point of view that it is probably more fruitful to ask what theory makes the most sense out of certain facts about alcoholism than to ask the broad question of what causes alcoholism. We need to ask, for example, why American men have a significantly higher rate of alcoholism and problem drinking than do women. To answer this question, we must look at differences in gender roles, expectations, and treatment. On the other hand, if we ask why one family has a higher rate of alcoholism and problem drinking than do other families in the same social categories, we must turn to physiological and psychological factors within the individuals. Although there is overlapping in the theories, it is still advantageous to consider them separately.

Proposed Solutions

The final part of sociological analysis is to consider the programs and policies that are intended to ameliorate and remedy each social problem. We shall review the ways in which private organizations, committees, legislative bodies, and other groups are attempting to treat and prevent each problem. We shall be especially interested in research on the effectiveness of an undertaking that is designed to change particular behavior or situations. There have been relatively few controlled studies of the effectiveness of programs; at times we shall point out the need for such studies. We are also interested in what assumptions current programs have made about causation and whether or not they rely on the theories which have been formulated regarding social problems. One reason we deal at length with theories is our conviction that sound theory is of vital importance in the effective treatment and prevention of the problem. If we can explain why something is happening, we are much more likely to be able to treat it or even to keep it from happening. It is in this sense that we contend that nothing is more practical than sound theory.

We suggest that in assessing current programs the reader may wish to reread the material on American values that we offered earlier in this chapter. It needs to be remembered that a situation is defined as a social problem when a widely held value is being violated, and that a program undertaken to remedy the problem has as its goal the restoration of that value. A fundamental test of the effectiveness of a program, then, is the extent to which the value is no longer being violated.

We have discussed the fourfold focus of sociological analysis: (1) the nature of the concern; (2) the dimensions of the problem; (3) explanations of the problem; and (4) proposed solutions. While these four steps will not be followed rigidly in the same way and to the same degree for each of the problems with which we will deal, they will give us a fundamental understanding before we present a Christian perspective on what should be done.

Topics for Review, Reflection, and Discussion

1. Is sociology more a science or an art?

2. Which of the major values of American society are most reflective of biblical morality? Which are most at variance with it?

3. Define the terms *cause, explanation,* and *theory* as they are used in sociological analysis.

3

Christianity and Social Problems

One of the greatest needs within contemporary Christianity is for the church to present a holistic gospel. For evangelicalism this means coming to grips with the imperative of Christian social involvement. That the evangelical church has not always suffered from a lack of social commitment is quite evident from the fact that during the early 1800s evangelical Christianity was a moving force, both in England and the United States, behind social reforms which addressed such problems as child labor, starvation wages for factory workers, prostitution, alcoholism, and slavery.

During the latter part of the 1800s, however, a great reversal took place: evangelicalism lost most of its zeal for social action. David Moberg (1972) believes that this reversal began when Christians came to view modern social problems as being so complex that biblical answers could not be found for them. He also notes that evangelical social concern was diverted into the struggle against evolutionism, defense of the Bible against the onslaught of modernist theology, and a fear of immigrating Catholics and Jews, who were seen at that time as contributing to some of the problems which plagued large American cities. Moberg also cites the emergence of dispensational theology, which offered the pessimistic premillennial view that since God is coming soon, we need to save all the souls we can now and forget about attempting to rectify unjust social structures. George Marsden (1980:85–93) has argued that the preparatory stage of the great reversal took place between 1865 and 1900, when the basically Calvinistic tradition, which viewed politics as being a significant means to advance the kingdom of God, gave way to a pietistic, dispensational view, which was primarily concerned with restraining personal vices.

41

Christian Theologies and Responses to Social Problems

A part of our definition of a social problem was "any situation which the members of a group think should be remedied by cooperative action." Genuine concern over a problem entails responsible action aimed at social change. Dick Simpson (1989) suggests that the attempts which various religious groups make at social change can be seen as a reflection of their theology of compassion. Within Judaism the ultimate goal of social action is justice. Within evangelical theology, where one is likely to start with an individual theology of compassion such as is expressed in Matthew 25, social action will take the form of attempts to provide direct assistance to those who are in need. In identifying the church with the larger culture, persons with a liberal theology will engage in action aimed at making the social system work. In contrast to liberal theology, which is written from the point of view of the elite, liberation theology is written from the perspective of the poor. In liberation theology the oppressed are enlightened regarding their situation and empowered to do something about it. Liberation is understood to be the heart of the gospel; God is viewed as on the side of the poor and as participating in social action aimed at releasing them from bondage.

Thus the response by Christians to social problems has been, to a very large extent, a reflection of their theological beliefs. Tragically, much of traditional theology has implicitly, if not explicitly, expressed a bias against attempts to bring about social change. In this section we shall examine elements within Christian theologies which have functioned as barriers to responsible action.

The Social Gospel of Liberalism

We will only briefly discuss liberal Christian theology because, rather than serving as a barrier, it has served as an impetus to Christian social involvement. With the emergence of liberal Christian theology during the latter part of the nineteenth century, a commitment to social involvement became a core part of the gospel. The major architect of this social gospel was Walter Rauschenbusch, who, in his book entitled *A Theology for the Social Gospel* (1919), propounded the idea that sin is culturally transmitted and thus resides within social structures rather than in individuals. The solution to the world's problems, then, is to reform evil social structures rather than to convert persons.

It is noteworthy that many of the early American sociologists were ministers who entered the field of sociology because they saw it as a way to work within the kingdom of God to defeat the kingdom of evil. In fact, during the early 1900s a Christian sociology was developed which sought to use sociological methods to eradicate evil social structures and establish God's perfect kingdom here on earth.

Given the optimism within liberalism and the pessimism within conservatism concerning the possibility of creating a perfect society, it was inevitable that these two wings of the church would clash. Because the conservatives affirmed certain fundamentals of the Christian faith which liberalism denied, for example, the virgin birth, the possibility of miracles, the bodily resurrection of Christ, and the verbal inspiration of the Bible, they came to be known as fundamentalists. A very important issue in the fundamentalist-modernist controversy of the early 1920s was the question of "What constitutes the Christian gospel?" The modernists held to a social gospel which emphasized that societal structures rather than individuals were in need of redemption. The fundamentalists, however, believed in a personal gospel which stressed the individual's need for salvation and minimized the social implications of the biblical message. The unfortunate result of this controversy has been a bifurcated Christianity which has failed to present the total biblical gospel, which has much to say about both individual and societal redemption.

In the more than fifty years since the beginning of the fundamentalist-modernist controversy, American Christianity has been struggling to implement a holistic gospel message. Some helpful writing has been done to assist us in this task, the most notable example being liberation theology (see pp. 286–89).

As we attempt to develop a theological rationale for a Christian response to social problems, we would do well to remember the truth in Rauschenbusch's declarations that social structures can be evil and that Christians must identify with the poor and oppressed of our world. However, we must question his denial of individual sinfulness as well as his attempt to Christianize the social order via socialism. Moreover, his biblical exegesis is at times wanting. For instance, his belief that Jesus propounded a realized eschatology, the view that the essence of God's kingdom exists at the present time here on earth, is certainly wrong.

The Psychological Captivity of Theological Conservatism

In his book *The Psychological Society* (1978) Martin Gross argues that psychology has lately come to be the basic American standard of behavior, replacing the Protestant ethic, which has weakened and is gradually fading from the scene. Although Gross has greatly overestimated the demise of the Judeo-Christian religion as the standard of behavior, there is an element of truth in his thesis. Americans do indeed place a psychological interpretation on all events in their lives. What Gross has failed to see is the extent to which Christians have held on to their religion by psychologizing or individualizing it.

Within Christian theologies there are two basic approaches that can be used to combat social problems. (We are admittedly oversimplifying here.) First, individuals can be changed, with the expectation that once they have been converted, they will bring about needed changes in social structures. Second, social structures can be changed, with the expectation that once they have been altered, the lives of the individuals they affect will change. The fundamentalist-modernist controversy can be understood in large part as an argument over the better way of implementing change. Fundamentalists opted for changing individuals, while modernists opted for changing social structures. These contrasting emphases came to be known, respectively, as the personal gospel and the social gospel.

By increasingly recognizing the legitimate social implications of the gospel, conservatives* are less likely today to emphasize the personal gospel at the cost of neglecting the social gospel. The conscience of conservative Christians has become sensitized to needed social change. However, there remains within conservative Christianity a carryover of an emphasis on individuals which has its roots in the fundamentalist rejection of the social gospel. While conservatives recognize the need for social change, for the most part they still believe that the most effective means of bringing about that change is to deal with individuals and not social structures. By substituting "Christian counseling" for "personal salvation" and "social reconstruction" for "social gospel" we have the fundamentalist-modernist controversy in modern dress. This is not to imply that conservatives no longer believe in personal salvation. They do! But in contrast to earlier fundamentalists, they no longer believe that personal salvation or conversion will totally change a person morally, socially, and psychologically. Conservatives now recognize that it is too simple to believe that all personal and social problems will dissipate when one turns to Jesus. Rather, the enlightened conservative recognizes the benefit of counseling and psychotherapy for the saved and unsaved alike.

Much of conservative Christianity today follows a three-step plan:

1. Actively seek the conversion of sinners to Christ.
2. Utilize the best principles of counseling and psychotherapy to make persons morally, socially, and psychologically whole.
3. Wait for the resultant change in social structures as these regenerated whole persons live their Christianity in society.

Under certain circumstances the first and second steps can be reversed. This is thought to be especially necessary when an individual is so psychologically disturbed as to be incapable of actually hearing and acting

*We are using the term *theological conservatism* to refer to views ranging from fundamentalism and the Moral Majority on the conservative right to organizations like Evangelicals for Social Action and publications like *Sojourners, Transformation,* and *The Other Side* on the conservative left. Although what we say in this section will be more applicable to some conservatives than others, we believe that all share a common heritage which has erected barriers against Christian social involvement.

upon the Good News of the gospel. Conservatives also stress that the gospel is best received when its hearers have full rather than empty stomachs (an old controversy from the foreign mission field as well). This is to say that theological conservatives are very attuned to meeting the social needs of the unconverted either before or simultaneous with the presentation of the gospel.

Theological conservatives are concerned about social, racial, and political problems and want to participate actively in the elimination of these problems. For the most part, however, they believe that the best solution to these societal problems is the conversion of individuals to Jesus Christ. A good illustration of this view can be seen in some representative statements of Bill Bright, the founder and president of Campus Crusade for Christ, the largest and most active theologically conservative college-student ministry in the world:

> There is no political structure, no social problem, no personal need anywhere for which Christ is not the answer.

> The world can be changed only as men's lives are changed. Jesus Christ is the one person who can change a man from within, who can give meaning, purpose, and direction to men's lives.

> It is not misleading to suggest that our twentieth century world can be changed in the same sense that the first century world was turned upside down. When individuals are changed in sufficient numbers, homes and communities will be changed. Cities, states, and nations of the world will feel the impact of the transformed lives of the men and women who have been introduced to Jesus Christ.

> Explo 72 can do more to bring peace to the world than all of the antiwar activity we have been seeing. Changed people in sufficient numbers make a changed world.

The psychological captivity of conservatism prevents it from seeing the naiveté in its assumption that changed individuals will automatically bring about changed social structures. Psychological blinders prevent conservatives from understanding that individuals are shaped and reinforced by social structures which they cannot escape. To concentrate on changing the individual, as opposed to the social structure, can be very inefficient when changed individuals are returned to the social conditions that were largely responsible for shaping and reinforcing their former selves.

Prevention and treatment

One result of the psychological captivity of conservatism is a concentration upon treatment rather than prevention. There is a case to be made, of course, that in a theological sense conservatism, by stressing the need for individual regeneration, deals more with prevention than liberalism does. Liberalism does not see humans as in need of regeneration and hence directs most of its effort to propping up social structures that fallen human beings keep perverting. The point being made here, however, is that individual counseling has the effect of changing the individual who is in need, but does very little about changing the social structures that most contribute to the problems of the individual. Another way of putting this is to say that alcoholism, mental distress, marital conflict, rebellious children, and the like are merely symptoms of deeper problems that are built into the social structure. When a troubled person is counseled, it is the symptom and not the cause of the problem that is being dealt with. We are not arguing that counseling should not be done, but that the Christian responsibility to a broken world does not stop there. Part of the Christian responsibility to a broken world is to attempt to change the alienating, dehumanizing, sinful social structures which are producing alcoholism, mental distress, marital difficulties, and rebellious children.

Attitudes and actions

Another result of the psychological captivity of conservatism is that conservatives tend to concentrate on changing attitudes rather than actions. This was especially evident in the resistance within the conservative wing of the church to any attempt on the part of government to force change in American society in response to the civil-rights struggle for justice and equality. Such resistance continues to manifest itself in reaction to racial tensions in South Africa. Even though most conservatives are not racially prejudiced, they are still resistant to any attempt to force change even by legitimate actions; legislation is thought to be unable to change the hearts of human beings. It is argued that people discriminate because they are prejudiced; therefore, racism will be eliminated by reducing prejudice. To attempt to reduce prejudice is, of course, to concentrate on changing attitudes, while attempting to reduce discrimination is to take action. The psychologizing of evangelicalism results in conservatives' interpreting the Bible in ways that lead them to attempt to change people from within rather than forcing change from without.

There are three ironies in the position conservatives take on the relationship between attitudes and actions. The first is that much of the early theorizing and research which concluded that reducing discrimination should have priority over reducing prejudice was done by a psychologist. It was Gordon Allport who first suggested that attempting to change people's hearts is infinitely less effective than changing the social structures that permit discrimination and thus forcing people to change their actions. The intellectual underpinning for the strategy of social change in the American civil-rights movement is Allport's conclusion that while racism cannot be substantially reduced by focusing upon prejudice, it can be effectively reduced by forcing change in behavior through laws modifying social structures.

The second irony is that when conservatives do advance a legislative agenda, it tends so to dissociate action from attitude, and individuals from social structures, as to be almost impossible to enforce. Evangelical campaigns against alcohol, abortion, and pornography tend ultimately to be unsuccessful because, while attempting to prohibit specific actions, they do not recognize the intimate connection between actions and attitudes.

The final irony has to do with the conservatives' selective inattention to Jesus' statement, "Where your treasure is, there will your heart be also" (Matt. 6:21 KJV). Jesus is here teaching that commitments (actions) determine attitudes. Understanding the implications of such statements might be a rich source for theological conservatism to develop a new view of social change.

Dispensational Theology

In the introduction to this chapter a special brand of conservative theology, dispensationalism, was targeted as leading to a fatalistic view of the human potential to eradicate social problems. Since this is not an uncommon accusation, we will discuss the possibility of a logical connection between dispensational theology and lack of social involvement.

The view of the future as painted by some dispensationalists is that (1) the end is near; (2) things will get worse and worse; and (3) any effort at structural change is futile (Grounds 1987). A cornerstone in dispensational theology is premillennialism—the view that the second coming of Christ, at which time all Christians will be taken from the world, will occur before his thousand-year kingdom on earth. Vernon Grounds (1987:1) summarizes the implications of this view for attempts at social betterment:

> [American premillennialism] holds out no hope for human betterment, no prospect of large-scale spiritual renewal and social progress before the Second Coming and the establishment of the Savior's earthly kingdom. All its hope is therefore concentrated on the supernatural termination of history when Jesus Christ returns to inaugurate a new terrestrial order. So its hope is entirely eschatological. As for the present order of human life, it will by a sort of prophetic necessity steadily degenerate. The world is destined to grow more and more evil, more and more violent, more and more anti-God until the Lord of history once more personally visibly breaks into time and space.

Grounds, himself a premillennialist, hastens to add that the pessimism which characterizes most premillennialists is a result of a mistaken interpretation of Scripture. Grounds lists three errors which he thinks have led to pessimism about the future.

First, there is a failure to recognize the element of conditionality in all of our relationships to God, where the key word is "if." Blessing comes *if* we respond to God in faith and obedience, while judgment comes *if* we respond to God in unbelief and disobedience.

Second, there is a failure to perceive that in the fulfilment of prophecy human responsibility often plays a decisive role. Since human beings are responsible agents, the fulfilment of a great deal of prophecy is not automatic and unconditional, but rather is contingent on human response. Grounds (1987:4) offers this hermeneutical principle: "In prophecy a conditional element is implicit unless its unconditionality is explicitly stated." God's not destroying Nineveh after its individual and collective repentance is an illustration of this principle.

Third, there is a failure to understand the meaning of the biblical expression *the last days*. Throughout the history of the church there have been persons who were convinced that they were witnessing the last days; they were less than shy in announcing that the second coming of Christ was just around the corner. Even the apostle John declared over nineteen hundred years ago that it was the last days. Grounds believes that "the last days" refers to "the age of the Holy Spirit when both evangelistically and socially there is no imaginable limit to what Christians can accomplish" (p. 5). Grounds's position is significant in that it holds that the premillennialists' pessimism about the future is due not to premillennialism itself, but to the mistaken biblical interpretations which often accompany it.

We should remember that theological doctrine reflects the social conditions of the period in which it was constructed. Historically, dispensational theology was developed by and for theological conservatives during a period when they were experiencing pain and alienation because of social changes (Mouw 1978). The reader should not think that other theological positions are immune from a self-interested interpretation of Scripture. It should be noted that H. Richard Niebuhr (1951:77–105) saw in the writings of John Calvin a theology which functioned to justify the social status quo and hence was suited for the well-to-do. More recently, Hendrik Hart (1987), a Calvinist himself, suggests not only that Calvin did not write much on social justice, but that what little he did write is dampened by (1) "an intellectual view of our faith, seeing it as a subscription to theological doctrines, that is, ideas," and (2) "a passive view of our faith, seeing it as opposed to works." Hart believes that as a result Calvinists are better at constructing rational theologies about the need for social action than they are at actually implementing social action.

Toward a Biblical Understanding of Social Relationships

From the sociological point of view, social problems are a reflection of dysfunction in both social relationships and social structures. From a Christian perspective, what we need to begin with is a biblical understanding of what form God desires social relationships and social structures to take. When the sociological and biblical perspectives are drawn together, the resulting insights are often such as could not have been obtained through either one of those perspectives by itself.

Our theological understanding of social relationships is based upon an examination of biblical writings concerning how God enters into and sustains relationships with his people. Biblical examples of God's relationships with his creation provide a paradigm of how human beings are to relate to each other today. We suggest that the biblical view of social relationships can best be understood in terms of four sequential, but nonlinear, phases: *covenant, grace, empowering,* and *intimacy* (Balswick and Balswick 1987, 1989).

Covenant: The Basis of Social Relationships

The concept of covenant has a rich heritage in biblical theology. In essence an unconditional commitment, covenant is demonstrated supremely by God. Our social relationships, then, should ideally be based on unconditional commitment. As the biblical meaning of covenant has eroded in modern society, however, social relationships have correspondingly come to be characterized as contracts rather than unconditional commitments.

The first biblical mention of a covenant is found in Genesis 6:18, where God says to Noah, "I will establish my covenant with you, and you will enter the ark" (NIV). God goes on to tell Noah what he must do: "[Take] your sons and your wife and your sons' wives with you. You are to bring into the ark two of all living creatures, male and female, to keep them alive with you." We are told in Genesis 6:22 that "Noah did everything just as God commanded him."

The second biblical reference in which God makes a covenant is Genesis 15:18, where a covenant is extended to Abraham. This covenant is later amplified: "I will establish my covenant as an everlasting covenant between me and you and your descendants after you for the generations to come, to be your God and the God of your descendants after you" (Gen. 17:7). Abraham's role in the covenant is specified in Genesis 17:9: "Then God said to Abraham, 'As for you, you must keep my covenant, you and your descendants after you for the generations to come.'"

What can we learn from these two accounts of God's establishing covenants with Noah and Abraham? First, we see that God was not offering either Noah or Abraham any choice in the matter. That is, God was by no means saying, "Now I am going to commit myself to you *if* this is your desire." Instead, the establishment of the covenant was based entirely on God's action. God's offer was in no way contractual; that is, it was not based upon either Noah's or Abraham's keeping his end of the bargain.

Second, God did desire and even commanded a response from both Noah and Abraham. Did this make God's covenantal offer conditional? Was God free to retract the offer if it was not reciprocated? The answer is a resounding no! The covenant which God offered was to remain an "everlasting covenant" (Gen. 9:16) regardless of what Noah or Abraham did.

Third, while the covenant itself was not conditional, the potential blessings it provided were. Thus Deuteronomy 11:26–28 states, "Behold, I set before you today a blessing and a curse: the blessing, if you obey the commandments of the LORD your God . . . and the curse, if you do not obey the commandments of the LORD your God" (NKJV).

Fourth, God extended his covenant beyond Noah and Abraham to include not only their immediate families, but generation after generation. That Abraham could not anticipate obedience on the part of his descendants is further evidence of the unconditional nature of the covenant. Again, however, the blessings of the covenant were to be conditional on the descendants' following God.

The biblical account of the covenant relationship between God and his people can best be understood by utilizing the analogy of an unconditional parental commitment to a child. For in the Old Testament, God forgave Israel every time they repented of some particular sinful action. And in the New Testament, the incarnation is the supreme expression of God's unconditional love for us, to which Jesus attested in his parable of the prodigal son.

Besides the unconditional nature of covenant love, the Bible stresses its reciprocal aspect. God's initial relationship with his creatures was a unilateral unconditional commitment. But he desired that this initial relationship mature into a bilateral unconditional commitment. By implication it is God's desire that all human social relationships be bilateral unconditional commitments. Joseph Allen (1984:32) neatly summarizes the covenantal aspects of an ideal social relationship: (1) it "comes about through interactions of entrusting and accepting entrustment among willing, personal beings; (2) as a result, the parties belong to the same moral community and have responsibility to and for one another as beings who matter; and (3) their responsibility in the relationship endures over time."

We should make it clear that there are two basic types of covenant. The inclusive covenant encompasses the whole of humanity and their relationship with God and with one another. God created all peoples of the world to be brothers and sisters to each other. It is to the inclusive covenant that we shall appeal when we call for a proper Christian response to global social problems such as poverty, world hunger, environmental destruction, and nuclear armament. There are also special covenants, which are relationships of "entrusting and accepting entrustment between two or more parties that arise out of some *special* historical transaction between the members and not only from their participation in the inclusive covenant" (Allen 1984:41). Examples of social ties based upon special covenants include marriage, parent/child relationships, and various community and political organizations which commit themselves to caring for their members.

We are suggesting that God's covenant love is to be the basic standard of human morality. Allen (1984:77) summarizes the goals of covenant love:

1. Always to see self and others as essentially belonging together in community
2. To affirm the worth of each covenant member; to regard each as someone who matters individually, irreplaceably, and equally
3. To include every category of person in the covenant community and therefore among those we affirm for their own sakes
4. To seek to meet the needs, both ultimate and proximate, of each person
5. To be faithful in our commitments to others, both in our ultimate commitment to all members of God's inclusive covenant and in our special covenants with specific people
6. To seek reconciliation wherever alienation exists

These are lofty ideals for human beings, who are fallen creatures and who live in a sinful world. Nevertheless, the ideal of covenant love is given by God as the standard for living in social community.

Grace: The Atmosphere for Social Relationships

From a human perspective, the unconditional love of God makes no sense except as an offer of grace. The word *grace* connotes relationship. In its biblical context "grace" refers to God's calling us to share in a relationship with him. The Hebrew word *ḥēn*, traditionally translated "grace," is in modern versions usually translated "favor" or "unmerited favor." Thus Genesis 6:8 reads, "Noah found favor in the eyes of the LORD" (NIV). The incarnation is the supreme act of God's grace to humankind. Christ came in human form to reconcile the world to God. This act of love and forgiveness is the basis for human love and forgiveness. We can forgive others as we have been forgiven, and the love of God within equips us to love others in the same unconditional way. Where there is an atmosphere of grace in a relationship, there will be a willingness to forgive and be forgiven.

Social relationships were designed by God for an atmosphere of grace and not law. Relationships which are based upon contract rather than unconditional love create an atmosphere of law, while relationships grounded in covenant engender an atmosphere of grace and freedom. The meaning and joy of being a Christian would be deadened if we conceived of our relation with God in terms of law instead of grace, and the same is true as well with regard to human relations. At both the individual and corporate levels, law leads to bondage while grace encourages freedom.

This is not to say that there is no place for law in human relationships. We need to note that the apostle Paul writes, "Christ ends the law and brings righteousness for everyone who has faith" (Rom. 10:4 NEB). It is not the case that the law itself is bad, for it points the way to live according to God's intention. However, since no human being is perfect, we can never fulfil the law. Christ is the end of the law in the sense that he is its perfect fulfilment. That we are righteous is due to Christ's perfection and righteousness, not to our having kept the law. Our salvation is not dependent upon our keeping the law, but upon our faith in Christ.

Although the covenant of grace rules out law as a basis for social relationships, people living in an atmosphere of grace will accept law in the form of patterns, order, and responsibility in their relationships. In reality, much of our daily routine must be performed according to agreed-upon rules, especially in large social organizations. Stuart McLean (1984:24) has insightfully observed that

> in the covenantal root metaphor, law and covenant belong together. The dyadic relationship necessarily involves creating specific forms, rules, and laws to guide community and personal relationships. The need for law, pattern, and form is mandatory, but the particular shape of law needs to be understood as relative to the actualization of dialogical-dialectical relationships, the creation of whole persons-in-community. The issue becomes which forms, which laws, which patterns are appropriate to the maintenance of humanity?

Empowering: The Action Needed for Mature Social Relationships

Power is the ability to influence another person. Research reveals that the most common way in which people use power in social relationships is to control others (Szinovacz 1987). Most social-science models in fact assume that when we use power, we are not attempting to increase the power of others, but to assure the maintenance of our own more powerful position.

Empowering is a biblical model for a use of power which is completely contrary to the common usage of power in society at large. Empowering can be defined as the attempt to establish power in another person. Empowering does not necessarily involve yielding to the wishes of another person or giving up one's own power to someone else. Rather, empowering is the active, intentional process of enabling another person to acquire power. The person who is empowered has gained power because of the encouraging behavior of the other.

Empowering is the process of helping another recognize strengths and potentials within, as well as encouraging and guiding the development of these qualities. It is the affirmation of another's ability to learn and grow and become all that he or she can be. It may require that the empowerer be willing to step back and allow the empowered to learn by doing and not by depending. The empowerer must respect the uniqueness of those being empowered and see strength in their individual ways to be competent. Empowering does not involve controlling or enforcing a certain way of doing and being. It is, rather, a reciprocal process in which empowering takes place between people in mutually enhancing ways.

If covenant love is the commitment and grace is the underlying atmosphere of acceptance, then empowering is the action of God in people's lives. It is supremely seen in the work of Jesus Christ. The celebrated message of Jesus was that he had come to empower—"I have come that they may have life, and have it to the full" (John 10:10 NIV). The apostle John puts it this way: "But to all who received him, who believed in his name, he gave power to become children of God; who were born, not of blood nor of the will of the flesh nor of the will of man, but of God" (John 1:12–13 RSV). Ray Anderson (1985) insightfully exegetes this text by noting that power "of blood" is power in the natural order, and "the will of the flesh" suggests tradition, duty, honor, obedience, and all that is a part of conventional power. In this passage, then, it is clear that the power is given by God and not by either physical or conventional means.

The power given by Jesus is power of a personal order—power which is mediated to the powerless. To us in our sinful and powerless condition God gives the ability to become children of God. This is the supreme example of human empowering. Jesus redefined power by his teaching and by his relating to others as a servant. Jesus rejected the use of power to control others, and instead affirmed the use of power to serve others, to lift up the fallen, to make the poor self-sufficient, to forgive the guilty, to encourage responsibility and maturity in the weak, and to enable the unable.

In reality, however, power resides in the hands of those who possess the most resources. Consequently, it is generally believed that power is a commodity which is in limited supply. This view contributes to many of the problems in contemporary society. The belief that power is limited results in a self-centered perspective, where each individual and social group try to reap maximum benefits for themselves at the lowest possible cost. On the collective level there is a tendency for the more powerful nations to keep poorer nations dependent upon them. In the frailness of our human insecurity we are tempted to keep others dependent upon us, and in so doing find a counterfeit security in having power over them.

The good news for Christians is that "according to Scripture, especially the New Testament, the power of God is available to human beings in unlimited amounts!" (Bartchy 1984:13). This unlimited power is seen in such passages as Ephesians 4:13 and Galatians 5:22–23, which rehearses "the fruit of the Spirit" (love, joy, peace, patience, kindness, goodness, fidelity, gentleness, and self-control) available to all Christians. This very character of God is available in unlimited supply because God's resources are inexhaustible!

Covenant love in action can free people from dependency. It is the mark of Jesus Christ which Christians need to emulate the most. They are called to model themselves after him and live in their communities and society according to patterns which are extraordinary. Even though we are sinners, God provides us with the ability to follow the empowering principle in our relationships. God empowers us, by the Holy Spirit, to empower others. The biblical ideal for all our relationships, then, is that we be Christian realists in regard to our own sinfulness and proneness to fail, but Christian optimists in light of the grace and power available to live according to God's intended purposes. In the chapters to follow, we will suggest that empowering (covenant love in action) is the Christian response to social problems.

Intimacy: Communication in Social Relationships

The ability of human beings to communicate with each other through language makes it possible for them to intimately know each other. Perfect intimacy is modeled by God in his relationships and communications with his children. For unlike the gods of Eastern religions, the God of Scripture wants to be personally related to us. In fact, the Holy Spirit dwells within us, and we are encouraged to share our deepest thoughts and feelings with him through prayer.

Adam and Eve in their perfect state stood naked before each other and before God and felt no shame (Gen. 2:25). They could be totally intimate. It was only after they sinned that they tried to hide from God out of a feeling of shame. Shame results in the playing of deceptive games—in putting on masks and hiding one's true self from others. Where shame is present, intimacy is difficult.

On the other hand, where social relationships are based on covenant and empowering is practiced in an atmosphere of grace, individuals will communicate with each other in a caring and concerned manner. When one talks, others will listen and want what is best for that individual. In this way we emulate Jesus, who selflessly promoted the welfare of others by being submissive and loving in his relationships.

The capacity to freely communicate feelings in our social relationships is contingent upon not fearing one another. John gives us insight into this in 1 John 4:16, 18: "God is love. . . . There is no fear in love. But perfect love drives out fear" (NIV). God is perfect love, and his love is unconditional. We thus return to the covenant basis of social relationships. Unconditional love allows us to freely communicate with each other because we do not fear rejection.

Jesus' closeness to his disciples serves as an excellent model of the type of communicative intimacy which we should strive to have with each other in our social relationships. Recall that at the end of his earthly ministry Jesus asked Peter three times, "Do you love me?" (John 21). Peter had earlier denied Jesus three times; Jesus was giving Peter the opportunity to assert what he had previously denied and to reaffirm his love for Christ three times. Because our relations with others often become strained, God desires that we verbally communicate our feelings to one another and in so doing bring our covenantal relationships to maturity.

Toward a Theological Understanding of Social Structure

Having presented a biblically based model of social relationships, we will now consider the context within which these relationships occur. The fabric of society consists of many interwoven layers. Most people can identify the social units of which their lives are a part. These several layers of social structure can be conceptualized as forming increasingly inclusive concentric circles. Figure 3 represents four different layers of social structure, along with a biblically prescribed ideal for each.

For most people the family is the central arena of social relationships. The biblically prescribed basis for family relationships is covenant.

Figure 3

Levels of Social Structure and Biblically Prescribed Ideals

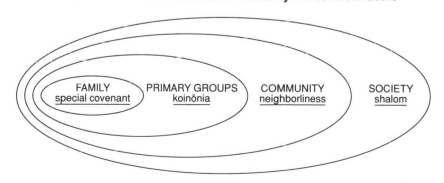

FAMILY
special covenant

PRIMARY GROUPS
koinōnia

COMMUNITY
neighborliness

SOCIETY
shalom

Beyond the family there exist primary groups within which we find a sense of belonging and personal identity. While these primary groups resemble family relationships, they are generally larger and more inclusive. The biblically prescribed ideal for primary groups is *koinōnia*. More inclusive than primary groups is the community, which consists of all those people who happen to reside in our neighborhood, town, or city. The biblically prescribed ideal for relationships at the community level, which are usually secondary and impersonal, is neighborliness. Finally, the most inclusive level is society. Here millions of people share identity through common membership in a nation-state or, even more inclusively, in the human race. The biblically prescribed ideal for societies is *shalom*. By discussing what the Bible says about each of these four levels of social interrelatedness, we will be in a better position to understand the theological dimension of the structural causes of societal problems.

Covenant Love in the Family

The basic unit in society, both sociologically and theologically, is the family. The family is the unit into which individuals are born; it is where they find their identity and are socialized. All that we have said about covenant, grace, empowering, and intimacy is supremely applicable to family relationships, since God intends for the family to be based on a mature (i.e., reciprocal) covenantal relationship between a man and a woman. It is for this reason that "a man leaves his father and mother and is united to his wife, and the two become one flesh" (Gen. 2:24 NEB). The marriage relationship is the archetype for all of the other types of social relationships. Moreover, it is the figure which the apostle Paul utilized to describe the unconditional bond between Christ (the bridegroom) and the church (the bride).

The family is meant by God to be an intimate environment where we can be ourselves without fearing rejection. Thus, although Adam and Eve were both naked, "they had no feeling of shame towards one another" (Gen. 2:25 NEB). The family is to be a place where unconditional love fosters intimate knowledge of and mutual caring for one another. Many contemporary social ills are at least partially attributable to the modern-day loss of this biblical perspective regarding family life (see chap. 8).

Koinōnia in Primary Groups

Most people find a sense of identity and social support in primary groups that exist beyond the family itself. Examples are churches, clubs, recreational associations, and other specialized interest groups. A primary group serves as a mediating structure between the isolated, private world of the family and faceless, remote societal structures. Unfortunately, an increasing number of people in modern society have been unable to locate supportive primary groups. Accompanying the decline in primary-group relationships has been a loss of effective social control. The result is that we have become vulnerable to our own moral laxity and to strangers around us. In this impersonal social environment an increasing number of persons can be categorized as members of the "lonely crowd" (Riesman 1950).

Some social scientists have suggested that networks are the modern substitute for traditional primary groups. Friends, co-workers, educational and religious groups—together these networks can satisfy virtually all of an individual's social needs. However, networks tend to be unstable and specialized and thus lack the virtues associated with primary groups—unconditional commitment and a sense of belonging which embraces the whole of a person's life.

There is a wide range of responses to the disintegration of traditional primary groups. At one extreme we see the trend toward a self-contained individualism which denies dependence on others and makes no commitment to them. At the other extreme we see people experimenting with various forms of primary groups which are focused around some common value such as economic sharing, family life, or religious devotion. In between these extremes we see many people searching for a sense of community in institutional contexts such as the church or in homogeneous neighborhoods such as housing developments, where names like Homewood, Pleasantdale, and Community Heights imply commonality and identity.

We live in a mass society in which the sense of identity and the relationships offered by primary groups are desperately sought after, yet prove to be exceedingly difficult to achieve. Moreover, the breakdown of primary groups is one of the root causes of such social ills as juvenile delinquency, adult crime, racial discrimination, alienation, substance abuse, poverty, and neglect of the elderly.

The key to understanding God's ideal for social relationships within primary groups is found in the New Testament concept of *koinōnia*. Scripture uses this term to refer to a group in which persons are united in identity and purpose. In the New Testament prototype, members of the church voluntarily shared all of their possessions. They joined together in both *politeia* (civic life) and *oikonomia* (family life). *Koinōnia* came to represent a new type of primary group between the all-inclusive, impersonal state and the exclusive, blood-based household (Banks 1980).

It is striking that the apostle Paul uses the family as a metaphor to describe the church, which is a primary group. Christians are to see themselves as being members of a divine family headed by God the Father. Thus Paul, quoting from the Old Testament, writes, "I will accept you, says the Lord, the Ruler of all being; I will be a father to you, and you shall be my sons and daughters" (2 Cor. 6:18 NEB). We are also told that "God has sent the Spirit of his Son into our hearts, crying, 'Abba! Father!'" (Gal. 4:6 RSV). And Ephesians 2:19 states that we "are no longer strangers and foreigners, but fellow citizens with the saints and members of the household of God" (NKJV).

In advocating that the church be a family the Bible implicitly rejects any notion of the family as an exclusive, self-contained group. In fact, there is much in the teaching of Jesus to suggest that one's loyalty is misplaced if it ultimately resides in the family. Jesus speaks of leaving, dividing, disuniting, and even hating one's family for the sake of God's kingdom. Of course, Jesus was not trying to undermine family life, but dramatizing the point that a Christian's loyalty must transcend familial bonds and reside ultimately in the church, which, if it practices *koinōnia*, will exude the characteristics of family life.

It is God's desire that strong family relationships not be simply ends in themselves, but also paradigms of how we are to care for each other in our primary groups. Jesus' attitude regarding the inclusiveness of the family is clearly shown in Mark 3:31–35. While speaking to a crowd, he was informed that his mother and brothers had arrived. His reply was, "'Who is my mother? Who are my brothers?' And looking round at those who were sitting in the circle about him he said, 'Here are my mother and my brothers. Whoever does the will of God is my brother, my sister, my mother'" (NEB). Common membership in the body of Christ binds all believers to him and to one another as family, and their relationships are to be based upon covenant, grace, empowerment, intimacy, and *koinōnia*.

The *koinōnia*-practicing New Testament church provides us with a model of an ideal primary group. In his book entitled *Paul's Idea of Community*, Robert Banks (1980:42) argues that since the first Christian churches, which reflected Paul's standard, met in the houses of believers, the size of any one fellowship was limited to about twenty or thirty persons. It is significant that recent social-science research has found that a typical individual is able to maintain intimate relationships with a maximum of twenty-five to thirty persons. Those attempting to develop a larger network of intimate friendships find that they lack the time, capacity, and energy to keep each relationship growing and vital (Pattison 1984).

The decline of primary groups is related to the nature of contemporary mass society with its impersonalization, urbanization, industrialization, rationalization, dehumanization, bureaucratization, and secularization. In the face of these societal changes, Christian churches which practice *koinōnia* can be a witness to how God intends for us to relate in primary groups. A primary group other than a Christian fellowship might also be able to fill this function, provided, of course, that the members share common beliefs, values, ideals, and goals. Nevertheless, we would argue that the New Testament example of *koinōnia* provides us with the best model of how all human beings may live meaningfully and harmoniously with themselves, others, and their Creator.

Neighborliness in the Community

Whereas the social relationships of family and primary groups are based upon special covenant commitment, such is not necessarily the case with respect to the relationships between people who live in the same community, be it a small town or large city. The relationships between persons living in the same community tend to be secondary rather than primary. A secondary relationship is usually temporary, focusing on the fulfilment of some immediate goal such as purchasing groceries or buying clothes. Is there a biblical basis for how persons are to behave in their secondary relationships?

Such a basis we believe was given by Jesus in one of his parables. In the parable of the good Samaritan Jesus sets forth the concept of neighborliness as the normative model for all of our secondary relationships in community life:

> On one occasion a lawyer came forward to put this test question to him: "Master, what must I do to inherit eternal life?" Jesus said, "What is written in the Law? What is your reading of it?" He replied, "Love the Lord your God with all your heart, with all your soul, with all your strength, and with all your mind; and your neighbour as yourself." "That is the right answer," said Jesus; "do that and you will live."
>
> But he wanted to vindicate himself, so he said to Jesus, "And who is my neighbour?" Jesus replied, "A man was on his way from Jerusalem down to Jericho when he fell in with robbers, who stripped him, beat him, and went off leaving him half dead. It so happened that a priest was going down by the same road; but when he saw him, he went past on the other side. So too a Levite came to the place, and when he saw him went past on the other side. But a Samaritan who was making the journey came upon him, and when he saw him was moved to pity. He went up and bandaged his wounds, bathing them with oil and wine. Then he lifted him on to his own beast, brought him to an inn, and looked after him there. Next day he produced two silver pieces and gave them to the innkeeper, and said, 'Look after him; and if you spend any more, I will repay you on my way back.' Which of these three do you think was neighbour to the man who fell into the hands of the robbers?" He answered, "The one who showed him kindness." Jesus said, "Go and do as he did." [Luke 10:25–37 NEB]

How convenient it would have been had Jesus simply made a clear distinction between those who are our neighbors and those who are not. Instead, he makes the startling assertion that every individual is potentially our neighbor. Neighbor-type relationships are created only when one person comes to the aid of another. Each of us is capable of both being a neighbor and having a neighbor. Thus, when I meet the needs of another, I am being a neighbor to that person. But when someone else serves me, then I have a neighbor.

The parable of the good Samaritan is a vivid illustration of Jesus' command to "love your neighbor as yourself" (Matt. 19:19). In our own lives, this commandment may be observed by such actions as not changing the television channel when the plight of the starving in Africa is shown. Or it may mean taking notice of a newspaper account of racial or sexist injustice. Or again, it may consist of not avoiding the homeless as we walk to work. We must come to the aid of others just as God in Christ has come to our aid.

When the call to be a neighbor is from God and not simply a desire to be needed, the resultant action is empowering (see pp. 52–54). In this regard, Eloise Frazier (1986:268) comments:

> A distinction must be made between the kind of aid that takes over and the kind that enables the recipient to continue the task. To take up the cause of another is not to give aid in the first sense. It is not to judge the other incompetent or weak or inadequate, and to set one's own self up as the superior deliverer of the needy. Rather it is to discern that point at which the other must be enabled to carry on a task, and to give that aid regardless of its seeming insignificance or lack of permanent value.

There is no promise that being a neighbor will result in having a neighbor. But regardless of whether neighborliness is reciprocated, God calls us to selflessly serve those in need. As we attempt to give a Christian response to social problems, we will stress the need for structural change on the community level which will render our secondary relationships more consistent with the biblical model of neighborliness.

Shalom in Society

The fourth concentric circle in figure 3 represents the many different large layers which exist in all societies. These include the faceless, impersonal structures of economic, educational, political, and religious institutions. Each of these social institutions is marked by patterns of position (status) and relationships (roles) which are reinforced by an integrated set of norms. The end result is that much of contemporary social life is spent in impersonal, hierarchical, rationally based bureaucracies.

Important determinants of social status include such factors as race, ethnicity, gender, class, occupation, religion, age, level of education, residential area, and verbal ability. These factors, which find in elaborate ideological systems their justification as determinants of status, are legitimately employed only in certain contexts. For instance, an individual's level of learning is certainly an appropriate yardstick for determining his or her status within the field of education. Because of her breadth of knowledge, a teacher should be accorded more honor than her students.

Suppose, however, that race or gender were used as the major criterion in determining an individual's status in education. If institutional racism or sexism were a part of the educational structure, there would be no way to mount an internal grievance. In approaching social problems from the vantage point of the Christian faith, we will employ the firm foundation of biblical truth as our basis for evaluating the justice or injustice of using certain factors to determine societal standing.

The Old Testament concept of *shalom* characterizes the type of society in which institutions function best. In most modern translations of the Bible, the term *shalom*, which is used more than two hundred times in the Hebrew Scriptures, is usually translated "peace." In Western cultures peace connotes the absence of conflict. However, in Scripture and Hebrew culture *shalom* is not seen merely as the absence of conflict, but as promotion of human welfare in both its material and spiritual aspects. It denotes a culture characterized by justice and righteousness. For *shalom* to exist there must be justice and righteousness in the ethical structures of society; there must be a fairness in the way human beings relate to each other at every level. Such a situation is poignantly described in Isaiah 11:6–8:

> The wolf also shall dwell with the lamb, and the leopard shall lie down with the kid; and the calf and the young lion and the fatling together; and a little child shall lead them. And the cow and the bear shall feed; their young ones shall lie down together; and the lion shall eat straw like the ox. And the sucking child shall play on the hole of the asp, and the weaned child shall put his hand on the cockatrice' den. [KJV]

Shalom carries with it a holistic connotation of societal well-being. It is "the human being dwelling at peace in all his or her relationships: with God, with self, with fellows, with nature" (Wolterstorff 1983:69). When any one of these relationships is out of focus, disrupted, at tension, or hurting, then *shalom* is not present.

Peace and justice find common expression in the Old Testament concept of *shalom*. Where *shalom* is lacking, social problems inevitably arise. These problems are often symptomatic of deeper spiritual and cultural injustices and inconsistencies.

Shalom is present only when social structures have been changed in such a way that they empower rather than make persons excessively dependent or vulnerable. Thus, for example, chronic unemployment and oppression with their attendant poverty must be eradicated before *shalom* is even approximated. Achieving *shalom* means eradicating the conditions which contribute to and perpetuate poverty. One way of eliminating poverty is to provide the poor with food, clothing, and shelter. Now this is a good beginning, but if the underlying oppressive conditions which cause poverty are not dealt with, *shalom* is not present.

Christians must work to prevent a situation in which persons who are able to help themselves are not provided with the means to do so. In sum, a society characterized by *shalom* treats its people neither unjustly nor paternalistically.

A nation whose foreign policies are biblically informed will try to implement *shalom* in international relationships. In a world where some people live in riches while others live in relative poverty, *shalom* is not present. A biblically informed foreign policy in a rich country such as the United States will seek to foster economic development in poor countries, even if releasing these poor countries from economic dependency means that those of us in rich countries will pay more for such commodities as coffee, bananas, sugar, and raw materials.

We have suggested that the biblically prescribed ideals for relationships at the family, primary-group, community, and society levels are

covenant love, *koinōnia*, neighborliness, and *shalom* respectively. In conclusion we suggest two guiding principles: (1) God calls us to give our
highest priority to the most exclusive social group of which we are members; and (2) commitment to this exclusive group is to be the basis for
developing inclusive commitments. Thus, our first priority is to our family, followed by commitment to primary groups, to community, and
finally to society. Families which are characterized by covenant love will
reach out to include members of their primary groups as brothers and
sisters. Primary groups which are experiencing *koinōnia* will be open to
include neighbors from the community as new members. Community
members who are willing to be neighbors to others and to let others be
neighbors to them are creating the type of society which will be characterized as *shalom*. We shall attempt to be consistent with these principles
as we give a Christian response to the social problems we analyze.

A Procedure for Analysis of Social Problems

In the previous chapters we emphasized that social problems are situ-
ational, that is, they are a part of the sociocultural milieu and cannot be
understood apart from that milieu. American society and culture are
exceedingly varied and complex, and it is not possible in the scope of a
single volume to present this milieu in detail. We have, of necessity, summarized and simplified. However, by illustrating how American values,
social variables, and certain other dynamic factors relate to social problems, we have tried to lay a foundation for analysis of the social problems in the United States.

We will, in general, ask five questions about each social problem we
analyze (this pattern will vary, however, whenever one of these questions
overlaps with another or is irrelevant to the topic at hand):

1. *What is the evidence and nature of the concern?* We will begin by
   examining (a) the evidence that members of American society
   consider a given situation to be a problem and (b) the reasons
   why they consider it to be so. We will also inquire into the values
   with which the situation is in conflict, whether there are certain
   groups in the society that are especially concerned, if the concern
   has changed over the years, and if there are conflicts among
   those who show concern.
2. *What are the dimensions of the problem?* We will give available
   statistics on the phenomenon being considered, with an indication of whether there is significant variation by age, sex, income,
   race, geographical location, and the like. Significant changes
   from past years will be noted.
3. *What are some of the explanations of the problem?* We will present
   and analyze various theories, especially those based on empirical

investigation. We will also point out related social changes that have taken place in America during this century.

4. *What programs for prevention and treatment are being used to ameliorate the problem?* Where empirical testing of these programs has been carried out, we will summarize the results. We also note that in some cases explanations of the problem are implicit in the programs.

5. *From a Christian perspective, what should be done?* We shall conclude our analysis of each social problem by suggesting types of action which Christians might consider taking in order to combat the problem being discussed. Our suggestions are an attempt to approach the problem from both a Christian and sociological perspective.

In our analysis we shall encounter gaps in knowledge, and these will be freely acknowledged. We devoutly hope that this lack of knowledge will not discourage students; rather, we hope that it will stimulate them to close the gap. The reader should bear in mind that the systematic, objective study of social phenomena, including social problems, is a relatively recent undertaking. In addition, the problems themselves and the factors associated with such problems are extremely complex.

An explanation of how we came to choose the particular problems analyzed in this volume is in order. There were two fundamental criteria. We have included those problems which are of greatest concern to members of American society and which have been studied by the sociological method. They are also the problems about which the authors are most knowledgeable. We feel, however, that our choice of the specific problems themselves is not of paramount importance. Nor are up-to-the-minute data on each problem of primary significance. What is most important for a general understanding of social problems is the development of the ability to analyze a social problem with objectivity and with appreciation of the complex factors involved. It is hoped that our analyses of the problems chosen will both help the reader develop this ability and provide pertinent information about areas of current interest.

Social change is a given in modern, technologically oriented societies. As members of modern society, we are embedded in this change. The question is whether we choose to consciously participate in it. Although God is changeless, he has a will for his creation which involves movement towards a desired end.

Topics for Review, Reflection, and Discussion

1. Why do theologically conservative Christians usually take politically conservative positions, while theologically liberal Christians often take politically liberal positions?

2. Is it theologically correct to think of sin as residing in social structures? Can social structures be thought of as evil?

3. Is there any conflict involved in emphasizing both a personal gospel and a social gospel?

4. Are there some social problems that are best combated by first converting individuals to the Christian faith?

5. Does dispensational theology necessarily entail a fatalistic attitude regarding attempts to combat social problems?

6. Give examples of theologies that can be understood as a product of the social upheaval of their times.

7. How realistic is it to believe that a Christian can apply the concepts of covenant, grace, empowering, and intimacy in all social relationships? In which relationships are these concepts most likely to be applicable?

8. Can you think of a specific family that exemplifies covenant love? a primary group that embodies *koinōnia*? a community that displays neighborliness? a society that has achieved *shalom*? For which group is it hardest to think of an example? Why?

Part 2

Analyses of Selected Social Problems

4

Crime and Juvenile Delinquency

All societies have regulations that prohibit behavior considered destructive of the social order; they require conduct which will maintain that order. Since violation of these regulations threatens the survival of society, we can assume that concern about such offenses is universal. Of course, societies vary widely in the kinds of regulations they develop and the extent to which their members violate these regulations. As urbanization and industrialization increase, so do the difficulties of social control. Consider also that the problems of regulating behavior in a democracy with relative freedom for the individual are different from those in a society with centralized control.

Evidence and Nature of the Concern

There is clear evidence that violation of the law has long been a concern of Americans; with the growth of cities, expansion of industries, and reinterpretation of individual freedom, this concern has increased. It is manifested in numerous ways, one of which is the development of voluntary organizations to prevent and combat delinquency and crime. For example, the National Council on Crime and Delinquency (NCCD) was established in 1907 and incorporated as a national service agency in 1921. Today the NCCD has throughout America regional, state, and community councils which provide consultation, training institutes, a clearinghouse for information, and other services for those at work in the areas of prevention, treatment, and control of delinquency and crime. The NCCD has combined with other organizations to sponsor conferences on ways to combat crime and delinquency.

A second illustration of concern can be found in governmental activities to legislate against, investigate, and punish those who violate the law. Congress and the legislative bodies of states and localities have as a fundamental task the passing of laws making certain actions illegal; they also change past laws so that they become more effective. For example, both houses of Congress developed and passed a bill with harsh penalties against the importation, manufacture, distribution, and use of illicit drugs; it was signed into law by the president in October 1988. Congress also from time to time sets up special investigative committees to look into allegations of the violation of laws, for example, the sale of American arms to Iran and the diversion of the profits to antigovernment forces in Nicaragua in 1986. Any candidate for political office who is

WHAT MAKES YOU THINK THAT I LIVE IN
A HIGH-CRIME-RATE AREA?

accused of being soft on crime has a difficult time being elected, unless the charge can be disproven.

A third illustration of concern is public-opinion polls which have shown the apprehension Americans feel about crime and delinquency. The Gallup Poll periodically asks Americans what they think are the most important problems facing this country. Crime has been consistently cited (Gallup 1988:89–90). Violations of the law that are cited separately as serious problems are the use of illegal drugs and vandalism, especially in schools.

The deep concerns Americans express about violation of the law reflect the values outlined in chapter 2 (pp. 28–34). Violation of law is a threat to life, liberty, and property. Its consequences include a loss of confidence in democratic government, a fear of bodily harm and loss of possessions, damage to legitimate businesses, and the enormous cost of protecting law-abiding citizens and prosecuting and imprisoning law violators. Most of these concerns have been summarized by the President's Commission on Law Enforcement and Administration of Justice (1967:59):

> There is the sheer cost of crime—billions of dollars every year spent on apprehending and adjudicating and treating offenders. There are the lives forfeited, the personal injuries suffered, the inconveniencing and sometimes irremedial loss and destruction of individual initiative, of productivity, of a basis of pride in and a sense of participation in society. And society . . . is inevitably diminished by the loss of a member's potential contribution.

Dimensions of the Problem

Expressions of concern about crime and delinquency show that Americans feel that the number of criminal and delinquent acts is far too high for the well-being of the nation. We need to ask, then, just how high the rates of delinquency and crime are, if they are increasing, and who the law violators are. But before doing this, we must clarify what is meant by "crime" and "delinquency."

Crime can be defined as an offense against the state. In criminal law the state as the injured party initiates the prosecution, and it punishes convicted offenders through fine, imprisonment, or execution. In civil law, on the other hand, the action is initiated and carried through by the person claiming to be harmed, and any judgment is rendered in behalf of the person who has been injured. Such judgment against the offender does not involve imprisonment unless the offender willfully disobeys the order of the court. It should be noted that violation of criminal or civil law is not to be equated with violation of informal rules about behavior considered to be offensive to good taste.

When criminal law is violated by children or youth, the violation is termed "juvenile delinquency." Until 1974, when Congress passed the Juvenile Justice and Delinquency Prevention Act, delinquency also included being ungovernable, running away from home, being truant from school, and other acts which adults could commit with impunity from the law. Congress labeled these and similar behaviors "status offenses" and urged that states no longer consider them violations of the law.

General Statistical Data on Crime

The most reliable statistical data on crime and delinquency in the United States come from *Uniform Crime Reports*, issued annually by the Federal Bureau of Investigation (FBI). The data for these reports are gathered through the voluntary cooperation of over twelve thousand law-enforcement agencies. The reports include violations known to officers of the law either from citizen complaints or through independent discovery.

Uniform Crime Reports characterizes eight types of violations as index crimes (or Part I Offenses). These eight types of crime are divided into two categories, crimes of violence against persons and crimes against property. In the former category are murder, forcible rape, robbery, and aggravated assault. In the latter are burglary, larceny-theft, motor-vehicle

Table 1

Index Crimes in the United States in 1978 and 1987

Index Crime*	Rate per 100,000		Percentage of change
	1978	1987	
Murder	9.0	8.3	−7.8
Forcible rape	31.0	37.4	+20.6
Robbery	195.8	212.7	+8.6
Aggravated assault	262.1	351.3	+34.0
Total crimes of violence	497.9	609.7	+22.5
Burglary	1,434.6	1,329.6	−7.3
Larceny–theft	2,747.4	3,081.3	+12.2
Motor-vehicle theft	460.5	529.4	+15.0
Total property crimes	4,642.5	4,940.3	+6.4
Total of all index crimes	5,140.4	5,550.0	+8.1

*Arson is not included, since it was not an index crime in 1978.

Source: U.S. Federal Bureau of Investigation, *Uniform Crime Reports—1987* (Washington, D.C.: Government Printing Office, 1988), p. 41.

theft, and arson (added in 1979). The FBI lists some twenty-one additional violations (Part II Offenses), which include embezzlement, vandalism, prostitution, and disorderly conduct.

Table 1 sums up the index crimes reported for 1987. For purposes of
comparison, the figures for 1978 are also given, along with the percentage of increase (or decrease) from 1978 to 1987. Note that except for murder and burglary, there was an upward trend in the number of crimes
reported.

Table 2

The Rate of Index Crimes
in Metropolitan and Rural Areas (1987)

Index Crime*	Rate per 100,000		
	Metropolitan areas	Other cities	Rural areas
Murder	9.2	4.5	5.7
Forcible rape	42.5	24.4	18.5
Robbery	268.6	49.9	14.7
Aggravated assault	399.7	272.0	138.7
Total crimes of violence	720.0	350.8	177.6
Burglary	1,484.8	1,042.0	670.1
Larceny–theft	3,440.0	3,302.7	942.7
Motor-vehicle theft	645.7	203.0	110.0
Total property crimes	5,574.5	4,547.7	1,722.8
Total of all index crimes	6,294.5	4,898.5	1,900.4

*Arson is not included because of insufficient data.

Source: U.S. Federal Bureau of Investigation, *Uniform Crime Reports—1987* (Washington, D.C.: Government Printing Office, 1988), p. 42.

Table 2 indicates that the rate of index crimes is consistently higher for
metropolitan areas than for smaller cities and rural areas. In fact, the rate
for metropolitan areas is more than three times that of rural areas, with
smaller cities falling in between. One of the tasks of a theory of crime is
to explain why the rate of index crimes is so high in metropolitan areas.

Characteristics of Persons Arrested

According to the *Uniform Crime Reports*, there were 10,795,869 arrests
in the United States in 1987. This, however, is only an approximate figure
of known criminals and delinquents, since some offenders are arrested
more than once during a year. It should also be borne in mind that arrest
figures are not an accurate reflection of the number of law violations.

Two or more persons may be arrested for the same crime; on the other hand, one arrest may cover several crimes committed by the same person. In addition, many complaints of violations never eventuate in the arrest of those who committed the offense. Finally, it is likely that various types of bias, especially in regard to socioeconomic status, race, and ethnic background, enter into who is and who is not arrested. In a sense, then, arrests are a measure of police activity, as well as an indication of who has been accused of breaking the law.

Age

A disproportionately large number of teenagers and young adults are arrested for violating the law. In 1987, for example, teenagers from fourteen through seventeen made up approximately 6 percent of the total population, but 25 percent of those arrested. Also, young adults from eighteen through twenty-four made up 11.5 percent of the population, but accounted for 32 percent of the arrests for index crimes. In contrast, people forty-five and over constituted approximately 31 percent of the total population in 1987, but less than 6 percent of those arrested for index crimes. It is clear, then, that those arrested for index crimes and other violations in America in 1987 were not randomly distributed by age but were predominately young.

Sex

Arrests of males greatly outnumber arrests of females. *Uniform Crime Reports* states that 82 percent of those arrested in 1987 were male, and 18 percent were female. In the population as a whole in 1987, males made up approximately 48 percent and females approximately 52 percent. Yet arrests of males outnumbered females in every category of index crimes and in all categories of nonindex crimes except prostitution–commercialized vice. From 1978 to 1987 arrests of females increased slightly more rapidly than arrests of males. Arrests of females increased 32.8 percent compared to an increase of 23.3 percent for males. Of the total arrests in 1978, 16.8 percent were of females, while in 1987 18 percent were of females.

Racial category

Similarly, statistics on arrests by racial category show another nonrandom distribution in the American population. In 1987, whites composed 84.6 percent of the total population and accounted for 68.7 percent of all arrests. Blacks made up 12.2 percent of the population and 29.5 percent of those arrested. Other races—American Indian, Asian, and Pacific Islander—made up 3.1 percent of the population and 1.8 percent of those arrested. It can be seen, then, that in 1987 blacks were arrested in disproportionately large numbers. When only index crimes are considered, the variation by race is even greater. Blacks were arrested for 35.5 percent of index crimes, whites for 62.6 percent, and other races for 1.9 percent.

Social status

Official statistics of those arrested do not include the social status of the offender. The social status of those arrested must be derived from special studies of arrest records, interviews, and questionnaires. While there has been some disagreement in research findings, mainly because of differences in the way social status has been determined, John Braithwaite's extensive review (1981) of more than a hundred studies of crime and social status has shown that there is a clear relationship between lower social status and arrests for serious crimes. Among the factors used to determine social status are amount of education, income, occupation, job stability, and neighborhood of residence. Some of these variables have been found to be more clearly associated with the likelihood of being arrested than have others. For example, one of the factors most clearly associated with juvenile delinquency has been low educational achievement. Another finding has been that adult crime is most prevalent when there is a significant gap between the incomes of the lower and upper class. It is also important to recognize that there are reciprocal effects between crime on the one hand, and unemployment or job instability on the other (Thornberry and Farnworth 1982).

Personality traits

Personality traits of delinquents have been measured in various ways; there have also been wide differences in the procedure for choosing subjects. In general, however, studies are in agreement that there are significant differences in the personality traits of delinquents and nondelinquents. One of the best known of these studies was carried out by Sheldon and Eleanor Glueck in Boston. They compared five hundred male delinquents with five hundred nondelinquents. In scrutinizing subjects who were similar in terms of neighborhood, age, racial/ethnic background, and intelligence quotient, the Gluecks found that the delinquents were more likely than the nondelinquents to be extroverted, uncooperative, hostile, defiant toward authority, impulsive, and suspicious of the motives of others (1950:215–43). In a follow-up study of most of their subjects after they became adults (1968), the Gluecks found that a large majority of those who had been delinquents as boys had been arrested for serious crimes as adults; the nondelinquent sample had been arrested far less frequently, and only for minor offenses.

In addition to the difficulties presented by the use of different procedures to measure personality and choose subjects, there has also been the persistent question of whether the delinquents developed the personality traits in question before or after they were labeled delinquents and kept in detention centers. There have been several attempts to deal with this issue. One such study was carried out by John Conger and W. C. Miller (1966). They reviewed the records of 2,348 males enrolled in the tenth grade in the Denver schools in 1956 and found that 271 had officially become delinquents by 1960. These 271 delinquents were matched with 271 nondelinquent classmates who were similar in age, racial/ethnic background, social status, and intelligence quotient. The researchers studied the biannual personal evaluations which the subjects' elementary-school and junior-high teachers had written. Conger and Miller found that those who later became delinquents had had difficulties in adjustment early on. Using several personality scales, they found that those who later became delinquents were less mature, less cooperative, less tolerant of frustration, and less likely to have stable social interests than were their nondelinquent counterparts.

Intelligence

A characteristic in which researchers have been vitally interested is intelligence. In one of the earliest studies of the relationship between intelligence and crime, Henry Goddard argued that every person of low intelligence is a potential criminal because of an inability to distinguish right from wrong. Goddard went as far as to say, "It is no longer to be denied that the greatest single cause of delinquency and crime is low-grade mentality, much of it within the limits of feeble-mindedness" (1920:73).

Reviews of Goddard's and similar studies of the comparative intelligence of delinquents and nondelinquents, however, have raised serious questions about the alleged correlation between low intelligence and delinquency. A general conclusion in the 1930s and 1940s was that there is at most a weak relationship between low intelligence and violations of the law. The matter is still being pursued, especially by those arguing that violations are directly related to low intelligence, for example, Travis Hirschi and Michael Hindelang (1977), whose "revisionist review" of the evidence challenges the notion that low intelligence is *not* related to delinquency and crime.

There are major problems in trying to relate lack of intelligence to crime. One of these has to do with the difficulties of measuring intelligence. Intelligence has been defined as the ability to solve problems, to learn from experience, to handle abstract concepts, to deal effectively with new situations, and so on. As a rule, measurement is done through intelligence-quotient (IQ) tests. Usually, then, when we refer to intelligence, we mean the score achieved on a particular IQ test. IQ scores, however, are an oversimplification of the concept of intelligence. Those who argue strongly that low intelligence contributes to delinquency and crime, for example, James Q. Wilson and Richard Herrnstein (1985:159), believe that low intelligence is associated with certain kinds of crime. They suggest that individuals with high intelligence will carry out low-risk crimes and do so with careful planning. At any rate, more research is needed before we can say with confidence that lack of intelligence and crime are related.

Physical characteristics

A number of studies have been carried out to see if those arrested for violating the law differ in physical traits from the rest of the population. One of the earliest investigations was conducted in the mid-to-late 1800s by Cesare Lombroso, an Italian military physician, who compared the traits of prisoners and nonprisoners. Lombroso reported that prisoners had more physical stigmata, including asymmetry of the face, ears of unusual size, and receding or excessively long chins. But contrary evidence soon questioned Lombroso's findings. In 1900 Charles Goring, an English physician, began an extensive study of English prisoners, comparing them with students at Oxford and Cambridge, hospital patients, and soldiers in the British army. Goring found no significant difference in physical traits between prisoners and nonprisoners. In contrast, Earnest Hooton, a Harvard physical anthropologist, took twenty-two standardized measurements of the bodies of hundreds of criminals and noncriminals, and found that criminals differed not only from noncriminals with respect to nearly all body measurements, but also among themselves according to the type of crime for which they had been convicted (1939). Hooton's work has been heavily criticized for both the methods and samples used.

A particular characteristic that has been associated with criminality is body type. William Sheldon (1949) applied the concept of somatotype to a study of two hundred delinquent youth in Boston and reported that the most seriously delinquent boys were mesomorphic (athletic in appearance) rather than ectomorphic (thin, linear, and fragile) or endomorphic (smooth, generally round, and fat). In the study by the Gluecks (1950) reported earlier in this chapter, the five hundred boys who had been apprehended for breaking the law differed significantly from the five hundred nondelinquents in body type, with the delinquent boys more likely to be mesomorphic. Specifically it was found that almost twice as many delinquents as nondelinquents were mesomorphic.

A final physical trait that we shall consider is the XYY chromosomal abnormality. The body cells of females have two X chromosomes; normal males have an X chromosome and a Y chromosome; some males have an extra Y or male-determining chromosome. This abnormality was first reported in 1961. It later came into prominence in murder trials in France and Australia in 1968, when defense lawyers claimed their clients were not responsible for their criminal actions because of the XYY characteristic, which reputedly led to violent and aggressive behavior over which they had no control. In a review of eighty-five studies of the XYY chromosomal abnormality, the National Institute of Mental Health (1970) reports that in imprisoned populations there is 1 XYY male for every 140 XY males; among nonimprisoned adult males there is 1 XYY male for every 1,036 XY. Two conclusions are clear from the review: the XYY characteristic is rare, and it occurs more frequently among imprisoned males than among nonimprisoned males.

Theories of Delinquency and Crime

One of the chief purposes of theories of delinquency and crime is to integrate the multitude of available facts on the subject. The more facts covered by a theory, and the more logical its correlation of those facts, and the more accurate its predictions, the more adequate is the theory. So, rather than trying to explain delinquency and crime as such, our task will be to look at various attempts to relate the facts to one another.

A further approach to theory that we shall take is to differentiate among the assumed loci of causation (see pp. 79–83). Physiological theories locate causation within the individual's genetic inheritance. Psychological theories also assume that causation is found within the individual, but in one's early experiences rather than one's innate makeup. Sociocultural theories, on the other hand, place causation outside the individual and in the norms and structure of society. We do not believe that one type of theory is stronger than or preferable to the others. Rather, we will utilize the different types of theories to deal with different kinds of data.

Among the facts with which a theory of delinquency and crime must deal are these: metropolitan areas have a higher rate of delinquency and crime than do smaller cities and rural areas; young people from fourteen through twenty-five make up a disproportionately large number of those arrested; males are more than four times as likely as females to be arrested; blacks are more likely than those of other races to be arrested, especially for index crimes; individuals of lower social status are more likely to be arrested than are those of upper social status; those arrested tend to be extroverted, uncooperative, defiant of authority, impulsive, intolerant of frustration, somewhat low in intelligence, and mesomorphic.

Before turning to specific theories, we need to take one more step in clarifying our approach. Frequently a multifactor explanation is offered. One of the best-known multifactor explanations is that of the Gluecks (1950). In explaining differences in the behavior of delinquents and nondelinquents, the Gluecks speak of "factors with probable causal significance." As they draw their data together, they point out that they do not regard any single factor as the cause of delinquency; rather, they take into account the interaction of several factors from which "a tentative causal formula of law emerges." Among the factors they cite are that delinquents are more likely than nondelinquents to be mesomorphic, restlessly energetic and aggressive, and hostile and defiant in attitude; they come from homes with little understanding, affection, and stability (1950: 281–82). The Gluecks go on to say that while in individual cases any one of these factors may account for delinquency, in general the interaction of all of these conditions and forces is needed to bring about delinquency.

A more recent multifactor explanation has been summarized by Richard Jenkins and his colleagues in a volume entitled *No Single Cause* (1985). The authors contend that several elements blend together in varying degrees to cause delinquent acts: failure to develop the capacity of feeling compassion for others; failure to develop appropriate behavior by empathizing with others; lack of opportunity to meet basic social needs; opportunity to fill some of these needs by violating the law; the influence of peers and older associates to engage in delinquent acts (1985:19–20).

The difficulty with such multifactor explanations is that a mere listing of contributory conditions does not explain how such factors bring about delinquency. Multifactor explanations have the merit of avoiding the oversimplification of single-factor explanations, but they fail to tie the various factors together in such a way that enables us to explain why law violation occurs. We must develop a broader principle that unites these factors. As we move into general theories, the inadequacy of multifactor explanations will become clearer.

Genetic and Physiological Theory

There is general agreement among the advocates of the genetic/physiological theory of law violation that there are probably no specific, identifiable genes that can account for law-violating behavior. Rather, certain physical traits or conditions that are genetically based or acquired during development in the uterus are sufficient to cause aggression, violence, and, possibly, criminal behavior. Lawrence Taylor in *Born to Crime: The Genetic Causes of Criminal Behavior* (1984) lists a number of them: brain dysfunction, hypoglycemia combined with temporal-lobe dysfunction, the XYY aberration, premenstrual syndrome, high levels of testosterone, genetic predisposition to alcoholism and drug addiction, and mesomorphism. While Taylor believes that these physical traits and conditions are sufficient to cause aggression and violence, he does not say that they inevitably in and of themselves lead to crime. He does, however, believe they are necessary prerequisites to crimes of aggression and violence.

Taylor and others who posit biological bases for crime spend considerable time and energy attacking what they call environmental determinists. But they seem to miss the point that different theories are needed to handle different facts about criminal behavior. Genetic/physiological theories appear to be most adequate in accounting for crimes of aggression and violence, especially assaults and murders that appear to be irrational, since the physical conditions which presumably produce such behavior are the result of genetic makeup and are not subject to the control of the individual. The genetic/physiological theory, however, needs to make clear how the allegedly inborn traits of aggression and violence lead to the breaking of criminal law. How can these traits be channeled, instead, into legitimate expression in highly competitive areas like sales, personnel recruitment, and sports?

Psychological Theory

Earlier in this chapter we reported studies that show that delinquents are more impulsive, more defiant toward authority, more suspicious of the motives of others, less cooperative, and less tolerant of frustration than are nondelinquents. Furthermore, at least one study shows that these characteristics precede rather than follow delinquent behavior. While it might be claimed that some of these traits are inherited or developed because of biological makeup, they can also be attributed to the way in which the individual has been brought up. In a review of numerous studies Jenkins and his colleagues (1985:23–33) conclude that children with such socially unacceptable characteristics are very likely to have suffered maternal rejection from birth and to have lacked adequate nurturing and affection as they reached maturity. Unable to get along with others, these children were a problem at home, in school, and in the community. They tended to drop out of school, run away from home, and commit antisocial and illegal acts. Their delinquent behavior could be explained, then, by their inability to conform to societal expectations.

A psychological theory that has received a great deal of attention was proposed by James Q. Wilson and Richard Herrnstein in *Crime and Human Nature* (1985), which claims to be "the definitive study of the causes of crime." The authors concentrate entirely on the individual criminal. Their theory states that those who break the law do so because the material and nonmaterial rewards of crime are perceived to be greater than the material and nonmaterial rewards of abiding by the law. The assumption is made that human behavior is determined by its consequences. If one's acts are rewarded, they are likely to be repeated; if they are punished, they are unlikely to be repeated. Delinquent behavior, then, results from conditioning. The authors describe how conditioning to delinquent behavior is related to mesomorphism, a background that includes a criminal father, low intelligence, impulsiveness, and an autonomic nervous system that has difficulty in responding to stimuli. As is true of those who advocate the genetic/physiological theory of crime, Wilson and Herrnstein are hostile toward social and cultural explanations, for they insist that it is the individual who acts and whose behavior must be explained.

Sociocultural Theory

The task of the sociocultural theory is to explain the high rate of delinquency and crime among specific social categories. It seeks, for example, to explain why the highest rates of criminal activity are to be found among young people, in males, in large metropolitan centers, among certain minority groupings, and among the lower socioeconomic classes.

Subcultures of delinquency

One sociocultural theory of crime is that there are delinquency areas characterized by relatively high rates of law violation. These areas are most likely to be found in the inner cities of metropolitan centers. Clifford Shaw and Henry McKay (1969) point out that those growing up in inner-city areas are exposed to social values, norms, and attitudes different from those of the rest of American society. A tradition of delinquency develops, perpetuated by gangs. Through contact with these gangs, youths growing up in the slums learn techniques of stealing and the norms and attitudes which enable them to form binding relationships with and to be accepted by gang members. This explanation of delinquency stresses the normality of law-breaking behavior. According to Shaw and McKay, "in cases of group delinquency it may be said . . . that from the point of view of the delinquent's immediate social world, he is not necessarily disorganized, maladjusted, or antisocial. Within the limits of his social world and in terms of its norms and expectations, he may be a highly organized and well-adjusted person" (1969:316).

Strain theory

The strain theory suggests that lower-class youth, especially in inner cities, cannot compete successfully for high status and material goods, values that are cherished by American society, and so they are placed under a severe strain (Vold and Bernard 1986:194–201). Sharing the conventional goals of society, which they are unable to reach through legitimate channels, these youth adopt illegal means of obtaining money and desirable material goods. At the same time they are gaining high status in the eyes of their peers.

Differential association

The final sociocultural theory at which we shall look is differential association, which has been advanced by Edwin Sutherland. His basic thesis is that "a person becomes delinquent because of an excess of definitions favorable to violation of law over definitions unfavorable to violation of law" (Sutherland and Cressey 1970:75). In other words, a person who has some form of association with criminal behavior patterns, attitudes, and values, as well as with delinquents and criminals, is likely to adopt criminal practices. And the greater the frequency, duration, and intensity of the association with criminal patterns, the more likely it is that criminal behavior will result. This theory has been both supported and challenged by numerous studies. A recent review of these studies concludes that while the theory remains viable inasmuch as "the extent of 'bonding' to conventional and delinquent peers is by far the most important predictor of delinquency" (Matsueda 1988:295), continued testing is needed.

All three of these sociocultural theories claim to be able to handle reasonably well the sociological data concerning delinquency and crime. The young, being less committed than adults to conventional ways and more apt to experiment with different behaviors, are more likely to be involved in crime; males are less restricted than females by social custom and are expected to be more daring; large metropolitan centers have greater anonymity than do small towns and rural areas, and thus offer more opportunity for deviant behavior; blacks tend to be concentrated in disproportionately high numbers in inner-city slums and to have fewer social controls than do other races; finally, those in the lower socioeconomic groupings are less likely to have legitimate employment opportunities than are those in the upper socioeconomic groupings.

The reader should note once more that sociocultural theories do not purport to explain why particular individuals violate criminal law while others do not. Rather, sociocultural theories attempt to explain why different social categories exhibit different rates of criminal behavior. On the other hand, the genetic/physiological and psychological theories concentrate on why particular individuals break the law. Of course, these three approaches can overlap. For example, the difference in the number of crimes committed by males and females has been accounted for by genetic theorists in terms of physiological makeup, by psychologists in terms of both biological predisposition and societal expectations, and by sociocultural theorists in terms of gender roles determined by the society and culture.

Sheldon Glueck (1956) has criticized sociocultural theory by challenging its basic assumption that criminal behavior is learned. According to Glueck, it is nondelinquency that must be learned. Delinquency, for Glueck, is nonconventional, nonconforming behavior that has a biopsychological base composed of "primitive tendencies" toward "asocial, dissocial, or anti-social impulses and desires" which must be "tamed" to win social approval. Glueck's position and that of sociocultural theory are irreconcilable. There is also an irreconcilable difference between the individualistic theory of Wilson and Herrnstein and the sociocultural position. According to Wilson and Herrnstein, all behavior, including criminal behavior, must be understood in terms of *individual* decisions

(1985:42–43). Their theory, which focuses entirely on the choices made by individuals, has no place for the influence of social structures and societal norms.

Jenkins and his colleagues (1985) have suggested what might be termed a division of labor among the three approaches to explaining the facts about delinquency and crime. They differentiate between unsocialized and socialized delinquents. The unsocialized (or undersocialized) delinquent cannot get along with others because of constitutional makeup, maternal rejection, and lack of affection during early childhood. The unsocialized delinquent, for the most part, acts alone or with temporary companions, while the socialized delinquent is part of a group which routinely violates the law. Biologists and psychologists can study the individual upbringing of unsocialized delinquents. Socioculturalists can study the influence of social structures and cultural norms on socialized delinquents. Cooperation among the approaches would be more productive than criticism of each other or the assumption that one approach can handle all of the facts regarding delinquency and crime.

Prevention and Treatment

What are some of the ways delinquency and crime are being dealt with, and how effective are they? In answering these questions it will be convenient to distinguish between two general approaches, prevention and treatment. Prevention includes programs that try to keep violations of law from happening, while treatment concerns ways of dealing with actual delinquents and criminals. These two approaches, however, are not strictly separable, for prevention may involve measures to keep youngsters who are having difficulties with their family or school from breaking the law. Treatment, on the other hand, has as one of its aims preventing convicted criminals from breaking the law again after they have been released.

The reader would do well to remember that assumptions about causation are present either implicitly or explicitly in the various attempts to prevent or to treat delinquency and crime. While we have a long way to go in developing theory to explain the facts about delinquency and crime, practice cannot await the full development of theory, for those with responsibility to do something about violations of the law are required to act. It is possible, of course, that practice can succeed without our understanding why. It is the conviction of the authors, however, that in the long run adequate theory is required before effective programs can be designed. In this sense, sound theory is highly practical.

Prevention

We noted earlier that law violators tend to be young and that once officially labeled delinquents, they are apt to break the law again. It is not surprising, therefore, that most of the work in prevention has been directed toward juveniles.

Strengthening the family and the neighborhood

In assuming that juvenile delinquency is likely to develop when the influences fostering conformity to societal norms are weak, it logically follows that weak and inconsistent control by one's family, association with delinquent peers, and neighborhoods with high crime rates serve to encourage a young person to violate the law. One approach to strengthening families and thus reducing delinquency has been an emphasis on family values. Families have been encouraged to do things together, including attending church or synagogue and participating in recreational activities. Parents are urged to become involved in their children's schoolwork and in parent-teacher organizations. If difficulties develop in relationships between parents, or between parents and children, family counseling is available. Governmental help has been provided to enable poor families to hold together. Such governmental programs include subsidized housing, aid to families with dependent children, food stamps, welfare payments, and job training. Because many mothers of small children now work outside the home, more and more attention is being paid by government and religious groups to child care. The objective is to make available to working parents places where their children can receive safe, well-regulated care from trained teachers who love children. Further, far more attention is being paid to child abuse; in many states, in fact, teachers, doctors, social workers, and others who have contact with young children are required to report suspected cases.

Another approach to the prevention of delinquency has been the establishment of supervised neighborhood facilities, housing for the homeless, and neighborhood-watch associations. To reduce violations of the law in areas of high delinquency, Shaw and McKay (1969) argue that there should be action by those most directly related to the problem, namely the residents of those areas. They set up what was known as the Chicago Area Project in ten neighborhoods of high delinquency, keeping outside leadership to a minimum and emphasizing the development of indigenous leaders. Neighborhood committees were formed to carry out numerous activities to attract residents toward conventional rather than illegal pursuits. A recent study of the Shaw-McKay approach (Heitgerd and Bursik 1987) points out that while it has merit, factors external to the neighborhood must be taken into account in trying to reduce violations of the law. This study states that external factors such as economic changes in the society, racial impingement on the neighborhood, and the development of unwanted expressways through the area may induce the residents to engage in illegal activities opposing those changes. We might add that such highly lucrative practices as the sale of crack cocaine may produce a form of gang warfare with a sharp increase in violence over which the neighborhood has little control. In other words, the neighborhood cannot be isolated from other developments in the city and in the society as a whole.

The recently developed and popular neighborhood-watch program involves collective surveillance of the neighborhood. The residents are encouraged to watch for anything suspicious going on and to report their observations to one another and to the police. Neighborhood meetings are held in the hope that cohesion will be increased and crime reduced. Signs are posted that the area is under special surveillance. A review of these programs, unfortunately, has not been encouraging. Although more than 80 percent of Americans approve of neighborhood-watch programs and say they would be willing to join one, only 5 percent are actually involved (Rosenbaum 1987:112). Furthermore, the programs in operation are in middle-class neighborhoods, not high-crime areas. Meetings to discuss strategy are not well attended, and fear of crime often increases after the exchange of information. The review concludes that although the watch programs have been oversold, a higher level of citizen participation in crime prevention is a commendable goal. Much more research on how to bring about neighborhood cohesion and cooperation to prevent crime needs to be done.

Work with juvenile gangs

Another approach to preventing delinquency has been for highly trained adults, known as detached workers, to direct youth gangs into constructive channels. In this way, the group dynamic can be used rather than combated. This approach also solicits and coordinates the aid of various social agencies in the community. Studies of the effectiveness of these programs, however, have not been encouraging. Malcolm Klein (1971) has found that attempts at adult direction of gang activities has had very little effect:

> By the time boys and girls become affiliated with a juvenile gang, they have experienced 12 to 18 years of formative processes from the family, the neighborhood and the society. They continue to be bombarded by the contemporary factors of group and social processes even as we work with them. . . .
>
> Arrayed against this veritable army of psychological, social, and cultural forces is the detached worker and the few resources at his disposal. David beat Goliath, but at least he had a slingshot. How would he have fared against a hundred Goliaths? How conceited we are to expect one worker, however reinforced, to overcome substantially the combined forces of family, neighborhood and society. [1971:52]

Klein proposes organizing alternative activities to reduce gang cohesiveness. His follow-up study of a juvenile gang in East Los Angeles shows that by restricting gang activities of any type and by making it difficult to recruit new members, a reduction in the number of violations of the law can be achieved.

Treatment

Treatment has both a negative and a positive aspect. Punishment, the negative aspect, carries the assumption that if pain results from law-violating behavior, such behavior will not be repeated. On the other hand, rehabilitation, the positive aspect, aims at changing convicted law violators so that they will adopt legitimate ways of behavior.

Punishment

Punishment can take the form of fines, imprisonment, and execution. One of the chief purposes of punishment is to keep the offender from repeating criminal acts in the future. The logic is that once punished, the offender will have learned a lesson and will avoid illegal acts in the future for fear of being punished again. There is, however, a high rate of recidivism among released prisoners, for as many as 65 to 70 percent are rearrested.

Studies of juvenile offenders show that some kinds of punishment are more effective than others in preventing recidivism. In a study of more than two thousand juvenile offenders from four Illinois jurisdictions, John Wooldredge (1988) found that close supervision in open community facilities is relatively more effective than mere probation or than high-security detention homes. If juveniles are sent to detention facilities, their stay should be short in order to reduce recidivism. A review of the correctional treatment of juveniles between 1975 and 1984 reported that recidivism was reduced most when there were strong external controls, full daily schedules, and surveillance by community agencies (Lab and Whitehead 1988).

Earlier in this chapter we mentioned the Juvenile Justice and Delinquency Prevention Act, which keeps status offenses by juveniles (e.g., truancy) from being dealt with as criminal offenses. There have been both favorable and unfavorable results of this law. On the one hand, it has helped to keep many juveniles from being sentenced by the justice system and labeled delinquent, although according to one finding, truants, runaways, and ungovernable children are now labeled sick instead of bad (Frazier and Cochran 1986). On the other hand, Anne Schneider (1984) found that it is difficult for children with status offenses to receive community services. Yet some form of such services is needed to keep runaways from having to support themselves through prostitution, the sale of drugs, and petty theft. Schneider points to the importance of ensuring that "children who are in need of assistance are not left to their own devices and ignored" (1984:349).

The form of punishment that should be the strongest deterrent to crime is execution. Yet there is a serious question as to whether it does deter crime. Sarah Dike (1982) asked three questions designed to find out if capital punishment has been effective in reducing homicide. Does the homicide rate increase when a state abolishes the death penalty? Do contiguous states, one with and one without the death penalty, differ in homicide rates? Do the number of homicides decline when there is an execution? Dike found that there is no direct relationship between homicide rates and the death penalty. Furthermore, there is a tendency for the homicide rate to increase after executions. Dike concluded that since most murders are impulsive acts of passion, the death penalty would be unlikely to prevent them. And as far as calculated murders are concerned, for example, by hired killers, the risk of being apprehended is low. Dike cites a study of over one thousand gangland murders in Chicago—there were only twenty-three convictions, four sentences to life imprisonment, and no death sentences (1982:42). It is also noteworthy that when the death penalty was put into practice again in 1977 (after a ten-year hiatus because of legal complications), five of the first eight men to be executed had insisted that all appeals be stopped. Such choices by individuals about to be put to death makes one wonder just how much a deterrent the death penalty is.

Regardless of the relationship between certainty of punishment and the rate of crime, there are several functions that punishment logically serves. First, it acts as a reinforcement of the sanctity of law, both for those who break the law and those who do not. It underscores the unity of society and the necessity for the individual to abide by its rules. Second, law enforcement is required if an urbanized, highly interdependent society like ours is to avoid chaos. Third, it is probable that efficient law enforcement does deter organized crime.

Rehabilitation

The high rate of recidivism indicates that much of the crime committed in the United States is by individuals who have been arrested previously. Therefore, a major way to make a reduction in the crime rate is to rehabilitate offenders so that they do not repeat illegal acts. Those who support rehabilitation efforts point out that convicted lawbreakers need special help if they are to become constructive citizens upon release from prison. Several different kinds of rehabilitation programs have been instituted, including intensive group therapy, occupational training, job placement, probation, and parole.

An illustration of group therapy is a program for juveniles at Highfields, New Jersey (Jenkins et al. 1985:106–7). The objective is to bring about self-rehabilitation, with the force of group pressure aimed at discouraging delinquent behavior and encouraging nondelinquent behavior in its stead. A follow-up study concluded that the program has been more successful than programs with comparable delinquents at a state detention center which does not offer such therapy. Further evaluations of the Highfields experience showed that certain carefully selected juvenile delinquents can be dealt with more effectively in small, short-term facilities than in state reformatories.

Programs of education, occupational training, and job placement are designed to enable the prisoner to take up legitimate work when released. The logic is that without something constructive to do, the released prisoner will likely resort to violating the law again. Most offenders have poor work records; so if rehabilitation is to be achieved, special efforts must be made to provide vocational training and a satisfactory job upon release. A few companies have developed work programs within the prison system; in other cases prisoners are released for the day to work at a regular job and then return to the prison at night. The purpose of such programs is to enable prisoners to contribute to the support of their families and to develop greater self-confidence and self-respect. Most of these programs have been successful; unfortunately, a few highly publicized exceptions, where prisoners released for work have committed violent crimes, have caused entire programs to be curtailed.

Probation and parole, accompanied by careful supervision, can be considered efforts at rehabilitation. Probation involves a suspending of the sentence on the condition of good behavior for a stipulated period of time. It is most often used for first-time offenders, in part as an incentive to avoid future violations of the law. Parole is granted to convicted offenders after they have served some part of their sentence. It is designed to remove prisoners from the institutional environment, place them in the outside community, and hasten their adjustment to civilian life. Probation and parole can be provided at a small fraction of the cost of imprisonment. The best risks for successful adjustment are paroled and given supervision, while the poorest risks are kept until their maximum sentence has been served; they are then released without supervision. Studies show that the great majority of all offenders could benefit from supervision as they reenter life outside prison.

A Christian Response to Crime and Juvenile Delinquency

Paul writes in Romans 13:1 that "everyone must submit himself to the governing authorities, for there is no authority except that which God has established" (NIV). The Bible seems to leave no room for an anarchist position—followers of Christ are to respect the law. But governmental law is to reflect biblical ideals of justice. Accordingly, the first duty of all Christians in society is to actively work for the implementation of just laws. And in regard to a response to crime and juvenile delinquency, they must develop a Christian view of just punishment.

In a society which has become increasingly relativistic, it is understandably tempting for Christians to take unambiguous and uncomplicated positions on a moral issue such as punishment. In seeking to use the Bible as their source, various groups have offered their own unambiguous "Christian" views of punishment, which are often contradictory. The biblical view of punishment is far from uncomplicated, however. What might be most helpful here is the development of a social theology which recognizes and incorporates the scriptural complexities on this subject.

To punish is to cause a person to undergo pain, loss, or suffering for a wrongdoing. As a legal concept, punishment is the penalty imposed on an individual for a criminal offense. A criminal offense is an offense against society; accordingly, we will keep today's society in view as we attempt to develop a theology of punishment.

The Biblical View of Punishment

Consideration of the wrongful act and the motive

A criminal offense includes two elements: the wrongful act itself and the intent of the perpetrator. In determining the type of punishment to be inflicted on the offender, our current legal system takes both of these elements into account. For example, an automobile driver who accidentally hit and killed a pedestrian can be charged only with manslaughter rather than murder, because the intent to kill was not present. On the other hand, an individual who picked up a gun and fired it at another with the intent to kill, but missed the would-be victim, would be charged only with intent to murder. In neither case would the offender be charged with first-degree murder, for this charge entails both a premeditated intent to kill and the accomplished fact. Nor, however, would the offenders in our examples go scot-free, for each would be held accountable for either the act or the intent.

That this is so is an encouraging sign that our criminal-justice system is at least in part a reflection of biblical ethics. The Bible clearly teaches that punishment for an offense must take into account both the act and the motive. This is perhaps most clearly stated in Exodus 21:12–14: "Anyone who strikes a man and kills him shall surely be put to death. However, if he does not do it intentionally, but God lets it happen, he is to flee to a place [God] will designate. But if a man schemes and kills another man deliberately, take him away from [the] altar and put him to death" (NIV). The Ten Commandments likewise strike a balance between act and intent.

Justice and mercy

In addition to considering both act and intent, punishment in the Bible must be understood as encompassing both justice and mercy. This dual concern is, of course, part of the larger biblical teachings about law and grace. Our understanding of the relationships between law and grace is perhaps most clearly addressed by Paul in his statement, "Christ is the end of the law so that there may be righteousness for everyone who believes" (Rom. 10:4 NIV). As Paul elaborates on this text, we learn that there is nothing wrong with the law itself, for it points the way to live according to God's intention. The problem is that because no one is perfect, we cannot fulfil the law. Christ is the end of the law in the sense that he is the perfect fulfilment of the law. Because of Christ's perfection and righteousness, our righteousness does not come from our keeping the law, but from our faith in Christ.

We can understand the relationship between justice and mercy in much the same way, for God in his holiness demands justice, but he demonstrates mercy through the giving of Jesus Christ. By his example God has taught us that when we exercise punishment within our society, we must also demand justice but demonstrate mercy.

In a general sense, justice shows concern for the victim, while mercy shows concern for the offender. The emphasis in the Old Testament seems to be on the victim. An attempt to build a philosophy of punishment only upon Old Testament teachings, as some Christians seek to do, yields a view which shows little concern for the offender. What the Old Testament says has to be tempered by the examples of mercy shown by Jesus. When the Pharisees brought to Jesus a woman who had been caught in adultery, they were quite right that the law of Moses demanded that she be stoned. (Actually, according to the letter of the law, both she and the man with whom she committed adultery were to be stoned—Deut. 22:22–24.) Jesus, however, showed mercy when he replied to the Pharisees, "If any one of you is without sin, let him be the first to throw a stone at her." After her accusers had left, Jesus turned to the woman and said, "Then neither do I condemn you. . . . Go now and leave your life of sin" (John 8:3–11 NIV). Before God all of us are accused and found guilty. But by giving Jesus Christ, God showed mercy to us. Christ's example has shown us how we might be merciful, too. It is with an eye toward God's great mercy that we are to understand Jesus' comments in Matthew 5:38: "You have heard that it was said, 'Eye for eye, and tooth for tooth'" (NIV).

A Social Theology of Punishment

Having considered the biblical view of punishment, we are now ready to develop a theology of punishment suitable for application in contemporary society. A social theology of punishment must strike a balance

Figure 4

A Social Theology of Punishment

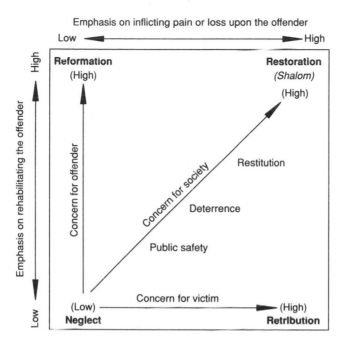

Emphasis on inflicting pain or loss upon the offender

between justice and mercy. Figure 4 is a visual conceptualization of various approaches to punishment. Where there is a low emphasis on both inflicting pain upon and rehabilitating the offender, we have a condition which can be called societal *neglect*. A society in which this is found would tend toward anarchy—the absence of government or law—for there is no collective mechanism to come to grips with the wrongs which one person may inflict upon another.

A society which has a high emphasis on inflicting pain upon the offender, but a low emphasis on rehabilitation, is practicing *retribution*. Retribution shows concern for the victim's need for revenge, ensuring that the offender pays for the offense committed. The law of revenge as practiced by the ancient Hebrews not only provided punishment similar in nature to the offense, but specified the maximum punishment allowable (Exod. 21:23–36). There is a sense in which retribution not only attempts to equal the score between the offender and the victim, but also serves to unify society by drawing attention to the legitimacy of the societal norm which has been violated.

A low emphasis on inflicting pain combined with a high emphasis on rehabilitating the offender constitutes *reformation*. There are some who believe that reformation is the only appropriate course. Those who hold to this position are often characterized as secular humanists who understand behavior as "determined by our genes, our environment, and the associations of infancy, . . . with the result that all too frequently the criminal is regarded not as an offender but as a victim of his circumstances who needs treatment rather than punishment" (Hughes 1983:113).

The problem with the reformation approach is not only that it fails to show concern for the victim, but also that it fails to treat the offender as a responsible human being. Not to hold a person responsible for his or her own behavior renders that individual less than the choice-making, accountable human being that God created. As C. S. Lewis (1970:287) has stated, "When we cease to consider what the criminal deserves and consider only what will cure him or deter others, we have tacitly removed him from the sphere of justice altogether; instead of a person, a subject of rights, we now have a mere object, a patient, a 'case.'"

There are three reasons for punishment: concern for the victim, concern for the offender, and concern for society. Punishment motivated by concern for the good of society is usually referred to as *deterrence*. The reasoning here is that punishing the offender will, by example, discourage others from committing the same offense. Inversely, if the offender is not punished or is only lightly punished, then others may be less resistant to committing the same offense. Where there is low concern for society, deterrence is not a strong motivational force. As concern for society increases, deterrence becomes a driving factor.

Punishing offenders for the good of society may entail considerations other than deterrence. At a lower level, the act of removing the offender from society can be motivated by a desire for *public safety.* Merely getting the offender off the streets is a less ambitious motive than holding the offender up as an example. By contrast, *restitution* and *restoration* are more ambitious motives than mere deterrence. Although punishment in modern society is rarely based on concerns for restitution and restoration, these are two of the dominant reasons for punishment given in the Bible.

In restitution the punishment recompenses in some direct way the harm done to the victim. Chapter 21 of Exodus contains a number of examples:

> If men quarrel and one hits the other with a stone or with his fist . . . he must pay the injured man for the loss of his time and see that he is completely healed. . . .
>
> If a man hits a manservant or maidservant in the eye and destroys it, he must let the servant go free to compensate for the eye. . . .
>
> If a man uncovers a pit or digs one and fails to cover it and an ox or a donkey falls into it, the owner of the pit must pay for the loss; he must pay its owner, and the dead animal will be his. [vv. 18–19, 26, 33–34 NIV]

Exodus 22:1 teaches that in certain cases restitution needs to be more than the loss inflicted on another: "If a man steals an ox or a sheep and slaughters it or sells it, he must pay back five head of cattle for the ox and four sheep for the sheep" (NIV). So strong was the Old Testament emphasis upon restitution that inability to pay back the victim could result in the offender's being "sold to pay for his theft" (Exod. 22:3). Chapter 22 of Exodus continues to detail punishments based upon the principle of restitution.

Our legal system today seeks to make the punishment given to the offender equivalent to the harm done to the victim. Only rarely, however, is the offender made to recompense the victim directly. Yet it is only through restitution that the victim can hope to be, even in part, recompensed for the loss incurred. The absence of restitution may be one of the reasons why victims in our society cry out so stridently for revenge.

Actually, restitution is in many cases an effective way to bring about the rehabilitation of the offender. Under the existing system most offenders leave penal institutions more hardened than when they entered. Part of the reason for this may well be the lack of logic between the offense committed and the punishment given.

Finally, there is the ideal situation, where there is high concern for the victim, for the offender, and for society. A society which combines these three motivations for punishment is practicing *restoration*. Restoration is in part the process of attempting to reestablish the interpersonal accord which was present before an offense occurred. Restitution can begin the process of restoration, because restitution focuses upon reestablishing equity in the relationship between the offender and the victim. Interpersonal restoration is possible only after there is a change in both the offender and the victim. The offender must go through a process of sorrow, confession, repentance, and asking forgiveness for the wrong committed.

The Christian basis for interpersonal restoration is the biblical model of reconciliation. In the Old Testament, reconciliation was achieved by offering a sacrificial atonement for sin (Lev. 6:30; 16:20). Jesus radicalized the concept of reconciliation by tying it to resolving any dispute one might have with an offending brother: "Therefore, if you are offering your gift at the altar and there remember that your brother has something against you, leave your gift there in front of the altar. First go and be reconciled to your brother; then come and offer your gift" (Matt. 5:23–24 NIV). It is noteworthy that the Greek word for "being reconciled" is *diallassomai*, which means "to be changed entirely." Reconciliation or interpersonal restoration is not merely for the benefit of the offender, but for the offended and for God, who desires that broken relationships be mended.

It is significant that Jesus taught that Christians should take the initiative in seeking reconciliation. The basis of this teaching is found in the reconciliation made possible by Christ's atoning death—"Be reconciled to God. God made him who had no sin to be sin for us, so that in him we might become the righteousness of God" (2 Cor. 5:20–21 NIV). The theology of the cross provides a basis for Christians to pursue and achieve reconciliation with offending brothers.

Reconciliation or restoration in the offender-victim relationship must not be superficially rushed, however. Victims must be given time to experience and admit to deep feelings of betrayal, grief, anger, rage, and desire for revenge. The last thing they need (quite literally) is to be urged to forgive the offender. Forgiveness is possible only after the victim has been able to let go and disarm the emotional power that the offense has wielded over his or her life. Forgiveness never means condoning or excusing the offense. It must be a conscious choice on the part of the victim, a choice which can be aided by the empowering of God's grace (see Lewis Smedes's *Forgive and Forget* for an excellent discussion of this matter). The other side of true reconciliation is that the person who committed the offense must be fully penitent for the wrong. When the offender truly repents and the victim forgives, there is interpersonal reconciliation, that is, restoration. The parties involved have become neighbors to one another.

In addition, the biblical view of punishment calls for restoration at the societal level. Social structures can create an environment within which certain types of criminal offense are likely to occur. For example, a situation which allows a few to accumulate vast wealth, while others are left poor and destitute, by its very nature encourages criminal activity. Such social structures are evil and must undergo restoration. The biblical view of justice leaves no room for a system in which the poor must steal in order to live. The Bible demands that Christians be the creators of justice, and not merely reinforcers of the existing order.

In contrast to Aristotle's classical model of preserving justice, biblical justice is creative justice. Whereas classical justice is oriented toward sustaining people in their place in the existing social structure, biblical justice is oriented toward re-creating social structures so that all members participate fully and equally in society. As Stephen Mott states (1982:65):

> The difference between scriptural and classical justice lies in the understanding of what is to be the normal situation of society. The Scriptures do not allow the presupposition of a condition in which groups or individuals are denied the ability to participate fully and equally in the life of the society. For this reason, justice is primarily spoken of by the biblical writers as activity on behalf of the disadvantaged.

Mott further argues that biblical justice is dominated by the principle of redress, "which postulates that inequalities in the conditions necessary to achieve the standard of well-being be corrected to approximate equality" (p. 67). He finds this principle in such biblical texts as Psalm 107:39–41: "Then their numbers decreased, and they were humbled by oppression, calamity and sorrow; he who pours contempt on nobles made them wander in a trackless waste. But he lifted the needy out of their affliction and increased their families like flocks" (NIV). Redress can also be seen in the Old Testament concept of the year of jubilee: once every fifty years all land which had been sold or foreclosed was to be returned to the family whose heritage it was (Lev. 25:25–28).

A biblically sensitive application of punishment, which incorporates high concern for the victim, high concern for the offender, and high concern for society, will include an attempt to make social structures conform to the biblical ideal. As we suggested in chapter 3, ideal social structures are characterized by *shalom*. Society will achieve a state of *shalom* when it is characterized by a just peace. Where peace and order are present without justice, there is no *shalom*. To punish offenders without addressing the problems of social injustice reflects a secular rather than a biblical view. The biblical view of justice requires that both interpersonal and societal restoration be motivating goals behind the use of punishment. Punishment is too narrowly focused when it concentrates only on retribution for the victim and rehabilitation for the offender; it must aim for a just peace at all social levels.

Capital Punishment

Few social issues are capable of dividing the church as much as does capital punishment. Because of the intensity of feelings on the issue of capital punishment, most discussions generate considerably more heat than light. We shall present the basic arguments for and against the use of capital punishment and encourage the reader to seek God's guidance.

The starting point in arguing for capital punishment is the value God places on and the seriousness of taking a human life. Chapter 21 of Exodus lists a number of offenses for which the death penalty was to be imposed, including striking one's father or mother, kidnaping, and cursing one's parents. In addition, anyone guilty of adultery, intercourse with animals, or idolatry was to be executed. If the letter of the law were to be applied to contemporary society, capital punishment would be imposed for offenses for which it is not now being exercised.

The principle which is seen as justifying capital punishment is summed up in Exodus 21:23–25: "But if there is serious injury, you are to take life for life, eye for eye, tooth for tooth, hand for hand, foot for foot, burn for burn, wound for wound, bruise for bruise" (NIV). Justice demands that what was borne as a cost by the victim be borne as a cost by the offender. Needless to say, the cost of an eye or hand to the offender does little to recompense the victim for the loss incurred.

Our theology of punishment would suggest that punishment be administered with a high concern for victim, offender, and society, and that restitution and restoration be key criteria in determining what is appropriate. In the case of murder (the crime for which capital punishment is most often applied), complete restitution is not a possibility. No act can bring back a life that has been taken.

A pragmatic argument against capital punishment is the difficulty of imposing it equitably. Although this can be used as an argument against any form of punishment, the severity of ending a person's life should give us pause. We ought to seriously question the use of capital punishment in any society where the poor and racial minorities are more likely than others to experience it.

It seems to us that the New Testament stops short of building a case against capital punishment, and may even be interpreted as suggesting that it be retained (Rom. 13:4; Rev. 13:10). If Jesus wished to speak against capital punishment, he could have done so in the Sermon on the Mount (see especially Matt. 5:21). However, in light of the unequal ways in which capital punishment has been administered, it seems to us that Christians need to be working for restraint in the use of capital punishment. Those who argue most strongly for capital punishment base their position on the seriousness of taking a human life unjustly. The same value should also demand that capital punishment not be used if it might involve taking the life of a wrongly accused person. The major argument for capital punishment is that God's justice demands the life of a person who has taken another human life. However, given today's sophisticated methods of detention, we find it hard to disagree with the Christian who argues for life imprisonment for murderers. We believe that one who elects to leave capital punishment to the hand of God should not be labeled a moral coward.

Topics for Review, Reflection, and Discussion

1. What is the relationship between, on the one hand, juvenile delinquency and crime and, on the other, the amount of freedom tolerated in society?

2. Who are more likely to be the victims of crime—affluent people or the poor? Why?

3. What social and personal characteristics are disproportionately represented among the criminal population?

4. Which of the theories of delinquency and crime makes the most sense?

5. Which are more likely to increase *shalom* in society—programs to prevent crime or to treat criminals?

6. Critique the statement, "In the matter of punishment for criminal offenses, the Old Testament focuses on the wrongful act itself, the New Testament on the motive of the perpetrator."

7. What would be a just punishment for each crime listed in table 1 (p. 72)?

5

Racial Discrimination and Prejudice

As a nation of immigrants, the United States is composed of people of varied racial and ethnic backgrounds. Many of them have moved into the mainstream of society and are no longer considered distinct. However, some racial and ethnic groupings continue to be identified as minorities. The United States Bureau of the Census recognizes blacks and those of Hispanic origin as the two chief minority populations. In addition, the Census Bureau includes in some of its analyses references to other minorities, for example, American Indians and Americans of Asian background. In 1987, 12 percent (29 million) of the total population was designated as black, and 85 percent was categorized as white, leaving 3 percent in other races (U.S. Bureau of the Census 1989:16). Americans of Spanish origin (an ethnic rather than racial designation) composed 8 percent of the population in 1987. The Census Bureau estimates that blacks will increase to 14 percent and those of Spanish origin to 11 percent of the population by the turn of the century (U.S. Bureau of the Census 1989:14–15).

At this point we need to clarify the way in which the terms *racial* and *ethnic* are being used. "Racial" is a biological term, referring to a human population that has distinctive physical characteristics. "Ethnic," on the other hand, is a cultural term, indicating a population that is considered distinct because of unique customs or language. Thus, black Americans compose a racial category, although, debatably, they do have some cultural traits that are distinct. Americans of Spanish origin, on the other hand, are an ethnic category; its members, according to the Census Bureau, fall variously into all of the major racial classifications. The use of the Spanish language is, of course, one of the chief characteristics making Hispanics a distinct ethnic grouping, but there are also other cultural traits that are different from those of the majority. It might be added that there are internal variations as well among those of Spanish origin, depending upon whether they or their ancestors came from Mexico, Puerto Rico, Cuba, or Central or South America.

Evidence and Nature of the Concern

Discrimination and prejudice, as defined in this book, are in and of themselves contrary to the American values discussed in chapter 2. Racial or ethnic discrimination means unequal or unfair treatment of an entire category of people regardless of the achievements and behavior of the individuals in that category. Prejudice, on the other hand, is an unfavorable attitude toward those in a racial or ethnic category; prejudice does not take into consideration any characteristics other than the undesirable stereotypes attributed to the entire category. In both discrimination and prejudice, it is membership in the racial or ethnic category that overrides all other considerations. Such behavior and attitudes are obviously in conflict with the American values of the inherent worth of every individual, equality in treatment and opportunity, and the freedom to develop one's talents without facing artificial barriers. Discrimination and prejudice can thwart the efforts of individuals to achieve through hard work and dedication. They frustrate the values of practicality, efficiency, improvement, fair competition, and the material, physical, and mental well-being of those in the racial or ethnic category, and consequently affect the well-being of the society as a whole.

Concerns about discrimination and prejudice are expressed in a number of ways. A prime example is the many organizations committed to monitoring and enforcing the civil rights of minorities. In a 1981 report the Commission on Civil Rights listed forty-one federal agencies, four hundred state and local agencies, and more than three hundred private organizations involved in protecting and extending minority rights (Simpson and Yinger 1985:418). Far-reaching civil-rights laws have been passed by the federal government and are being upheld by the courts. The mass media have condemned prejudice and discrimination against minorities, and have also made special efforts to represent American society as multiracial and multiethnic and to combat the stereotyping of minorities.

There are at least three areas of concern that appear to bother many Americans. One is the continuation of discrimination and prejudice despite attempts to reduce and eliminate them through ad hoc organizations, legislation, and educational programs. Another is the effect of past discrimination and prejudice, which placed racial and ethnic minorities in disadvantageous positions. And closely related to both of these concerns is the problem of how present-day inequities should be eliminated.

While there is general consensus in American society that discrimination and prejudice against minorities should be combated, there is a dispute over whether or not to use what has been termed affirmative action, especially if it is perceived to involve preferential treatment of those who have suffered from discrimination and prejudice in the past.

In analyzing these concerns, we shall first consider the factual data available about the status of minorities compared to that of the majority in such areas as education, income, unemployment, occupation, election to public office, and depiction in the mass media. In doing so we shall pay special attention to whether or not the situation of minorities has changed significantly since the time of major court decisions and legislative acts some thirty years ago. Then, after a consideration of the causes of discrimination and prejudice, we shall look at ways of reducing inequities.

Factual Data about Discrimination and Prejudice

Racial and ethnic minorities in America have a number of problems in common; yet because they have different histories of development and vary in size and geographic location, they also have certain problems that are unique. We cannot in the short space of this one chapter consider each of the minorities separately as we present factual data on discrimination and prejudice. So what we shall do in this section is to concentrate on what we know about black Americans, who constitute our largest and most visible racial minority. They have suffered extensively from discrimination and prejudice, and have also been the subject of a considerable amount of research. While the factual data will deal with the situation of black Americans, the succeeding sections on causation and remedial action will apply to minorities in general.

In presenting data that demonstrate the continuation of discrimination and prejudice against black Americans, we shall look at both absolute and relative changes. Absolute change is measured by comparing present-day findings about black Americans with raw data on their situation twenty-five to thirty years ago. Relative change, on the other hand, is a measure of whether the discrepancy between the circumstances of blacks and whites has decreased or increased over the years. Actually, relative change is more significant than absolute change in determining status, for the difference between blacks and the majority is the clearest indicator of unfair and unequal treatment. Accordingly, sociologists have utilized the concept of "relative deprivation" as their determinant of whether inequity exists within a society.

A debate is going on among sociologists today as to whether blacks in American society are moving toward equality with whites in such areas as educational attainment, income, and employment. Some studies claim that progress toward equality has been notable (e.g., Gilder 1981), while others question whether any significant advance has been made (e.g., Hill 1981). Still others claim that generalizations are difficult, for while some blacks have done well, others have slid deeper into poverty, creating a sizable underclass (Wilson 1980, 1987). Although it is not our goal to resolve the issue of whether the status of blacks has significantly improved, we trust that the data we present will throw some light on the debate.

Discrimination

Education

Over the past twenty-five to thirty years there has been a steady move toward a convergence in the number of years of schooling completed by blacks and whites. In 1970 the median number of years of school completed by persons twenty-five years of age and older was 9.8 for blacks compared to 12.1 for whites; by 1987 the median for blacks was 12.4 and for whites 12.7 (U.S. Bureau of the Census 1989:131). This improvement in the educational attainment of blacks is due to the fact that young blacks are staying in school longer; the situation of older blacks, however, has not changed appreciably. For example, in 1987 the number of blacks twenty-five through twenty-nine who had completed four years of high school was 83.4 percent, but for blacks sixty-five and over the figure was only 24.7 percent (U.S. Bureau of the Census 1989:131). It needs to be noted that these statistics do not reveal if there have been improvements in the quality of education received, and if black children are more likely than white children to be enrolled at a grade level below what is typical for their age.

While the percentage of blacks completing four or more years of college increased notably from 1970 to 1987, there continued to be a considerable difference by race. In 1970, 4.4 percent of blacks and 11.3 percent of whites had finished four or more years of college. In 1987, the figures were 10.7 percent for blacks and 20.5 percent for whites (U.S. Bureau of the Census 1989:131).

Income

In comparing income on the basis of race a number of cautions must be observed if we are to make sound inferences about discrimination and prejudice. The category of data being examined must be precisely the same for all races. We need to make sure, for example, that only personal, household, or family income is being compared. If we are looking at personal income, we must decide whether to include those who work part-time or seasonally. We must decide whether to include both sexes as well as workers with different educational attainments and levels of experience. If we are comparing family income by race, we must be consistent as to whether we include all types of families or only those where a married couple is present. Without providing control on these and other variables, we will be comparing aggregate data. Such data can give an over all picture, but factors other than race may account for differences in income.

One type of comparison frequently made to see if the gap between the income of blacks and whites is changing is to look at family income. The Census Bureau reports both household and family income. These designations need to be differentiated. According to the Census Bureau, "a 'household' comprises all persons who occupy a 'housing unit,' [while] 'family' refers to a group of two or more persons related by birth, marriage, or adoption and residing together in a household" (U.S. Census Bureau 1989:5). Comparing median income we find that black families made 55 percent as much as whites in 1960 (U.S. Census Bureau 1989:445). This increased to 61 percent in 1970, but it decreased to less than 60 percent in the 1980s, dropping to 56 percent in 1987. If we compare only those families where a married couple was present, we find a smaller difference: black families made 77 percent as much as white families in 1987 (U.S. Bureau of the Census 1989:446). Furthermore, the income of black families where the father was absent was only 36 percent of that of black families where a married couple was present. At the same time it should be noted that single-parent white families headed by a female made only 48 percent as much as white families with both a husband and wife present. In such figures we see a feminization of poverty for both blacks and whites.

Is it possible that these differences in income are due to differences in education, experience, and number of hours worked rather than to racial and sexual discrimination? Reynolds Farley in an extensive analysis of data on personal income developed a procedure to control these variables (1984:90–95). He found that in 1979 black men earned 89 percent as much as white men with the same amount of education, experience, and hours worked; twenty years earlier blacks earned 75 percent as much as whites. Farley concluded that black men had evidently benefited from decreases in discrimination. At the same time, the differences that remained could logically be attributed to discrimination. Using the same procedure, Farley found that black women had also improved in relative earnings, making 60 percent as much as white men and equaling the income of white women. While the difference between the earnings of blacks and whites decreased in all occupational categories from 1959 to 1979, there was no corresponding change in the gap between the incomes of white men and white women.

Unemployment

The rate of unemployment, by which is meant the percentage of those seeking work and unable to find it, has consistently been higher for blacks than for whites. Studying data covering the years 1950 to 1982, Farley found that the unemployment rate for blacks was uniformly twice that for whites; in addition, it is likely that many blacks became so discouraged about employment prospects that they gave up the search for a job (1984:38–40). If so, the unemployment rate for blacks was even higher than that reported.

In 1987 the average unemployment rate for whites was 5.3 percent, while the rate for blacks was 13.0 percent (U.S. Bureau of the Census 1989:393). The rate was particularly high for young blacks: 34.7 percent for those sixteen to nineteen years of age, and 21.8 percent for those from twenty to twenty-four years of age. It should be added that these differences in unemployment rates persisted even among people from twenty-five to forty-five and of the same educational level. In 1988, for example, for white high-school graduates the unemployment rate was 4.6 percent, while for blacks who had finished high school the rate was 11.2 percent (U.S. Bureau of the Census 1989:394).

Occupational status

Occupations can be classified into upper- and lower-status categories. People in managerial, professional, sales, and clerical positions hold what have been termed white-collar jobs, which carry a higher status than do jobs involving manual labor, for example in factories, which have been termed blue-collar jobs. Blacks have long held a disproportionately small number of high-status jobs, and a disproportionately large number of low-status jobs. This inequity, however, has been gradually decreasing since 1960, when 14 percent of blacks and 39 percent of whites held high-status jobs (Farley 1984:47). By 1982 the proportion of blacks in high-status jobs had more than doubled, to 30 percent, while that of whites had increased far less rapidly, to 44 percent. Still, a gap of fourteen percentage points remained. Blacks continued to be overrepresented in service occupations, particularly in janitorial positions.

Differences in occupational status remain even when educational attainment is the same. For example, white high-school graduates who have not received additional training are almost twice as likely to hold managerial or professional jobs as are blacks with the same amount of education (U.S. Bureau of the Census 1987:387).

Election to public office

The number of blacks elected to public office increased by over 450 percent between 1970 and 1988, from 1,479 to 6,793 (U.S. Bureau of the Census 1989:255). There is little question that this increase is related to the decrease in discrimination against the registration of black voters since the passing of the 1965 Voting Rights Act. Blacks have been elected mayors of such large cities as New York, Los Angeles, Chicago, Philadelphia, and Detroit. A black senator in the Virginia state legislature was elected lieutenant governor in 1986 and governor in 1989; and an

increasing number of blacks have been chosen to be judges, congress-
men, state legislators, sheriffs, and members of state educational agencies, school boards, and city councils.

Depiction in the mass media

Although no definitive study has been made, it is clear that the mass
media are increasingly depicting blacks as an integral part of American
society. The Children's Television Workshop, for example, makes a point
of including blacks and other nonwhites in prominent roles. Blacks are
appearing ever more frequently in important television dramas, as commentators on talk shows, and in various kinds of advertising. Blacks
have also become highly visible as star athletes in sports watched by millions of Americans.

Poverty level

A government-prepared index classifies individuals and families as
being above or below the poverty level (see p. 251). In 1959, 55.1 percent
of black families fell below the poverty line, compared to 18.1 percent of
white families (U.S. Bureau of the Census 1989:452). By 1970 the percent-
ages had declined to 33.5 for blacks and 9.9 for whites. Since 1970 there
has been little change in either rate: 33.1 percent of all black households
and 10.5 percent of white households fall below the poverty line. Thus
the rate for black families in poverty has stayed at approximately three
times that for whites. As would be expected from the data on income
given earlier in this chapter (p. 103), the families most likely to fall below
the poverty line are families with dependent children headed by a single
female. In 1987 the rate for such families was 54.7 percent (U.S. Bureau of
the Census 1989:453).

Racial segregation

Racial segregation in education, housing, and access to public facilities
has long been considered an overt manifestation of discrimination, especially against black Americans. The Supreme Court decision in 1954 that
all state laws requiring racial segregation in public schools were unconstitutional marked a fundamental turning point in race relations. The
court reasoned: "To separate them [Negro children in public schools]
from others of similar age and qualifications solely because of their race
generates a feeling of inferiority as to their status in the community that
may affect their hearts and minds in a way unlikely ever to be undone."
This decision set the stage for a number of civil-rights acts making racial
segregation illegal. The 1964 Civil Rights Act prohibited discrimination
in places of public accommodation, public facilities, public education,
and employment; and the 1968 Housing Act by Congress forbade discrimination in renting and selling houses.

While there has been some movement toward racial integration in all
school districts, progress has been greatest in small cities and in cities

with a relatively small proportion of minority children. There has been far less racial integration in large cities with a high proportion of minority students. It is likely that as long as there are separate school districts for urban and suburban areas, de facto segregation will persist.

Similarly, while the former rigidity in racial segregation in residential areas has been broken, studies have shown little movement toward integration. A study of twenty-five central cities with large black populations reported a mixed pattern of change from 1970 to 1980 (Farley 1984:33–35). In five cities there were notable decreases in segregation; but in two of the cities, Philadelphia and Cleveland, there was an increase in residential segregation; and in Chicago, St. Louis, Washington, and Newark there was virtually no change at all. The clearest move toward racial integration had been in hotels, motels, restaurants, and other establishments open to the public.

Prejudice

As stated earlier, racial prejudice is an unfavorable attitude toward all the members of a racial category; it is a preconceived judgment without regard to objective criteria and rationality. In this section we shall rely almost entirely upon a definitive study of racial attitudes by Howard Schuman and his colleagues (1985). They summarized data gathered from 1942 to 1983 by three major survey organizations: the Institute for Social Research, the National Opinion Research Center, and the Gallup Poll. To determine the attitudes of white Americans, Schuman looked at answers to thirty-two questions that the survey organizations had asked at least twice over the forty-one-year period. The subject matter of the questions fell into three categories: (1) broad principles of equal treatment; (2) implementation of these principles; and (3) racial integration at a personal level. The researchers found a steady increase in whites' acceptance of equal and fair treatment for blacks, especially in the areas of public accommodations, jobs, and support for a qualified black candidate for president of the United States. While there was increased opposition to laws forbidding marriage between blacks and whites, there was far less approval of racial intermarriage itself. Schuman and his colleagues concluded: "What has changed is the normative definition of appropriate relations between blacks and whites. Whereas discrimination against, and enforced segregation of, blacks was taken for granted by most white Americans as recently as the 1940s, today the dominant belief is that blacks deserve the same treatment and respect as whites, and that some degree of racial integration is a desirable thing" (1985:202).

Although the Schuman study found that there had been a significant increase in whites' acceptance of the principles of equality, far less support was expressed for implementing equality by government intervention, except in the area of public accommodations. It should be added that despite the finding that most whites believe that blacks deserve equal treatment and respect, there have been isolated, highly publicized antiblack incidents (e.g., in Howard Beach, N.Y., in 1986, and in Forsyth County, Ga., in 1987) which show that some whites continue to have deep feelings of prejudice against blacks. At the same time, in support of the Schuman conclusion that the normative definition of race relations has changed, these incidents were strongly denounced by whites as well as by blacks, and the whites who were found to be responsible for the incidents were arrested and sentenced to prison terms.

Schuman and his coresearchers could not find as much data on the racial attitudes of blacks as they had for whites, but they did find that by 1964 a few questions had begun to be asked of black Americans on a regular basis (1985:139–62). These questions can also be classified as dealing either with basic principles or implementation of those principles. Black respondents, from the first, gave almost unanimous support to the principle of racial equality. Almost all said that they would vote for a well-qualified black presidential candidate, that blacks should have the right to live in whatever area they can afford, and that black and white children should go to the same schools. About three-quarters of the respondents approved of interracial marriage. In response to the question, "Are you in favor of desegregation, strict segregation, or something in between?" a declining number (though still a majority) favored "desegregation," while an increasing number preferred "something in between."

In regard to implementation, blacks express much stronger support for government intervention than do whites. There are, however, some convergences between blacks and whites on the matter of implementation. For example, in response to the question, "Do you think that the government in Washington should see to it that black and white children go to the same schools, or should stay out of this matter as it is not its business?" both blacks and whites have shown declining support for government intervention. Black support for federal intervention dropped from 90 percent in 1968 to 60 percent in 1978, while white support dropped from a peak of 48 percent in 1966 to 25 percent in 1978 (Schuman et al. 1985:148–49).

Explanations of Discrimination and Prejudice

The next step in sociological analysis is to attempt to account for some of the facts presented in the preceding section. One of those facts is that despite a decrease in some areas, racial discrimination and prejudice continue in American society, a society in which the individual and equal treatment are highly valued. We need to try to explain why discrimination and prejudice persist amid the changes that are taking place.

Another finding with which we need to deal is that while racial prejudice, as measured by responses to survey questions, has decreased significantly over the past thirty years, support for the implementation of racial equality has not increased commensurately. In this section we shall summarize three general theories that attempt to account for racial discrimination and prejudice, and then we shall combine two of them.

The Physiological Approach

The physiological or genetic explanation of racial discrimination and prejudice is based on the conviction that race is a crucial variable in differentiating a person not only physically, but also emotionally, morally, and mentally. It is believed that common emotional, moral, and mental characteristics give members of the same race a natural affinity for one another. There exists, according to this explanation, an inherent racial unity or integrity.

What do physical anthropologists who have made extensive studies of race say about this theory? They begin with a general agreement that any classification of human beings into distinct biological categories is arbitrary. There is no fixed number of clearly identifiable races; and "pure races," whatever that term might mean, have never existed, nor could they exist. Races are open genetic systems: members of any race, no matter how the race is delineated, can interbreed with members of any other race. Some of the variations in physical traits like skin color and nasal index may be related to natural selection or geographical isolation. However, no human group has ever become so different from other human groups that it developed into a separate species; rather, all human beings belong to a single species—Homo sapiens. At one time it was thought that there were three major stocks or races—Caucasoid, Mongoloid, and Negroid—and that several subcategories, each related in some way to one of the three major stocks, could be delineated. Anthropologists, however, now generally agree that such a three-way typology is so contrived and abstract as to be meaningless. More and more anthropologists are suggesting that in scientific studies we eliminate the term *race* altogether and in its place use a more functional expression like "human biological variation." In any event, anthropologists deny that the manifest physical differences used in the past to designate races have anything to do with behavior, emotion, or mentality. In short, scientific evidence that racial discrimination and prejudice are natural and inherent is completely lacking.

In spite of the scientific conclusion that races are arbitrary constructs, some societies still firmly believe that there are distinct races and that membership in a particular race is a determinant of one's behavior and ability. We are reminded of the dictum of sociologist William I. Thomas that if people define an imaginary situation as real and act as if it is, it is real in its consequences (Thomas and Thomas 1928:572). C. Loring Brace, an anthropologist, has gone as far as to say that "the reality of races as biological entities, then, is to be found in the human conviction that they exist. . . . They [races] are real because people believe that they are, and social reality—the human world—is determined by human belief" (1971:5).

Anthropologists recognize, of course, that human beings vary in physical traits like the color of skin, hair, and eyes, in nasal and cephalic index, and in other observable ways. Each of these differences, however, is on a continuum on which no hard-and-fast divisions can be made, and on which it is therefore impossible to set up distinct, nonoverlapping categories of people. And yet some of those physical differences have occasionally been seized upon as a means of differentiating populations into what are *believed* to be racial categories. But such cases entail a shift from a strictly physiological or genetic explanation to a psychological and sociocultural one.

The issue of whether or not distinct races can be delineated is complicated by the way in which racial categories have actually been determined and recorded by the Census Bureau, which makes the disclaimer that its designation of race "does not denote any clear-cut definition of biological stock" (U.S. Bureau of the Census 1989:4). Prior to the 1960 census, race was determined by the enumerator, who did face-to-face interviews at residences; persons of mixed parentage were classified according to the race of the nonwhite parent. From 1960 on, however, race has been determined by the self-identification of the respondent. In the 1960 census, those of mixed parentage continued to be classified as nonwhite; in 1970 the race of the father was recorded, and in 1980 the race of the mother. Obviously, then, race is not a fixed concept, and the theory of an inherent racial unity entailing emotional, moral, and mental characteristics is wrong.

The Psychological Approach

The psychological approach locates the cause of racial discrimination and prejudice within the individual, and specifically within the patterns of behavior learned in childhood. One theory sees a correlation between prejudice and an authoritarian personality (Adorno et al. 1950). Researchers have found that those who are highly prejudiced and insist on discriminatory practices are likely to have been reared in families in which discipline was arbitrary and severe, relationships were characterized more by dominance and submission than by equality, and duties and roles were strictly defined. Children raised in such an atmosphere tend to develop an authoritarian personality and to fixate on power, both in others and in themselves. Furthermore, they see their world in clear-cut dichotomies of good and evil and cannot tolerate ambiguity. They are contemptuous of those whom they consider to be weak, yielding, compromising, and indecisive. Racial prejudice and discrimination are *functional* for individuals with such a personality, that is, serve to meet their psychological needs. Being prejudiced and discriminating against people who have little power, especially racial minorities, bring satisfaction to those who have an authoritarian personality.

Another psychological explanation is the scapegoat theory, which holds that one of the chief responses to frustration is aggression, and that aggression, which is usually unacceptable, is often displaced by hostility toward minorities, who provide scapegoats. Members of minorities provide relatively safe targets, for they do not have sufficient status and power to be able to protect themselves. Once again, prejudice and discrimination are functional for (i.e., meet the needs of) individuals with a deep-seated problem.

The Sociocultural Approach

The sociocultural approach finds the cause of prejudice and discrimination in the basic structure and norms of society. This approach assumes that behavior mimics social values; thus if a society divides its members into racial categories and assigns to each category a hierarchical ranking in status and power, members of the highly ranked group(s) will be prejudiced and discriminate against those in the lower categories. Furthermore, children growing up in such an environment will adopt the racial attitudes and discriminatory actions that are embodied in the norms of that society. Prejudice and discrimination, then, are normative, that is, they conform to expected behavior.

Research has found that preschool children in societies stratified by race have far more bias than do children in societies without such stratification (Morland and Hwang 1981). Such studies lend support to the sociocultural explanation of prejudice and discrimination, which stresses society's influence on the young child:

> If we take it for granted that children begin early in life to see differences in persons around them, the [sociocultural] theory leads us to believe that they will consider these differences important only if their society makes them the basis for categorization and calls for a particular kind of response to those in the category. Thus, in a multiracial society, we assume that children can see variations in skin color, hair form, and the like. However, it is the society which determines how much attention is to be paid to these variations and whether or not certain groupings are to be recognized on the basis of selected characteristics. Furthermore, it can be assumed that it is in the socialization process that children learn not only what physical traits are used as a basis of classification but also what attitudes are to be held toward those in the classification. [Morland 1969:372]

According to the sociocultural explanation, then, prejudice and discrimination are built into the structure of the society and supported by social norms. The majority in the society come to regard prejudice and discrimination as normal. The attitudes and behaviors that result can be termed *conforming* prejudice and discrimination. By giving higher status, power, and privilege to the dominant race, continuing the dominant-subordinate relationship from which they presumably grew, such attitudes and behaviors ensure their own perpetuation in the norms.

Conforming prejudice and discrimination are to be distinguished from functional prejudice and discrimination. The former are expressions of expected attitudes and behavior, an adherence to what is conventional. The latter, however, are more deep-seated in that they are needed by individuals with psychological difficulties—an authoritarian personality or an inability to deal with frustration. Conforming prejudice and discrimination against minorities provide a ready outlet for individuals with functional prejudice and discrimination.

Combining the Psychological and Sociocultural Theories

Since our discussion to this point has assumed the existence of racial and ethnic minorities vulnerable to prejudice and discrimination, it is a fair question to ask how these people have actually come to be afforded a second-class status. It is logical to look to past events. For example, in the case of black Americans, their ancestors were forcibly brought to this country as slaves. The initial justification for setting blacks apart was their "uncivilized" condition. As time went on, however, physical appearance was relied upon more and more to justify unequal treatment, which was then supported by law, religion, science, and literature (Williams and Morland 1976:3–19). The blacks' low status and lack of political and economic power continued after the Civil War under legally enforced racial segregation, undergirded by the Supreme Court decision in *Plessy v. Ferguson* (1896), which permitted laws requiring segregation as long as the situations of the races were equal. The situations in voting rights, schools, public accommodations, housing, occupations, transportation, and the like were, however, never equal, and thus perpetuated a social structure and norms that relegated blacks to a lower status than whites. Moves to change the structure came with the Supreme Court's 1954 reversal of the Plessy "separate but equal" decision and with civil-rights legislation passed by Congress in the 1960s. The effects of past discrimination and prejudice, however, could not be readily erased by such moves, although there have been a general increase in equal treatment and a general reduction in racial prejudice. At the same time there have been some resistance to equal treatment and a continuation of racial prejudice by some Americans.

Against this background of the development and subsequent modification of the American social structure vis-à-vis the black minority, we can bring the sociocultural and psychological explanations of discrimination and prejudice together. The sociocultural approach accounts for the conforming discrimination and prejudice that led the majority to repress blacks. The sociocultural approach also accounts for the general reduction in discrimination and prejudice as the social structure has been changed to provide equality in the treatment of minorities. The psychological approach accounts for the continuation of discrimination and prejudice by some Americans for whom such behavior and attitudes are functional.

We should add here that conforming discrimination and prejudice are more readily changed than functional discrimination and prejudice. The reason is that discrimination and prejudice are vital outlets for those who have authoritarian personality traits or low thresholds of frustration. Also to be kept in view is that while we have discussed conforming and functional discrimination as distinct, most discrimination is not strictly one type or the other, but falls somewhere on a continuum between the two.

Alleviating the Problem

In our discussion of the sociocultural and psychological approaches we saw that the existence of racial discrimination promotes conforming prejudice and provides an outlet for those with functional prejudice. Furthermore, it is clear that behavior (in the form of discrimination that is customary or required by law) can be more readily changed than feelings (in the form of racial attitudes). There is considerable research in psychology, sociology, and anthropology that supports these views and by implication suggests steps for alleviating the problem of racial discrimination and prejudice.

Disseminating Scientific Knowledge about Race

When we considered the physiological approach, we indicated that from the scientific point of view it is based upon false premises about race. Scientists have shown that any racial classification is arbitrary, for there can be no distinct, fixed categories within the human species. Further, no race, however delineated, is by any objective criteria superior or inferior to any other racial category. While there are individual differences in intelligence and creativity, it is wrong to claim that there are significant racial differences in ability, as some have done (Jensen 1969).

Although the majority of Americans agree that no race is more intelligent than any other (Schuman et al. 1985:118), about one-fourth of the respondents in opinion polls continue to believe that races do differ in intellectual ability. Even more widespread is the notion of racial integrity or racial unity. Given the history of race relations in this country, it is not surprising that there is widespread belief in what has been termed the mystique of race, that is, an air of mystery and sanctity that supposedly surrounds one's racial affiliation. Obviously, little scientific information about race is being taught in elementary and high schools. Yet although the relationship between knowledge on the one hand and attitude and behavior on the other is a complex one, we can safely assume that sound information on race would be enlightening and reduce misunderstandings in the relations between races. That accurate knowledge about race is a necessary (though not a sufficient) condition for reducing racial prejudice is a hypothesis that deserves extensive testing.

Changing the Social Structures

The aim of the civil-rights movement has been to change the structure of American society so that racial and ethnic minorities are not forced by law and custom to occupy a second-class status. Such a goal obviously presupposes the sociocultural explanation of racial discrimination and prejudice as a product of social structure and norms. The movement has proved to be largely successful in altering social structure by removing legal barriers to equal treatment. Much of the success is due to the work of a number of organizations that have challenged the inequities in the system: the National Association for the Advancement of Colored People (NAACP), founded in 1909 and focusing on litigation, legislation, and education; the National Urban League, founded in 1910 to help minorities gain equal opportunity especially in urban areas; the Southern Regional Council, founded in the 1930s to give Southerners a special channel for removing racial inequities; and the Southern Christian Leadership Conference, founded in 1957 by Martin Luther King, Jr., to produce change by nonviolent disobedience of segregation laws (Garrow 1986).

These and other civil-rights organizations have been successful in helping to bring about court decisions and congressional laws that bar racial and ethnic discrimination in many areas of American life. These rulings and civil-rights acts require Americans to treat members of minorities equitably, thereby reducing prejudice and breaking down stereotypes. The court decisions and laws resulting from the civil-rights movement, however, have done little to overcome the effects of past discrimination and prejudice. In order to lift minorities from their disadvantaged position, what came to be known as affirmative action was adopted.

Promoting Affirmative Action

The expression *affirmative action* was first used by John F. Kennedy and Lyndon B. Johnson in executive orders; it is also found in the Civil

Rights Act of 1964. The intention of affirmative action is to ensure equality of opportunity and treatment without regard to race, color, national origin, sex, or creed. The method is to implement the court decisions and congressional laws requiring equal treatment of all Americans by advertising job openings so that members of minority races and ethnic groupings know about them and can be recruited and trained to fill them. The reasoning behind this approach was given by President Johnson in a commencement speech at Howard University on June 4, 1965:

> You do not wipe away the scars of centuries by saying: Now you are free to go where you want and do as you desire and choose the leaders you please. You do not take a person who, for years, has been hobbled by chains and liberate him, bring him to the starting line of a race, and then say you are free to compete with all the others, and still believe you have been completely fair. Thus it is not enough just to open the gates of opportunity. All our citizens must have the ability to walk through those gates. This is the next and more profound stage of the battle for civil rights. We seek not just freedom but opportunity. We seek not just legal equity but human ability, not just equality as a right and a theory but equality as a fact and equality as a result. [quoted in Johnson 1971:166]

The first attempts to provide equal opportunities for racial and other minorities were made voluntarily by employers and schools. Word went out that members of minorities were welcome to apply for positions from which they had been virtually excluded, and parents were given the freedom to choose the schools their children would attend. Such efforts, however, brought about little change; so government agencies and courts began to require that minorities be employed and that schools be integrated in actuality. Numerical goals began to be set to make sure that minority members were really being afforded the opportunities created by the civil-rights laws. There was a move, then, from a policy of being color-blind to being color-conscious, and members of minorities had to be identified and their number recorded by employers and schools. The threatened loss of federal funds and contracts loomed over those communities and institutions that did not make clear progress toward the integration of minorities.

In 1966 the Department of Health, Education, and Welfare began to require evidence that schools were being racially integrated; and in 1968 the Supreme Court ordered dual systems eliminated so that there would no longer be schools identifiable as white or black. Likewise, statistical proof of movement toward racial integration of work forces began to be required. In May of 1968 the Office of Federal Contract Compliance required that every institution with more than fifty employees and a government contract of at least fifty thousand dollars submit a written plan "of specific goals and time-tables for the prompt achievement of full and equal employment opportunity" (quoted in Glazer 1975:46). Stronger and more specific guidelines were issued in 1970 and 1971, the latter stating:

> An acceptable affirmative action program must include an analysis of areas within which the contractor is deficient in the utilization of minority groups and women, and further, goals and timetables to which the contractor's good faith efforts must be directed to correct the deficiencies and, thus to increase materially the utilization of minorities and women, at all levels and in all segments of his work force where deficiencies exist. [quoted in Glazer 1975:48]

In order to comply with these and other directives, businesses and school systems began to develop plans to promote racial integration. A number of these plans have been challenged in the courts, both by plaintiffs who claim the plans do not eliminate discrimination against minorities, and by plaintiffs who feel the plans discriminate against whites. This has been called "reverse discrimination" or, to use Nathan Glazer's term, "affirmative discrimination."

We will briefly examine a select few of the cases that have been decided by the Supreme Court since 1970. As we take up this approach, bear in mind that (1) it oversimplifies what has been a highly complex process, (2) divisions in the Court have resulted in decisions that are not always clear, and (3) the makeup of the Court and the mood of the country have changed over the two decades being considered.

A landmark case for public schools was *Swann v. Charlotte-Mecklenburg County Board of Education* in 1971. The Supreme Court upheld the order of a district judge that the ratio of black and white pupils be the same in every school throughout the 550-square-mile county and that this goal be brought about through busing. Later decisions by the Court, however, rejected attempts to integrate predominantly black school districts in the city with predominantly white districts in the suburbs.

An important test of preferential treatment in college admissions came when Alan Bakke, a white, was denied entry to the University of California Medical School at Davis in 1973 and 1974. The university had set aside for minorities sixteen of its one hundred openings. Although Bakke's entrance-examination scores were significantly higher than those of the minority students admitted, who competed only among themselves and not with whites, and although some of the openings reserved for minority students remained unfilled, Bakke was refused admission. He sued the university, claiming that the special program for minorities operated to exclude him solely because of his race, and thus was in violation of the Fourteenth Amendment, a provision of the California

Constitution, and Title VI of the 1964 Civil Rights Act, which states that no person can on the basis of race be excluded from a program receiving federal financial assistance. In 1978 the Supreme Court upheld Bakke's claim and compelled the university to admit him.

In a far-reaching decision the following year, however, the Supreme Court ruled that a plan devised by the United Steel Workers and Kaiser Aluminum to increase the number of minority workers in skilled jobs at the Kaiser plant in Gramercy, Louisiana, was not a violation of the Fourteenth Amendment or Title VII of the 1964 Civil Rights Act, which prohibits discrimination in employment on the basis of an individual's "race, color, religion, sex, or national origin." The plan to increase the number of minority workers in skilled positions required that half of the openings in an on-the-job training program be given to minority members, regardless of seniority. A white worker, Brian Weber, was denied admission to the program, while blacks with less seniority were admitted. Weber sued, claiming that his constitutional rights had been violated in that he had been discriminated against on the basis of race. The Court, however, held that because the plan had not been mandated by the state, the Fourteenth Amendment did not apply, and that Title VII permits voluntary affirmative efforts to correct racial imbalance. In a similar case in 1986, the Court sanctioned a plan to increase the number of minority firefighters in Cleveland by hiring or promoting a minority member for every white hired or promoted. In a decision in 1987 the Court approved the promotion policies of the Transportation Agency of Santa Clara County, California, which aimed at remedying "imbalances" in the number of women and racial minorities in "traditionally segregated job categories."

In other decisions, however, the Supreme Court has permitted seniority systems to take precedence over preferential treatment designed to bring about racial and sexual balance in the work force. For example, in 1982 it ruled that the collectively bargained seniority system at Pullman-Standard's plant in Bessemer, Alabama, was not illegal; the Court pointed out that even though the difference in treatment of employees tended to perpetuate the effects of past discrimination, it was not motivated by "an intent to discriminate on account of race." In a 1987 ruling, *Wygant v. Jackson [Mich.] Board of Education*, the Supreme Court rejected as unconstitutional a school-board policy that laid off white teachers, but continued to employ black teachers with less seniority in order to maintain racial balance of the teaching staff. And in 1989, in *Ward Cove Packing Co. v. Atonio*, the Court ruled against minority workers at two salmon canneries in Alaska who claimed that they were being discriminated against by being kept in low-paid, unskilled jobs. The Court found that the workers had failed to prove that the companies' employment practices were discriminatory; furthermore, statistics showing dramatic racial or ethnic imbalances in job categories are not enough to prove discrimination. This decision has the effect of shifting the burden of proof. It is now incumbent on the employee to prove discrimination rather than on the employer to prove nondiscrimination.

Almost all of these cases have been decided by a five-to-four vote, indicating a sharply divided Supreme Court. The reactions to these decisions have likewise been strongly divergent, demonstrating serious conflicts in American society. As has already been noted (p. 106), there is a general agreement that overt racial discrimination and prejudice are anachronisms which have no place in American society. At the same time, there is less agreement that preferential treatment should now be given to minority groups against whom there was discrimination in the past. The unresolved issue is how the nation can overcome the effects of past discrimination without discriminating against others in the process. The objection has not been to affirmative action per se—taking steps to make sure that minorities know about job opportunities and are actively recruited for them. Rather, the objection comes when affirmative action really means preferential treatment. Those who are bothered by what we referred to earlier as reverse discrimination believe that hiring and promoting on the basis of race, ethnicity, or sex in order to reflect the composition of the population are incompatible with individual rights and individual merit. On the other hand, those who defend the Court's decision in allowing race, ethnic background, and sex to be given weight in employing and promoting are equally convinced that preferential treatment is the only way to make up for past discrimination. They contend, further, that in preferential treatment only individuals who qualify for the job are hired or promoted; that flexible, temporary, narrowly drawn numerical goals cause a minimum of burden to those in the majority; and that it is unrealistic to believe that racial and ethnic minorities and women can move into the mainstream of economic and political life without some sacrifice by the majority.

Disagreement as to how to overcome the effects of past discrimination will likely continue in American society, for those on both sides of the issue base their position on the same widely shared values: the worth of all individuals and equality in treatment and opportunity. One suggestion that might reduce confusion when the matter of affirmative action is debated is to limit the meaning of affirmative action to recruitment and special training of racial minorities and women as a means of overcoming past inequities. Preferential treatment, on the other hand, would refer to giving special consideration to the race, ethnicity, and sex of the applicant in order to achieve a more equitable balance in the work force.

There is one point of agreement between those who believe that preferential treatment is necessary to overcome the effects of past discrimination and those who do not: both affirmative action (in its restricted meaning) and preferential treatment are limited in the extent to which they can and should be applied. Members of minority groupings cannot be benefited by affirmative action or preferential treatment if they are not qualified for the training program, position, or promotion in question. Yet a relatively large proportion of blacks, Hispanics, and other minorities, for whom affirmative action and preferential treatment are designed, do not have the basic qualifications for being given special consideration in the marketplace. They belong to what has been termed the underclass (Auletta 1982) or the truly disadvantaged (Wilson 1987); among their numbers are the homeless, unemployed teenage dropouts, single parents on welfare, and ex-offenders who have recently been released from prison. Members of this underclass, which includes all races and ethnic backgrounds, require special assistance that affirmative action and preferential treatment as presently practiced cannot give. For these individuals are affected by problems of American society that go beyond racial and ethnic considerations and involve dire poverty itself (see chap. 12).

A Christian Response to Racial Discrimination and Prejudice

A Christian response to racial discrimination and prejudice must begin with the clear biblical message that "God does not show favoritism" (Rom. 2:11 NIV). In one inclusive statement, Paul wrote against the major forms of discrimination in his day: "There is neither Jew nor Greek, slave nor free, male nor female, for you are all one in Christ Jesus" (Gal. 3:28 NIV). But although the church affirms this biblical message, it has been something less than decisive in supporting minority groups in their struggle against discrimination. Except for the leadership given to the black civil-rights movement by a few outstanding Christian leaders, the church as a social institution has in many instances taken an obstructionist position.

In his now classic article, Gary Marx (1967) demonstrates how even traditionally oriented black churches have served to retard the fight against racial discrimination. Blacks living in a society that discriminated against them experienced tremendous frustration. This frustration, as Marx explains, was sublimated into emotionalism and escapism within the black church. The brand of Christianity that was first taught to slaves and later passed on within the black church stressed that blacks should fix their hopes on the afterlife and pay no attention to their deprivation of temporal rewards here on earth. This otherworldly religion that was practiced in the black church actually functioned, according to Marx, as an opiate to keep blacks from protesting against discrimination.

Paradoxically, however, the civil-rights movement gained much of its inspiration from within this same black church. The spiritual power of the civil-rights movement came from persons like Martin Luther King,

Jr., who found in the life of Jesus a model for radical, nonviolent noncompliance with discriminatory laws and social structures. Many conservative Christians, rather than supporting King because of his nonviolent approach, attacked him because he advocated breaking the law. Such attacks were obvious signals that many within the church placed a greater value on order than on justice. They reasoned that the breaking of a "whites only" law would lead down the slippery slope to breaking any law deemed inconvenient.

The Bible clearly teaches, however, that the church is to set an example. James 2:1–4 declares that Christians are to show no partiality or discrimination:

> My brothers, as believers in our glorious Lord Jesus Christ, don't show favoritism. Suppose a man comes into your meeting wearing a gold ring and fine clothes, and a poor man in shabby clothes also comes in. If you show special attention to the man wearing fine clothes and say, "Here's a good seat for you," but say to the poor man, "You stand there" or "Sit on the floor by my feet," have you not discriminated among yourselves and become judges with evil thoughts? [NIV]

God abhors discrimination or elitism of any kind; in fact, if God shows any favoritism at all, it is in behalf of the poor and disinherited of the world, the victims of discrimination, prejudice, and elitism. In his examination of the four Gospels, Donald Kraybill (1980:399) points out that "Jesus focused his ministry primarily on individuals who were members of stigmatized groups in Palestinian society in the first century A.D." The stigmatized groups to whom Jesus ministered include the Gentiles (Matt. 8:5–13; Mark 5:18–20; Luke 4:14–30), women (Mark 5:25–34; Luke 7:11–17, 37–50; 8:1–3; 10:38–42), the poor (Luke 4:18; 6:20–26; 7:22–23; 14:13), and the powerless and outcasts (Matt. 11:19; 25:31–46; Mark 2:15; Luke 4:18; 7:22; 15:1–2). It is also significant that Jesus selected a Samaritan as the model of perfect love. The Samaritans were the most disparaged ethnic group in Palestine at the time. In utilizing a Samaritan in his parable, Jesus not only elevated the status of this ethnic people, but also demonstrated in a profound way the equal value of all members of humankind, regardless of social or physical characteristics.

In addition to the charge of breaking the law, many Christians leveled the accusation that the civil-rights movement of the 1950s and 1960s was trying to change people's actions without changing their hearts. It is only a slight overgeneralization to suggest that conservative Christians believed that converting people to Christ in sufficient number and thus transforming their racial prejudice would bring about needed change in social structures that support discrimination. Liberal Christians, on the other hand, believed that preventing people from practicing racial discrimination would, in time, lead to a reduction in prejudice. While conservatives charged that liberals were being unbiblical in trying to legislate change in people's hearts, liberals charged that conservatives were doing nothing, and by their inaction were actually perpetuating unequal treatment.

The fruit of the civil-rights movement has been both a change in social structures (Farley 1984) and a reduction in, but not the elimination of, racial prejudice (Schuman et al. 1985). The persistence of prejudice means that people will continue to discriminate. Unfortunately, the social-science evidence on the subject indicates that prejudice cannot be eradicated by direct means; the only way to change attitudes is to change behavior and actions first.

What does the Bible have to say about how to confront racism? Conservatives point out that Scripture does present a model for reducing prejudice by changing the individual. But nearly all biblical examples entail a radical personal change; Paul's transformed attitude towards Christians, for instance, resulted from his dramatic conversion. However, the Bible also suggests that attitudes are affected by behavior. In pointing out the foolishness of storing up treasures on earth rather than in heaven, Jesus says, "Where your treasure is, there your heart will be also" (Matt. 6:19–21). The storing up of treasures (behavior), Jesus tells us, determines where one's heart will be (attitudes). All truth is God's truth, so we should not be surprised when the teachings of Jesus correspond to that which is discovered through social-science investigation.

For our purposes, however, a more important point is that Christians must not selectively use Scripture to fit their preconceived notions of how an evil like racism should be challenged. As Christians, we must be actively working for the elimination of both discrimination and prejudice; we must not focus our attention on just one or the other. Legal changes during the last thirty years have all but eliminated formal racial discrimination. There are still much informal discrimination and prejudice towards minority people in the United States, however, and Christians cannot be content until all racial injustice has disappeared.

Even the elimination of racial discrimination, however, will not undo its past effects. Many of those whom we identify as the underclass or the truly disadvantaged owe their unfortunate position to previous discrimination. *Shalom* is present in inverse proportion to the size of a truly disadvantaged underclass in society. Although one might have ideological reasons for opposing preferential treatment, Christians must support and engage in efforts to empower the powerless, which can be done in a variety of ways. For example, local churches can offer after-school tutoring programs to disadvantaged children and language classes to minorities for whom English is a second language, give financial support towards the college education of an academically qualified but poor youth, provide child-care instruction and housekeeping help for disadvantaged mothers, or train the underprivileged so that they might qualify for an adequate-paying job.

Attempts at empowering will be defeated where churches settle into a type of benevolent paternalism. True empowering is achieved only when the disadvantaged become independent and self-sufficient. By sharing our time, material resources, knowledge, and skills on a personal basis with the disadvantaged, empowering becomes a distinct possibility. The establishment of *shalom*, which is our ultimate social goal, entails undoing the sins of our fathers and mothers against minority people. In the eyes of secular society this may seem to be a radical response; a biblical people, however, regards it as following Jesus and his example.

Topics for Review, Reflection, and Discussion

1. What is the difference between racial discrimination and racial prejudice? Can one practice discrimination without being prejudiced? Can one be prejudiced and yet not practice discrimination? If so, give examples.

2. Which have proved to be more effective—attempts to reduce racial discrimination or to reduce prejudice?

3. How effective has affirmative action been as a strategy for combating racial discrimination? Has it created any new problems?

4. Has religion served more as an inspiration to the civil-rights movement or as an opiate to keep blacks from protesting against racism?

5. Is there more racial prejudice within theologically conservative or theologically liberal churches? What accounts for the difference?

6

Alienation and the Crisis of Modernity

Nature of the Concern

We began this book by suggesting that life in modern society can be described as both the best of times and the worst of times. On the one hand, technological development has given us the opportunity for undreamed-of material wealth and personal leisure. On the other hand, modernity has unexpectedly also produced a cultural environment in which people have increasingly felt a sense of alienation.

Historically, the concept of alienation has been used within the Judeo-Christian context to refer to human separation or estrangement from God. Karl Marx was the first to use the concept of alienation in a sociological sense; in his *Economic and Philosophical Manuscripts* (1964), he describes the capitalistic economic system as having an alienating effect upon the working class (the proletariat). Both social scientists and policy-makers have become increasingly concerned about alienation in present-day mass society, which by its very nature prevents the establishment of intimate primary relationships and breaks down those that already exist.

There is no lack of examples illustrating alienation in modern society: the factory worker who performs the uncreative and meaningless task of assembling one minute part of a total product; the elderly person who, after a useful life in society, finds retirement a time of uselessness, loneliness, and boredom; the youth who enthusiastically enters school only to find that much of what is called education is actually a process of molding and fitting the individual to rules, regulations, and the demands of the curriculum; the educated and intelligent housewife whose life consists of washing dishes and clothes, watching soap operas, taking care of children, and getting together with other housewives to talk about the dull routine; the black who aspires to the good life only to find that a job or a house is not available because one's skin is too dark; and the corporate executive who is alienated from family and community by high stress and long hours.

Although alienation is felt in a variety of ways, there is always an underlying sense of despair. This despair comes from experiencing modern life as so complex, so out of control and balance, that it seems nothing can be done to improve the situation. Another theme associated with alienation in modern society is the disintegration of traditional forms. Nathan Glazer has said that modernity entails "a sense of the breaking of the seamless mold in which *values, behavior,* and *expectations* were once cased into interlocking forms" (cited in Seeman 1957:411). In the past, the interlocking forms or cultural glue holding society together was an acceptance of the Judeo-Christian belief system. This belief system, however, has been gradually eroded by what is popularly referred to as secular humanism, or what sociologists refer to as modernity. The effect of modernity is all-encompassing, for it includes change

> (1) in the *political* sphere, as simple tribal or village authority systems give way to systems of suffrage, political parties, representation, and civil service bureaucracies; (2) in the *educational* sphere, as the society strives to reduce illiteracy, and increase economically productive skills; (3) in the *religious* sphere, as secularized belief systems begin to replace traditionalist religions; (4) in the *familial* sphere, as extended kinship units lose their pervasiveness; (5) in the *stratificational* sphere, as geographical and social mobility tends to loosen fixed, ascriptive hierarchical systems. [Smelser 1973:748]

The contributions of modern artists yield a glimpse of the alienation in modern technological society. Contemporary art and drama reflect the self-estrangement, lostness, and meaninglessness that many individuals are experiencing (Reichart 1969; Rookmaaker 1970). Sandford Reichart suggests that the development of modern art reflects a combination of some of the ideas of Albert Einstein and Sigmund Freud. The ideas behind Einstein's theory of relativity can be seen in the artist's search for new freedoms of self-expression. Freud's emphasis can be viewed in the artist's attempt to articulate the irrational dictates of the subconscious mind. The movement to free art from traditional pictorial representations led to the development of expressionism, where form and order were shattered much as social form and order were shattered prior to World War II. The development of pop art in the 1950s and 1960s suggested societal "worship of the god of the manufactured item—blown up to a gigantic size" (Reichart 1969:140). Drawings of giant soup cans and soapboxes satirized the age of increased automation and depersonalization.

Drama, especially in the theater of the absurd, acts out the message that life is meaningless. Samuel Beckett's *Waiting for Godot* involves two characters sitting under a tree and asking each other when Godot will come. As the play ends, the two characters are still asking the same question. Godot never does (and never will) arrive! Godot, to many, represents God. Beckett's message is clear: there is no God, and there is no ultimate meaning to life. With the erosion of traditional Judeo-Christian beliefs and values, no alternative beliefs and values have emerged upon which an integrated cultural life can be built. In such a state, alienation will be the order of the day.

Dimensions of the Problem

Traditional societies can be characterized as an integrated whole. The different layers of sociocultural life—personal experiences and understandings, social interaction and communication, and institutional and group life—all fit together. In modern society, however, there is discontinuity between these layers. We shall analyze four evidences of alienation in sociocultural life—fragmentation of consciousness, complexity of communication, disintegration of community, and dominance of commodities.

The Fragmentation of Consciousness

Consciousness refers to the individual's subjective experiences, including thoughts, beliefs, images, and emotions. Crises in this area can occur both within and between individuals—both subjectively and intersubjectively.

Within the individual, consciousness is fragmented between different spheres of life. The individual must negotiate between the impersonal competition of the marketplace and the intimacy of friendship and family, between rationality in the school and faith in the pew, between the fast-paced solutions of television and the routine open-endedness of daily life. Even the best of minds and the most stable of personalities can quickly lose a sense of centeredness, a clear grasp of meaning and reality.

This fragmentation of thought has resulted in a disjunction between faith and life. We ask the questions, How do our beliefs and values affect the structure of our lives? Do our Christian commitments and beliefs distinguish us from other people? Do competing values and beliefs shape different areas of our lives?

In *Ideology and Social Psychology* Michael Billings (1982) suggests that people today live in a state of cognitive dissonance. We have adapted to apparently inconsistent beliefs and lack of congruency between values and behavior. For example, interpersonal commitments and intimacy are highly valued, but relationships are often unstable. Many Christians speak about having compassion for the poor, but avoid those in need. To paraphrase the apostle Paul, we are trapped in a sociological "body of death," doing not the good we want, but the evil we do not want—and we do not understand our actions (Rom. 7:15–25).

A diversity of world-views is available to us. The more modern we become, the more aware we are of this diversity and the more relative our own views appear. Peter Berger (1967) refers to this as the pluralization of consciousness. For some, this opens the door for a challenging dialogue with others to help in the construction of one's own value system. This can be an awesome and lonely task. Others will try to mold a new consensus either by creating a new synthesis through dialogue or by cutting the dialogue short and imposing their own beliefs on the other participants. Another possible way of proceeding is subjectivization. As James Hunter (1983:40) puts it:

> When institutional routines and ideologies are rendered implausible, modes of conduct and thought, *morality included*, are deliberated. If institutions no longer provide consistent and reliable answers to such questions as "What do I do with my life?", "How do I raise my children?", "Is it acceptable to live with a member of the opposite gender outside of marriage?", etc., the individual must necessarily *turn inward* to the subjective to reflect, ponder, and probe for answers. The process of "turning inward" is the process of subjectivization.

As Hunter further suggests, the process of subjectivization is not negative—it is simply a structural feature of modern society. It can, however, foster "an incessant fixation upon the self . . . [an] abiding absorption with the 'complexities' of individuality."

Complexity of Communication

Communication in modern society both shapes and reflects the fragmentation, pluralization, and subjectivization of modern consciousness. Significant symbols—terms which everyone understands in precisely the same way—are the basis of communication. But in modern society we cannot assume that everyone will understand a term in precisely the same way. Even the words *family* and *church* have a variety of meanings which can arouse emotional debate. The denotative or referential meanings of words vary considerably—consider the multitude of meanings of the word *love*. The connotative or associative meanings are even more diverse. Lack of consensus on meanings creates a dilemma. On the one hand, our diverse backgrounds and uniqueness as individuals make communication more necessary than ever. On the other hand, our lack of significant symbols makes communication more problematic than ever.

A variety of questions arise in the context of our attempts to communicate: How can we communicate if we cannot assume that others will understand our words as we understand them? How is dialogue possible if there is no shared basis of interpreting language? Are our vocabularies authentic? How free are we to create new vocabularies and to give new meanings to words? What is the relationship between experience and language? Can we trust the very process of communication? Will language become, like advertising, one more technique to mystify and control others?

The difficulties of communication are compounded today by the proliferation of technical and professional languages which mystify the common person. We also see attempts to transcend the traditional means of symbolic communication through various forms of nonverbal communication. In general there is an impoverishment of everyday language and conversation because of the impossibility of capturing complex and confusing realities in simple words.

Disintegration of Community

The breakdown of traditional (homogeneous and geographically based) communities has been lamented by many as the major crisis of

HOW CAN YOU SAY WE ARE ALIENATED FROM OUR NEIGHBORS WHEN WE DON'T EVEN KNOW THEM?

the modern era. Without such communities we have no means of social control and are thus vulnerable to ourselves (to our own moral laxity) and to strangers around us. What Peter Berger and others have called the homeless mind (1973) is in search of a new home or community in which to find meaning and purpose. What is often forgotten when we lament the loss of traditional communities, however, is the provincialism and lack of autonomy which are characteristic of them. Isolated villages and tribal groups are noted for their ethnocentrism.

Concurrent with the disintegration of community life is the centralization of economic and political functions in corporate and governmental bureaucracies. The picture that emerges is of the isolated individual and nuclear family confronted with the faceless image of mass society. The community which once mediated between the individual and larger institutions is no longer there. Judicial and political institutions are called upon to settle more and more family, church, and community disputes. Government encroachment into areas previously considered private or sacred has become a serious social question to which there are no apparent answers.

Some social scientists have suggested that networks are the modern substitute for traditional communities. Friends, co-workers, social, educational, cultural, and religious groups—together these networks can satisfy all or almost all of the individual's needs. However, networks tend to be unstable and specialized and thus lack the virtues associated with community—unconditional commitment and a sense of belonging which embraces the whole of a person's life.

There is a wide range of responses to the disintegration of traditional communities. At one extreme we see the trend toward a self-contained individualism which denies dependence on others and makes no commitment to them. At the other extreme we see people experimenting with various forms of communities focused around some common value such as economic sharing, family life, or religious devotion. In between these extremes we see many people searching for a sense of community in institutional contexts such as the church, where the community metaphor is familiar, and in homogeneous neighborhoods such as suburban housing developments, where names like Homewood, Pleasantdale, and Community Heights imply commonality and identity.

Dominance of Commodities

In advanced capitalism the economic sphere has been largely secularized. Economic life develops unguided by any particular religious ideology. This differentiation of economic life is characteristic of modern institutions. Fragmentation of consciousness, complexity of communication, and disintegration of community make integration of life around economics seem viable. Richard Fenn (1974:41–42) argues that religion has not served to integrate modern society and that uniformity or consensus will most likely be limited to political and economic issues. Remaining unanswered is the question whether a society based solely on economic and political consensus can maintain itself.

Economic principles do dominate modern social life. Jacques Ellul notes in *The Technological Society* (1964) that the principle of technique or rational efficiency has moved from the economic realm to all other areas of life, including the political, educational, and interpersonal. As the principles and values associated with economic life enter other areas, we can see a pattern of the "commodification" of social life developing (Wexler 1983).

Karl Marx maintained that the capitalist emphasis on commodities results in the alienation of the worker. The intrinsic meaning of work is lost. Work becomes only a means to the end of making money. Consequently, workers define themselves and others in terms of their ability to make money. Money has become a spiritual force in society as well as a moral criterion for judging people and their activities (Ellul 1984). Social interaction and the creative process are subservient to the goals of efficiency and production. Given the disintegration of traditional communities and other significant mediating structures between individuals and the economic-political institutions, many people experience great tension between their inner selves and the objective economic realities that determine the direction of their lives.

Explanations of Alienation

We will consider some of the more traditional and then some contemporary sociological explanations of alienation. Marx viewed alienation as resulting from the dual class system produced by capitalistic economics. Both the bourgeoisie (property owners) and the proletariat (workers) are alienated, but especially the proletariat, because they are estranged from the products of their labor, and therefore from themselves and their own creative expressions. As Marx stated:

> The worker becomes all the poorer the more wealth he produces, the more his production increases in power and size. The worker becomes an ever cheaper commodity the more commodities he creates. With the *increasing value* of the world of things proceeds in direct proportion the *devaluation* of the world of men. Labor produces not only commodities: it produces itself and the worker as a *commodity*—and this in the same general proportion in which it produces commodities.
>
> This fact expresses that the object which labor produces—labor's product—confronts it as *something alien*, as a *power independent* of the producer. The product of labor is labor which has been embodied in an object, which has become material: it is the *objectification* of labor. Labor's realization is its

objectification. In the sphere of political economy this realization of labor appears as *loss of realization* for the workers; objectification as *loss of the object* and *bondage to it*; appropriation as *estrangement*, as *alienation*. [1964:107–8]

For Marx, alienation occurs when individuals begin to experience themselves as a commodity or an object, a view which we are going to see has persisted to the present day.

Although differing from Marx, Max Weber was another early social theorist who wrote on the alienating aspects of mass society. Weber believed that the modern emphasis on rationality and the social structures it produces alienates the individual from community and culture. Traditionally, social relationships had been primary and communal, but with the ascendancy of rationality, social relationships became impersonal and bureaucratic. Weber was especially aware of the tendency for people to become little more than cogs in the bureaucratic machinery. Gigantic institutions define the rights and duties of humans, who perform their role accordingly. At the same time they view other people not as personalities with selves, but rather as the occupiers of positions which also carry assigned rights and duties. Weber saw bureaucratization and alienation as inevitable in most segments of industrial society, especially government and education.

Like Marx before him, Weber saw capitalism as being based upon rationalism and as contributing to alienation in society. Capitalism involves rational restraint from the irrational impulse to spend money, and then rational reinvestment of the money to produce further profit. Calvinistic Protestantism, with its suspicion of feelings and its emphasis upon the objective results of faith, provided the spirit or climate within which rationalistic capitalism could develop. In turn, capitalism led to the destruction of traditional values and helped subjugate persons to the rational structures of society. Over seventy years ago Weber lamented the future in a prophecy which many modern critics believe has been fulfilled:

It is horrible to think that the world could one day be filled with nothing but these little cogs, little men clinging to little jobs and striving toward the bigger ones—a state of affairs which is to be seen once more, as in the Egyptian records, playing an ever increasing part in the spirit of our present administrative system, and especially in its offering, the students. This passion for bureaucracy . . . is enough to drive one to despair. It is as if in politics . . . we were deliberately to become men who need "order" and nothing but order, who become nervous and cowardly if for one moment this order wavers, and helpless if they are torn away from their total incorporation in it. That the world should know no men but these: it is in such an evolution that we are already caught up, and the great question is, therefore, not how we can promote and hasten it, but what can we do to oppose this machinery in order to keep a portion of mankind free from this parceling-out of the soul, from this supreme mastery of the bureaucratic way of life. [quoted in Mayer 1943:127]

Contemporary discussions of the concept of alienation have generally been more social-psychological than those of Marx and Weber. These recent treatments have endeavored to subject definitions of alienation to empirical testing, and tend to view it as a multidimensional concept. Melvin Seeman (1959), for example, suggests that alienation has five basic dimensions:

1. *Powerlessness*: the belief that the individual is incapable of influencing the world under the present social and political ground rules
2. *Meaninglessness*: the lack of any clear system of meaning by which individuals can interpret events
3. *Normlessness*: the inability of the system to direct individual behavior
4. *Isolation*: a sense of estrangement from society and a questioning of its beliefs
5. *Self-estrangement*: the feeling that there is no meaning in one's inner life, with a consequent emphasis on external rewards

Martin Gold (1969) has posited three types of alienation: (1) *Resistance to influence* means that the individual is not regulated by the social system. In terms of Seeman's categories, this includes meaninglessness, normlessness, and isolation. (2) *Inability to influence*, the converse of (1), means that individuals cannot affect their environment. This corresponds to Seeman's concept of powerlessness. (3) *Self-estrangement* means that "the individual is *not part of himself*, and the concept of influence is irrelevant."

Perhaps the most devastating analysis of modern society's potential to alienate the individual is found in Jacques Ellul's *Technological Society*. Ellul's main thesis is that we live in a technological rather than a natural environment. This technological environment involves much more than machines; it is, in fact, all-encompassing. Ellul is primarily interested in the relationship between technique and society, technique being defined as the "*totality of methods rationally arrived at and having absolute efficiency in every field of human activity*" (Ellul 1964:xxv). Although technique has been present to some degree in past societies, it has become all-pervasive in modern society.

Today's technical phenomenon has two basic characteristics: rationality and artificiality.

Rationality, which is best exemplified in systematization, division of labor, creation of standards, production norms, and the like involves two distinct phases: first, the use of "discourse" in every operation; this excludes spontaneity and personal creativity. Second, the reduction of method to its logical dimension alone. Every intervention of technique is, in effect, a reduction of facts, forces, phenomena, means, and instruments to the schema of logic. Examples of the application of rationality can be seen in the formation of any large bureaucratic organization.

Artificiality refers to the fact that "technique is opposed to nature," and that the "world that is being created by the accumulation of technical means is an artificial world and hence radically different from the natural world." [Ellul 1964:79]

In fact, the major problems of society today are not only natural ones like floods, earthquakes, and physical distance, but manmade ones like air, water, and noise pollution, and the threat of nuclear fallout.

Ellul's two basic characteristics of modern technique, rationality and artificiality, combine to establish efficiency as the major criterion in making decisions. Decisions today are based on a very simple philosophy: the most efficient means constitute the best means. Consequently, the important decision-makers in society are the technical experts, who alone are capable of determining the most efficient means.

Five less well known characteristics of modern technique are automatism, self-augmentation, monism, universalism, and autonomy. (1) Automatism refers to technique's tendency to become self-directing at a certain stage of development. Thus heart transplants had to be performed simply because they could be performed, and supersonic transports had to be built because it was technically possible to do so. Whatever is technologically possible must be done, regardless of the long-term effect upon society. (2) Self-augmentation refers to technique's ability to reproduce itself geometrically. This phenomenon can be seen in the fact that many of the problems which technique creates can be solved only by further technical applications. For instance, technique-generated problems such as contaminated rivers, deforestation, and air pollution must look to technology for solutions. Ellul fears that at a certain point technical progress may become irreversible, and that none of the problems which it creates in the world will be solvable through natural means, but only through technical means. (3) Monism refers to the fact that technique can be applied in only one way, that is, according to its own inherent rules. Moral terms like "good" and "bad" have no bearing. While it is true that an automobile can kill or, on the other hand, help to save a life, in either case the technical use of the automobile is the same. Automotive technique is the same everywhere it is applied, whether it is used for good or ill. (4) The universalism of technique refers to the fact that all people and organizations in modern society must conduct themselves according to technical principles. (5) The autonomy of technique means that the goals to which it is applied become secondary or may even be lost in the concentration upon technical means. In short, the means becomes the end. Efficiency comes to determine all moral and technical judgments.

The reader should by this time have guessed that Ellul believes that the technological society is doomed to become a totalitarian society. Examination of the methods which are being used to solve societal problems in the United States reveals that they are all technical in nature. All problems have become political problems, and the government is continually developing an ever larger bureaucratic machinery to handle an ever expanding number of problems. The life of the average citizen is becoming more and more absorbed into the life of the state. Ellul's ideas are applicable equally to capitalistic, socialistic, and communistic countries. Technique is the same in all technological societies, each of which is fully capable of alienating its citizenry.

Each of the explanations we have discussed leads to the conclusion that modern society is by its very nature alienating. Two terms which often appear in this connection are "modernity" and "mass society." Modernity refers to the type of sociocultural structures that emerge when a society's economic system becomes closely linked to technology (Levy 1967; Berger, Berger, and Kellner 1973). James Hunter defines modernity as "the inevitable period in the history of a particular society that is characterized by the institutional and cultural concomitants of a technologically induced economic growth" (Hunter 1983:6). Its threats to our social and moral tasks of determining our own beliefs and reconstructing institutions appear overwhelming. We are trapped between our personal needs and desires and a series of modern realities which Ellul (1976:27) describes as a "collection of mechanisms of indescribable complexity—techniques, propaganda, state, administrative planning, ideology, urbanization, social technology." The conditions of modernity by their very nature alienate the individual.

The concept of mass society refers to individual identity's being lost in a primary homogeneous group, for example, the national community. The characteristics of mass society include anonymity, impersonalization, mechanization, and bureaucratization. In describing America as a mass society Daniel Bell (1960: 21–22) states:

> The revolutions in transport and communications have brought men into closer contact with each other and bound them in new ways; the division of labor has made them more interdependent; tremors in one part of society affect all others. Despite this greater interdependence, however, individuals have grown more estranged from one another. The old primary group

ties of family and local community have been shattered; ancient parochial faiths are questioned; few unifying values have taken their place. Most important, the critical standards of an educated elite no longer shape opinion or taste. As a result mores and morals are in constant flux, relations between individuals are tangential or compartmentalized, rather than organic. At the same time, greater mobility, spatial and social, intensifies concern over status. Instead of a fixed or known status, symbolized by dress or title, each person assumes a multiplicity of roles and constantly has to prove himself in a succession of new situations. Because of all this, the individual loses a coherent sense of self. His anxieties increase.

Mass society by its very nature is, then, in many respects an alienating force.

Overcoming Alienation

Concern about alienation as a social problem can focus on either the alienating society or the alienated individual. In our explanation of alienation we stressed that individual alienation is largely a product of an alienating society. Before presenting a Christian response to the problem, we shall summarize three secular strategies for overcoming alienation: cultural pluralism, cultural reform, and cultural revolution.

Cultural Pluralism

One method of overcoming alienation is to encourage individuals of like ideals, beliefs, and values to form homogeneous subgroups within a culture. Under such an approach diversity is encouraged as long as it does not lead to direct conflict. Individuals have their choice of hundreds of different philosophies and are allowed the lifestyle that most approximates their taste.

The rationale here is the diversity of perspectives about society. Some people see change as a disastrous breakdown in institutional norms; others view it as a healthy move. The former group view modern society as alienating because traditional norms are being rejected; the latter group view it as alienating because those who have vested interests in the institutional norms attempt to force everyone else into a rigid, traditional pattern of behavior. A valid response to this lack of agreement is to accept cultural pluralism. According to this view, the consensually accepted monolithic social institutions of the Middle Ages are neither desirable nor necessary in modern society. Members of society should live and let live, and in so doing find their identity with persons of like beliefs, values, and behavior.

Cultural pluralism seems most workable in the areas of education, religion, and the family. American family and religious life are already noted for their cultural diversity. And educational institutions are increasingly trying out new types of experimental programs such as open classrooms. Cultural pluralism may be more limited in its application to political and economic institutions, since governmental and economic organizations have become so entrenched and bureaucratized as to limit the development of alternative forms. Also, since it is the task of the political structure to establish the ground rules within which life is conducted, it must necessarily enjoy the consent of the majority if society is to continue to function.

Although America could be more pluralistic than it now is, there is a point at which pluralism would begin to be disruptive. It must be remembered that society can survive only if the majority of its people agree upon basic ground rules. So although the forming of like-minded subgroups may give relief from individual alienation, all of these subgroups must agree on certain fundamental principles which will allow society to function as some sort of whole.

Cultural Reform

Virtually all attempts to overcome alienation through cultural reform start with the premise that there is nothing inherently wrong with the basic structure of society. While our system is not perfect, any needed overhaul or change can be accomplished within the existing structures. The wisdom of this approach is supported by the success of the many reform movements that have improved conditions throughout the history of our society. Proponents of cultural reform can cite the success of the early feminist movement in helping reduce alcoholism and eliminate slavery and child labor. Other examples include the labor movement's achieving fair wages for workers, the suffrage movement's obtaining the right to vote for women, and the civil-rights movement's gaining equal opportunities for blacks.

Reformers agree that bureaucratic social structures alienate the persons within them. The reformers' response consists of developing new organizational and managerial models rather than radical social upheaval. Take, for example, the area of education. Reformers agree that much of our current educational system, which treats students as impersonal entities, is dehumanizing and alienating. The solution, they argue, is not to tear the system down, but rather to humanize it. Educational reformers have already introduced alternative types of schools, open classrooms, and on-the-job training as part of high-school programs.

Many Christians have come to feel increasingly alienated in modern megachurches, which seem to be obsessed with lavish buildings (Fulton Sheen spoke of our "edifice complex"), fund raising, and the development of large staffs. Their end seems to be served rather than to serve, and their evangelism efforts take place largely inside the church instead of in the marketplace. But even here a multitude of examples could be given of attempts to reform the church from within: the emergence of the small-group movement offering church members opportunities for Bible study, meditation, spiritual growth, and encounter-type experiences; the forming of parachurch organizations which attempt to present the gospel in the marketplace; and alternative forms of worship incorporating drama, dance, multimedia art forms, and folk singing.

Cultural Revolution

Reform is most successful in a democracy such as ours. Wherever change is not likely to be forthcoming within the existing system, people can be tempted to resort to more radical tactics. Cultural revolutionaries believe that reforms are merely cosmetic changes to a system that is by nature alienating. What is needed, therefore, is a thoroughgoing upheaval that will replace existing social structures with more humane forms. Marxists, for example, argue that alienation is an inevitable concomitant of an economic system based on private property. The only way to get rid of this alienation is to overthrow the capitalist system and replace it with communism.

The most recent examples of radical attempts to deal with alienation in the United States are the student revolts and counterculture movement of the 1960s. Major university campuses were the scene of student demonstrations, sit-ins, strikes, and violence. These actions brought a variety of responses from the Establishment, including suspension of students by university administrators and arrests by the police. The student revolts, which began at the University of California at Berkeley in 1964, spread throughout the country. Major revolts took place at large academic institutions like San Francisco State, Columbia, Cornell, and the University of Wisconsin.

The Berkeley revolt was the first coherent student challenge to the authority system of a university (Horowitz and Friedland 1970). This type of radicalism had never occurred before in American universities. Irving Horowitz and William Friedland attribute this revolt against the authority structure to the university's relationship with the Vietnam War effort. Students became aware of the divergence between their interests and the interests of other groups involved with the university. The result was what Howard Becker (1970) refers to as the "campus power struggle."

To assert power and identity, it became necessary for the radicals to mobilize large segments of the student body. The involvement of moderate students was achieved through the politics of confrontation (Horowitz and Friedland 1970). The confrontation involved various acts of disobedience such as seizing university facilities and interfering with campus recruitment activities. These confrontations were "calculated to mobilize an otherwise apathetic majority by forcing it to take positions on issues" (Horowitz and Friedland 1970:82). Confrontation was not, then, an end in itself; rather, its goal was to arouse the majority. Success depended upon the response of the administrators to the behavior of the activists. On several occasions police intervention—particularly at Berkeley and Columbia—mobilized the student body in favor of the activists.

Out of the climate created by the student revolts of the 1960s emerged a less confrontational movement which was variously referred to as the hippie movement, the counterculture movement, or the effortless revolution. It consisted of youth who, in response to an alienating society, elected to drop out and "turn on" to an alternative lifestyle. In place of what they perceived to be a standardized, future-oriented, restrictive, unequal, and anxiety-ridden society, the hippie lifestyle emphasized spontaneous self-expression, living for the full enjoyment of the moment, freedom, equality, and mind expansion. The ideology of the effortless revolution was reduced in Charles Reich's *Greening of America* (1968:241) to three commandments:

1. *Thou shalt not do violence to thyself*—do not allow the Corporate State or one of its impersonal organizations to use you. Rather than becoming a "prostitute" of the Corporate State, one must "be true to oneself."
2. *Thou shalt not judge anyone else*—recognize the absolute worth of every individual, of every self. One does not require that everyone must measure up to a certain standard: there are no true objective standards whereby human worth can be measured; each self is different and unique. This commandment also means that competition, outside of sports, is an unhealthy condition that only serves to judge individuals on the basis of some superficial criteria.
3. *Thou shalt be wholly honest with others, and use no other person as a means*—indict our consumer-oriented society, where we are taught to view people as objects to be manipulated for our own ends. The manipulation of others not only degrades the other person, but it also means altering oneself to become something that one is not. These values, which place a high value on self and human life, lead to a radical critique of society. . . . The high value placed upon the self also leads to a high premium on community—not a community where human relationships are governed by law or politics, but one which, instead, is like an extended family which has great respect for individuality.

We have seen that the encouragement of cultural pluralism may in part serve to give individuals a greater sense of identity, but in the long

run will do little to alter those elements in the social structure that produce alienation. And although the effortless revolution may have legit-
imized some aspects of the counterculture morality, history demonstrates
that change is rarely effortless and that its direction is almost never predictable. Whether student rebellion has been an effective force for positive change is still debated. That student rebellion has had an impact
upon the mood of the country and the attitudes of its people is undebat-
able. But some would argue that student rebellion has done more to hinder than advance the cause of progressive change. There is some evidence that student rebellion may have created a backlash effect against
the very goals the protestors were striving to promote. Such a reaction, it
is argued, was evidenced in the popular cry for law and order and in the
cutbacks of funds for colleges and universities in the 1980s.

Although student rebellion undoubtedly does alarm many people into
taking a reactionary position, it can be argued that it also serves to open
the way for less radical attempts at changing the social structure. The
requests for societal change made by liberal reformers seem mild next to
the demands made by student radicals, thus resulting in an increased
likelihood that reform will be accepted in society. Accordingly, the radical should not view the liberal reformer as an enemy. Many radicals hold
to the theory that conditions do not get better until they get worse, and
since the reformer is making conditions slightly better, the needed revolution is being delayed. Philip Slater (1970:122) has insightfully observed,
however, that "revolution does not occur when things get bad enough
but when things get better—when small improvements generate rising
aspirations and decrease tolerance for long-existing injustices. The 'make
things worse' approach is not only not strategic, it is not even revolution-
ary—it seeks unconsciously to preserve, while at the same time discrediting . . . authority." Slater believes that the reformer may actually be
doing the softening-up work which makes more-radical social change
possible. According to Slater, in the effort to improve an alienating society, "liberal reform and radical change are thus complementary rather
than antagonistic" (1970:124).

Some would argue that the lasting effects of the youth counterculture
have proved to be more superficial than significant in that its success
amounts to little more than the introduction of an alternative lifestyle
and amelioration of some of the conditions which had alienated the
youth themselves; the basic flaws that are inherent in any technological
society and alienate virtually everyone, however, have not been dealt
with. Although there may be some truth in this argument, it is impossible to overlook the fact that in the 1960s our country underwent some
rather significant and visible structural alterations in which young people played a significant role. Among those changes and their aftereffects:

1. Legal and extralegal events have advanced the cause of civil rights for blacks.
2. A president chose not to run for reelection because he could not organize sufficient popular support for the war in Vietnam.
3. The United States did eventually withdraw from the Vietnam War.
4. Young women have joined the feminist movement and have seen their efforts pay off in legislation that has opened doors to education and employment previously closed to them.
5. Eighteen-year-olds have been given the right to vote.
6. The ecology movement has resulted in a reexamination of the use of natural resources.

In these and other ways, young people have seen society respond to their wishes and demands; they have had tangible proof of their influence and effectiveness in the public sphere.

A Radical Christian Response to Alienation

Alienation is not a new phenomenon—it first appeared when Eve and Adam sinned and felt a sense of shame due to their nakedness. The sin of Eve and Adam alienated each of them from self, from the other, and from God. The biblical solution to alienation is redemption. Where there once was estrangement, redemption works to restore wholeness at three levels: (1) between human beings and God; (2) between human beings themselves; and (3) within individuals. We must be aware that redemption is not an abstract system, but an unfolding creative work of God in our lives, a work in which his church is to participate by being a redeeming community in the world. Redeemed at great cost ourselves, we must not minimize God's call for us to help bring restoration in all areas of life, both individual and collective.

Christians, like Christ, are called to make a radical response—to be light and salt—in a world of broken relationships. This means that Christians must seek to restore wholeness at the family, primary-group, community, and society levels. It also means working toward release from bondage to commodities, which can assist in bringing about a reconstruction of community, which can lead to a revitalization of communication, which can in turn help achieve a reintegration of consciousness. The Christian's task is nothing less than attempting to bring about *shalom* in society, neighborliness in communities, *koinōnia* in primary groups, and covenant love in the family. Though we might be overwhelmed at the magnitude and complexity of this task, there are specific ways in which Christians, as part of the body of Christ, can work to change alienating social structures.

Release from Bondage to Commodities

One need not be a Marxist to acknowledge that capitalism dominates all of modern life. We see virtually everything in economic terms. Even time spent on the freeway is viewed essentially as money lost. When we evaluate individuals and social relationships in terms of how they will profit us, the possibility of effecting *shalom* and being a neighbor to the stranger are doomed hopes. We are, alas, a people for whom the term *productivity* automatically connotes commodities. Clearly, God's ideal for human life cannot be accomplished without liberation from the pervasive influence of our economic system.

Without a revolution to free us from our bondage to commodities we will inevitably be pulled toward conformity to the system that promotes it. Techniques, money, careers, and material growth have become spiritual forces in society. We cannot count on society to change by adopting our Christian values; rather, we must be willing to sacrifice and risk appearing foolish in resisting the power of worldly values.

Given the dominance of the economic realm, many needed changes must begin within it. Christian employers can take the lead. They can, for example, establish policies which provide ways for their employees to give priority to family and community relationships. One option is to offer flexible schedules for both mothers and fathers who desire to be with young children. A strategy which reverses the two-hundred-year-old trend of giving economic institutions priority over parenting would make a significant contribution.

Similarly, Christian employers could make advancement opportunities available locally to employees who elect not to move their families to a new community. The average young American family moves every three years. It is inconceivable that the community support systems which families need, especially during periods of stress and crisis, can develop within such a mobile society.

There also need to be commitments from employers to the welfare of their employees, as well as commitments from the employees to produce high-quality work. The present economic system, which makes the profit motive the major consideration, works directly against the development of any sense of loyalty or pride in the quality of work performed. Christian employers must provide, in addition to salary, a context in which the employee is given incentives and rewards for creative service and pride in production.

The church also has a role to play in the task of freeing society from its bondage to commodities. It should, for example, support anyone who makes financial sacrifices for the sake of relationships. A willingness on the part of church members to share—be it of their time, possessions, or skills—will minimize the impact of these sacrifices and protect the individual from the brute economic forces of modern society. In addition, when a brother or sister is in need, the church must see that person as a neighbor and respond with love rather than merely funneling the need through committees and budgets. To be a redeeming community to a broken world may mean developing programs directed at empowering the least lovable members of society. This will be unpopular with members who want their church to be a Christian country club. The Christian gospel, however, should not be diluted in order to keep nominal church members content. Drawing on his many years in the ministry, Samuel Shoemaker (1965:144) points out that "the 'means of grace' with which the church is endowed are not satisfactions for the comfort of the 'ins,' so much as gifts for their equipment and empowering as they seek to reach the 'outs.'"

Finally, to reduce its economic and technical orientation, the church must avoid commodifying the gospel in order to appeal to large numbers. In a commodity-dominated society it is all too easy for churches to judge their success solely on the basis of size and growth. This approach necessitates complex programs and specialization. The church should, instead, concentrate on delivering a genuine message. Fewer may be involved, but more will be accomplished.

Reconstruction of Community

One of the strongest contributors to alienation is the disintegration of community in modern life. As a community of faith based upon covenant commitment, the church can be an example of the koinōnia the world so desperately needs. The church can realize this goal if it keeps several basic principles in view: (1) The church must be a community of diversity, including people of various social classes, races, ages, backgrounds, and religious experiences. It must avoid a unity based on similar images or subjective experiences, for true unity is based only in Jesus Christ. When a diverse group of people worship and serve God together, God is indeed glorified. Disagreements and conflicts will inevitably arise, but when they do, they should not be feared. (2) The church must be a community whose members have a genuine knowledge of one another. This does not necessarily mean intimacy between all members, but a knowledge which is based on a sharing of burdens and joys. (3) The church must create roles for all of its members. Youth, single persons, and the elderly need to be integrated into the body. Rather than being mistrusted because of their youth, singleness, or age, they should be respected, nurtured, and disciplined so that the whole community may be enriched by their perspective and insight.

The gap between clergy and laity must be minimized so that the pastorate is not viewed as just another career. Laypersons must be regarded as ministers of the gospel and not merely as sheep who show up at church to be fed. True *koinōnia* will develop when the members become mutually dependent, knowing and caring for one another deeply, and when the support they give to and receive from each other leads not to an exclusiveness, but an inclusiveness open to the needs of those outside the fellowship. Alienated individuals without a sense of community can be helped immeasurably by a church that models or exemplifies what true community can be.

Revitalization of Communication

Communication is vital in reconstructing our community life and re-integrating our consciousness. It should reflect our individual uniqueness and our shared values and activities. One way of revitalizing communication is for the church no longer to rely solely on experts to interpret the Word of God. Hermeneutics could be integrated into the life of the local church as a tool to help us reconstruct our relationships with one another and with God. This would serve to diminish the boundaries of exclusiveness that are set up by technical theological language. Instead of being abstract, individualized activities, Bible studies and sermons could focus on church life itself. In this context individuals ought to be given the freedom to create and express their own languages of faith. At the same time, they should be willing to confront one another without automatically declaring false any experiences in contradiction to their own.

Including the laity in the interpretive process and diminishing reliance on traditional symbols and language will give us opportunity to explore and experiment with new expressions of our experience of God. We must be liberated from our fixation on words which have impoverished communication. One example of what can be done is the inclusion of female imagery for God and our experience of her as the nurturing mother. Perhaps we need more guidance now from our artists, poets, dancers, and dramatists than from our systematic theologians and Bible interpreters.

Reintegration of Consciousness

On the personal level, alienation is the disintegration of consciousness—a disjunction between thought and meaning on one hand, and experience on the other. Reintegration of consciousness can be achieved by participating in and experiencing genuine, caring, meaningful relationships. At the primary-group level this means that every individual needs to be a part of a family-type body within which one experiences what it is to love and be loved (covenant), to forgive and be forgiven (grace), to serve and be served (empowering), and to know and be known (intimacy). When personal integration and wholeness develop from such a fellowship, we can reach out as neighbors to the stranger or foreigner who appears to have nothing in common with us. On the individual level we can be light and salt in a needy and broken world, and collectively we can challenge the dehumanizing and unjust social structures which hinder the realization of *shalom*.

Christians must strive together to manifest the value of relationships grounded in a love which is patient, kind, hopeful, and enduring. Only as a concrete witness to this love from God can the church enable its members to resist the alternatives provided by the world. The structures of the world are firmly entrenched, ready at all times to oppose the Word of God. This has always been the case; the modern situation is unique only in its specific challenges and temptations. Our service and witness to Christ will be only partially effective in this world, but we have a great hope in him. The disintegrating effects of modern society will be overcome now in part, but someday in perfection. "For we know in part, and we prophesy in part. But when that which is perfect is come, then that which is in part shall be done away. . . . For now we see through a glass, darkly; but then face to face: now I know in part; but then shall I know even as also I am known" (1 Cor. 13:9–10, 12 KJV).

Topics for Review, Reflection, and Discussion

1. In what type of social situation do you feel most alienated?
2. In what ways is alienation related to the absence of *koinōnia*? of *shalom*?
3. Give examples of the dominance of commodities in everyday life.
4. How is alienation in a state-controlled economy (socialism or communism) likely to differ from the type of alienation found in a capitalistic economy?
5. Why are mass societies likely to be alienating?
6. Which of the five basic dimensions of alienation—powerlessness, meaninglessness, normlessness, isolation, or self-estrangement—do you personally experience most?
7. Which of the secular strategies for overcoming alienation—cultural pluralism, cultural reform, or cultural revolution—seems to be most realistic?
8. How realistic is the suggested radical Christian response to alienation?
9. Do you agree that change on any of the four levels—reintegration of consciousness, revitalization of communication, reconstruction of community, and release from bondage to commodities—is interdependent with change on each of the other levels?

7

Redefinition of Gender Roles

So God created man in His own image; in the image of God He created him; male and female He created them.

Genesis 1:27 NKJV

The Nature of the Concern

The question of what it means to be male or female is a matter that every society faces and deals with in its own way. The definition of gender roles is probably not an issue in most societies since they simply assume that males will grow up behaving like males and females will grow up behaving like females. Likewise, most Christians interpret Genesis 1:27 to mean that whatever sexual differences exist in their particular society are a direct result of God's creation.

It is only since the emergence of the social and behavioral sciences that we have begun to question the view that physiology is the sole factor in the formation of sexual temperament and behavior. Cross-cultural research has led social scientists to conclude that culture rather than nature is the major influence in determining the temperamental differences between the sexes.

The United States has undergone such a rapid rate of social and cultural change in recent decades that gender roles have increasingly been called into question, thus necessitating a continuing process of redefinition. The nature of the concern with regard to the female role centers around its expansion to include more than wife and mother. The key element here is the liberation of women from suppressive conditions that previously denied them the opportunity to pursue options other than

145

those traditionally defined as suitable for them. The concern becomes a social problem wherever there is a perception that (1) women are treated unequally and have fewer opportunities to achieve positions of power and prestige than do men, and (2) the situation should be remedied by cooperative action.

With the increasing freedom of females, many men have come to feel insecure about their masculinity and position in society. Men have traditionally been defined as independent, task- and achievement-oriented, competitive, rational, unsentimental, and inexpressive, while women have been defined as dependent, interpersonally oriented, supportive, emotional, sentimental, and expressive. As many of these stereotypes undergo modification, related changes will occur in such areas as family life, religious organizations, and educational and economic institutions.

The Christian community is currently far from united in its evaluation of the change in gender roles. Some say that women should return to their rightful place in the home, while others argue for increased participation by women in all occupations, including the ordained ministry. The redefinition of gender roles certainly places Christians in a difficult position. For while we must affirm the distinctions between male and female as intended by God, we must also be aware that many of the differences we see are unique or peculiar to given cultures. Such culturally defined and produced differences God never intended to exist. Only after we recognize this fact may we explore such issues as authority in marriage, female participation in the church, and heterosexual and homosexual relationships.

Our concern in this chapter, however, will be much broader. We will focus on the nature of gender differences in society in general. To do this, it is necessary to first understand some of the background for the changes that are taking place. It may be no accident that it was a woman, the late Margaret Mead, who did the classic study demonstrating that temperamental differences between the sexes are to be explained primarily in terms of culture and not physiology or biology. In *Sex and Temperament* (1935) Mead reported on the gender differences in three societies in New Guinea. Using ethnocentric Western stereotypes as a standard for comparison, she found that among the Arapesh both the male and female were essentially feminine, among the Mundugumor they were essentially masculine, and among the Tchambuli the males were feminine and the females masculine. That is to say, the Tchambuli's definition of gender roles was opposite that which is found in America.

Following Mead's early work, the environment-versus-heredity argument swung in the direction of emphasizing environmental factors in the determination of gender differences. Recently, social scientists have been taking a more balanced view, stressing the interactive effects of both biological and environmental factors. In her presidential address to the

American Sociological Association, Alice Rossi (1984) reported five compelling evidences that biology accounts for some gender differences: (1) correlations between the social behavior and the physiological attributes of each sex; (2) gender differences in infants and young children prior to socialization; (3) the emergence of gender differences with the onset of puberty, when body physiology and hormonal secretion change rapidly; (4) stability of gender differences across cultures; and (5) similar gender differences among the higher primates.

Figure 5
Differences Between Male and Female Behavior

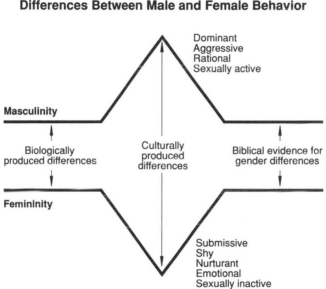

On the basis of both physiological and social-scientific research, it may be said that males and females are born with general tendencies (but not directional predispositions) which are then exaggerated by patterns of socialization to fit in with the prevailing definition of masculinity and femininity. (See figure 5, where the distance between the horizontal lines represents the difference between male and female behavior.) We would suggest that it is culture and not biology which molds males to exhibit primarily dominant and rational characteristics and shapes females to be submissive and emotional. It is essential for Christians to keep this in mind when they ask the fundamental question, "What is God's intent for the development of full manhood and womanhood in modern society?"

Dimensions and Explanations of Gender Redefinition

The redefinition of gender roles is currently at the center of a storm of controversy. On the one hand, many persons, especially those involved in the feminist movement, view the traditional way in which sex roles have been defined as the problem. They argue that we need to accept an alternative, modern definition which allows for greater flexibility and interchangeability in gender roles. On the other hand, those who tend toward religious and political conservatism view the drift away from traditional definitions and toward new ones as the problem. Neither group is content with the present situation of flux, which is characterized by conflicting and contradictory definitions of manhood and womanhood.

Redefinition of the Female Role

In our society, females have traditionally acquired status through being wives and mothers. However, this situation is rapidly changing as women assume extrafamilial responsibilities, particularly in the work force. Although competing images are not introduced into the traditional socializing process of females, many women experience contradictory expectations when they begin to pursue professional careers or work

...AND THEY SAY BEING A WOMAN IS EASY TODAY!

full-time outside of the home. Magazines, films, and television add to the confusion by encouraging romance, marriage, and childbearing, and at the same time glorifying the independent, career-oriented woman. The message women hear is that they can have the security and enrichment of marriage and family, and the excitement and independence of a career at the same time. Many women, however, have found the competing demands upon their time, energies, and loyalties too much to bear. This is especially true of women who work full-time and find their role as wives and mothers impoverished. Many today are rightly concerned about the confusion and contradictions with regard to women's role(s) in our society. The issue, however, is not whether change should occur, but rather what the nature of this change should be and how it will affect current societal patterns.

Historical roots of women's liberation

Western civilization has both glorified woman and viewed her as inferior to man. As the dominant institution during much of the history of Western civilization, the church set the pattern for society's attitude toward women. The early churchman Tertullian, for instance, believed that woman, by arousing lust, is the gate of hell and the destroyer of God's image in man. Later saints took equally harsh views. Bernard described woman as a scorpion, ever ready to sting. Chrysostom stated that of all the wild beasts, the most dangerous is woman. In the sixth century the Council of Macon decided by only a one-vote majority that women have souls (Vernon 1962:101).

It is necessary to keep this historical backdrop in mind when considering the low view of women that was prevalent in colonial America. Women were regarded as creatures who are inferior to men intellectually, legally, socially, and politically. Educationally, girls could hope for little more than a few years of schooling, and college was totally out of the question. Legally, a wife could not sign a contract and had no right even to her own earnings. Socially, she was "put on a pedestal to be looked down upon," or, as one writer put it, "woman was treated like a cross between an angel and an idiot." In addition, women could not vote. Andrew Sinclair may not be too severe when he states that "early American women were almost treated like Negro slaves, inside and outside the home. Both were expected to behave with deference and obedience towards owner or husband; both did not exist officially under the law; both worked for their masters without pay; both had to breed on command, and to nurse the results" (1966:4).

Women first began to organize in the early 1800s in New England and Western towns. The first feminist leaders and organizations arose when women became involved in various reform movements including welfare, antislavery, and temperance. Women were encouraged to go outside the home to do good work, and in the process inadvertently began to redefine their own existence and sphere of influence. In working against slavery, for example, women began to realize their own state of bondage.

Before the Civil War, the feminist movement consisted of geographically scattered groups and individuals addressing themselves to local interests. After the war, however, women organized at the national level with the forming in 1868 of the National Woman Suffrage Association (NWSA) through the efforts of a rather radical group in New York. This was followed in 1869 by the more conservatively oriented American Woman Suffrage Association (AWSA), which was based in Boston. Like women's liberation today, these early movements had both their liberal and conservative factions.

Besides the NWSA and the AWSA, many suffragists engaged in club work, education, and various charitable activities. Rather than making women's rights an end in itself, these women (sometimes referred to as social feminists) sought to demonstrate by their example that their spheres of influence should be expanded. These feminists were not so much opposed to the goals of their more radical sisters as they were convinced that their own methods of social involvement were both more useful to others and thus more fruitful in the quest to gain equality for women. The social feminists were especially successful in showing prostitution to be degrading to womanhood; they triggered masculine guilt by pointing out that most prostitutes were compelled to engage in such activity out of economic necessity produced by an inequitable social order. In attempting to cope with all kinds of social problems—from poverty, inadequate housing, and disease to prostitution, alcoholism, and crime—the social feminists not only redefined and expanded the role of women in American society, but also were forerunners of the social-work movement.

The major victory of the feminist movement came in 1920 when women gained the right to vote. Once this victory had been won, many women felt there were no further battles to fight. The social feminists, though, viewed suffrage as being only a necessary first step in effecting still more change.

Some have argued that because of the changing nature of American culture during the last one hundred years, increased rights for women would have developed independently of feminist activity. It should be kept in mind, however, that cultural change is never automatic nor its direction predictable. The evidence from social-science research, including studies of the black civil-rights movement, indicates that substantive societal change rarely occurs apart from collective assertive efforts.

We have seen that the roots of the contemporary women's movement may ultimately be traced back to the feminists of the 1800s. Interest revived in 1963 with the publication of Betty Friedan's *Feminine Mystique*.

In 1966 Friedan was instrumental in establishing the National Organization of Women (NOW), the largest of the present-day feminist groups. Although this body has consistently fought for an end to legal and economic discrimination against women, its goals are sometimes labeled conservative by more-radical feminists.

Because of their extreme zeal the radical female liberationists are often found in small splinter groups. In the early 1970s, their tactical strategy consisted of entering (by force if necessary) all-male bars and clubs, picketing stores which they believed discriminated against women, and in some cases even disassociating themselves from men. In their view, males were the enemy, and the only meaningful alternative to living in a male-constructed society was to become a female separatist.

Today at least three factions can be identified within the radical wing of the women's movement: (1) Traditional Marxist feminists stress that private property is the primary cause of the oppression of women, and that equality is possible only in a classless society. Thus, women are encouraged to join the proletariat class and in so doing help to undermine capitalism. (2) Radical feminists, by contrast, believe that the oppression of women is inherent in the nature of male/female relationships and thus predates the emergence of private property. Therefore, the abolition of social classes will not eradicate the oppression of women. Instead of joining men in the proletariat class, women are urged to form their own economic associations and businesses. For the only way to effect change in a male-dominated system is for women to seize power. (3) Socialist feminists see some truth in both the Marxist and the radical thinking. Capitalism and sexism are understood to reinforce each other. By stressing that both economic and sexual oppression must be eliminated, socialist feminists have attempted to synthesize the Marxist and radical views.

Unfortunately, many Christians make the mistake of classifying most women liberationists as radical feminists. But most women want merely to be treated equally, which they believe can be achieved by enacting and enforcing laws which will forbid employers to discriminate against women in the areas of hiring, pay, and advancement.

The Equal Rights Amendment and opposition to women's liberation

Although a resolution was introduced in every session of the United States Congress since 1923, it was not until 1972 that the House of Representatives and the Senate both overwhelmingly passed the Equal Rights Amendment (ERA). In order to become the Twenty-seventh Amendment to the Constitution, however, it needed to be ratified by three-fourths of the state legislatures within seven years. At this point a countermovement arose. Led by Phyllis Schlafly, most of the opposition centered on the negative effects that the ERA might have on women. It was argued that if all laws that treat men and women differently were declared unconstitutional, females would lose certain rights and privileges enjoyed in the past. More specifically, a male would no longer be required to financially support his wife and children. Laws protecting females against sex crimes would be nullified, and women would be subject to the draft and combat duty. In addition, their chances of obtaining custody of their children in the event of divorce would be lessened (Schlafly 1972).

In retrospect, it is amazing that so much opposition could have been mounted against an amendment that merely stated, "Equality of rights under the law shall not be denied or abridged by the United States or any state on account of sex." One of the curiosities here is the extent to which the evangelical church has sided with the anti-ERA forces, supposedly for the sake of maintaining certain God-ordained practices in our society and preventing sexually integrated rest rooms, the drafting of women into the armed forces, and the payment of alimony by women. In actuality, the Bible presents no justification for discriminating against women in the area of employment practices. Moreover, what the anti-ERA groups predicted would have happened if the ERA had passed can as a matter of fact take place under existing legislation. The government does have the right to draft women, business establishments need not provide separate rest rooms for men and women, and some women are already paying alimony to their ex-husbands. The anti-ERA position taken by many Christians today is reminiscent of the anti-civil-rights stance which many Christians took several years ago. It is a tragedy that the church rather than being an initiator must often learn of social justice from secular groups.

Women in society today

Currently, 52 percent of all adult women hold full-time jobs; as of 1981 they were earning less than two-thirds of what their male counterparts were making ($11,684 and $18,044 respectively). It is significant, however, that this difference has been decreasing during the last thirty years. Part of the reason is the increased number of women who have entered the higher-earning professions. For instance, the proportion of new graduates from dental school who are female increased from less than 1 percent in 1960 to 14 percent in 1981; the figures for medical school rose from 6 percent in 1960 to 25 percent in 1981, and for law school from 3 to 32 percent. Furthermore, from 1950 to 1980 the proportion of bachelor's, master's, and doctoral degrees that were awarded to women increased from 33 to 49 percent, from 32 to 49 percent, and from 9 to 21 percent respectively. And in the area of government, the proportion of state legislators who are women increased from 5 percent in 1971 to 13 percent in 1983, while the proportion of women mayors in cities with populations over thirty thousand increased from 1 percent in 1971 to 8 percent in 1983.

By almost any objective criteria, women have achieved a large measure of economic and professional equality in the United States during the last few decades. There continue to be, however, a multitude of subtle informal ways in which women are discriminated against. One of these involves the societal norms governing the aging process. It can be argued that it is much more difficult psychologically and sociologically for a woman to grow old in our culture than it is for a man. For instance, a male who is widowed often marries a much younger woman, and society does not react unfavorably. In fact, it even seems to expect such an eventuality. However, similar behavior on the part of females is usually frowned upon. This form of discrimination, coupled with the fact that women typically live longer than men, greatly reduces a female's chance of remarrying. In fact, for those widowed between the ages of forty-five and sixty-four, 70 percent of the men remarry while only 2 percent of women do so.

Although it seems almost too obvious to mention, it is still the case that women are reduced to sex objects by advertisers, who know all too well that sex sells. And magazines such as *Playboy* and *Penthouse* preach that a woman is to be used and discarded at a man's convenience.

Professional women also encounter sex discrimination in the form of a protégé system under which new employees or associates must serve an apprenticeship under an experienced sponsor. The sponsor is very likely to be a male with reservations about or even resentments at having to give guidance to a female. Also, the informal social patterns within many professions often serve to exclude women since females are typically not invited to many of the activities of their male associates.

The Redefinition of the Male Role

Within the last few years, increased attention has been given to the issue of men's liberation. This movement typically elicits one of three responses. Most people ask, "What do men need to be liberated from?" Others enthusiastically say, "It's about time. Women's liberation has gone too far!" And still others comment, "That's just like men, trying to capitalize on a good thing that women started. They're attempting to divert attention away from females and towards themselves."

In reality, female and male roles are two sides of the same coin, since one cannot be redefined without also redefining the other. Thus, when we call the traditional role of females in our society into question, we cannot help questioning the male role as well. Although men are not in need of liberation in the same sense as are women, they do need to be freed from the culturally prescribed ways in which they have been molded. They have been conditioned, for instance, to regard the achievement of tasks as the touchstone of self-worth, to be compulsively competitive, and to put on a tough, unsentimental, and inexpressive façade.

Many recent popular books have focused on the subject of masculinity in our culture. For instance, *Women Who Love Too Much* (Norwood 1985) describes the dilemma facing females who have emotionally invested themselves in relationships with men but receive very little emotional support in return. It is significant that the subtitle to the book is *When You Keep Wishing and Hoping He'll Change*. The author believes that many a woman whose husband cannot return love is living with the illusion that if she will love just a little bit more, then surely he will reciprocate. The tragedy is that there is often little chance of this occurring.

On the other hand, *Men Who Hate Women and the Women Who Love Them* (Forward and Torres 1986) states that many women are involved with men who love them yet cause them tremendous pain. These men may intimidate by yelling or withdraw into angry silence. Or they may withhold love, money, approval, or sex as a form of punishment or control.

The McGill Report On Male Intimacy notes that "most wives live with and love men who are in some very fundamental ways strangers to them—men who withhold themselves and, in doing so, withhold their loving. These wives may be loved, but they do not feel loved because they do not know their husbands" (McGill 1985:74). As a father, the average male is found to be more of a "phantom man" than a "family man," for even "when he is present he is absent—he is there in body, but in every other respect he is removed from the family. Present or absent, the father is reliant on his spouse to relate to the children for him. Whatever closeness he has with his daughter is more likely to be based on imagery and illusion than on substantive information about himself. His relationship with his son is circumscribed by competition, where proving oneself is more important than presenting oneself" (p. 155). Men do not fare much better in their relationships with other men, which are typically "superficial, even shallow." Even the best of friends "reveal so little of themselves to each other that they are little more than acquaintances. There is no intimacy in most male relationships and none of what intimacy offers: solace and support" (p. 184).

Perry Garfinkel's *In a Man's World: Father, Son, Brother, Friend and Other Roles Men Play* offers still another pessimistic analysis of the way in which relationships between males are typically devoid of intimacy. In reflecting on what a boy can expect to gain from his father, Garfinkel states, "If he has learned well—about the importance of power, achievement, competition, and emotional inexpressiveness—he will enter relationships with other men with great caution and distrust" (1985:43). And what is the most important lesson which a boy can learn from his brother? It is that "rivalry rules. He who comes in first—who is born first, scores higher, earns more—is better. Like an endless game of one-upmanship from cradle to coffin. The lessons of competition and emotional inexpressiveness come through the brother bond as well" (p. 95).

One of the most discouraging statements is Samuel Osherson's *Finding Our Fathers: The Unfinished Business of Manhood*. He suggests that "boys grow into manhood with a wounded father within, a conflicted inner sense of masculinity rooted in men's experience of their fathers as rejecting, incompetent, or absent" (1986:3).

Evidence from social-science research indicates that the cultural imprint begins early in life. In one noteworthy study a hospital placed male names on female newborns and female names on male babies. The researchers reported that observers described the girls as active, robust, and strong, while they referred to the boys as darling, cute, and sweet.

When a young boy expresses his emotions by crying, his parents are often quick to scold, "You're a big boy, and big boys don't cry!" or "Don't be such a sissy!" And when parents use the phrase, "He's all boy," they typically mean that their son is aggressive and mischievous. As he matures, he is expected to display anger, boisterous humor, and competitiveness. On the other hand, such feminine emotions as tenderness, compassion, and sentimentality are not to be expressed. Society in general and parents in particular are communicating to male children that it is improper for men to express their emotions. By the time a boy reaches school age, he is afraid to act in any way that might be labeled feminine.

As the boy moves into the sphere of male peer groups, the emphasis on being tough and the taboo against expressing one's feelings are reinforced. According to studies of male subcultures in schools and juvenile gangs, being affectionate, gentle, and compassionate is, to say the least, not encouraged. The mass media convey a similar message when they define masculinity in terms of aggressiveness and virility. Confronted with this machismo image projected by the powerful triumvirate of family, peer group, and mass media, most young males quickly learn that whatever masculine behavior might be, it is not characterized by gentleness, tenderness, compassion, verbal affection, and sentimentality.

Overcoming the Problem:
Defining Christian Womanhood and Manhood

The present confusion with respect to gender roles provides the church with an excellent opportunity to define maleness and femaleness from a Christian perspective. But we must look first at three approaches that emerged within the women's movement: assimilation, androgyny, and accommodation.

The earliest approach was assimilation. Women had become conscious of their economic and political disenfranchisement in a male-dominated society. So the goal which women set for themselves was simply to prove that they too could be successful in the rational, competitive worlds of business and politics. Although many women did prove to themselves and others that they were tough enough to compete directly with men, they began to wonder if they had not sacrificed their womanhood in the process.

The shortcomings of assimilation led in turn to the androgynous approach, which emphasized the desirability of taking the best from ideal masculinity (andro-) and the best from ideal femininity (-gyny) and incorporating both into existing social structures. In practice, this meant that women should be allowed to create their own roles in those institutions traditionally monopolized by men. And in a female-dominated institution such as the family, the goal was increased participation by the father. Rather than being assimilated into the social structures dominated by the opposite sex, men were to participate in them as men, and women as women, the result being the creation of androgynous social structures.

As a consequence of the androgynous approach, much research was generated demonstrating the dehumanizing effects which the worlds of work and home have produced because they are dominated by one sex. It was shown that the competitive, impersonal workplace was producing anxiety, fatigue, ulcers, career burnout, and midlife crises. Also demonstrated were the ill effects upon children who were deprived of their father's nurturing.

Although the androgynous approach has been fruitful in bringing about some needed social corrections, when carried to its logical extreme it leads to a blurring of gender distinctives. While some feminists delight in the possibility of a unisex world, the notion has not garnered unanimous support. Recently, other feminists have suggested accommodation or differentiation, an approach which recognizes fundamental differences between the sexes. Now although we recognize much value in the androgynous approach, we believe that differentiation is most consonant with a Christian world-view.

The reader will recall that in figure 5 (p. 147) we visually suggested that the biologically produced differences between males and females are quite small; they are nevertheless accentuated, and in many cases exaggerated, in the socialization process. As Christians we must take care not to defend culturally produced images of gender differences. However, this is precisely what happens when some of us argue for the preservation of traditional gender roles. Still others need to guard against wholeheartedly embracing the androgynous approach.

Genesis 1:27 states that "God created man in His own image; in the image of God He created him; male and female He created them" (NKJV). At least one important implication to be derived from this statement is that there are only two ways to be a human being, that is, as either a male or female. But what are maleness and femaleness? We will turn to the Scriptures in order to explore this subject.

The Bible gives no reason why Christians should not be involved in the process of liberating women from the suppressive societal conditions that have kept them from having the same opportunities as men and pursuing options other than, or in addition to, those of wife and mother. Likewise, we see no biblical reason why Christians should not be actively working to liberate males from the traditional definitions of masculinity that have hindered them from developing healthy male-female, marital, and parental relationships. If there is to be a true liberation of women, there must also be liberated men who, feeling secure in their own masculinity and position in society, can support increased freedom for women. Secure Christian manhood means that one is so mature that he need not confirm his masculinity at a woman's expense. Such a man will be able not only to work with a woman as an equal, but also to work under a female supervisor. In addition, within the family he will be willing to wash dishes and change diapers.

We must keep in mind that true Christian womanhood and manhood are not to be equated with a specific culture's definitions of femininity and masculinity. In fact, many of the ways in which different cultures define femininity and masculinity are consistent with the Bible. From God's point of view, it is neither right nor wrong that certain activities are done by women in one culture and by men in another. The essential question that we should ask is, At what points do our cultural norms prevent males and females from becoming fully human as intended by God? Those Christians who argue for rigidly separate roles for men and women can do so only by misconstruing the message of Scripture. Some use a proof-texting method that ignores the context of the verses cited. Another faulty use of Scripture is to view historical descriptions of gender roles as if they were normative.

The Bible has much more to say about Christian temperament in general than it does about distinctions between female and male temperament. Paul writes in Galatians 5:22–23: "The fruit of the Spirit is love, joy, peace, patience, kindness, goodness, fidelity, gentleness and self-control" (NIV). It is noteworthy that our culture considers most of these attributes to be feminine. On the basis of these verses, we would argue not only that males and females should be more alike, but that males need to develop the qualities that have been traditionally defined as feminine.

Still another means of viewing gender roles from a Christian perspective is to examine the person of Jesus during his earthly ministry. That is to say, what was Jesus really like as a human? To begin with, we read about a person who experienced a wide range of emotions, but compassion and love were pervasive. The compassion of Jesus is seen in his relationship with the blind man, the lepers, the bereaved widow, the woman at the well, and children. Consider also his actions toward people in need—feeding the hungry, healing the sick, and reaching out to the lost as to sheep without a shepherd.

The compassion and love of Jesus were also expressed in his sorrowful emotions during experiences of despair and loss. Jesus wept over Jerusalem because of the unbelief of its people, and he cried after the death of Lazarus. At other times Jesus was elated and expressed great joy. For example, when the seventy whom he had sent out to witness returned, Jesus "rejoiced in the Holy Spirit" (Luke 10:21 RSV). He also told his disciples that if they would abide in his love, his joy would be in them (John 15:10–11).

In addition to meekness, Jesus openly expressed anger and indignation. In a world under the curse of sin, he responded appropriately with anger. When he witnessed unbelief, hypocrisy, and acts of inhumanity, he took action. Jesus openly expressed his emotions, whether it was to nurture the little children or to upset the tables of the moneychangers in the temple. Enraged at the hypocrisy of the Pharisees, he called them whitewashed tombs, snakes, and a brood of vipers. His language was equally severe when he called Herod a fox, unreceptive audiences swine, and false prophets savage wolves.

The picture that emerges in the Gospels is that Jesus was not traditionally masculine or feminine by current cultural standards but, rather, distinctively human. He incorporated the characteristics of both sexes and presented to the world a model of an integrated and whole person.

We would suggest that womanhood and manhood, properly defined, are far more similar to one another than our culture often realizes. Scripture gives no indication that mothering is more important than fathering. In fact, an examination of how God parented his children Israel reveals that the Old Testament places more stress upon the father-child relationship than upon the mother-child relationship. Perhaps God has created males and females to be differentiated more in terms of style than role. There is, then, probably more room for variation within each gender than there is between the genders.

The question arises, How do we go about implementing the Christian definition of manhood and womanhood? Scientific research indicates that it is easier to change attitudes by changing behavior than vice versa. Many Christians may be surprised to find that this discovery by modern social science is completely consistent with the wisdom of Jesus. For in Matthew 6:21 Jesus states, "Where your treasure is, there will your heart be also" (KJV). Notice that Jesus did not say that a proper attitude ("your heart") brings about right behavior (investing "your treasure" in the kingdom of God), but rather that right behavior—the act of investing our treasure in an appropriate way—results in the right attitude. So then, the most effective way to change gender roles that prevent us from attaining full Christian womanhood and manhood is not to attempt to change sexist attitudes directly, but to change behavior. Sociologically, this means attempting to change social structures rather than personalities.

An examination of the history of the feminist movement reveals that significant cultural improvements came about when attempts were made to change social structures. For instance, the early feminists were successful in working for laws against child labor, slavery, and prostitution; and the suffragettes were successful in getting women the right to vote. From their experience we learn that sociocultural change is not automatic. Rather, changes occur when collective assertive efforts are made to alter the structure of society.

We should also mention the massive changes brought about by industrialization as well as by World Wars I and II, which created a demand for women workers. Once afforded these new opportunities, women were reluctant to relinquish them.

Today, over half of all married women work outside of the home. Instead of reacting negatively, Christians should encourage husbands and fathers to devote more time to emotion-laden tasks such as child rearing. If fathers committed as much of their time to relating to their children as their wives do, they would undoubtedly become more expressive and better parents. Part of the needed structural change has already been initiated by women's redefining their role in society, which will in turn force men to commit greater amounts of time to tasks that demand expressiveness. Further change will be realized as men are educated regarding the potential gains which a more expressive role can bring.

We conclude by noting that when any aspect of our culture is in the process of change, such as is presently the case with regard to gender roles, Christians must, before either accepting or rejecting that change, carefully examine its nature in the light of the Bible. We therefore encourage each reader to diligently search the Scriptures to see how they define maleness and femaleness.

Topics for Review, Reflection, and Discussion

1. Why have gender roles been changing?

2. Is it possible to redefine the role of one gender without redefining the role of the other?

3. Is there evidence that the Bible prescribes specific behavior for each gender?

4. Which explanation of gender differences makes the most sense?

5. What does it mean to be a Christian feminist? What is a proper response to a person who claims that this is a contradiction in terms?

6. In what ways has the traditional definition of gender roles kept women dependent on men and men dependent on women?

7. Give examples of both formal and informal gender discrimination.

8. In what ways have men been discriminated against on the basis of their gender?

9. How adequate are assimilation, androgyny, and differentiation as responses to the need for redefining gender roles?

10. Much of the recent writing on redefining gender roles has called for greater participation by men in the home. Is this consistent with the Christian view of family life?

11. From what the Gospels tell us, make a list of words that characterize Jesus. Using traditional stereotypes, categorize each trait as masculine, feminine, or gender-neutral.

8

Family Instability

The Nature of the Concern

"The family is in trouble today!" That sentiment is heard from the pulpit, television evangelists, and news commentators, and appears in current magazine and newspaper articles analyzing contemporary family life. They point out, for instance, that the highest rate of divorce in our nation's history occurred during the last fifteen years, and that millions of children come from broken homes. A fact often unrecognized, or at least unstated, is that the family has been profoundly disrupted by the tremendous rate of cultural and social change during the twentieth century. Unlike the extended-family systems of more traditional societies, our isolated-nuclear-family system has been unable to absorb the shock of this change. The result has been the emergence of both problem families and family problems.

Some families are in deeper trouble than are others. Many of the social problems discussed in this book—juvenile delinquency, crime, alcoholism and drug addiction, poverty—have their origin in problem families as a common denominator. On the other hand, there are a variety of family problems which potentially affect all families. These include marital difficulties and divorce, parent-child conflicts, teenage rebellion, premarital sex, extramarital sex, pornography, homosexuality, and abortion.

It is right to be concerned about the condition of family life because the overall well-being of both society and the individual is dependent upon the health of the family. In view of the importance which Scripture places upon the family, Christians have given vocal expression to this concern. However, unless the church has some understanding of the causes of family instability, and is willing to engage in critical analysis of the changes now going on, it will be in no position to effectively apply a Christian perspective to the problems of family life in contemporary society.

Nearly half of all persons who vow, "Till death do us part," part sometime before their marriage is naturally terminated. In the past it was not enough that a husband and wife agreed to get a divorce; rather, one of them had to be proven guilty of breaking a state marriage law. With the introduction of no-fault divorce all of this has changed, making divorce on demand available in almost every state. If both spouses want to end the marriage, they are legally entitled to do so.

Although no-fault divorce was meant to correct what had become a hypocritical system which demanded that there be a plaintiff and a defendant, it has had some disastrous results. A study of the effects of the California no-fault divorce law concludes that "the major result is the systematic impoverishment of divorced women and their children. They suffer an immediate 73% drop in their standard of living . . . [while] ex-husbands are actually better off, with standard-of-living increases of 42% in the first year after divorce" (Weitzman 1985:338). Beyond the economic effect of a divorce upon family members, our concern should be with the millions of children who cannot expect to spend their growing-up years with both parents.

We should also make mention of a number of other contemporary problems which are perceived by society as real threats to stable family life. Most of these problems involve some element which has traditionally been defined as deviant: premarital sex and pregnancy, abortion, motherhood without marriage, extramarital sex, homosexuality, and pornography. An increased rate in these activities raises societal concern proportionately. Each remains a threat to family stability until society manages to curtail it or cultural norms change to include it. Thus, whereas premarital sex used to be regarded as a violation of social norms, it is now considered acceptable by a large number of persons, provided affection is involved. Unwed mothers and homosexuality, on the other hand, continue to be seen as a challenge to family stability. Should large numbers of unmarried women become pregnant and opt to keep their babies, the family as it is now conceived in American society would indeed be threatened. The increasingly vociferous gay-liberation groups have also created concern among those who fear the effect the legitimization of homosexuality would have upon family stability. Those behaviors which pose the strongest challenge to family norms are causing the greatest social concern.

Adding to the current problems are a host of technologically generated possibilities—artificial insemination, in vitro insemination, artificial wombs, surrogate motherhood, and prenatal gender determination—whose likely effects upon family life boggle the imagination. Public discussions of most of these possibilities are so recent that they are best classified as social issues rather than social problems.

The Dimensions of Family Instability

The most obvious dimension of family instability is marital disruption. This section will begin with a consideration of divorce, continue with a discussion of changing sexual norms and behavior, and conclude with a brief look at other issues affecting family life.

Divorce

In the developed world the United States has both the highest divorce rate and the highest proportion of children affected by divorce (Cimons 1990). The rate has steadily risen from three divorces for every ten thousand people in 1867 (when statistics first became available) to fifty-three divorces in 1979. Thereafter the rate has leveled off to around fifty

NO, I WAS MARRIED TO HANK BEFORE I WAS MARRIED TO GEORGE, WHICH WAS BEFORE I WAS MARRIED TO BILL.

divorces for every ten thousand people. There have, of course, been occasional fluctuations. During the Great Depression of the 1930s, for example, couples who would otherwise have divorced settled for a separation because of legal costs. And after World War II there was a spurt in the number of divorces. The reason is that during emotionally charged wartime situations, couples find themselves swept into marriages, which under normal circumstances would be the culmination of a gradual courtship. Also, the separation of the father from his family as well as his sudden return resulted in significant stress.

In terms of total numbers, approximately 1,200,000 divorces take place each year, which is approximately one divorce for every two marriages. It may very well be that the high divorce rate reflects a change in societal norms. While most persons still hold to the ideal that marriage is to be a permanent bond, the individualistic search for self-fulfilment has become so strong that many are willing to terminate the marriage contract when it no longer serves their personal needs. Most sociologists believe that the divorce rate has reached a plateau; they do not foresee either a dramatic rise or fall in the near future.

Education and divorce

Among the factors that are significant in divorce statistics is the level of education, which is closely related to age at marriage, income, occupation, and social class, which also affect the probability of divorce. The correlation between education and divorce is not the same for men and women. For men there is a curvilinear relationship: the divorce rate is low among men with little education, increases among those who have had some high-school training, and declines among men who have a college degree. Since the socioeconomic status of a couple usually reflects the education of the husband, the probability of divorce depends more upon the education of the husband than of the wife. For women, the probability of divorce tends to increase proportionately with an increase in educational level.

Educational level is also related to the likelihood of remarriage. A poorly educated male with a low income finds it much more difficult to remarry than does a poorly educated female. Well-educated males are able to afford remarriage, while well-educated females can afford not to remarry and may choose instead to support themselves. Since well-educated men are desirable marriage partners and divorced men who want to remarry tend to look for a woman younger than themselves, the older, well-educated divorced women may have difficulty finding well-educated unmarried men of comparable age to marry.

Age and divorce

The average age at marriage is comparatively low today. It dropped from around 26 years for men and 22 years for women in 1900 to 23.2 years for men and 21.0 years for women in 1974, and has risen slightly in recent years to just over 22 years for women and just under 24 years for men. Note that the age gap is smaller than ever before

Studies consistently show that those who marry young, especially in their teens, are much more likely to divorce than are those who marry in their mid-twenties. A number of interrelated factors may also be at work here. Those who marry young are typically from a lower socioeconomic class (which increases the probability of financial difficulties); they marry after a very short engagement and perhaps because of a pregnancy. Given their stage of individual development, most teenagers are socially and psychologically unprepared for a relationship as demanding as marriage. Inadequacies in role performance, unfaithfulness, disagreement, and lack of understanding and companionship have been found to contribute to divorce among those who married while very young (Booth and Edwards 1985).

Next to teenage marriages, the most unstable are those between people who marry after age thirty. Among the most common complaints are a lack of agreement and the tendency of the partner to be domineering and critical (Booth and Edwards 1985). The underlying dynamic here is that those who marry late in life have become so set in their ways that they have a hard time adjusting to the expectations of a spouse. On the other hand, people who marry in their mid-twenties tend to have the most stable marriages.

The average length of marriages that end in divorce is seven years. Although there has been an upsurge in divorce since 1960 among adults of all ages, the increase has been highest among those under forty-five years of age, those "who have grown up during a period when divorce was generally looked upon with less disfavor than during earlier years" (Glick and Lin 1986:738). Since reaching a peak in 1980, the rate of divorce has leveled off for all age groups except teenagers, whose rate in 1984 was two and a half times the national average.

Four out of five persons who get divorced eventually remarry. In general, the younger a person is at the time of divorce, the greater the likelihood of remarrying. Since peaking in 1965, the proportion of persons who remarry has been declining in all age groups. The more children a divorced woman has, the greater is the likelihood that she will remarry, and that she will do so quickly. A divorced woman with children does not have the luxury of carefully choosing before marrying again. Unless she has a good income, economic necessity demands that she find a husband to assist in providing financial support. This is especially true in cases where the ex-husband is not paying child support or where the court has allocated inadequate child-support payments.

Other factors

In terms of ethnic differences, the divorce rate is highest among blacks, moderate among whites, and lowest among other ethnic groups, particularly those of Far Eastern origin. In terms of religion, divorce rates are lowest among Jews, moderate among Catholics, and highest among Protestants (Chalfant, Beckley, and Palmer 1987:224–28). Finally, heterogeneous marriages are more likely to end in divorce than are homogeneous marriages. Thus divorce is more likely when there is a sizable age gap or differences in religion, social class, or ethnic origin.

Changing Sexual Norms

Any definition of family stability is based upon prevailing social norms. Behavior that is in violation of these norms can be considered deviant and potentially challenging to the family. The most salient norms in this regard are those that govern sexual behavior. The sexual norms of American society have been subject to a great deal of questioning in recent years. And when such norms are questioned by large numbers of people, they are likely to be changed.

We will now consider three forms of behavior—premarital sex, extramarital sex, and homosexuality—which deviate from traditional patterns. Sexual norms in the United States have in the past been based upon the Judeo-Christian religion, which has formally taught a standard of premarital abstinence. Present attitudes, however, do not closely conform to the traditional norm of abstinence. In light of changing standards, it may even be a misnomer to call premarital sex deviant. Extramarital sexual activity and homosexuality, however, remain beyond the pale of acceptable behavior. Most Americans are less receptive to extramarital sex than to premarital sex, and they are even less tolerant of homosexuality. Homosexual behavior is considered an extreme deviation. But with the recent development of outspoken gay-liberation groups, it appears that homosexuality may well become more than an ephemeral threat to traditional norms. (Since the redefinition of acceptable practices and the corresponding increase in behavior formerly considered deviant are more likely to prevent the establishment of traditional families than to disrupt those that already exist, which is the basic subject at hand, we will in succeeding sections of this chapter focus on divorce rather than the changes in sexual norms. For the moment, however, it is important that we take a brief look at these other threats to family stability.)

Premarital sex

There are no reliable data on the amount of premarital sex in America before 1900. The best available sources suggest that considerably more males than females engaged in premarital coitus during the 1800s (Terman 1938:321). Most of these men had done so only with women other than their future spouse, while the majority of females who had engaged in premarital coitus had done so only with their future spouse. The picture which begins to emerge is that there was a double standard which allowed far more freedom to males than to females. Further, the double standard meant that men placed females into two categories: "good women," with whom one did not have sex, but whom one might marry; and "bad women," with whom one might have sex, but would never think of marrying.

Sexual standards throughout most of Western history have been more lenient toward male than toward female violators, with the United States being no exception. The Puritan ethics of colonial America probably came the closest to giving Western society a single standard. However, Nathaniel Hawthorne's *Scarlet Letter* illustrates that the Puritans were more concerned about female than male adultery. Could not the male as well as the female have been forced to wear the letter *A*, thus signifying that he too had participated in adultery? So although the Judeo-Christian tradition has formally endorsed a standard of abstinence for both males and females, that standard has been applied to women more vigorously than to men. Thus males have always enjoyed greater sexual freedom than females have.

Studies indicate that a dramatic increase in the incidence of premarital sex took place during the post–World War I years. In 1938 Dorothy Bromley and Florence Britten reported in *Youth and Sex* that fear of pregnancy rather than moral objections was the primary reason young people gave for not engaging in premarital coitus. Already by the 1930s, then, there had been a weakening of religious sanctions, and it was obvious that the advent of adequate means of preventing pregnancy would greatly affect sexual behavior.

The most famous of the studies on sexual behavior, the Kinsey reports on *Sexual Behavior in the Human Male* (1948) and *Sexual Behavior in the Human Female* (1953), illustrated the range of premarital sexual activity in America, a topic which had formerly been taboo. These studies brought public attention to the fact that most Americans were not living according to a standard of abstinence before marriage. They also revealed the wide differences between the sexual behavior of males and females and supplied evidence of the double standard in America.

In his study of a thousand college students, Winston Ehrmann (1959) gave further insight into the double standard. He found that the males engaged in premarital coitus because of the sexual gratification received, while the females engaged in premarital coitus only when they felt they were in love. While the females were person-centered, the males were body-centered in their premarital sexual involvements.

To piece together the historical information we possess on premarital sexual norms and behavior in the United States: after a formal standard of abstinence (there is evidence that males were less likely than females to abide by this standard), there was a rather startling liberalization in attitudes and behavior during the post–World War I years, which was followed by a more gradual liberalizing process through the 1950s. The change in standards during the first sixty years of the twentieth century was more of a sexual evolution than revolution, with the standards for females evolving at a more rapid rate than the standards for males. The result was a convergence of the standards for both sexes.

There is evidence to suggest that a second sexual revolution, comparable to the changes that took place in the 1920s, occurred in the wake of the counterculture movement of the 1960s. This revolution entailed a rapid liberalization of attitudes regarding the sexual behavior of females, which further reduced the double standard. Much of the impetus for this change undoubtedly came from the women's liberation movement, which has consistently spoken for equal sexual rights and freedoms for women.

Although there has been a liberalization in attitudes toward premarital sex, it would be a mistake to think that all persons hold to a permissive standard. The recognized authority in the field of sexual standards, Ira Reiss, has suggested that there are four major philosophies on the subject of premarital sex (1971:156):

1. *Abstinence*: premarital sexual intercourse is wrong for both men and women, regardless of circumstances
2. *The double standard*: premarital intercourse is more acceptable for males than females
3. *Permissiveness with affection*: where there is a stable, affectionate relationship, premarital intercourse is right for both men and women
4. *Permissiveness without affection*: premarital intercourse is acceptable for both men and women regardless of the amount of affection or stability in the relationship

Of these four standards, abstinence is still dominant. While the double standard continues to have its share of proponents, many now advocate instead permissiveness with affection. Furthermore, since our increasingly permissive society has come to view sex as recreation, there has been some recent movement toward permissiveness without affection. Needless to say, the threat of AIDS and other communicable diseases has restrained many persons from freely acting on their permissive sexual standards.

Extramarital sex

Americans are more strongly opposed to extramarital than to premarital sex. Every state grants a divorce on the grounds of adultery, and it is a rare marriage counselor who forthrightly condones extramarital affairs. As is the case with premarital sex, there is a gap between what Americans hold as their ideal and their actual behavior. Alfred Kinsey found that in the late 1940s 50 percent of the men and 26 percent of the women in his study had been involved in extramarital coitus by the age of forty. Given the movement toward more liberal attitudes, an educated guess would be that the figures are even higher today. Recent evidence suggests that while the rate of extramarital affairs has risen for both sexes, the increase has been greatest among young married women (Macklin 1987:332).

The vast majority of Americans (70 to 80 percent) continue to disapprove of extramarital sex. Those who approve of it disassociate sex from love and marriage. A recent study found that most of the people who approve of extramarital sex approve of premarital sex as well, lack strong religious commitments, and reside in metropolitan areas (Weis and Jurich 1985). Eleanor Macklin (1987:333–34) points out that actual involvement in extramarital sex depends upon four factors: (1) perceived opportunity—a potential partner and sufficient privacy must be available; (2) readiness to take advantage of the opportunity—here marital dissatisfaction, moral values, and personal needs come into play; (3) expectation of satisfaction—past experiences and the degree of attraction to the potential partner are good indicators of what to expect; (4) fear of negative consequences—there is anxiety over what would occur if one were found out. Although extramarital sex can be the cause of marital unhappiness, there is evidence that most extramarital sex is an indication rather than a cause of marital problems (Spanier and Margolis 1979).

Homosexuality

Americans are even more strongly opposed to homosexual behavior than to premarital and extramarital sex. The extent to which homosexuality is practiced in the United States is a difficult question to answer. Kinsey (1953:452) found that about 13 percent of the females and 37 percent of the males in his sample had experienced orgasm through homosexual activity. It would be a mistake, however, to think of all of these people as homosexuals, since a majority of them had only one or two homosexual encounters and did not adopt homosexuality as a life pattern. For our purposes, we shall define a homosexual as one who engages in extensive, but not necessarily exclusive, sexual activity with a member of the same sex. An acknowledged limitation in this definition is that it includes only those persons who are practicing homosexuals, thus excluding latent homosexuals, that is, those who are attracted to members of their own sex, but who for various reasons do not act upon their attraction. It is estimated that one out of every twenty adults in the United States has a preference for the same sex.

There are various biological, psychological, and sociological explanations of homosexuality. According to traditional psychoanalytic theory, at about the age of four or five every male child entertains romantic fantasies about his mother, possibly even to the extent that he may have the urge to eliminate his father to gain possession of her (the Oedipus complex); correspondingly, every female child desires an exclusive love relationship with her father and may have an urge to eliminate her mother (the Electra complex). In a family where the mother and father love each other deeply, children surmise that they are unable to compete with the parent of the same sex for the love of the parent of the opposite sex. In the usual or normal process of development, the child then represses both the romantic fantasies about the parent of the opposite sex and the desire to eliminate the parent of the same sex; instead, the child consciously identifies with the parent of the same sex. But in a family where there is little love or where there is conflict between the mother and father, the child may conclude that the parent of the same sex does not have the love of the parent of the opposite sex. The child may then compete with the parent of the same sex for the other parent's love. Should the parent of the opposite sex encourage this pursuit, the child will not repress the undesirable fantasies, but will instead proceed to identify with that parent in an attempt to win love.

The most complete attempt to identify the factors in homosexual orientation is reported in *Sexual Preference: Its Development in Men and Women* (Bell, Weinberg, and Hammersmith 1981). Data from interviews with 979 homosexual and 477 heterosexual men and women do not support the psychoanalytic explanation of homosexuality. Nor do they support such sociopsychological explanations as a lack of adequate heterosexual experiences during childhood, negative experiences with members of the opposite sex, or early contact with homosexuals. The one sociopsychological factor that was found to be somewhat important is that homosexual men, more than heterosexual men, report that their fathers were cold and detached. While these findings do not constitute direct evidence that homosexuality (or heterosexuality) has a biological base, they "are not inconsistent with what one would expect to find if, indeed, there were a biological basis for sexual preference" (p. 216).

What actually causes sexual preferences remains, then, an open question. Our present understanding suggests that very little of what we call human behavior (including sexual preference) can be attributed exclusively to either biology or socialization, but is in reality a result of the interaction between the two. Should stronger evidence for biological causation appear, Christians will have the task of explaining how homosexuals can be held responsible for their behavior.

Other Issues

There are a number of other broadly debated issues which may be on their way to becoming family problems—pornography, abortion, surrogate motherhood, and artificial insemination. Of these issues, pornography, given the widespread agreement as to its harmfulness, comes closest to qualifying as a social problem. The remaining question here centers on the definition of pornography. At one extreme is the view that pornography is in the eye of the beholder; at the other is the belief that any novel which describes a sexual encounter should be banned from public libraries.

Explanations of Family Instability

General Societal Change

The rapidly changing nature of American society is certainly a major source of family instability. First, the typical family today does not live in a rural agricultural community, but rather must learn to survive in an urban, technological, industrial complex. Second, today's society places upon every individual family member pressures making it difficult to develop consistent relationships. Family relationships are undermined by the demands of the workplace, the school, the church, and various social organizations and activities. Third, family instability is in part a result of the changes that have taken place in the basic institutions of society. Shifting patterns of moral authority within religious institutions have affected family norms. Educational institutions have usurped much of the family's prerogative to socialize children. With the increasing emphasis on expansion, many business organizations have inadvertently caused the uprooting of family life by making occupational advancement dependent upon geographical transfer. And political institutions have steadily been relieving the family of many of its traditional functions, such as the care of the elderly.

Factors Contributing to Marital Difficulties

There are no simple explanations for marital difficulties and divorce. Research indicates that factors that existed prior to the marriage, elements in the marriage itself, and the breakdown of barriers to divorce can all play a role (Lewis and Spanier 1979). An important predisposing factor is personal incompatibility; this may entail wide differences in age, intelligence, attitudes and values, and socioeconomic, ethnic, and religious background. Divorce is also more likely for persons who are socially immature, who have emotional and psychological problems, or whose parents were poor role models. In addition, getting married at a very young age, because of a pregnancy, or without the approval of family and friends can contribute towards family instability.

With regard to elements in the marriage itself, a general dissatisfaction with life may portend divorce. This could entail dissatisfaction with socioeconomic status, with the wife's working outside the home, or with the size of the family. Another possible factor is a lack of support from friends. On the other hand, all those elements which make life a satisfying experience can also contribute to marital quality. A marriage will be greatly enriched if it involves a high regard for one another, emotional gratification, communication, and meaningful interaction.

In the past, couples who were dissatisfied with their marriage usually elected to stay together because of a number of barriers to divorce. In recent years, however, there has been an erosion of strict divorce laws, of the social stigma against divorce, and of rigid adherence to religious doctrine. Furthermore, as various alternative lifestyles gained acceptance, the high degree of commitment to marriage and of tolerance for marital conflict and tensions waned.

Intense and dramatic social change contributes to divorce by putting additional pressure on the contemporary marriage. There are new expectations of marriage, namely, unqualified personal happiness and gratification of one's own needs (Price-Bonham and Balswick 1980). In an age of narcissism and hyperindividualism, most people believe that they have a right to complete happiness and self-fulfilment. When marriage does not bring complete self-fulfilment, it is discarded so that the individual can search for fulfilment elsewhere. In a society which places emphasis on individual rights and fulfilment instead of collective obligations, it is no wonder that marital relationships are being sacrificed for the sake of the individual.

Responses to Family Instability

A multitude of methods and programs have been proposed to overcome family instability and improve family life. Each proposal begins with an assumption about what constitutes a desirable family. In most cases what is in view is a two-parent nuclear family in which close relationships are developed and maintained. Programs to strengthen family life range all the way from enormous government-sponsored projects with million-dollar budgets to small neighborhood and religious organizations with budgets of several hundred dollars. The methods used may emphasize education and prevention, enrichment, or therapeutic intervention. The object of help may be an individual, a married couple, a family unit, a community within which family life is lived out, or detrimental conditions in society.

Family Enrichment

The story is told of an isolated community that could be reached by only one road which wound its way over a mountain. As the road descended from the summit, there was a particularly dangerous turn which claimed many an unwary traveler. For years the people of the community had shown their concern by stationing an ambulance at the spot, thus facilitating speedy assistance to any who might survive an accident there. One day a member of the community suggested that perhaps they should place a warning sign just ahead of the dangerous turn. Someone else suggested that perhaps a guard rail would also prevent potential disasters. Still another suggested that for the cost of maintaining the ambulance service, the dangerous curve could be straightened out.

One response to family instability consists of enrichment programs, which can take a variety of forms. A low-level program will provide road signs warning family members of probable difficulties ahead. This type of program is usually known as family-life education. Family-life education within the church can most effectively be done within existing organizational structures, such as Sunday-school classes. Good Sunday-school material will not only be directed at fostering individual growth in the Christian life, but also be cognizant of the fact that individuals belong to families. Effective programs and materials will foster healthy family relationships. Good road signs within the local church will focus on the issues and potential problems that may arise as the family and its members move into new stages of development.

At a higher level are enrichment programs which act as guard rails. They enable family members to better communicate with each other, resolve conflict, and make decisions together. The majority of mid-level enrichment programs that have been developed assume that the family will travel a bumpy and winding road. Their purpose is to empower a family with inner strength and resources which will allow for growth instead of disillusionment when difficulty comes.

It may very well be that the road on which marriages and families are expected to travel in modern society needs to be straightened out. This is to say that a host of societal factors—the sexual revolution, the redefinition of gender roles, unrealistic marital expectations, individualism, materialism, secularism—may lie behind the difficulties in family life today. Working for change at this broad societal level, although certainly needed, is beyond the scope of family enrichment. All the evidence suggests that if there are to be long-term positive effects, we must have programs aimed at changing whole social structures in addition to those aimed at changing individuals.

Divorce

A second response to family instability is divorce, which is more and more being taken as the easy out. Wherever marriage is not defined in terms of mutual commitment, the partners will not be predisposed to work out their difficulties. The fact that subsequent marriages are also likely to end in divorce suggests that incompatibility is not necessarily the reason why marriages fail. It may be that some persons would be incompatible with anyone, simply because they have no concept of the work and commitment required for a healthy marriage. Marriage is basically not much different from any other social relationship, except that it is much more demanding and intense.

People vary greatly in terms of maturity, but there is no reason to fatalistically accept one's personality and level of development as unalterable. The human personality is dynamic and capable of great change and adjustment, as periods of economic depression, war, and other crises can attest. It must be remembered, however, that personality change and growth do not take place in a vacuum, but in the context of interpersonal relationships. Every encounter contributes either toward personal growth and the development of a relationship, or toward personal stagnation and barriers impeding relationship. The daily encounters between spouses are no different. Either an encounter leads to the personal growth of each partner and the building of the marital relationship, or to the destruction of personalities and the tearing down of the relationship.

It must be admitted that there are marriages within which a healthy relationship may be near to impossible because of the social circumstances or personality difficulties involved. However, what we are arguing against is the developing American pattern of using divorce as an escape mechanism. Upon finding difficulties in their marriage, couples today are propelled away from facing their problems and toward the path of least resistance—escape through divorce. Instead of acknowledging their problems and attempting to work them out through personal encounter, the couple chalk the marriage up as a costly learning experience.

This escapist approach to marital problems is part of an overall philosophy found in society today. Many Americans have divorced themselves from the problems of our large metropolitan areas by escaping to the suburbs. Philip Slater (1970:15) has coined the term *toilet assumption* to refer to the view that "unwanted matter, unwanted difficulties, unwanted complexities and obstacles will disappear if they are removed from our immediate field of vision." Divorce is just such an attempt to solve a problem by eliminating it from one's field of vision. Where there is no marriage, there is no marital problem. But in eliminating a bad marriage, divorce may be eliminating what is only a symptom of a deeper problem which will inevitably resurface in other relationships.

Nontraditional Family Forms

The traditional family involves a "legal, lifelong, sexually exclusive marriage between one man and one woman, with children, where the male is primary economic provider and ultimate authority" (Macklin 1980:905). However, the traditional family is becoming an endangered species, as it is estimated that only 16 percent of all households fall into this category. Macklin (1987) identifies a variety of alternatives to the traditional family: never-married single nonmarital heterosexual cohabitation, voluntary childless marriages, coparenting binuclear families, joint custody binuclear families, step-families, single-parent families, open marriages and open families, dual-career families, commuter marriages, sexually open (swinging) marriages, sexually open coprimary marriages, same-sex relationships, multiadult households, and communes.

A current strategy for dealing with family instability is to forgo any attempt to prop up the traditional family, and instead encourage people to become involved in an alternative form more suited to their personal needs and situation. In responding to the new family forms, we Christians must be careful to avoid two improper reactions. First, we must not regard as the Christian standard the traditional patriarchal family that existed around the turn of the century. Some Christians start with the assumption that the golden age of family life occurred about one hundred years ago, and everything would be all right again if we would only return to the traditional form of family life. These Christians wrongly idealize the nineteenth-century family, and then proceed to insert this ideal into their reading of Scripture. They incorrectly associate the biblical view of family life with nineteenth-century patriarchy. The second improper reaction is the relativistic assumption that in a changing society the family can take any form desired. While avoiding the pitfall of idealizing a particular cultural and temporal form of the family, proponents of this approach fail to acknowledge any lasting normative structures or functions for the family.

A Christian Response to Family Instability

To evaluate the various responses to family instability and to come up with a distinctly Christian approach, we need to begin with the question of what purpose God wishes to fulfil through the family (Anderson 1985). Then we need to ask whether the meaning and purpose of family life can be fulfilled within a specific family form. For example, can God's intention for family life be fulfilled within the nuclear family? the extended family? We believe that God can be honored by either a nuclear- or extended-family system; each has its own inherent strengths for fulfilling God's purpose.

Some other family forms, such as premarital cohabitation, open marriages, and same-sex relationships, will not be acceptable in a Christian framework because they cannot fulfil God's purpose for the family. On the other hand, we need to affirm that while the single-parent family may not be God's ideal, it is in many cases an honest attempt to fulfil God's purpose in a broken and fallen world. Instead of adopting condemning and condescending attitudes, the church needs to fill the void in incomplete families. The church needs to be reminded that Jesus radically redefined the concept of family. In Mark 3:31–35 we are told that when informed that his mother and brothers had arrived and were asking for him, Jesus responded, "Who is my mother? Who are my brothers? . . . Whoever does the will of God is my brother, my sister, my mother" (NEB). Membership in the body of Christ binds all believers to him and to one another as family (Anderson 1985).

Many family-enrichment strategies and programs of the type we have described are being effectively used within the church to improve family life. However, as effective as these programs are, they are limited to those families who are already in the church. They can do little to change the broad social structures which together constitute a less than healthy environment for the development of strong family life. The family is currently being plundered on one side by the demands and intrusions of mass society, and on the other by an individualism which has become increasingly narcissistic. Family life needs protection from a multitude of forces which are currently sapping its vitality.

The type of protective action needed is perhaps best illustrated by examples of changes which can be made in the economic realm. To begin with, the business world must adjust to the needs of the family rather than requiring the family to adjust to its needs. To reiterate a point made earlier (p. 140), employers can make local advancement opportunities available to employees who elect not to move their families to a new community. Businesses should also develop a system of flexible schedules for both mothers and fathers who need to be with their children at certain times. Nurseries and day-care centers can be provided for parents who must work while their children are young. There are various creative ways in which the economic world can change in order to allow strong family life to develop.

In the religious sphere, some churches, realizing that a heavy calendar of activities can pull family members away from each other, purposefully do not schedule any activities on certain nights, which they encourage their members to regard as family nights. Such sensitivity to the needs of the family ought to be emulated in other areas. The examples we have given could be multiplied by analyzing ways in which other social institutions could create more favorable environments for family life.

The Covenant Family

In chapter 3 we suggested that the biblical view of social relationships can best be understood in terms of four phases: covenant, grace, empowering, and intimacy. Bringing these elements into family relationships will help to overcome instability.

First there is the matter of covenant. The relationship between God and the children of Israel can be thought of as an unconditional parental commitment to a child. A reading of the Old Testament Scriptures reveals the cycle of Israel's turning away from the true God and getting into difficulty, God's reaching out to and forgiving them, Israel's being reconciled into the intended parent/child relationship, and Israel's being blessed and renewed in their relationship to God. This cycle is the central message of the Book of Hosea.

Figure 6

Types of Commitment in Family Relationships

	Conditional	Unconditional
Unilateral	Modern Open Arrangement	Initial Covenant
Bilateral	Contract	Mature Covenant

Figure 6 depicts the various types of commitment found in family relationships. By emulating God's covenant with Israel, that is, by making unconditional commitments, family members can take a giant stride toward reducing instability. Note that the concept of covenant can be used in reference to both unilateral (one-way) and bilateral (two-way) relationships. We have labeled a unilateral unconditional relationship an initial covenant, and a bilateral unconditional relationship a mature covenant. All biblical references to the covenants which God initiated (e.g., with Noah, Abraham, and Israel) are examples of initial covenants. It would be erroneous to think of an unconditional unilateral relationship as partial, because from the individual's perspective a personal covenant without restrictions is being offered. From a relational perspective, unilateral unconditional commitment entails the attractive possibility of someday becoming a two-way street. The desire of God in each covenant he initiated was that the unconditional commitment would eventually be reciprocal and mutual.

This is exactly what God intends to happen in the parent/child relationship as well. When a child is born, the parents make an unconditional commitment of love to that child. The infant or young child is unable, at that time in life, to make such a commitment in return. When the child gives very little back, it is often a battle for parents to follow through on their unconditional love. However, as the child matures, the relationship which began as an initial (unilateral) covenant will (ideally) develop into a mature (bilateral) covenant. True reciprocity occurs when parents themselves age and become socially, emotionally, and physically more dependent on their adult children. Here, in a mature bilateral commitment, reciprocal and unconditional love is especially rewarding.

Figure 6 also shows that there are two types of conditional family relationships. An emerging type, which we call the modern open arrangement, is symptomatic of a society in which persons are hesitant to make commitments. A typical example is a person who begins a marriage with the unspoken understanding that as long as his or her needs are being met, all is well; but as soon as those needs are no longer met, the relationship will end. When both partners adopt this conditional stance, the marriage amounts to a contract, a quid pro quo arrangement. Both husband and wife consider they have fulfilled the marital contract if they get about as much as they give. If marriage is understood in this way, divorce is likely to be viewed as the solution whenever difficulties arise. How much wiser it would be to view marriage and family as unconditional commitments!

The Family of Grace

What we said earlier about grace as the proper atmosphere for social relationships (pp. 51–52) is especially relevant in the context of the family. Family relationships as designed by God are meant to be lived out in an atmosphere of grace (unmerited favor) and not law. Family life based upon contract leads to an atmosphere of law, while family life based upon covenant leads to an atmosphere of grace, acceptance, and forgiveness. A family based upon law is a discredit to Christianity. For as is true in our individual relationships with God, law in our family relationships leads to legalism, whereas grace provides a freedom from legalism. In an atmosphere of grace family members act responsibly out of love and consideration for one another.

Although not based on law, family relationships characterized by grace will accept law in the form of order and responsibility. A certain amount of regularity and rules is simply unavoidable in daily family life, as one of the authors learned all too well about ten years ago. He announced to his family that all rules regarding chores would be eliminated; each family member was to live out a covenant of grace in the home. When the garbage needed to be taken out, someone would take care of it. When dishes needed to be washed, someone would adopt an attitude of servanthood toward the other family members. In just three short days, the garbage piled up and the dishes were stacked high in the sink. Everyone in the family seemed to have a legitimate excuse for not having done the kitchen chores.

The application of grace to family relationships allows us to throw off purely cultural patterns of behavior which are devoid of biblical grounding. Grace will challenge a system in which marital roles are segregated, where, for example, women wash dishes, cook meals, and change diapers, and only men mow lawns, tend to light fixtures, and work outside of the home. Grace will also challenge a parenting system in which fathers are more emotionally distant from their children than are mothers. In addition, if there were more grace in contemporary family life, perhaps there would not be such anarchic overreactions against family rules. For grace recognizes that order and regularity function for the sake of each family member's needs and enhancement and not as a means of repressing them.

The Empowering Family

As we suggested in chapter 3, empowering is the biblical model for the use of power. Employing one's own strengths to build up others could revolutionize the way authority is handled in families. The secular view, on the other hand, is that power is a commodity which has a limited supply and determines social hierarchies. It should therefore be jealously guarded. People with the most power, the most resources, are on top. In marriage, whatever one partner has to offer and the other values—money, sex, love, nurture, protection—can be converted into power. Each partner, from a rather self-centered perspective, tries to maximize the returns on his or her investments in the marriage. Not surprisingly, research has indicated that wives who work outside the home have greater power in the marriage relationship than do wives who do not work. The money earned can be converted into power, thus elevating the authority of the wife in the marriage.

Christians, on the contrary, need have no concern about holding on to what power they have or accumulating more for themselves. They have the assurance that the power of God is available in unlimited amounts. The fruit of the Holy Spirit is inexhaustible. The Spirit indwells believers and enables them to enable others. So individuals need not subordinate others to maintain their own position in the hierarchy. As this spiritual growth takes place in family members, it is possible for them to serve and give to each other in unlimited ways, in extraordinary ways. Family members will use their areas of strength to build each other up. This is the essence of 1 Corinthians 8:1: "Knowledge puffs up, but love builds up" (NIV).

An empowering approach to parenting begins by reconsidering the nature of power and authority. In the biblical sense, parental authority is an ascribed power. The Greek word for authority, *exousia*, literally means "out of being." It refers to a type of influence which is not dependent upon any personal strength, achievement, or skill, but rather comes forth "out of the being" of a person. The Greek word for power, *dynamis*, is the word from which "dynamo" is derived. The authority of Jesus flowed from his personhood. It was dynamic. Parents, too, have authority over their children which flows from their personhood as they earnestly and responsibly care for their children's physical, social, psychological, and spiritual development. The process of empowering children certainly does not mean giving up this position of authority, nor does it mean that parents will be depleted or drained of power as they parent. Rather parents and children will both achieve a sense of personal power, self-esteem, and wholeness. Successful parenting has to do with children's gaining personal power and parents' retaining personal power throughout the process.

Unfortunately, our human nature often stands in the way of family members' empowering each other. In the frailness of our human insecurity we are tempted to keep others dependent upon us, and in so doing find a counterfeit security in having power over them. Attachment which is based upon dependency is not love but addiction. Covenant love, by contrast, draws people to a mature attachment, which is free from dependency. It is a love that is loyal and supportive even when differences or adversity threatens the relationship. It is a love whose ultimate aim is to empower another to self-responsibility, a rewarding and mutually satisfying achievement for both parties.

The Intimate Family

In their perfect creatureliness, Adam and Eve were naked before each other and felt no shame (Gen. 2:25). They were able to be themselves without pretense. The biblical description of the nature of the prefall human family thus places major emphasis on intimacy—on the knowing of the other. Members of a modern family that patterns itself after this example will earnestly listen to and try to understand one another. Each individual will want what is best for the others. Differences will be acknowledged and appreciated, and the others' needs and desires will be respected. There will be a willingness to give up one's own wishes at times, so that relationships are enhanced and the family can live in love, harmony, and unity.

The capacity for family members to communicate feelings freely and openly with each other is contingent upon trust and commitment. Then they are not afraid to share and be intimate with one another. This brings us back to unconditional love, which is the key to family communication and honest sharing without the threat of rejection and criticism.

In summary, the Christian response to family instability calls for a radical change. Family life is to be based upon a covenant commitment, providing an atmosphere of grace within which family members can empower and become truly intimate with one another. These four elements of Christian family relationships are a continual process: intimacy leads to deeper covenant love; unconditional commitment fortifies the atmosphere of freely offered grace; this climate of acceptance and forgiveness encourages serving and empowering others; and the sense of self-esteem that follows leads to the ability to be intimate without fear of rejection. The result is a maturing of relationships that eventually enables family members to reach out even to persons beyond the boundaries of the family.

Topics for Review, Reflection, and Discussion

1. What are some of the major explanations for the rise in the divorce rate during the last thirty years?

2. What can the church do to support persons who have experienced a divorce? to support reconstituted families (i.e., families that include stepchildren)?

3. Given the trend toward permissiveness, is it legitimate to consider premarital sex part of the problem of family instability?

4. Do nontraditional family forms offer any solutions to family instability?

5. How can the concepts of covenant, grace, empowering, and intimacy be applied in families that have been broken by divorce?

9

Alcoholism and Problem Drinking

Nature of the Concern

In the words of the National Council on Alcoholism (1987:1), "Alcohol is the most widely used and destructive drug in America." It can be argued that Americans are deeply concerned about the excessive use of alcohol because it violates every one of the basic values described in chapter 2. Not only are the individuals who drink heavily affected, but also their families, friends, and coworkers are hurt. The detrimental effects reach into almost every aspect of American society.

The physical, mental, and social price paid by excessive drinkers themselves is very high. Although occasional moderate drinking apparently does little if any physical damage to the body, prolonged heavy drinking has been found to have disastrous effects. Just a decade or so ago it was thought that most of the physical damage from drinking was due to nutritional deficiency, since heavy drinkers do not eat properly. Alcohol provides virtually no vitamins, minerals, proteins, or other nutrients, but only a high level of calories; and as someone has said, "Man cannot live by fuel alone." Furthermore, alcohol interferes with the digestion of what little food one does eat. The most recent studies also indicate that alcohol has direct toxic effects on almost every part and function of the body: the liver, the gastrointestinal tract, the pancreas, the heart, the brain, the immune and endocrine systems, respiration, metabolism, the bones, the muscles, and the hematologic system (Lieber 1985; Roach 1985; and Gordis 1987). The mortality rate from heart disease is 400 percent greater for heavy drinkers than for others; and birth anomalies, mental disorders, and motor and cognitive impairment are also associated with heavy drinking. Robert Straus (1985) found that heavy drinking adversely affects perception, reaction time, and reasoning, and that it causes aggressive and even violent behavior. Such deleterious effects prevent heavy drinkers from ever achieving the American ideal: individual worth, freedom of expression, equality of opportunity, the ability to compete successfully, and general well-being.

The effects of excessive drinking are not limited, of course, to the drinker. The families of those who drink heavily are likewise affected. A Gallup survey in the summer of 1987 found that 24 percent of a random sampling of Americans reported that drinking was a problem in their homes, twice the level recorded in 1974 (Gallup 1987a:35). Tangible effects can be seen in spouse and child abuse. Even when physical and mental abuse are not obvious, the children of heavy drinkers pay a heavy price. Constance and Henry Cutter (1987:29) report that these children may suffer lifelong problems of low self-esteem, excessive feelings of responsibility, inability to reach out to others, depression, and susceptibility to alcoholism.

Excessive drinking also leads to substandard behavior necessitating police action. According to the Federal Bureau of Investigation (1987:164), in 1986 there were 933,900 arrests for public drunkenness and 676,400 arrests for disorderly conduct, most of which involved heavy drinking. Drinking was likewise a factor in many of the arrests for aggravated assault and for spouse or child abuse. Perhaps the most striking statistic is that more people were arrested for drunken driving than for any other offense. Driving while intoxicated accounted for 1,793,300 arrests, over 14 percent of the total. Not surprisingly, a high percentage of fatal accidents involve alcohol. In 1982 the Department of Justice reported that 48 percent of fatally injured drivers were intoxicated, another 5.4 percent were legally impaired, and an additional 5.7 percent had some alcohol in the blood (McGarrell and Flanagan 1985:445). In addition to the death and suffering we should consider the time and effort that police, lawyers, judges, and insurance companies must expend because of excessive drinking.

And then there is the matter of monetary cost. The Association of Labor-Management Administrators and Consultants on Alcoholism (ALMACA) has estimated that the total cost to American society for 1986 was $136.5 billion, of which $80.7 billion was lost in the workplace. In addition, according to ALMACA, eighteen thousand persons died in on-the-job accidents involving alcohol (Knobelsdorff 1987).

One way Americans give expression to their concerns about the effects of alcohol abuse is to form private and governmental organizations committed to dealing with the problem. Alcoholics Anonymous (AA), one of the best known of the private organizations, was established in 1935. In

1984, AA estimated that it had six hundred thousand members in some thirty thousand groups in the United States, and more than one million members worldwide (Rudy 1986:131–32). Run by and for alcoholics, AA helps its members achieve sobriety and then stay sober. Al-Anon, an off-shoot of AA, is composed of family and friends who seek to learn how best to handle their relationship with the alcoholic. Alateen is a similar organization for the teenage children of alcoholic parents. Children of Alcoholics is designed to help the adult children of alcoholics better understand and deal with the difficulties they have faced and will continue to face (Leerhsen 1988).

The National Council on Alcoholism (NCA), which was organized in 1944, currently has some two hundred affiliates throughout the United States. Unlike AA, which concentrates on self-help and mutual support among problem drinkers, the NCA is more outwardly directed, with four major areas of activity: medical research and training programs; educational and treatment programs in industry; dissemination of information through the mass media and a national resource center; and services for its local affiliates. The NCA has been a pioneer in promoting an understanding of alcoholism and in developing prevention and treatment programs.

The Center of Alcohol Studies at Rutgers University promotes research on all aspects of alcoholism. It publishes the *Journal of Studies on Alcohol* and book-length monographs, sponsors summer institutes, and aids in establishing clinics and programs in industry. Many professional organizations have special committees devoted to the problem of alcoholism; for example, the American Medical Association has a Committee on Alcoholism and Drug Dependence. Several church denominations have developed programs to help both clergy and laity understand compulsive drinking (Hancock 1985).

Several activist groups were formed during the 1980s to prevent people from driving while intoxicated. Mothers Against Drunk Driving (MADD) and Remove Intoxicated Drivers (RID) have helped institute more severe penalties against those convicted of driving while intoxicated, have sought to educate teenagers about the perils of drinking and driving, and worked for the passage of the National Minimum Drinking Age Act of 1984. Also worthy of mention are Students Against Driving Drunk (SADD) and Business Against Drunk and Drugged Driving (BADDD).

Among major governmental expressions of concern is the National Center for Prevention and Control of Alcoholism, which was established in the mid-1960s within the National Institute of Mental Health to develop and administer federally supported programs on problem drinking. An additional step was taken when Congress passed the Comprehensive Alcohol Abuse and Alcoholism Prevention, Treatment, and Rehabilitation Act of 1970. One of its major provisions was the establishment of the National Institute on Alcohol Abuse and Alcoholism (NIAAA), which has two principal objectives: to make treatment and rehabilitation available to alcoholics at the local level, and to develop effective methods of preventing problem drinking.

Dimensions of the Problem

The Effects of Alcohol

Before we look at the characteristics of problem drinkers, we need to review how alcohol affects human beings. Unlike most foodstuffs, alcohol is not digested but absorbed through the wall of the stomach and intestines into the bloodstream. Most of the alcohol is oxidized in the liver, which breaks it down into carbon dioxide and water. In this process, energy in the form of heat is given off. While most foods also give off heat when oxidized, alcohol differs in that it has toxic effects.

At one time alcohol was thought to be a stimulant, but by the 1940s most scientists considered it exclusively a depressant of the central nervous system. Most research now views the effects of alcohol as biphasic—it acts as both a stimulant and a depressant (Keller 1985a). At relatively low concentrations alcohol is a stimulant, leading most people to be more active, more talkative, more sociable, and more aggressive. To explain the outgoing behavior, those who believed that alcohol is always a depressant maintained that alcohol depresses the cortex of the brain, releasing it of its inhibitory function. Current research, however, indicates an initial stage of stimulation after one or two ounces of whiskey; following more drinks, a second phase occurs. The nervous system is depressed, affecting reaction time, vision, speech, coordination, and balance. If sufficient alcohol is taken, confusion, disorientation, stupor, coma, and even death may result. The particular effect will depend not only on the number of drinks, but also on the type of beverage, the size of the drinker, and the particular body chemistry. Other factors include how fast the drinks are consumed, how much food is in the stomach, and how much experience the person has had with drinking.

An Operational Definition

We have used such terms as "excessive drinking," "heavy drinking," "alcoholism," and "problem drinking" in a general, almost interchangeable way. At this point we need to clarify their meaning and to develop a single definition that will enable us to measure the number of persons who encounter serious difficulties because of their drinking. All of the terms we have used suggest an indulgence that exceeds the limits deemed acceptable by society and interferes with one's ability to function effectively. In his article "Alcoholics Do Not Drink" (1958), Selden Bacon distinguishes between social drinking and consuming alcohol. Rather than following the social norms for drinking, alcoholics develop a special need for alcohol; its consumption becomes the most important part of their existence. According to Bacon, an alcoholic "is no more a drinker than a kleptomaniac is a customer or a pyromaniac is a campfire girl. Alcoholics may consume alcohol. They do not drink" (1958:63).

Of the several terms we have used, "alcoholism" has received the most attention. A consensus appears to be emerging that "alcoholism" should be restricted to a physiological condition in which the individual has lost control and cannot stop drinking once it has begun. It should be considered a disease that is largely or entirely inherited. In a review of the ways in which the term *alcoholism* has been used, Mark Keller concludes that alcoholism is a medical diagnosis. He repeats his own earlier definition as still satisfactory, namely, "alcoholism is a psychogenic dependence or a physiological addiction to ethanol, manifested by the inability of the alcoholic to control either the start of drinking or its termination once started" (1985b:120).

The view that alcoholism is genetically based means that it is a condition over which the individual has no control; it should therefore be treated as an illness rather than a deliberate flouting of behavioral standards. Alcoholics, according to this concept, should not be lectured or punished or shamed for their condition any more than those suffering from severe arrhythmia should be blamed for their heart problems. While this view is not a new one, it is quite in contrast to the traditional moralistic approach to alcoholism as a weakness of character. Certainly it is a far cry from the attitude attributed to a social scientist who is reputed to have said at the turn of the century, "If a drunkard is in the gutter, that is where he belongs."

While those involved in the treatment of alcoholics and problem drinkers have welcomed the move away from a moralistic, punitive approach, others have expressed concern about the current popular concept that alcoholism is a disease. For example, Stanton Peele asserts that the claim that alcoholism is a genetically based disease "does not accurately reflect the state of knowledge in this area" (1986:63). Peele then proceeds to point out the contradictions and complexities entailed in this claim. For instance, it leads to the conclusion that alcoholics are destined from birth to be unable to control their drinking. Such a view poses difficulties for treatment, for it can serve as a self-fulfilling prophecy by convincing alcoholics that they have been biologically preprogramed and therefore are not responsible for their excessive drinking.

One way to avoid the dispute over whether alcoholism is a disease (and, indeed, over how alcoholics are to be characterized) is to use the descriptive, nondiagnostic term *problem drinking* to include alcoholism, excessive drinking, and heavy drinking. Given this use of the term, all alcoholics are problem drinkers, but not all problem drinkers are alcoholics. Keller has proposed that problem drinking be defined as "heavy, deviant or implicative drinking that causes private or public harm—that is seen to cause problems for the drinker or for others" (1985b:129). Alcoholism, then, may be thought of as the most serious form of problem drinking.

Through interviews carried out with a random sample of Americans over twenty-one years of age, Don Cahalan (1970) determined that 9 percent of the sample could be categorized as problem drinkers. Seventeen years later, in 1984, Michael Hilton and Walter Clark (1987) replicated the study, separating Cahalan's original questions into two groups: (1) questions designed to determine dependency on alcohol; and (2) questions focusing on its negative consequences. To determine dependency, respondents were asked if they ever skipped meals, drank to the point of intoxication, or went on drinking sprees. The questions focusing on negative consequences asked if drinking had harmed one's social life, marriage, health, or finances; or if it had ever caused accidents, created legal troubles, resulted in the loss of employment, or brought forth comments from friends or physicians. The follow-up survey showed significant increases for both men and women in dependency upon alcohol and an increase in negative consequences for men. The number of problem drinkers had clearly risen over the seventeen-year period.

It might be argued that the line of demarcation between drinkers with problems and those without problems is arbitrary. This, however, is the nature of all such definitions. The surveys found that the drinking problems people experience fall at virtually every point along a continuum. Thus there is no way to make a hard-and-fast distinction between those who have severe problems with drinking and those who have relatively few and less severe problems. Yet the line needs to be drawn somewhere if we are to identify problem drinkers, and Cahalan and his colleagues have made a logical argument for drawing it where they do. Over the past twenty-five years, from 65 to 75 percent of Americans responding to annual Gallup polls have said that they drink (Gallup 1987b:8). The great majority have few if any problems with drinking. So we have the task of trying to explain why only a relatively small percentage of those who drink have problems.

Characteristics of Alcoholics and Problem Drinkers

The National Institute on Alcohol Abuse and Alcoholism has estimated that in 1987 there were eighteen million alcoholics and problem drinkers in the United States (cited in Chafetz 1987). We must now see if these problem drinkers and alcoholics are significantly different from the rest of the population in terms of sociocultural traits, psychological characteristics, and genetic makeup. We need such data in order to develop theories regarding problem drinking and alcoholism.

Sociocultural traits

A consistent finding, not only in the United States but in other societies as well, is that men are far more likely than women to be alcoholics and problem drinkers. The Cahalan study (1970) found that almost four times more men than women were problem drinkers, and the replication of the study (Hilton and Clark 1987) similarly reported that far more men than women are dependent on alcohol and experience harmful consequences in their relationships at home, at work, and in the community.

Both the 1970 study by Cahalan and its replication seventeen years later also found that the respondents under fifty years of age were more likely to have drinking problems than were those who were over fifty. The peak age for problem drinking, according to the 1970 report, was twenty-three to twenty-nine for males and thirty to thirty-nine for females. In the 1987 report, however, drinking problems for both men and women were highest among those between twenty-three and twenty-nine.

Another area of interest has been socioeconomic level. In the national survey reported in 1970, socioeconomic level was defined in terms of educational attainment and type of occupation. It was found that almost two-thirds of the problem drinkers were in the lower socioeconomic level (Cahalan 1970). The 1984 study, which defined socioeconomic level solely in terms of educational attainment, found that the highest percentage of problem drinkers occurred among males who had not gone beyond high school and females who had less than a high-school education.

Finally, there have been studies that attempt to determine whether there is any correlation between ethnic, racial, and religious background on the one hand, and rates of alcoholism and problem drinking on the other. While there has not always been a consistency of findings for the various groups, in part because of variations in the ways in which alcoholism and problem drinking have been defined, the results in a number of cases do permit generalizations. Comparatively high rates of alcoholism have been reported for American Indians, Hispanic Americans, and Irish Catholics, while comparatively low rates of alcoholism have been found among Americans of Jewish, Italian, and Asian descent. When such studies were expanded to include all problem drinkers, similar results were reported.

Psychological characteristics

One of the questions that has intrigued researchers is whether certain personality traits or combinations thereof contribute to the likelihood of becoming a problem drinker. Research in the 1950s was largely inconclu-

sive. The authors of these studies cited several difficulties they encoun-
tered. There was variation in the ways in which personality traits and
alcoholism were defined. Another problem was the lack of representative
samples to draw upon (most of the individuals studied were institutionalized or were being treated in clinics for what had been diagnosed as
alcoholism). Still another problem was the difficulty of separating the
personality trait from the sociocultural setting (it is logical to suppose
that a certain trait may lead to alcoholism in one setting but not in
another). Finally, there was the issue of determining whether the personality trait in question preceded or followed the development of the
drinking problem.

   In a review of the research on the personality traits of alcoholics,
Gordon Barnes (1979) reiterated the need to distinguish between the
"prealcoholic" personality and the traits that develop after an individual
has become an alcoholic. From longitudinal studies of persons both
before and after they developed drinking problems, Barnes identified
several traits of personality that may contribute to alcoholism: impulsiv-
ity, nonconformity, gregariousness, antisocial behavior, and poor self-
concept. In a later review of research on personality traits, Edith
Gomberg concluded that the supporting evidence for Barnes's findings is
somewhat ambiguous. Nonetheless, Gomberg acknowledged that there
are personality "predispositions" to problem drinking: "Alcoholism is
not a hit-or-miss affair. One learns in early life, in childhood, and in ado-
lescence patterns of behavior and ways of dealing with problems, and it
is a safe assumption that some patterns are more likely to occur in persons who will later become alcoholics. Perhaps it is a particular combination of patterns" (1985:195).

   A number of studies have found that problem drinkers have a more
favorable attitude toward drinking than do those who are not problem
drinkers. In the Cahalan study of 1970, attitudes toward drinking were
measured by asking how much the respondent would miss drinking if it
were necessary to give it up, whether drinking does more good than
harm, how many drinks are appropriate, and whether the respondent
enjoyed getting drunk once in a while. The findings showed a strong correlation between highly favorable attitudes toward drinking and problem drinking. Once more, however, the question arises as to which came
first, the favorable attitude or the problem drinking, or whether they
developed concurrently. This question can be answered only by longitudinal studies which measure the individual's attitudes over a period of
time and relate them to the extent of problem drinking.

   Physiological characteristics
   A logical argument can be made that those who become alcoholics
and problem drinkers have a particular genetic or constitutional makeup

that differentiates them from the rest of the population and makes them more vulnerable to the development of alcoholism and problem drinking. Three types of research tend to support this argument: (1) the search for a genetic marker for alcoholism; (2) comparison of identical and fraternal twins; and (3) studies of adoptees who had alcoholic parents (Goodwin 1985).

1. A genetic marker is a trait that is known to be inherited, usually in a straightforward Mendelian process; for example, blood group, eye color, sickle-cell anemia, and Tay-Sachs disease. If a genetic marker could be located in alcoholics, either exclusively or more frequently than in nonalcoholics, we could conclude that alcoholism is related to heredity. Donald Goodwin (1985) found that a number of studies associate alcoholism with some genetic marker, but that these studies are inconsistent and in some cases conflicting. On the other hand, studies which show that the children of alcoholics are more likely than the children of nonalcoholics to develop alcoholism have convinced some geneticists that a marker for alcoholism does exist. Research into the way alcohol affects alcoholics and their children has promise for the discovery of a genetic marker or a combination of genetic traits that makes some persons more vulnerable to alcoholism than others. This research will also have to determine whether such a genetic marker, if and when found, is a necessary, sufficient, or contributory condition.

2. An extensive study conducted in Sweden found identical twins to be more concordant in regard to alcoholism (i.e., either both became alcoholics or neither did) than was the case for fraternal twins (Goodwin 1985). Since identical twins are exactly alike in genetic makeup while fraternal twins are not, the implication is that genetic factors could be involved. Other studies, however, have been critical of the Swedish findings. These studies point out, for example, that environmental factors were not effectively controlled, for even twins do not necessarily have exactly the same upbringing (Peele 1986).

3. The purpose of studies comparing how the children of alcoholic and of nonalcoholic parents fare when they are raised in nonalcoholic foster families is to separate genetic, or at least congenital, factors from the influences of upbringing. From numerous studies of adoptees both in the United States and other countries, Goodwin drew three tentative conclusions: "(1) Children of alcoholics are about four times more likely to become alcoholic than are children of nonalcoholics, whether raised by their alcoholic biological parents or by nonalcoholic foster parents; (2) Their alcoholism developed at a rather early age . . . ; (3) The alcoholism is particularly severe" (1985:165).

While these recent studies have consistently pointed to a genetic (or congenital) factor in alcoholism, at least one classic investigation raises questions about them. Anne Roe (1945) studie sixty-one adults who had been placed in foster homes at an early age; thirty-six of them were children of alcoholics. While two of the latter group and one subject whose biological parents were not alcoholics experienced drinking problems as adolescents, by the time they were in their late twenties or early thirties, there were no excessive drinkers in either grouping.

Goodwin attempted to explain Roe's findings by suggesting that the biological parents of the thirty-six may not have been "truly" alcoholic, since none of them was being treated for alcoholism at the time the child was placed in the foster home. These parents, Goodwin conjectures, should instead have been classified as "heavy drinkers with syndrome," which means that they were overaggressive and disorganized, lost jobs repeatedly, engaged in disorderly conduct, and neglected or mistreated their spouses and children—presumably because of their drinking. Goodwin's suggestion that a genuine form of alcoholism can be distinguished from other types of alcoholism implies that a sharp line can be drawn. Evidence from the Cahalan study and its follow-up, however, indicates that problem drinking falls along a continuum in which there are no sharp breaks. Alcoholism and problem drinking are matters of degree, and the lines of separation are arbitrary. It seems, then, that attempts to explain Roe's findings might better concentrate on uncontrolled factors like the child's age at entering the foster home, the attitudes of the foster parents toward drinking, the amount of affection shown the foster child, and the kind of discipline exercised in the home.

Explanations of the Facts on Alcoholism and Problem Drinking

The Sociocultural Approach

The sociocultural approach to explaining the facts on alcoholism and problem drinking assumes that the locus of causation is the social structure and the norms supporting that structure. This approach purports to make clear why the rates of alcoholism and problem drinking vary from one culture or social category to another. It cannot explain, however, why particular individuals become alcoholics or problem drinkers, which is a matter to be handled by theories that concentrate on the individual, namely, the psychological and physiological theories.

The sociocultural hypothesis draws upon the research of Robert Bales (1946), Albert Ullman (1958), and Charles Snyder (1958) among others. This hypothesis states that the rate of alcoholism will be relatively low in those societies where the patterns of drinking are consistent and clear-cut, there is moderate drinking at mealtime, and intoxication is strongly condemned. The converse is that the rates will be relatively high where there is strict prohibition or ambivalence concerning drinking, the amount is not rigidly controlled by social norms, and intoxication is not strongly disapproved. The hypothesis was derived by comparing ethnic and religious groups in which the rates of alcoholism and problem drinking are low (Jewish, Italian, and Chinese Americans) with groups in which the rates are high (American Indians, Irish Americans, and Hispanics).

We might consider, for example, the relatively low rate of alcoholism and problem drinking among Jewish Americans and the higher rate among Irish Americans (Snyder 1958; Glassner and Berg 1980). It is to be noted that Jewish tradition regards drinking as a sacred activity of the family. Especially among Orthodox Jews it is related at an early age to religious symbols, ideas, and feelings. Sobriety is prized, while drunkenness is deplored. In contrast, Irish Americans drink for enjoyment; their drinking is both utilitarian and hedonistic. It is not an integral part of family or religious activities, but rather facilitates fellowship and helps individuals meet crises.

Various cross-cultural studies also lend support to the sociocultural hypothesis. Roland Sadoun, Giorgio Lolli, and Milton Silverman (1965) compared the general drinking patterns in France, which has a high rate of alcoholism, with those in Italy, which has a relatively low rate. Drinking in childhood is viewed differently in the two countries. The French have rigid parental attitudes, either strongly for or against allowing children to use alcohol. In contrast, Italians are more relaxed about the matter, regarding it as a normal, relatively unimportant part of a child's development. There are other differences as well. Italians abide by social limits and usually confine their drinking to mealtime, while the French drink as much as and whenever they please. The French accept (or at least tolerate) intoxication as humorous or even fashionable, while the Italians consider intoxication disgraceful for both the individual and the individual's family. And in France, unlike Italy, drinking is considered a sign of virility.

A major contention of the sociocultural hypothesis is that a society's ambivalence toward drinking contributes to alcoholism. Paul Chalfant and Robert Beckley (1977) have noted that country music portrays alcohol as both "beguiling and betraying." On the one hand, drinking is depicted as a solution for loneliness, proof of manhood, and a source of relief and escape. On the other hand, it disrupts families, provides false security, and leads to illicit sex, punishment by God, and death. In a society so uncertain about alcohol, it is no wonder that there are problems.

While the sociocultural hypothesis most clearly helps to explain the differences in the rates of alcoholism of various ethnic and religious groups, it can also account for the differences in the rates of men and women. In American society there are different expectations for young men and women. Women do not have to prove themselves by drinking. Men, however, use drinking to establish their masculinity; accordingly, intoxication in men is frowned upon less than it is in women. In other words, American society puts more pressure on men to drink in a utilitarian and hedonistic way, making them more vulnerable to alcoholism. The sociocultural hypothesis is also able to account for the higher rates in large cities, among young people, and at lower socioeconomic levels, where, it is argued, social controls are not as strong as in small towns, among older people, and at upper socioeconomic levels.

Arnold Linsky and his colleagues have tested two aspects of the sociocultural hypothesis. In a 1985 report they demonstrate that where social structures and norms create great stress and tension, there are high consumption rates of alcohol and high death rates from cirrhosis, alcoholism, and alcoholic psychosis. In a second study (1986) they rank some of the United States in terms of the extent to which drinking is prohibited or frowned upon. The data include the percentage of persons living in legally dry areas, the number of liquor outlets, restrictions on the sale of alcoholic beverages, and the percentage of the state's population belonging to religious denominations that prohibit or severely restrict drinking. The researchers found a significantly high rate of disruptive alcohol-related behaviors in the states that have "the strongest biases toward beverage alcohol."

A Psychological Approach: The Reinforcement Theory

Psychological theories of alcohol abuse assume that the locus of causation is the individual, specifically, what one believes about drinking and what one experiences from using alcohol. One psychological theory is built on the assumption that alcoholism and problem drinking result from an acquired reliance on alcohol to reduce strain, stress, and anxiety, to meet crises, and to get through other unpleasant situations. Basic to this approach is evidence that persons are likely to repeat behavior that offers them some sort of reward and avoid behavior that entails unpleasant consequences. Furthermore, the sooner and more consistent the reinforcement, the greater is the likelihood that the behavior will be repeated. Many people find that drinking alcohol has a special set of rewards: it provides relief from depression and boredom; it creates a congenial and relaxed feeling that fosters social relationships; it helps one to avoid unpleasant and threatening situations, at least for the moment; it serves to change one's perspective. Such people will be inclined to repeat the experience.

Since the great majority of persons who drink do not develop problems, the question arises, Why are the normal, socially acceptable functions of alcohol insufficient for those who become alcoholics? The reinforcement theory leads us to suggest that excessive drinking may reduce tension much more effectively in some people than in others. It can be logically assumed that the former group will find heavy drinking far more rewarding than will the latter. We must caution here, however, that the tension-reduction hypothesis has been tested directly and received only partial support (Pandina 1985:56–57).

Another significant psychological factor is one's beliefs about drinking. We stated earlier that problem drinkers, including alcoholics, have a more favorable attitude toward drinking than do non–problem drinkers. It is possible that favorable expectations before drinking episodes override any negative aftereffects. Thus, remembrances of one's drinking tend to be positive and result in renewed expectations of the pleasant feelings that occur when one begins to drink. A related theory holds that the guilt and anxiety produced by drinking may precipitate still another episode.

A Physiological Approach: Alcoholism and Heredity

Underlying the physiological approach is the assumption that alcoholism and problem drinking are related to the physical makeup of the individual. It is postulated that because of inherited traits, congenital peculiarities, or biochemical characteristics that developed after birth, some persons are likely to have a special reaction to alcohol, lose control over their drinking, and become physically addicted. It is difficult at times to know whether the researchers in this area consider physiological factors necessary, sufficient, or contributory conditions in drinking problems. The majority of researchers apparently believe that certain constitutional characteristics contribute to alcoholism, for they use such expressions as "an inherited predisposition," "influenced by heredity," "vulnerability to developing alcoholism," and "heavy genetic load for alcoholism."

In any event, the facts on alcoholism that a physiological approach can deal with most effectively were mentioned earlier in this chapter, namely, signs of a genetic marker, the correlation between identical twins in regard to alcoholism, and the likelihood that the children of alcoholics will develop alcoholism. A question pursued by physiological studies of alcoholism is, "If heredity is a factor in alcoholism, just what is inherited?" In his review of the literature on the relationship between alcoholism and heredity, Donald Goodwin (1985) points to several clues. One is that genes provide enzymes which metabolize alcohol, and the way alcohol is metabolized may relate to a person's vulnerability to alcoholism. Goodwin points out that identical twins, unlike fraternal twins, metabolize alcohol at almost identical rates. It may be concluded, then, that the rate of metabolism is largely genetic.

A simple description of the metabolism of alcohol is in order here. While alcohol, like carbohydrates and fats, has a high caloric content, unlike them it cannot be stored in body tissues. Nor can it be eliminated through the lungs or the kidneys. Consequently, most of it must be oxidized. Most of the oxidation of alcohol takes place in the liver, but the brain is involved as well, with the possible consequence of bringing about a dependence on alcohol. One of the products of oxidation is the chemical acetaldehyde, which has toxic effects. Studies have shown that the concentration of acetaldehyde is significantly higher in alcoholics than in nonalcoholics, even when both have ingested the same amount of alcohol. The different levels of acetaldehyde after drinking may well be a factor in the development of alcoholism.

Another possible clue to the relationship between heredity and alcoholism is the fact that the enzyme monoamine oxidase, which affects neurotransmitters, is found in low levels in alcoholics and their relatives. Obviously, the physiological effects of ethanol are complex; even the cause of intoxication is not fully understood. Yet the search for physiological factors that predispose to alcoholism offers great promise of our someday comprehending why some individuals can drink socially while others lose control.

A recent study by Lars vonKnorring and his colleagues (1987) shows promise in this search. They differentiated between what they termed Type I and Type II alcoholics. Among the factors determining the two categories are the age at which alcohol-related problems first appeared, one's age at first treatment, alcohol-related aggressiveness, absence from or loss of a job, and arrests for being intoxicated.The problems of Type I alcoholics come on later and are far less frequent and serious than the problems of Type II alcoholics. The study concluded that Type II alcoholics have a high genetic proclivity toward alcoholism, while for Type I alcoholics genetic factors are, at most, minor in importance.

Ralph Tarter, Arthur Alterman, and Kathleen Edwards (1985) have suggested another way in which heredity may be related to alcoholism. They review the psychological and biological traits associated with vulnerability to alcoholism and hypothesize a relationship between temperament and genetics. They claim that there are genetically determined characteristics—hyperactivity, low attention span, difficulty in handling stress, an antisocial personality—that predispose an individual to alcoholism. Thus, in their view, the relationship between genetics and alcoholism is indirect.

Treatment and Prevention

To be effective, programs for the treatment and prevention of alcoholism and problem drinking should be based on sound theory. However, as has just been seen, we have a long way to go in the building of adequate theory. At the same time, we do have the results of substantial research on contributory conditions, results which provide leads on how to treat and prevent excessive drinking. In any event, doing something about alcoholism and problem drinking cannot wait until explanations are fully developed. In fact, current programs for treatment and prevention can give insight into causes and generate hypotheses that should be tested. Also, some methods work without our knowing why.

Treatment

The treatment of alcoholism and problem drinking covers a wide range of medical, psychological, and social activities. In order for treatment even to begin, however, alcoholics and problem drinkers must acknowledge their predicament and want to do something about it. While some alcoholics and problem drinkers can recover without the aid of hospitalization, aversion therapy, professional counseling, or the support of recovered alcoholics, the majority need a great deal of help to control their drinking problems. Indeed, persuasive pressure from family, friends, and employer may be required simply to get the individual into treatment in the first place.

Physical rehabilitation

For a number of problem drinkers, especially those diagnosed as being addicted to alcohol, a vital first step in treatment is detoxication. Those who are acutely intoxicated need professional supervision and medication to deal with withdrawal symptoms and delirium tremens. Intensive nursing care, high-potency vitamins, and electrolyte balancing are required. If there has been excessive use of alcohol over a long period of time, there may be damage to the liver, heart, pancreas, brain, and central nervous system, all of which will require special treatment. It is significant that in recent years insurance companies have begun to recognize alcoholism and problem drinking as medically treatable and therefore offer coverage for such conditions. In 1985 a Bureau of Labor Statistics survey of over thirteen hundred health-insurance plans covering more than twenty million employees reported that 68 percent provided some such coverage, an increase from 61 percent in 1984 and 38 percent in 1981 (Gordis 1987:583). While government agencies continue to be the major providers of such coverage, there has been a rapid move into the area by private insurers.

One way to prevent the patient from drinking during the rehabilitation period is the use of aversion therapy and deterrent agents. In aversion therapy, patients are allowed to have their favorite alcoholic beverage and at the same time are given a powerful nausea-producing drug like emetine. The result is a very unpleasant experience associated with drinking. Repeated treatments establish a conditioned response so that alcohol itself produces the same unpleasant reaction as does the emetine. One of the most widely used deterrent agents is disulfiram (Antabus). This drug interferes with the metabolism of alcohol, causing pounding headaches, severe nausea, and other disagreeable reactions. One relatively mild experience under a physician's supervision is usually sufficient to convince the patient not to drink while disulfiram is in the system.

Unfortunately, detoxication and aversion therapy are not enough to prevent relapses. One study in Canada found that more than half of its 522 subjects had been readmitted to treatment centers within six months of being discharged from detoxication programs (Annis and Smart 1978). Additional types of treatment are clearly required.

Psychotherapy

One type of additional treatment is psychotherapy, which gives patients insight into their drinking problems so that they might change their behavior and adopt more rewarding patterns of living. While helping patients to gain insight into their condition and to acknowledge their need to change, therapists avoid lecturing, moralizing, and frightening them, which not only are counterproductive but might very well raise the level of anxiety. Nor do therapists attempt to exact promises of sobriety, which have not been found to be helpful.

If patients stop their drinking, they must face an accumulation of problems that have long been neglected. To enable the patient to deal with these problems, treatment might well last for a year and involve other members of the family. Occasional follow-up sessions might be required for some time after that. Therapy of shorter duration may be effective with patients who maintain strong family ties, are determined to remain sober, and can face up to their situation quickly.

While psychotherapy is most often given on a one-to-one basis, group therapy is also employed. Several patients are guided in a discussion of their drinking problems. As they discuss their problems, they begin to see through one another's defenses. They are able to recognize the subterfuges others rely on, for they themselves often use such devices. Thus there is the possibility of a double channel of insight. Each patient learns both from observing the others unmask their defenses and from seeing oneself in their behavior. The therapist also learns a great deal from the exchanges between patients.

Social therapy

One of the major consequences of problem drinking is the disruption of family life; in some cases, as a matter of fact, the problem drinker may be completely excluded. Because the entire family is so directly involved, all of its members may be brought into the therapy process. It is possible that the spouse of the excessive drinker contributes to the problem and even unconsciously blocks attempts at recovery. There is, consequently, a growing tendency to treat both husband and wife when one of them has a drinking problem. The assumption here is that the marriage relationship is either contributing to the drinking or placing an excessive burden on the nondrinking partner.

THE FAMILY OFTEN COLLUDES TO DENY THE SERIOUSNESS
OF A MEMBER'S DEPENDENCE ON ALCOHOL.

Various organizations have been established for the families of problem drinkers. Among them is Al-Anon, which provides an opportunity to share the experiences of others who live with alcoholics. This can be therapeutic in two ways. It offers a chance to unburden one's problems in the company of understanding and accepting listeners, and it gives assurance that one is not the only person facing such a situation. A recent study found that Al-Anon members benefit in several ways: they are depressed less frequently and more assertive; they come to accept their own emotions; they no longer feel personally responsible for the problem; and they gain a new awareness about alcoholism (Cutter and Cutter 1987:31). Alateen, which is an offshoot of Al-Anon, helps teenagers deal with the problems that arise from living with an alcoholic parent. The goal is to enable teenagers to adopt attitudes and behavior that will help their parents deal more effectively with their drinking problems.

Problem drinking not only leads to conflicts and difficulties in the family, but frequently entails a loss of friends, social acquaintances, and professional and business contacts; in short, a general social rejection. To remedy this situation, Alcoholics Anonymous (AA) provides a supportive fellowship for individuals who want to stop drinking. The very problem that caused social rejection becomes the basis of membership in an accepting, understanding group. The liability is turned into an asset. The purpose of AA is stated in its preamble, which is read at the beginning of each meeting:

> Alcoholics Anonymous is a fellowship of men and women who share their experience, strength and hope with each other that they may solve their common problem and help others to recover from alcoholism. The only requirement for membership is a desire to stop drinking. There are no dues or fees for AA membership; we are self-supporting through our own contributions. AA is not allied with any sect, denomination, politics, organization or institution; does not wish to engage in any controversy, neither endorses nor opposes any causes. Our primary purpose is to stay sober and help other alcoholics to achieve sobriety.

Note from the preamble that membership in AA is self-determined. One becomes a member simply by expressing a desire to stop drinking; and no matter what an individual may have done or may do in the future, one remains a member if one so wishes.

The guiding principles of AA are the Twelve Steps, the first of which is: "We admit that we were powerless over alcohol—that our lives had become unmanageable." Other steps involve belief in a higher power that can restore health, and a resolution to make amends to those people who have been harmed by one's drinking. There is a strong nonsectarian religious emphasis in AA. Accepting the philosophy of AA and becoming totally absorbed in the community and its way of life bring about a radical change in one's world-view and self-identity. "Such a radical reorganization of identity, meaning, and life," asserts David Rudy (1986:42), "is profitably viewed as conversion."

Personal accounts of recovery from alcoholism give credit to AA time and again for success in achieving sobriety (Stromsten 1982). Several aspects of the group therapy found in AA can help account for its success with self-acknowledged alcoholics and problem drinkers. Individuals whose drinking has led them into serious problems are accepted by the group without question, so that their guilt and anxiety can be replaced by dignity and self-confidence. AA members do not condemn but extend sympathy and understanding, for they know firsthand what the excessive drinker has experienced; and the drinker realizes that they know. In this supportive setting, the drinker can verbalize feelings in open give-and-take sessions. Such verbalization itself can be therapeutic. With the group's encouragement, the new member resolves to remain sober. Once success has been achieved, the recovered AA member is able to help others stay sober, further enhancing one's feelings of ability and self-worth.

It is very difficult to know how many alcoholics and problem drinkers are permanently helped by AA. Follow-up studies of the effects of AA are exceedingly complex to conduct. One of the difficulties is the diversity of individuals. Most who attend meetings do so voluntarily, and genuinely wish to achieve sobriety. Others are ordered by the courts to attend. Some mature to the point of abstinence; and then there are those who attend AA meetings, relapse into excessive drinking, return to AA and then relapse again. George Vaillant found that individuals are more likely to be helped by AA if their alcoholism is less severe and if they experienced affection during childhood. Although AA has its limitations, each year it is able to reach twice as many excessive drinkers as do clinics and medical practitioners combined (1983:199).

Prevention

We will look briefly at three aspects of prevention. In keeping with the preceding discussion, we turn first to efforts aimed at preventing the recovered alcoholic from a relapse into excessive drinking. The other two aspects—education about the problems associated with drinking and attempts to change the climate of drinking in America—are much broader in purpose and directed toward a much larger population.

Efforts to keep recovered alcoholics and problem drinkers from relapsing

We have already explored various medical, psychological, and social programs that try to keep the individual from abusing alcohol again. What needs emphasis here is that both AA and the National Council on Alcoholism insist that recovered alcoholics and problem drinkers should not drink at all because of the likelihood of the loss of control and a relapse into excessive drinking. Reports in the 1960s and through the middle of the 1970s, however, took issue with the contention that recovered alcoholics cannot learn to drink in moderation. These reports claimed that 18 percent of the alcoholics who had undergone treatment became non–problem drinkers. Research since the mid-1970s, however, has challenged the notion that recovered alcoholics can drink in moderation without great risk. A reexamination found the earlier studies contradictory, too lenient in defining what was meant by "controlled drinking," and too short-lived to determine whether the moderate drinking was a permanent situation or the beginning of a relapse to problem drinking. The reexamination concluded, "The data from the majority of studies reviewed here indicate that moderate drinking among ex-alcoholics is an uncommon, perhaps even a rare, occurrence" (Taylor et al. 1986:120).

Although abstinence is the best course, it is not without its problems. Vaillant (1983:213–16) points out several problems that can rise from abstinence. First, release from dependence upon alcohol rarely brings instant relief. The early stages of remission may be accompanied by depression, severe marital and family disruption, and occupational difficulties. Another problem is that the alcoholic must begin to function as an independent person liberated from both the slavery of alcohol and medical supervision, overcome the loss of self-esteem that accompanies excessive drinking, make up for the loss in occupational proficiency, and repair family relationships. Vaillant emphasizes that "abstinence is a means not an end. . . . It is justifiable as a treatment goal only if moderate drinking is not a viable alternative and only if sight is not lost of the real goal—social rehabilitation" (1983:215).

Education

The educational programs of such organizations as the NIAAA and the NCA do not use scare tactics, nor do they urge everyone to abstain from alcohol. Rather, they accept social drinking as a part of American life and do not take a position for or against drinking per se. The basic principles of these educational programs for youth stress that it is not necessary to drink and that heavy drinking does not demonstrate adult status or virility. Those who choose to drink should do so responsibly; this entails sipping drinks slowly, diluting the alcohol, eating some food as one drinks, and, above all, learning not to indulge to the point where judgment and movement are impaired.

The NIAAA, through the National Clearinghouse for Alcohol and Drug Information, provides posters, pamphlets, and booklets that promote responsible attitudes toward drinking. "Think. You Don't Have to Drink" and "Be Smart! Don't Start!—Just Say No!" inform young people that one should never apologize for abstaining and that there are healthy alternatives to drinking. Other publications inform parents, teachers, and business, church, and community leaders about conferences on alcoholism and problem drinking. Education might not be sufficient to produce abstinence, but it can persuade individuals to control their drinking.

Attempts to change the climate of drinking in America

A part of the goal of the educational programs is to create a realistic view of the drinking of alcoholic beverages. There are, of course, more direct ways of changing the drinking patterns of American society. One approach is to enact state and federal laws limiting the availability of alcohol. Legislation has already raised the drinking age to twenty-one in most states, required warning labels, increased the federal excise tax on alcoholic beverages, and banned advertising altogether or required equal time for warnings about the dangers of heavy drinking. There have also been direct campaigns to keep people from driving an automobile or operating machinery if they have had too much to drink. Heavy punishments, including jail sentences, have been instituted in some states; and there are moves to make a concentration of .05 percent alcohol in the bloodstream—the equivalent of two beers—legal proof of alcohol-impaired driving.

There is evidence that beliefs about and attitudes toward drinking have undergone some change during the 1980s. A Gallup poll comparing responses from a representative sample of Americans in 1982 with responses from 1987 reported an increase in the percentage of Americans who seek professional help for drinking problems. There were corresponding increases in the percentage of those who believe that alcoholism is a disease, that it may be hereditary, that the use of alcohol by pregnant women can cause birth defects, and that recovered alcoholics cannot drink moderately (Gallup 1987b:37, 24–31). Large majorities of the American population support passage of a federal law making twenty-one the minimum drinking age, think the federal excise tax on alcoholic beverages should be doubled, and favor a designated-driver program in which certain persons agree not to drink alcoholic beverages at parties in order to serve as drivers for those who do.

Ironically, just as the Gallup survey was reporting that 87 percent of the American population agree that alcoholism is a disease, the Veterans' Administration denied an extension of educational benefits to two honorably discharged veterans whose education had been delayed by their need to recover from alcoholism. The Veterans' Administration ruled that their alcoholism was due to "willful misconduct" and therefore did not qualify as a legitimate handicap. The United States Supreme Court, in a decision announced on April 20, 1988, upheld the Veterans' Administration ruling. The Court stated that it was not its prerogative "to decide whether alcoholism is a disease whose course its victims cannot control. It is not our role to resolve this medical issue on which the authorities remain sharply divided" (U.S. Law Week 1988).

Despite the changes in attitudes and beliefs about alcohol and alcoholism, new concerns have been expressed in at least two areas. One has to do with the kind of information that is being transmitted to the American population by the mass media. For example, a study of 122 hours of prime-time television programs aired in the fall of 1984 found that alcohol appeared in 78 percent of the programs, with an average of eleven drinks per hour. The authors of the study stated that the message was not neutral:

> Alcohol is ubiquitous in television life. The strong suggestion conveyed to viewers is that alcohol is taken for granted, routine and even necessary, that most people drink and that drinking is a part of everyday life. The drinkers are frequently glamorous; for many viewers they are setting an example regarding lifestyle. These images are at variance with the problematic nature of alcohol in society. It would be difficult to make the case that alcohol is being presented in a balanced way on prime-time television. [Wallack et al. 1987:37]

The other concern is the proliferation of treatment centers that have sprung up around the country, and the expansion of "problem drinking" to include behavior that had previously been designated "social drinking." Morris Chafetz, the founding director of the NIAAA, believes that, as a result, we have failed to reduce alcohol problems, which is the main mission of the NIAAA. According to Chafetz,

> The definitions and descriptions of alcohol problems have been broadened to the point that they are meaningless. Whatever the reason for the increase [in the number of alcoholics and problem drinkers], more people are needed to feed the treatment mills, and the wider manifestations of alcohol problems increase the number of people to whom consumer activists can appeal. The prevailing wisdom seems to be that if alcohol itself would just go away, so would the problems. [1987:30]

Herbert Fingarette, a professor at the University of California at Santa Barbara, makes a similar point by stating that as health professionals in the alcoholism field began to expand their services, economic incentives came into play. Programs aimed at getting people to stop drinking have become an unmanageable billion-dollar-a-year industry (1988).

A Christian Response to Alcohol Abuse*

The positions held by Christians on the subject of alcohol use range from total abstinence on the one hand, to an acceptance of alcohol as a gift from God to be enjoyed in the celebration of life on the other. We need to examine these two extremes in the light of biblical evidence and the potential excesses to which each can lead.

There is merit to the position of abstinence. For while alcoholic beverages have almost no nutritional value, they are made from raw food products like grapes and grain which could otherwise be used to help feed a hungry world. Added to this is the estimated $136.5 billion that alcohol abuse costs society annually. Furthermore, one cannot even begin to estimate in monetary terms the value of the human lives lost in alcohol-related automobile and on-the-job accidents. We find it hard to disagree with the assertion that society would be better off if there were absolutely no alcohol consumption. In tallying up the total personal, social, physical, and economic cost of alcohol abuse, it is understandable why many Christians consider alcohol the tool of the devil.

A danger to be kept in mind, however, is that abstinence can easily become a single-issue approach to solving social problems. Anyone who looks on alcohol as the sole cause of poverty, crime, marital instability, and related social problems will be blind to other evils in the social structure which also contribute to these problems. Like the man who saw the

---

*Since alcohol and drug abuse raise similar moral questions, much of the discussion in this section is also relevant to the final section of chapter 10, and much of the discussion found there is relevant to this discussion.

speck in his brother's eye but was unaware of the beam in his own (Luke 6:41–42), we can preach against the evil of alcohol use among the poor or ethnic minorities, but fail to see our own evil participation in unjust and discriminatory social structures. This is exactly like the unobserved sin within the church at the time of the civil-rights movement. In his book *Religion and the Solid South,* Samuel Hill (1972:52) notes that the strong taboo against alcoholism held in the southern United States led to the belief that alcohol lay at the root of all social problems. By pointing to the evils of alcohol, Christians conveniently escaped taking responsibility for such social problems as racial discrimination and poverty.

The Biblical View of Alcohol

We believe that the Bible supports neither of the two extremes, as "the biblical writers reflect a variety of views on the use of alcohol" (Hayes 1987:13). The Bible does offer injunctions against drinking alcoholic beverages in certain places (the tabernacle [Lev. 10:9] and the inner court of the temple [Ezek. 44:21]) and during certain periods (a special consecration [Num. 6:3–20] or particular pregnancies [Judg. 13:4; Luke 1:15]). Alcohol is recognized as a potential evil in Proverbs 20:1, "Wine is a mocker and beer a brawler; whoever is led astray by them is not wise" (NIV), as well as in several other passages (Isa. 5:22; 28:7; Prov. 23:29–35). The Bible also warns that drunkenness can be confused with the presence of the Spirit (1 Sam. 1:13–18; Acts 2:13).

On the other hand, anyone who would build a case for abstinence will not find support in the teachings of Jesus, for he not only used wine as a sacramental element (Luke 22:20), a teaching tool (Luke 5:37–39), and a sign for the people (John 2:1–11), but also stated that "what goes into a man's mouth does not make him 'unclean,' but what comes out of his mouth, that is what makes him 'unclean'" (Matt. 15:11 NIV). Paul likewise did not teach against drinking alcohol, but only against drunkenness, for he states, "Do not get drunk on wine, which leads to debauchery. Instead be filled with the Spirit" (Eph. 5:18 NIV).

Alcohol Use and Guilt

Our conscience—that which makes us feel guilt or shame—is a product of both our culture and our spirituality. Some Christians have restrictive attitudes about alcohol use which are not based on Scripture; others have such libertine attitudes that they do not feel guilt or shame when they become intoxicated. This is akin to the problem which Paul addresses in Romans 14: some Christians were offended by other Christians who were eating meat which had formerly been offered to idols. Similarly, Jewish Christians were offended because the Gentile Christians did not observe Jewish holy days. Paul says that in such cases the failure to abide by someone else's standards is not sinful in and of itself, but that "each one should be fully convinced in his own mind" (Rom. 14:5 NIV).

Christians who experience neurotic guilt over the use of alcohol—guilt which has been produced by their cultural conditioning rather than by the convicting power of the Holy Spirit—must reeducate their conscience while taking care that they do not kill it in the process. To ignore guilty feelings is to violate one's conscience and is both spiritually and psychologically harmful. To repeatedly violate one's conscience serves to render it inoperative in our lives. By so doing, we may come to the point where we are no longer able to feel guilty about anything. Reeducating conscience, on the other hand, entails carefully examining and prayerfully considering the biblical evidence on alcohol use. Another good practice is to seek the advice of mature Christians who have shown evidence of spiritual discernment.

In Romans 14:14–18 Paul gives some additional counsel which can help us think clearly about the relationship between alcohol use and guilt:

> As one who is in the Lord Jesus, I am fully convinced that no food is unclean in itself. But if anyone regards something as unclean, then for him it is unclean. If your brother is distressed because of what you eat, you are no longer acting in love. Do not by your eating destroy your brother for whom Christ died. Do not allow what you consider good to be spoken of as evil. For the kingdom of God is not a matter of eating and drinking, but of righteousness, peace and joy in the Holy Spirit, because anyone who serves Christ in this way is pleasing to God and approved by men. [NIV]

Since wine was considered a regular part of the meal during New Testament times, we should probably understand Paul as saying that even alcoholic beverages are not unclean in themselves. He seems to reinforce this in verse 17—"For the kingdom of God is not a matter of eating and drinking, but of righteousness. . . ." Paul's statement here reminds us of Jesus' statement in Matthew 15:11.

This is not to say that God may not, in a given social or cultural circumstance, call upon a person to abstain from alcohol. On an interpersonal level, a Christian may choose to practice abstinence for the sake of another. As Paul says, "If anyone regards something as unclean, then for him it is unclean." We must be sensitive to others who may be offended by our imbibing. Nor are we to belittle or look down upon anyone who chooses abstinence. Instead, we should acknowledge that God leads people in different directions with regards to the use of alcohol, and we should affirm and appreciate the differences.

At the same time, the Bible has much to say about respecting Christian freedoms. As Romans 14:5 states, "One man considers one day more sacred than another; another man considers every day alike. Each one should be fully convinced in his own mind" (NIV). Our own behavior and our reaction to the behavior of others should be based upon Christian convictions rather than cultural conditioning.

Christian Attitudes Towards the Treatment and Prevention of Alcoholism

The Christian community should give enthusiastic support to the many programs that are designed to treat and prevent alcoholism. The AA philosophy that alcoholics can do little to help themselves, but need instead to draw upon a "higher power" to gain victory over their problem, is especially consonant with Christian belief. Churches should show compassion for persons struggling with alcoholism and be willing to provide material, social, and emotional support.

To show its support for the prevention of alcohol abuse, the Christian community needs to participate in attempts to change the climate of drinking in America. Raising the national drinking age to twenty-one and banning the advertising of alcoholic beverages on television and radio have much merit, but more radical changes are also needed. We need to be alarmed that prime-time television depicts drinking as glamorous behavior. Even more serious is the way people associate drinking with desirable mood changes and relief from the tensions and problems of everyday life. As Philip Walter (1982:14) states, "While there are appropriate uses for some mood-altering drugs, nevertheless, to use alcohol and other drugs as the means of coping with life's everyday problems is inconsistent with a spiritual understanding of life as a process of growth which includes natural highs and lows."

Each day millions of Americans routinely find it necessary to have several drinks after work in order to calm their nerves. This practice should alert us to the probability that the work situation for many is anything but ideal. High rates of alcoholism in technologically advanced societies may be an indication that the price being paid for such advancement is shallow and superficial relationships.

The extreme pressure to produce and compete militates against *koinōnia* in the workplace. Therefore, work in modern society must be reformed to meet the needs of human beings, and not just the bottom line. The Christian community needs to challenge a work ethic that makes productivity the sole concern and fails to consider the toll upon personal emotional health as a cost to be entered in the debit column of a business ledger.

At a broader level the lack of *shalom* in society has disinherited millions, many of whom turn to alcohol and drugs as a means of escaping their feelings of failure and alienation. Addiction to drugs and alcohol is most common among urban minorities, the very groups whose unemployment rates are the highest in the nation. Unemployment not only deprives a person of a decent living, but also of a positive self-identity, for in an achievement-oriented society such as ours, one is known and comes to know oneself by what one does. Granted, some persons may choose not to work. For the vast majority, however, unemployment is not a choice, but the result of an economy that defines a large number of persons as nothings—as worthless creatures. Any attempt to prevent alcoholism and drug abuse must confront this situation head-on. For without a greater level of *koinōnia* and *shalom* at all levels of society, such problems are bound to continue.

Topics for Review, Reflection, and Discussion

1. What is the difference between problem drinking and alcoholism? Does one necessarily precede and lead to the other?

2. Is there such a condition as being prone to alcohol?

3. Are males and females likely to take different paths in becoming addicted to alcohol?

4. How can we explain the finding that "children of alcoholics are about four times more likely to become alcoholic than are children of nonalcoholics"?

5. What biblical insights can help us understand the relative success of Alcoholics Anonymous and similar programs in assisting people with addictions?

6. Evaluate the statement, "The best prevention for alcoholism is never to take the first drink."

7. What is a healthy Christian attitude toward the drinking of alcoholic beverages?

10

The Use of Illegal Drugs

Evidence and Nature of the Concern

The American reaction to the use of habit-forming drugs has tended to follow a pattern of moving between tolerance and intolerance, between a low level and a high level of concern. We can gain perspective on today's problem by tracing briefly America's attitudes toward drug use over the past one hundred years, especially as seen in legislative acts and the debates leading up to those acts.

Until the latter part of the nineteenth century, there were no restrictions on supplying and using habit-forming drugs. The first restriction came in an 1875 city ordinance in San Francisco, which banned opium dens (Brecher 1986). This restriction was followed by ordinances and laws in other cities and states against the unlimited distribution and use of narcotics.

In 1914, after several years of intense debate about drug legislation, Congress passed the Harrison Narcotic Act, which made unlawful the production and distribution of narcotics and cocaine for other than medicinal purposes. The bill was passed in large measure because of pressure placed upon the United States by the international community. When the Harrison Act did not stop the use of narcotics for nonmedical purposes, the nation entered a period of strong intolerance for drugs. The Eighteenth Amendment to the Constitution went into effect in January 1920, making it illegal to manufacture and sell alcohol. From 1919 to 1921 Congress passed laws increasing the penalties for producing and distributing the drugs restricted by the Harrison Act; state laws called for life imprisonment and even execution for supplying or taking illegal drugs.

During much of the 1920s and into the 1930s the enforcement of the Harrison Act was overshadowed by the attention given to Prohibition. Fear about marihuana, however, began to increase in the 1930s, culminating in the passage of the Marihuana Tax Act of 1937, which placed marihuana under the same restrictions as had been placed on narcotics and cocaine in the Harrison Act. At the same time, a more tolerant approach was evident in the establishment of federal hospitals in Lexington, Kentucky, and Fort Worth, Texas, for the purpose of treating those who were drug dependent.

World War II disrupted the importation of opium, cocaine, and marihuana, so the drug issue was given less attention. However, the fears of Soviet intrigue and a Communist conspiracy during the McCarthy era of the early 1950s brought about a demand for harsh, mandatory minimum sentences for supplying and using illegal drugs. Congress passed bills in 1951 and 1956 which increased the penalties for first-time offenders and permitted capital punishment for those who sold illegal drugs to anyone under eighteen years of age. Toleration of the use of drugs was criticized as softhearted weakness that would eventually destroy American youth.

The 1960s saw a relaxation of punitive attitudes and actions, as marihuana became a popular drug. The synthetic narcotic, methadone, appeared in the mid-1960s as a substitute for heroin. Dispensed in clinics, methadone offered a nonpunitive approach to the treatment of heroin dependence and helped reduce the crime rate, since many heroin addicts no longer had to steal to support their habit.

The Comprehensive Drug Abuse Prevention and Control Act of 1970 represented a move away from reliance on heavy punishment to an emphasis on research, rehabilitation, and education. The law did away with mandatory sentences, and it permitted first-time offenders convicted of possessing a small amount of marihuana to be placed on probation for one year or less. If there was no further evidence of drug abuse during the probation period, the conviction could be expunged. In 1973, many of the federal programs for combating the supply and distribution of illegal drugs were consolidated into the Drug Enforcement Administration (DEA). The following year the National Institute on Drug Abuse (NIDA) was established to combine federal efforts aimed at reducing the demand for drugs. It collects information on the extent of drug abuse and sponsors research into its causes and possible treatments.

The 1980s witnessed a steady decline in American tolerance of drug use. There were harsher punishments for suppliers, distributors, and users of illegal drugs. One evidence of the increased concern is public-opinion polls. Each year the Gallup Poll asks a random sample of

Americans, "What do you think is the most important problem facing this country?" In 1985 drug abuse ranked eighth; in 1986 it was fourth; and in 1987 it was third, just behind economic problems (e.g., unemployment and the budget deficit) and international tensions (Gallup 1988:89). To the question, "What is the biggest problem facing schools in this community?" the use of drugs has been the leading response since 1981. And in 1986 the poll found that 90 percent of Americans believe that schools should require instruction regarding the dangers of drugs, 78 percent hold that students using drugs at school should be expelled, and 69 percent think that schools should provide counseling and treatment for drug abusers (Gallup 1987b:222–23).

Other evidences of concern about the use of illegal drugs include advertisements published in newspapers and magazines and shown on television. For example, in 1988 a newspaper printed a full-page plea for parents to become "pushers" of books, sports, camping, and scouting, for when children become "hooked" on something constructive, they are much less likely to become dependent on drugs. Various groups have been formed to combat drug use in schools; for example, the National Federation of Parents for Drug-Free Youth, which was organized in 1980. The stringent attitude toward the use of drugs was epitomized by Nancy Reagan, who stated, "Each of us has a responsibility to be intolerant of drug use anywhere, anytime, by anybody. . . . We must create an atmosphere of intolerance for drug use in this country" (quoted in Musto 1987:273).

Americans are concerned about drug use because it violates many of the values they hold dear. Foremost among their anxieties is the damage to physical and mental health, including the spread of acquired immune deficiency syndrome (AIDS) by the sharing of needles for intravenous drug use. There are also reductions in freedom, individual worth, competition, and efficiency. At the same time there is an increase in crime: users frequently must rob to support their drug dependence; suppliers have been known to bribe public officials; and distributors have murdered their rivals. The concern about the relationship between drugs and crime has been neatly summarized by Attorney General Richard Thornburgh's declaration that illegal drug use is Public Enemy Number One.

Dimensions and Explanations of the Problem

The drugs with which we shall deal in this chapter are either regulated or forbidden by law. Certain of these drugs may be legally used if prescribed by physicians, but there are strict regulations regarding amounts and renewals. The sale, possession, and use of other drugs are completely proscribed by law, except for cases of scientific research.

Before looking in detail at a few of these drugs, we shall list the major classifications as established by the National Clearinghouse for Alcohol and Drug Information.

Narcotics are drugs containing opium or its derivatives. Included in this classification are morphine, heroin, and codeine, and various synthetics such as dihydromorphinone (Dilaudid), meperidine (Demerol), and methadone. These drugs are used in medicine to relieve pain; they can also produce euphoria. They are addicting in the sense that if used in sufficient quantities long enough, they create physical dependence. Once this dependence develops, the user requires larger and larger doses for the same effect, because a tolerance for the drug has built up. The dependent user will suffer withdrawal pains if the drug is stopped, leading to an intense desire to secure more of the drug to prevent such effects. Persons who use narcotics can also develop a psychological dependence that may be stronger than and persist beyond the physical dependence.

Amphetamines are synthetic stimulants which bring about a state of alertness and activity, and are therefore called "uppers." Included in this group are amphetamine (Benzedrine), dextroamphetamine (Dexedrine), and methamphetamine (Methedrine or "speed"). Medically they are used to relieve mild depression, control appetite, and treat narcolepsy. While it has not been demonstrated that amphetamines create physical dependence, there is evidence of psychological dependence and organic damage.

Barbiturates are also synthetic drugs and include phenobarbital, pentobarbital (Nembutal), and amobarbital (Amytal). Their chief medical use is as sedatives; hence they are called "downers." Users can become highly dependent on barbiturates, in which case severe withdrawal symptoms appear if they are stopped. Continued use carries a potential for both mental dependence and organic damage.

Cocaine, made from coca leaves, is a stimulant that produces increased physical activity, euphoria, and excitation. Ingesting large amounts can result in intoxication and even respiratory or heart failure. Cocaine has been called the epidemic of the 1980s.

Hallucinogens include lysergic acid diethylamide (LSD), dimethyltriptamine (DMT), mescaline (from the peyote plant), and psilocybin (from a Mexican mushroom). These drugs bring about exhilaration and a distortion of the senses, including imaginary visual and aural perceptions. While there is no evidence that these drugs create physical dependence, whether or not they create psychological dependence and organic damage is unclear.

Marihuana comes from the Indian hemp plant (Canabis sativa). It is produced by crushing or chopping the dried leaves and flowers into small pieces. Concentrated resin from the hemp is made into hashish, a more potent form than the crushed leaves and flowers. Marihuana is a relaxant, a euphoriant, and, in high doses, a hallucinogen. It has been used medically to treat glaucoma and the nausea that results from the chemotherapy given to cancer patients; research indicates that it may also be an antitumor agent. Of all the illegal drugs in the United States, marihuana is the most widely used.

It is obvious from our brief survey that illegal drugs cover a broad range of substances which have different effects. Some cause physical dependence; some do not. Some are quite powerful in the effect they have on behavior; others are comparatively mild. Some bring about a feeling of euphoria and relaxation; others produce exhilaration and hallucinations. Therefore, there is limited value in discussing drug abuse in general. Instead of trying to deal with all illegal drugs in a single category, we shall consider marihuana, heroin, and cocaine in detail. We have selected these three because they represent different types of drugs and are very widely used.

Marihuana

The marihuana plant, or Indian hemp, has been cultivated for several thousand years. Long before the psychoactive properties of its leaves and flowers were discovered, the fiber found in the stalk was used to make twine, rope, and matting. The American colonies cultivated the marihuana plant for its fiber content. In the Western Hemisphere its earliest use as an intoxicant was in Central and South America in the nineteenth century; it was not until the early 1920s that it began to be smoked in the United States, this practice having entered the country with Mexican immigrants. Fear of the drug, largely from an exaggeration of its effects, grew until in 1937 the Marihuana Tax Act placed it under strict control. Some of the beliefs about the drug at that time can be seen in this condemnation by H. J. Anslinger, head of the Federal Bureau of Narcotics:

> From time to time, instances are brought to life of acts committed by persons under the influence or addicted to marihuana, which illustrate the viciousness of this drug. In Colorado, a man under the influence of marihuana attempted to shoot his wife but killed his grandmother instead, and then committed suicide. A Florida youth, while under the influence of the drug, murdered five members of his family with an ax. In Baltimore, a twenty-five-year-old Puerto Rican charged with criminally assaulting a ten-year-old girl entered a plea of not guilty on the grounds of temporary insanity caused by smoking marihuana cigarettes. [cited in Bonnie and Whitebread 1974:149]

There was no scientific support for such claims that marihuana use leads to violence; only anecdotal evidence was cited. It was backed up by a widespread belief that those who used marihuana were members of deviant minorities.

Up until the passage of the Comprehensive Drug Abuse Prevention and Control Act of 1970, marihuana was mistakenly treated as a narcotic; accordingly, its use carried exceedingly heavy penalties. In this act it was reclassified as a hallucinogenic substance; possession of and giving away small amounts of marihuana were now treated as misdemeanors rather than felonies (although such acts could bring imprisonment and a fine of up to $1,000). During the 1970s a number of states decriminalized the possession and use of small amounts of the drug, imposing moderate fines under civil law. These changes reflected the view of the Select Committee on Crime of the House of Representatives, which, in its report on marihuana, concluded: "Certainly, savage repressive and punitive laws cannot be defended as a solution to the marijuana problem. It destroys our criminal justice system to have penal statutes that are not uniformly enforced—and perhaps in some instances are unenforceable" (1970:114). Such a conclusion was a reaction against the exaggerated assertions about the dire consequences of smoking marihuana. Subsequent research, however, has shown that heavy use of marihuana, while not leading to violence, can create serious health problems and have a detrimental effect on reaction time.

Effects of marihuana

Controlled studies of the consequences of smoking marihuana are very difficult to design and carry out. While recognizing the problems involved, Miriam Cohen (1985: 59–67) in a summary of the research concludes that continued marihuana use does affect health. In the first place, it is clear that smoking any substance is harmful to the respiratory system. Marihuana smoke is more irritating than tobacco smoke, for it has much more tar and may be contaminated with fungi, bacteria, and the herbicide paraquat or other harmful chemicals. Marihuana also has injurious effects on the cardiovascular and immune systems. It increases the heart rate and often the blood pressure, while at the same time it decreases the amount of oxygen delivered to the heart just when the heart needs more oxygen to function. This situation is particularly serious for those who have hypertension or heart disease. Heavy use of marihuana alters the immune system by interfering with the work of T-lymphocyte cells, which are essential in resisting viruses.

Research has also found that smoking marihuana causes changes in brain chemistry by inhibiting the neurotransmitter acetylcholine, which transfers information from one nerve cell to another. This may explain why marihuana impairs the coordination essential to operating machinery and motor vehicles. Using marihuana has been found to cause mood changes and bring about short periods of memory loss, anxiety, and confusion. While some research has shown detrimental effects on human reproduction, it has not been clearly established that marihuana smoking interferes with fertility or is harmful to the fetus.

Finally, while research does not clearly indicate whether marihuana smoking produces physical dependence, sudden cessation of long term heavy use has unpleasant consequences. Among these are irritability, sweating, abdominal cramps, nausea, tremors, restlessness, and weakness. Research has not established whether the damage to the respiratory, cardiovascular, immune, mental, and motor-coordination systems is permanent. There is little question, however, that the smoking of marihuana over a long period of time involves a risk to health.

Extent of use and characteristics of users

As is true of other illegal drugs, information on the number of marihuana users and their characteristics depends largely upon self-reporting. This fact makes our data open to question, since it is unlikely that all the respondents who have actually used illicit substances will be willing to admit that they have broken the law. Most of our knowledge about the extent of marihuana use comes from two annual surveys conducted by the National Institute on Drug Abuse. One covers a random sample of the entire American population; the other is restricted to high-school seniors and a follow-up of their drug use in subsequent years. While these surveys give us the most valid and reliable data we have, they must nevertheless be used with caution.

The surveys in 1987 showed that more than sixty million Americans, or almost one in three persons twelve years of age and over, had used marihuana at least once. Some twenty million of these, or about one in ten of the teenage and adult population, had used marihuana within the past twelve months. In that same year, 51 percent of the high-school seniors had tried marihuana, 39 percent had used it in the past year, and 23 percent in the last thirty days. At the same time, 91 percent had tried alcohol, and 68 percent had smoked cigarettes at least once. The percentage of high-school seniors using marihuana daily almost doubled from 1975 to 1979, jumping from 6 to 11 percent. Since 1979, however, that figure has steadily dropped, moving below 6 percent by 1987.

Do those individuals who smoke marihuana on a daily basis differ in social characteristics from the rest of the population? Some reports state that daily users are found at all age, income, and educational levels, and include both sexes, making the point that everyone is vulnerable. While this is not disputed, it does not help in building theories of marihuana use. What have proven helpful are studies and interviews of regular marihuana smokers which have brought the following to light: marihuana use is usually preceded by use of alcohol and tobacco, both of which continue to be consumed after marihuana smoking has begun; marihuana use is social in origin and practice; the highest rates of involvement are found among the young, males, and individuals without religious affiliation. While in the 1960s and 1970s there were proportionately more whites than blacks who used marihuana, by 1985 there were proportionately more blacks than whites. Prior to the 1980s the average marihuana user was a highly educated, upper-income professional. By 1987, however, there was no clear distinction by income, occupational, and educational levels. One difference that did continue into 1987 was that regular users of marihuana were more likely to be found in large cities than small towns and rural areas.

A noteworthy study is that of Barry Glassner and his colleagues (1986), who carried out in-depth interviews with a hundred twelve- to twenty-year-olds, including forty daily users of marihuana. They found that users typically come from nonconventional homes, are ambivalent about goals, like to take risks, and smoke marihuana to fit into peer groups.

Finally, there have been no reports of significant differences in physiological or genetic makeup between those who smoke marihuana regularly and those who do not. And no one has as yet tried to make the case that regular smoking of marihuana is a disease.

Explanations of the facts about regular use of marihuana

We shall begin with those facts most adequately handled by sociocultural explanations of the regular use of marihuana. First, one of the most persistent findings is that marihuana smoking is sociogenic, that is, it has a social origin. Also, continued use of the drug appears to hinge upon the approval and support of other marihuana smokers. When asked how they started, the overwhelming majority respond that they were introduced to the drug by close friends on social occasions, and that subsequent use has been in congenial surroundings.

In his pioneering study "Becoming a Marihuana User," Howard Becker (1953) reported that the first-time user rarely feels the effects of the drug without careful coaching from companions on how to inhale and hold the smoke in the lungs and what effects to notice. Thus the user's reaction to the experience as euphoric and relaxing is in part a response to the expectations and encouragement of the group. In a similar study Andrew Weil and his colleagues found that only one of nine first-time marihuana smokers had a definite "marihuana reaction" (1968:1238). The inability to obtain a feeling of euphoria was attributed to the neutral laboratory setting—no friends were present to encourage the smokers and to tell them what to look for.

The sociocultural explanation, then, presupposes a setting in which marihuana use is both approved and encouraged. Such a setting might be said to be a necessary but not a sufficient condition, for some of those in the group, especially those who do not smoke tobacco, might not join in smoking marihuana. If marihuana smoking should become a requirement of membership in the group, it is doubtful that the nonsmokers will remain members.

Where are such groups that approve and encourage the smoking of marihuana most likely to be found? It is logical to assume that they are to be found among the young, many of whom experiment with different kinds of behavior as they seek an identity separate from that of their parents and other adults. The great majority of these young people are already using alcohol and tobacco, substances that are restricted by law to older persons.

Similarly, users are more likely to be found among males than females, for males are expected to be more rebellious and are given less strict supervision. Furthermore, it is logical to believe that marihuana use will more likely be found among the nonreligious, since they tend to be more nonconventional than those affiliated with a religious organization. Finally, groups that use marihuana are most likely to be found in large cities, where there is a ready availability of the drug.

Locating the cause of marihuana use within the individual's own development, psychological explanations point toward nonconventional family backgrounds and the particular kinds of groups the individual happens to fall in with. A number of studies indicate that those who use marihuana feel that it is less harmful than do nonusers. It is difficult to know which came first, the belief that marihuana is not harmful or the use of marihuana.

There is also the matter of chance. In a study of drug use among college students, Richard Blum and his associates (1969) found that different schools have different rates of marihuana use. They also found that dormitories on the same campus vary significantly in the proportion of residents who smoke marihuana. Students who attend colleges and live in dormitories where most of their peers use marihuana are likely to pick up the habit themselves.

While there have been no reports on genetic and physiological differences between users and nonusers of marihuana, such differences cannot be ruled out. It is entirely possible that users can tolerate and enjoy marihuana smoking because of a particular physiological makeup. As with alcohol, certain genetic traits may make some individuals vulnerable to becoming marihuana users once the drug is tried.

Heroin

Heroin or diacetylmorphine was first synthesized from morphine in 1874, but it did not become widely known until 1898, when it was synthesized again by a chemist of the Bayer Company (Zackon 1986:33). Ironically, heroin was initially promoted as a substitute for morphine and even declared to be a "heroic" cure for morphine addiction; hence the name. It was found to be more potent than morphine, and gave quick relief for the distress accompanying withdrawal from morphine dependence. Heroin was used in cough syrups and as a pain reliever and sedative until 1925, when it was banned as a dangerous narcotic. Since then it has had no legitimate medical use, and its preparation, importation, and possession have been subject to heavy penalty.

The experience of Americans with heroin since the mid-1960s illustrates how an illegal drug can become very popular with users and increasingly feared by the general public and the authorities, and then gradually decrease in popularity and fade from the limelight. The use of heroin leveled off and then declined by the 1980s, when greater attention began to be directed toward cocaine abuse, along with a continued concern about marihuana. Although it has moved from the center of attention, heroin remains a serious concern. It is a powerful drug, highly addictive and highly attractive to its users.

Effects of heroin

Heroin can be taken orally, but it has a more immediate effect when it is injected either subcutaneously ("joypopping") or intravenously ("mainlining"). The latter procedure is favored by addicts, for it brings about results more quickly and effectively. The immediate feeling of euphoria ("rush") when heroin is injected directly into a vein can bring about addiction quickly, even after a few doses. With addiction come an increased tolerance for the drug and a need for ever-larger amounts.

Heroin can diminish both physical and mental pain to a considerable degree. By inducing a sleepy, dreamlike state, it relieves tension and anxiety. Sensation and memory are dulled and stimuli have reduced effects. The user is said to be "on the nod," a condition experienced especially by persons who are suffering from physical pain or emotional distress at the time they take the drug. Physiologically, the primary effects of heroin are a diminishing of the heart and respiratory rate, a moderate drop in blood pressure, a contraction of the pupils, and a decrease in brain activity.

The effects of heroin begin to wear off in about four hours. In another twelve to sixteen hours, withdrawal symptoms appear: yawning, sweating, irritability, and a moistening of the eyes and nose. These symptoms become steadily worse, accompanied by a desire to sleep but inability to do so, loss of appetite, and gooseflesh. Thirty-six hours after the last dose, the addict experiences muscle twitching, heavy perspiration, diarrhea, vomiting, and severe cramps in the back, legs, and stomach. These reactions reach greatest intensity in two or three days, and then slowly decrease over the next one to two weeks. Because withdrawal is so painful, addicts will go to any extreme to obtain more heroin or some other narcotic.

There are several dangers in heroin addiction. The most serious of these is overdosage, which can result in death. This is an ever-present danger, for the buyer has no way of knowing how much pure heroin is in the dose purchased. Before reaching the consumer, heroin is diluted ("cut") with such substances as milk sugar, quinine, and baking soda so that the bags sold on the street rarely contain more than a 5 percent concentration of the drug itself. Any package of the drug that contains more than 20 percent heroin is usually too strong (Louria et al. 1970). The user rapidly passes into a deep sleep or coma. Breathing slows to such an extent that the brain is starved for oxygen, and the victim dies. This can happen so quickly that addicts are sometimes found with the needle still in the vein.

Another danger is infection from contaminated needles. The possibilities include tetanus, inflammation of the heart, and hepatitis, an inflammation and disease of the liver. The most recent is contraction of AIDS. Not surprisingly, the death rate among heroin addicts is considerably higher than that of nonaddicts of comparable age.

Extent of use and characteristics of users

The number of persons who have ever used heroin is estimated from national surveys, the number of addicts from police, hospital, and rehabilitation-center records. These estimates vary widely because of the enormous difficulties inherent in self-reporting of illicit activity and projecting from the number of addicts listed in official records the total number of actual addicts.

While acknowledging the difficulty of obtaining accurate figures, we can nonetheless state categorically that there was a rapid increase in the number of heroin users from the mid-1960s to the mid-1970s. By 1971 heroin use had reached what *Newsweek* called a plague and other news media termed an epidemic. According to one report (Hunt and Chambers 1976:111–13) the number of heroin users increased more than 300 percent from 1968 to 1974. The number began to decline, however, in the late 1970s. A report by the Bureau of the Census (1987:112) shows that while 4.5 percent of those between eighteen and twenty-five years of age had used heroin in 1974, there was a decline to 1.1 percent by 1985. The decrease in numbers was from approximately 1,240,000 to 290,000. Despite this decline there was still a sizable number dependent on the drug in the mid-1980s. While he did not give a source for his figures, Fred Zackon estimated that there were more than six hundred thousand heroin addicts in the United States in 1985 (1986:47). No matter which report is accepted, it is clear that heroin dependence continued to be widespread in the 1980s.

Known heroin addicts are not distributed randomly in American society. Rather, they are concentrated in large cities, with New York, Chicago, and Los Angeles being among the major centers. And within these and other large cities, the areas of highest heroin addiction are the slums, that is, the neighborhoods that rank lowest socioeconomically. Among the known addicts, there are far more males than females, at least three times as many. Blacks are represented in numbers three times their proportion of the total population. Addicts on the average are in their twenties, although most narcotic users begin in their late teens. Once one is addicted to heroin, it is extremely difficult to break the habit, and most addicts relapse after leaving treatment centers. The case of Riverside Hospital in New York City is proof of this point. Set up in 1952 to treat drug addicts, it closed after several years of operation because of the high percentage of its patients who returned to heroin.

Explanations of heroin use and addiction

There are at least two necessary conditions for developing heroin addiction—availability of the drug and human associations that teach the techniques of heroin use. Whether there are physiological characteristics that lead to addiction is not known. The usual assumption is that anyone can become addicted regardless of physiological makeup.

It can be argued that heroin addiction is found primarily in large metropolitan areas because these are the places where illicit trade can function most effectively. Another factor is that drugs tend to be available where there is a large demand. At the same time, it must be noted that availability is not a sufficient condition for developing addiction. Only a small fraction of those persons who have direct access to narcotics, namely, physicians, nurses, and pharmacists, become addicted. Furthermore, only about one-fourth of all those who have reported trying heroin are believed to have become addicted.

Most narcotic use begins as a recreational experience within a peer group. Young boys who want to obtain status in a neighborhood or school group will likely start taking drugs if that is the way the group seeks excitement and adventure. Why drug use instead of something else? One answer is the constant exposure to drug use in big-city slums. At the same time it must be emphasized that the individual is not coerced into drug use. Rather, the individual begins in order to be accepted by those whom one considers important, especially one's peers.

Another question is why some individuals become addicted to heroin and others do not. Joseph Brenner and his colleagues assert that the key factor is the "psychological readiness" of the user:

> For those who live lives of intolerable pain and indignity, for those who see death as a blessed relief, the choice of heroin as an escape is one of the few choices left; and clearly many will make that choice in full knowledge of the dangers, in the conviction that life offers them nothing better. . . .
>
> We would do well to remember that the combination of ghetto, heroin, and hopelessness is a particularly lethal one. [1970:81–82, 85–86]

The point is that young people who are psychologically susceptible because of their desperate situation are very likely to be attracted to heroin-using peers, find heroin use rewarding, and become addicted.

A study by Daniel Glaser and his colleagues (1971) throws further light on the question. They compared thirty-seven pairs of addicted and nonaddicted siblings residing in a slum area of New York City. Through extensive interviews the researchers found that treatment in the home had been essentially similar for the addict and the nonaddict. However, the addict had entered into illegitimate activity on the street at an early age, and was much more likely to have been arrested than his nonaddicted sibling. The addicted sibling also left school at an earlier age, largely because his gang and drug habits were incompatible with the world of education. The crucial difference between the user of heroin and the nonuser appears to be that by participating in illegal behavior and being arrested, the addict built barriers against moving into legitimate activities. He was then thrown more and more into the intimate circle of his heroin-using peers. Rejected by all those who conformed to social norms, the addict was likely to seek support from his nonconforming peers. This explanation is supported by the principle that we adopt behaviors and seek associations that we find personally rewarding. Glaser and his associates noted that when addicts congregate, there is an excitement as they exchange tales of how they stole to support their drug habit and how they reacted to various drugs. Amid such companionship the addict experiences a feeling of acceptance and accomplishment not possible in the legitimate world. Alternating with the excitement are drug-induced periods of euphoria during which the worries and pressures of daily life are eased.

Cocaine

The illegal drug that increased most rapidly in use and attracted the most concern in the 1980s was cocaine. This drug has been known and used for thousands of years, particularly in the Andean mountains of South America. Cocaine comes from the coca plant, which grows in abundance in the warm valleys on the eastern slopes of the Andes, and a large part of the population of Peru and Bolivia chew coca leaves today to combat hunger and fatigue (Grinspoon and Bakalar 1976:9–13). In addition to being ingested by chewing, cocaine can be sniffed, smoked, and injected into the veins.

Cocaine use first became popular in the United States in the 1880s when it could be purchased in drugstores as an inhalant and for cigarettes and cigars. Cocaine was promoted by physicians as an anesthetic, as a treatment for digestive disorders and asthma, and as a means of relief during morphine withdrawal. Coca-Cola, which contained cocaine when first manufactured (long since replaced by caffeine), was known as the intellectual beverage. Cocaine was endorsed as an elixir by such well-known people of the time as Pope Leo XIII, the Prince of Wales, Alexandre Dumas, Jules Verne, Emile Zola, and Thomas Edison (Grinspoon and Bakalar 1976:26). A manufacturer of cocaine told the medical profession, "Cocaine can supply the place of food, make the coward brave, the silent eloquent, free the victims of alcohol and opium habits from their bondage, and, as an anesthetic, render the sufferer insensitive to pain" (quoted in Musto 1986). Such praise of cocaine and its unrestricted availability led to what David Musto has termed "the first cocaine epidemic," which lasted from the mid-1880s to the 1920s, a period of about thirty-five years. Cocaine fell into disfavor when its harmful effects became widely noted and Americans began to put a greater emphasis on health.

Several researchers believe that cocaine reappeared as a popular drug in the late 1960s and early 1970s because of an all-out effort to curb illicit amphetamine manufacture and importation. According to Edward Brecher (1986:13), "By 1969 the street price of amphetamines had been driven so high that, for the first time in thirty years, it became profitable once more to deal in cocaine." Cocaine was a logical substitute for amphetamines, since both are stimulants.

There are various estimates as to how much cocaine is being smuggled into the United States. Federal agencies reported that as much as nine hundred kilograms, or enough for eighteen million doses, entered in 1969, and that by 1984 the figure had risen to seventy-five thousand kilograms. With the discovery at that time of a less expensive way to produce a form of cocaine called "crack" or "rock," the drug has become more affordable and more widely used.

Concern about the dangers of cocaine use in America reached new levels in 1986 with the highly publicized deaths of two prominent athletes. One was Len Bias, a basketball star at the University of Maryland who, having been drafted by a professional team, celebrated with friends by taking cocaine and died of cardiac arrest shortly thereafter. Americans realized that cocaine could strike down young adults in their prime. As a result, new and intensive campaigns against cocaine were undertaken.

The effects of cocaine

The strength and speed of the effects of taking cocaine depend in large measure on the form in which the drug is taken (Johanson 1986:22–27). Chewing the leaves, as has been done by Peruvian Indians for centuries, releases a relatively low amount of the drug, even when the leaves are stored in the cheeks so that cocaine is ingested over several hours. Cocaine hydrochloride (street cocaine) is produced when coca leaves are placed in a press along with sulfuric acid, kerosene, or gasoline, and crushed to form a mash, which is then treated with hydrochloric acid. In this form cocaine can be inhaled or "snorted," causing in five minutes a mild euphoria and high level of energy which peak in ten to twenty minutes and gradually subside within sixty minutes. Cocaine hydrochloride can also be taken intravenously, providing a much more rapid absorption of the drug, so that the user feels a strong "rush" within a minute or two. This exhilaration and energy subside within half an hour, when the user might feel a compelling urge to take another intravenous dose.

The most rapid way to bring about a sense of euphoria, exhilaration, and increased energy is by smoking the drug. In order to be smoked, cocaine hydrochloride must be treated with baking soda and converted to cocaine sulfate. One can then use a fast-acting solvent like ether; this process is called "freebasing." Or one can apply heat without relying on inflammable chemicals; "crack" is produced in this way. Smoking cocaine brings an intense "high" almost immediately and is therefore replacing the intranasal and intravenous methods of ingesting the drug. The National Institute on Drug Abuse points out that those forms of a drug which produce an immediate intense effect eventually replace those whose effects are slower and less intense. This is borne out by the increased popularity of "crack."

Cocaine acts upon the central nervous system to produce a euphoric excitement that comes very quickly when the drug is injected or smoked. Users state that they have feelings of well-being which they describe as "soaring." These feelings are accompanied by expansive good humor, talkativeness, and a conviction that one's mental and physical powers have increased. These effects are short-lived, but they are implanted in the mind in such a way that the user wants to repeat them by taking more cocaine, without which there are depression, irritability, restlessness, and apprehension. Eventually a form of cocaine psychosis resembling paranoic schizophrenia can develop. With continued heavy doses paralysis of the muscles, retardation of the reflexes, and damage to vital functions can occur.

Another effect of cocaine is the constriction of blood vessels, causing an increase in heart rate and blood pressure. More of the drug can produce a rapid, irregular heartbeat, and eventually cardiac arrest and death. Cocaine also increases the respiratory rate; heavy doses may lead to rapid and irregular breathing, a gasping for air, or even complete respiratory failure. Finally, the drug increases the activity of the areas of the brain associated with mood, emotion, and feelings of pleasure. Such effects are like those produced by direct electrical stimulation of the brain.

Whether an increased tolerance for and physical dependence on cocaine develop with continued use has not been clearly established (Johanson 1986: 43–44). There is no question, however, that the chronic user will continue to take more of the drug to reproduce the euphoria experienced from earlier doses and to overcome the severe depression that occurs when the elation subsides. As we have seen, continued large doses of cocaine can have lethal effects.

Extent of use and characteristics of users

On the basis of interviews in 1985 with 3,038 randomly selected individuals who were assured confidentiality and anonymity, the National Institute on Drug Abuse (1987a: 14–15) estimated that more than twenty-two million Americans over the age of twelve, 11.7 percent of the population, had tried cocaine at least once. Twelve million, or 6.3 percent of the population, had used cocaine within the past year; and 5.5 million, or 2.9 percent, had used it during the past month. The largest proportion of persons who had ever tried the drug—25 percent—was found among those between eighteen and thirty-four years of age. Twice as many males as females had used the drug at least once, in the past year, and in the past month. While proportionately more whites than blacks had tried the drug at least once, a higher proportion of blacks had used it during the past year and during the past month. Higher figures were found in the West than in any other region of the United States.

At the beginning of the current epidemic, most cocaine users were high-income professionals. It was an expensive drug for which only the privileged could readily pay. With the increased supply, and especially with the introduction of "crack," more people in the lower socio-economic categories began to use cocaine, so that at the present time there is no clear-cut difference in the economic status of users and nonusers. Nor are there are significant racial or ethnic differences.

The annual studies of high-school seniors funded by NIDA and carried out by the Institute for Social Research at the University of Michigan report that there was an increase in the use of cocaine from 1975 (the first year of the survey) until 1981, at which time the figures began to level off: 16 percent had used the drug at least once, 11 to 13 percent had used it in the last year, and 5 to 6 percent had used it in the past month. In 1987 there was the first clear-cut decline in the percentage of high-school seniors who had ever used cocaine; 15 percent reported they had used the drug at least once. The percentage using "crack," however, had increased. With this relatively inexpensive and widely available form of the drug, it is possible that the use of cocaine will increase once again.

Explanations of the use of cocaine

Cocaine use, like that of marihuana and heroin, must be learned from others, most often from social peers. High-school seniors who use drugs are far more likely than nonusers to have friends who use cocaine or other illegal substances. Young people tend to form small, close-knit groups called "peer clusters." The members not only use the same drugs, but also indulge to about the same extent. Furthermore, it is when the group is together that the individuals are most likely to take drugs. Indications are that they join not for the sake of the drugs, but the general congeniality. One way of maintaining that congeniality is to use whatever drug the group is using. Boys, given greater freedom in our society than are girls, are more likely to be a part of a peer cluster that experiments with drugs.

Another factor is that the attitudes of users and nonusers toward cocaine differ. Those who use the substance are less likely than those who do not to believe that the drug can cause serious damage. There have been no definitive studies, however, to indicate whether this belief came before or after using the drug. Nor has there been any evidence that those who use cocaine differ physiologically from those who do not use it. The current implication, as is the case with heroin, is that anyone can develop an addiction for cocaine.

We need to note at this point that the great majority of those people who report having tried the drug did not continue to use it. While in 1985 more than twenty-two million reported having tried the drug, fewer than six million used it on a regular basis. Why one in four people who experiment with cocaine continue to use it on a regular basis can be accounted for in various ways: their peer cluster requires it; it meets their psychological needs; or it complements their physiological makeup and provides a special sense of exhilaration and well-being. Further research is required to find out the extent to which any or all of these factors may be involved.

Prevention and Treatment

Although marihuana, heroin, and cocaine are quite different in their effects, in their addictive power, and in the number of persons they hold victim, American society generally looks upon them as a single issue when it comes to prevention and treatment. For this reason our discussion in this section will focus not on individual substances, but on illicit drugs in general. We will see that there are two basic approaches to prevention. One is to fight against the supply of drugs, and the other is to decrease the demand for them.

Prevention

Reduction of supply

The greatest effort by the United States government in its war on drugs has been to enforce the law against suppliers and dealers. During the 1980s the funds for law enforcement tripled and arrests increased each year. In 1987, of the nearly four billion dollars spent on the federal drug program, three billion were applied to law enforcement, with the remaining amount used to reduce the demand and to treat addicts (Struck 1988).

Federal officials estimate that as much as 90 percent of the illegal drugs used in the United States is smuggled in from other countries. To stem this flow, two types of interdiction have been attempted. One is to patrol the borders of the United States to prevent illicit drugs from entering, and the other is to halt their production in foreign countries.

How successful have these efforts been? In 1984, American agents in cooperation with the Colombian police confiscated in a single raid ten metric tons of cocaine from a jungle factory. The Drug Enforcement Administration hoped that the size of the seizure would substantially reduce the supply and raise the price of cocaine. But neither happened. Despite this and other successful raids, the interception of drugs at points of entry, and an increasing number of arrests of suppliers and distributors, illegal drugs are as available as ever and street prices have gone down. For example, in 1985 a kilogram of cocaine sold in Miami for $34,000; it cost half that amount in 1988, according to the Drug Enforcement Administration. In that same year the secretary of health and human services was reported to have told the president that we are not winning the war against drugs; and the mayor of Baltimore, Kurt L. Schmoke, called for a national conference to discuss what can be done about the drug situation, for "the things we have been doing over the past 25 years have not worked" (Struck 1988).

A major obstacle to controlling the supply has been the enormity of the profit made from the importation and sale of illegal drugs. The amount of money is so great that some officials can be bribed to cooperate. In Latin American countries desperately in need of the money that can be made from producing and selling drugs, members of drug cartels have testified that they would arrange to have some illegal drugs seized by their government to show that the country was serious about trying to keep drugs out of the United States. At the same time, the exporting countries have expressed resentment that they are blamed for the production and shipment of drugs, when it is the insatiable demand by Americans that creates the problem in the first place.

Another move to reduce the supply of illegal drugs has been to impose harsher sentences on drug traffickers. A bill presented to the House of Representatives in 1988 proposed the death penalty for drug dealers convicted of murder, denial of student loans and other federal benefits to convicted drug users, and judicial admissibility of improperly seized evidence, provided the police had acted "in good faith." Such proposals indicated the strong antidrug feelings of Congress and the nation. The effectiveness of harsh punishment is questionable, however, for only a comparative few are actually arrested for drug trafficking. In view of the enormous profits to be made, most suppliers are more than willing to take the risks.

Perplexed as to what can and should be done about the situation, a small minority of Americans are calling not for eradication, but for the legalization of illicit drugs. The drug that has been most intensely debated is marihuana. The National Organization for the Reform of Marijuana Laws (NORML) advocates decriminalization of the production, distribution, and use of marihuana. At the same time, NORML proposes that marihuana be strictly regulated, in much the same way alcohol is.

One of the main arguments for the legalization of marihuana and other drugs is that the enormous profits now being made would be drastically reduced. It would no longer be profitable for producers, smugglers, and distributors to stay in business. The billions of dollars now spent to enforce the laws could be greatly reduced, and officers would be freed to deal more effectively with crimes of violence, theft, embezzlement, and the like. The advocates of legalization point out that in 1987 there were more than twice as many arrests for marihuana offenses as for rape, robbery, and murder combined. Legalization would help ease the overburdening of the criminal-justice system. Furthermore, drug users would no longer be considered criminals, but would be treated for an illness, in much the same way as those who develop health problems from smoking tobacco or drinking alcohol.

Those who oppose legalization say that it would increase the supply of drugs and the number of users. The sanctity of law would no longer deter suppliers and users. Although the attempt to rid America of illegal drugs is expensive, legalizing them would cost even more. The opponents of legalization point out that approximately 150,000 deaths a year can be attributed to alcohol and 350,000 deaths to tobacco. With legalization it is logical to expect that deaths from cocaine, heroin, barbiturates, and amphetamines would be far greater than they are now. Some opponents claim that legalization would be a surrender to and tacit approval of drugs. The proponents of legalization deny both of these claims, and say further that it is not a foregone conclusion that legalization would increase the supply of and demand for drugs.

The assumptions of what would happen under legalization are very difficult to support or refute by research. In any event, the present mood of Congress and the public is such that it is highly unlikely that any steps will be taken toward legalization. Indeed, there is a strong move toward enacting laws that provide for more stringent control and more severe punishment of those involved in supplying, distributing, and using illegal drugs.

Reduction of demand

There is widespread agreement that the demand for drugs can be decreased by education, but there is little consensus on what type of education is most effective. A recent NIDA publication (1987b:33–57) summarizes the traditional approaches, the most basic of which is for teachers, physicians, police, and ex-addicts to present factual information about the dangers of using drugs. Related to this approach is the more recent admonition to "Just say no to drugs." The assumption is that if young people are made aware of the dangers of drugs, they will make rational decisions not to use them. Another traditional program involves helping youth to achieve self-esteem, learn how to make decisions in a responsible way, and participate in activities that will keep them away from drug use. While such approaches have increased awareness of the dangers of drugs and changed some attitudes, they have not been found to be particularly effective in preventing or decreasing drug use.

New approaches have concentrated on teaching students to become aware of and to deal with the social influences that lead to the use of drugs. We saw earlier in this chapter that peer influence is of critical importance in promoting drug use. So young people are being made aware of the social pressures to use drugs, are taught specific skills to enable them to resist these pressures, and are being shown the incorrectness of the belief that everybody uses drugs. Supplementing this approach is training that increases personal and social competence and makes it clear that drug use poses risks to valued relationships. The result is a reduction in the motivation to use drugs.

Testing to see if people are using illegal drugs is another way of trying to reduce the demand. The assumption here is that people who are subject to testing, even if only on a random basis, will not use drugs for fear of losing their jobs, of having job applications rejected, or of being dismissed from an athletic team. This approach has not been adequately tried, in part because it is so new and its legality has not been settled. A major objection to mandatory testing is that it may be in violation of the Fourth Amendment to the Constitution, which guarantees freedom from unreasonable search and seizure. There is also the concern that test results are not always reliable and that innocent nonusers could be unjustly charged. The chief argument in favor of testing is that it can protect organizations from the risks that drug users pose.

In March 1988, the United States Department of Justice adopted a policy of "zero tolerance" in order to reduce the demand for drugs. Under this policy an individual caught with a very small amount of illegal drugs is treated in the same way as are dealers who distribute large quantities. The individual is arrested, and the boat, plane, car, or motorcycle where the drug was found is confiscated. The philosophy embodied in this approach is clear—America should eliminate the demand for illegal drugs and thus become a drug-free society. But while government officials claim that the policy is too new to determine its effectiveness, a survey of chief prosecutors indicates that it is having little if any effect on drug traffic (McBride 1988).

Treatment

To be successfully treated, the person who has become dependent on drugs must acknowledge that a problem exists and that help is needed.

Even then, however, drug dependency is very difficult to overcome, and those who provide treatment warn that there is no quick, easy, or final cure. In fact, they do not speak of cures at all, but use terms like "reduced dependency on drugs" and "remission." A complicating factor is that most of those who are addicted use more than one drug, quite often alcohol, and thus make diagnosis and treatment very difficult.

Medical procedures

The first step in treatment is detoxication or withdrawal from the drug, a process that can be made less painful by various types of medication. Clonidine, which reduces hypertension, has recently proved to be effective in heroin withdrawal. Not itself a narcotic, it can ameliorate withdrawal symptoms. For persons dependent on cocaine, withdrawal is very difficult because of the tremendous craving for the drug and the severe depression that follows. The antidepressant medication desipramine has been reported to decrease both the craving for cocaine and the depression. Also, lithium has been found to work for some cocaine-dependent persons. The fundamental approach to marihuana users is to persuade them not to smoke for two or three months so that they can see the connection between marihuana and their apathy, confusion, and loss of energy.

After detoxication medical steps are also employed to keep the patient from relapsing and returning to the drug. Opiate antagonists like naltrexone, which is not an opiate itself and not addicting, occupy opiate receptors and thereby prevent heroin from exerting any effect. After withdrawing from heroin, the patient is given naltrexone two or three times a week to provide protection against taking heroin impulsively and becoming readdicted. There is no unpleasant reaction to naltrexone, as there is for recovering alcoholics who take emetine or disulfiram. Rather, the feeling of euphoria that heroin induces is blocked. A problem is that naltrexone has appeal only to patients who are highly motivated to give up heroin-induced euphoria, and it is not especially effective for those who are less motivated.

For those patients who are not sufficiently motivated to stop taking heroin or who relapse shortly after detoxication, methadone can be used. Methadone is a synthetic narcotic which blocks the effects of heroin. A number of clinics give oral doses on a regular basis to patients who are willing to have a periodic urinalysis to make sure they are staying away from other drugs. It is reported that 65 to 85 percent of the heroin addicts who start the methadone program continue for twelve months or more; many of them are able to turn from crime to gainful employment (NIDA 1987b:70–71). Methadone programs are controversial, however, because they are not compatible with the goal of a drug-free society. Opponents say that such programs merely substitute one narcotic for another; they give the illusion of a solution, but do not get at the underlying causes of addiction. Those who support methadone respond that it enables former heroin addicts to turn away from crime, to hold legitimate jobs, to be helped by doctors and social workers, and to avoid the dangers of contaminated needles and overdose.

Pharmacologists are hard at work trying to develop a cocaine antagonist, but have not yet succeeded. Beta blockers can combat some of cocaine's effects, namely hypertension and arrhythmia. Tranquilizers like diazepam are used to treat cocaine-induced seizures and acute anxiety, and lithium carbonate has been found to help reduce the craving for the drug.

Contingency contracts

Another means of treatment consists of what might be called contingency contracts, explicit agreements drawn up between patient and therapist. For example, the patient might sign a letter that would jeopardize his job. This letter is entrusted to the therapist, who will mail it to the patient's employer if there is a relapse. Such contracts obviously work only in the case of patients who have jobs to lose. Studies have found that 90 percent of cocaine addicts who enter into such a contract abstain from the drug for the duration of the contract (NIDA 1987b:157–58).

Psychotherapy

Still another treatment is psychotherapy, which helps patients to gain insight into their drug problem and to deal with it directly and realistically. The assumption is that facing one's drug dependence honestly with professionals who understand the problem and offer help can enable the patient to manage without drugs. And indeed, experiments have shown that addicts who receive psychotherapy are far more likely to stay away from drugs than are those who do not receive therapy (NIDA 1987b:71–72).

Group therapy

We have seen that social influence plays a crucial role in starting and continuing drug use. Group therapy relies on the same principle to help patients become free of drug use. Skilled therapists lead discussions in which patients are encouraged to share their feelings freely and openly. The exchanges can be confrontational: patients may challenge one another to be honest about their drug-dependent behavior. Such sessions provide insight and excitement, and release emotions that used to be submerged by taking drugs.

Therapy sessions carried out with the family of the patient are aimed at reestablishing trust and communication. Family members come to understand and appreciate the powerful attraction of drugs and the difficulty of giving them up, and patients gain a new realization of how much they have hurt and burdened their families. The restoration of family ties can be an effective therapy in itself.

Drug-free communities like Phoenix House in New York City can be viewed as a form of group therapy. While these communities vary, they do have similarities. For example, addicts who enter do so voluntarily and may leave when they wish. As a rule, they are not slowly detoxified, but must withdraw completely and immediately, their only support being the companionship of former addicts who stay with them, encourage them, and let them know that others have suffered similar withdrawal pains and were able to survive. All members of the community are given job assignments. Several times a week they meet in small groups for a free and open exchange of feelings about themselves and others. These therapeutic communities provide close human associations and mutual encouragement to keep away from drugs. One study of seven such communities found that only 4 to 12 percent of the residents stay for as long as twelve months, but those who do remain fare better than do those who leave (NIDA 1987b:71).

Finally, there are self-help groups like Narcotics Anonymous and Cocaine Anonymous, modeled after Alcoholics Anonymous. Regular meetings are held in which members tell of their struggles to stop taking drugs. Long-term members are assigned to help new members maintain abstinence. Because of the constant danger of relapse, continued association with and the help of other former addicts can be of vital importance after treatment in medical facilities and residence in therapeutic communities.

A Christian Response to Drug Abuse*

Drugs as God's Gift

Given the tremendous destructive power of drug use, it might seem out of place for us to suggest that drugs are a gift from God. And yet this is certainly the case, for God has said, "I give you every seed-bearing plant on the face of the whole earth and every tree that has fruit with seed in it. They will be yours for food" (Gen. 1:29 NIV). In giving plants for food, God expects us to care for and use them responsibly. Virtually every society on the face of the earth uses drugs derived from plants as part of the physical healing process. This is certainly a responsible use of plants. Since modern medicine depends so heavily upon drugs, we need to begin by thanking God for the gift of drugs. Unfortunately, what can be used for good can also be abused. Philip Walter (1982:5) states, "As with all of God's creation, chemicals are neither good nor bad; but the way they are used determines their potential benefits or risks." Christian discernment is needed if we are to use drugs wisely.

---

*Since the ethical questions pertaining to drug use are similar to those pertaining to alcohol use, the material within the last section of chapter 9 is equally relevant here.

The Wise Use of Drugs

In judging the morality of drug use, society asks whether a particular drug is legal or illegal. From a Christian perspective, however, the matter of legality versus illegality is of less consequence than are the *motive for* and *effect of* drug taking. There is perhaps more legal than illegal drug abuse in our drug-oriented society in which many people use over-the-counter or legally prescribed drugs to either feed a dependence or keep from facing a problem. One cannot tune in the evening news without being bombarded by a host of commercials promoting drugs to relieve every imaginable irritation—from headaches, hangovers, and inability to sleep, to upset stomachs and hemorrhoids. In many cases these irritations are in reality merely symptoms, messages from our body telling us that it is being misused. While taking a pill may relieve the symptom, what is often needed is a change in lifestyle. From a Christian perspective, an indiscriminate use of pills to relieve such symptoms is drug abuse.

The apostle Paul gives us some assistance in formulating a Christian perspective on legitimate drug use. In 1 Corinthians 6:12 he states: "'Everything is permissible for me'—but not everything is beneficial.

'Everything is permissible for me'—but I will not be mastered by any-thing." At the same time that Paul is arguing for a freedom from legal-ism, he declares that he will refrain from certain activities because of the ultimate effect of excess. Following this Pauline principle, we should make sure that proper use of drugs does not lead to dependence upon them.

Drug Addiction and Sin

The term *addiction* has become commonplace in modern society. We now have professional groups dealing with drug addiction, alcohol addiction, nicotine addiction, food addiction, gambling addiction, sex addiction, and even pleasure addiction (Hart 1988). With the concept of addiction becoming so common, it is necessary to examine whether it may have begun to erode, or even replace, the concept of sin. Christians are understandably suspicious of the free use of the term *addiction*, for it seems to fly in the face of the biblical emphasis upon individual choice and personal accountability. Is it not a legitimate fear that the label of addiction might lead to the belief that one is not responsible for one's condition?

How are we to think Christianly about addiction? A beginning point might be Romans 1:24–28, where the phrase "God gave them over to . . ." is used three times. It is used in verse 24, where we read that "God gave them over in the sinful desires of their hearts to sexual impurity for the degrading of their bodies with one another" (NIV). In verse 26 we read that "God gave them over to shameful lusts." Verse 28 states that God "gave them over to a depraved mind, to do what ought not to be done." It is significant that verse 24 begins with the word *therefore*. This is a ref-erence back to verses 18–23, where we are told that "men . . . suppress the truth by their wickedness" and that they "are without excuse. For although they knew God, they neither glorified him as God nor gave thanks to him." They also "exchanged the glory of the immortal God for images made to look like mortal man and birds and animals and rep-tiles" (NIV). Quite clearly, God "gave them over to" their shameful behav-ior only after they had volitionally rejected and sinned against him. Richard Mouw sees the essence of addiction here: "We rebel against God and suppress the truth in unrighteousness"; then, and only then, are we "'given over' to where it's not enough to 'just say no'" (1988:44). Thus we must recognize that drug addiction in almost all cases begins with a wil-ful act on the part of the individual. Only after the volitional act does the person, both physically and psychologically, come to the point where the taking of drugs can be thought of as addictive or beyond one's control.

This whole issue is complicated by the fact that some addictions do not stem from a wilful act of the addict. This is most obvious in the tragic cases in which a baby is born addicted to heroin. Even here, however, the addiction has its beginning in a volitional act—the mother chose to take heroin. But the fact remains, the infant is a drug addict through no choice of its own. Similar addictions occur when patients who are given drugs for medical purposes recover from their illness, but continue to be dependent upon the effects of those drugs. Does the blame for such addictions lie with the doctors who prescribed the drugs, or with the patients themselves?

In both of these examples the drug addict cannot be held accountable for having become addicted. We must offer sympathetic understanding and full support to the nonvolitional addict. But while these individuals cannot be held responsible for having become addicted, honoring their full humanity will mean that we do hold them responsible for seeking to overcome their drug dependency. This means they must be willing to be empowered—to be released from and gain the victory over the bondage imposed by their dependency. It also means the Christian community must be willing to provide the support and empowering which the addict needs, and must make sure that no stigma attaches to the addict's condition.

The Radical Christian Response:
Restoring Koinōnia, Shalom, and Meaning

A radical Christian response to drug abuse must go beyond concern for the individual drug abuser, important as this is, and address the social conditions which contribute to the problem. The United States government's war on drugs has placed its greatest efforts on enforcing the law against suppliers and dealers. Such concentrated efforts ignore the root of the problem. That many Americans, both rich and poor, take illegal drugs should suggest that there must be something radically wrong with our society.

We earlier suggested that prevention of drug abuse can take the form of reducing the supply or reducing the demand. Our discussion of how to reduce the demand for drugs conspicuously lacked any mention of programs that are aimed at correcting some of the social problems which contribute to drug abuse. Most notably, racial discrimination, alienation, family instability, and poverty are known to create a climate within which drug abuse is common. A holistic Christian response to drug abuse must include an attack on these social problems, all of which result from a lack of either *koinōnia* or *shalom*. A holistic response will include attempts to restore *koinōnia* by restructuring community life so that alienation will be eliminated and family life will be strengthened. A holistic response will also include attempts to restore *shalom* by changing the social structures which perpetuate discrimination and poverty.

Finally, a radical Christian response to drug abuse will recognize that Blaise Pascal was right when he said that there exists within the heart of human beings a vacuum which only God can fill. Drug taking for the purpose of expanding one's mind or escaping reality can be seen as an attempt to fill this existential void. We Christians need to point out the futility of drug use as a means for finding purpose in life. And while we must be cautious about using terms from the drug culture to describe the Christian life, we would do well to reiterate the message of the Jesus People movement that Jesus is the only "trip" that can offer a continual "high."

Topics for Review, Reflection, and Discussion

1. Why is it that some drugs are addictive and others are not?

2. Which of the methods of dealing with the drug problem—interdiction, harsher punishments, legalization, education, testing for the presence of drugs, or a policy of zero tolerance—is most realistic?

3. Do you favor legalization of the use of marihuana? Why or why not? What would be the likely effect on society if marihuana were legalized?

4. Critique the campaign that advises young people to "Just say no to drugs."

5. To what extent are commercials and advertisements responsible for the current drug problem?

6. Is there any relationship between drug use and the economic circumstances of a country?

7. Is the use of the term *drug addiction* rather than *sin* consistent with the biblical emphasis on individual freedom and personal accountability?

11

Environmental Quality

Nature of the Concern

As a nation we discovered our environmental problems in a dramatic way in the 1960s. Although conservation efforts and concerns about pollution and sanitation had become a part of the public consciousness much earlier, in the 1960s these efforts and concerns became much more tightly woven into our social fabric. In 1962 Rachel Carson's curiously titled *Silent Spring* documented the vast destructive effect our booming industrial economy was having upon the environment. She argued that the problem lay not just with urbanization and industry, but also with the agricultural use of pesticides which gradually kill off wildlife. Spraying a field with dichlorodiphenyltrichloroethane (DDT) to get rid of crop-damaging insects is only the beginning of a deadly chain. For the insect is eaten by the rodent, and the rodent is eaten by the bird. While virtually all the foods ingested by a predatory animal will then undergo some sort of metabolic change, the DDT remains intact. Thus the springs have become silent, Carson explains, because the birds which once sang there have been killed off inadvertently by pesticides.

The warning of the silent springs does not stop there, however. Humans are part of the food chain, too. The insects killed by DDT are swept into the river, where they are eaten by small fish, which are eaten by larger fish, which are eaten by still larger fish, which are then eaten by human beings. Not only that, but vegetable and fruit crops are also contaminated.

Another reason for concern is the ability of insects to develop immunity to pesticides. Some scientists fear that the use of pesticides is gradually causing species of insects to evolve which will be able to resist any attempt at controlling their numbers. As a result, some biologists argue for natural means of pest control, such as the introduction of infertile insects into pest populations.

Although everyone wants a quality environment, some people do not see environmental quality as a serious problem. Any environmental problems that do exist, they argue, are short-term conditions that every society temporarily encounters on the way to full industrialization. They believe that most of the fear and concern over environmental issues is generated by radicals and socialists who want to replace the free-market economy with a system in which all of the land and resources are owned by the state. This view that ecology is not a major problem was most noticeably exemplified in the early 1980s by Secretary of the Interior James Watt, who sought to release government-owned land for the purpose of private development. The idea was that ecological problems will be taken care of not by directly protecting the environment, but by allowing the capitalist economy to work itself out. The evidence seems to suggest, however, that environmental problems are greatest where economic development has grown fastest. We would seek to temper both the undue optimism that thinks the environmental problem will take care of itself and the undue pessimism that thinks any efforts to confront the environmental crisis will be too little, too late.

Dimensions of the Problem

There are a number of aspects to the problem of environmental quality. All of them are either directly or indirectly related to the present and potential size of the world's population. If there were only one million people in the world, they would have a hard time causing noticeable damage to the environment. But with an estimated population of six billion, and still growing, the sheer volume of natural resources consumed and waste discarded is nearly incomprehensible. As might be expected, the most serious environmental problems are associated with the most densely populated areas of the world. However, density of population is not the only contributor to environmental problems—technological development is also a major factor. Indeed, environmental problems in densely populated but technologically undeveloped cities in China are relatively small when compared to the problems of densely populated, technologically developed cities in Western countries. Although we shall describe many different dimensions of the environmental problem, it should be kept in mind that in actuality they are inherently interrelated and incredibly complex. Thus solutions in one area often lead to problems in another area.

Water Pollution

While Love Canal (Niagara Falls, N.Y.) and similar toxic-waste sites dominate the headlines, the main sources of water pollution are household and common industrial waste together with the fertilizers and pesticides used in farming. Water pollution is especially acute in rivers that flow through large cities. This was dramatized in 1969 when the Cuyahoga River in Cleveland caught fire as a result of its high chemical content. The pollutants that are dumped into rivers eventually make their way into lakes and oceans. The Public Health Service has declared that the fish caught in Lake Erie and New York Bay are unsafe for human consumption. There are also times when the beaches of major seaside cities are declared unsafe for swimming. Recently in Los Angeles a recommendation was made to close all beaches after rainstorms, since the runoff carries so much chemical waste.

Less frequent but still potentially dangerous are the accidental spills from oil wells being drilled in coastal waters and from oil-carrying tankers. In 1969 the beaches of Santa Barbara were coated with oil from an uncapped well a few miles out. And in 1989 a tanker accident off the coast of Alaska caused environmental havoc. The natural ecology of existing seasides is put in danger by such mishaps.

Air Pollution

Air pollution has been linked to lung cancer and various respiratory problems. The major source of air pollution is carbon monoxide, produced by the incomplete combustion of carbon. Automobiles are responsible for fully half of the air pollutants in a typical American city, while industry and domestic heating account for three-quarters of the rest. The pollution generated in Los Angeles often causes unhealthy conditions as far as eighty miles away, and it can even hinder visibility at the Grand Canyon, some four hundred miles away. Pollutants in the air eventually settle on grass, bushes, and trees, where they may remain until they re-enter the atmosphere in the smoke produced by a brush or forest fire.

When air is polluted with sulfur dioxide and nitrogen oxide from industrial plants, there is the danger of acid rain. Acid rain has been cited as the cause of extensive damage to plants and animal life in southeastern Canada and the northeastern United States. Mishaps at nuclear-energy plants are another potential source of acid rain. After the disaster at Chernobyl in 1986 acid rain was found at dangerously high levels in the Scandinavian countries and in measurable quantities throughout the rest of the world. After eating radioactive moss and lichen, reindeer herds in Lapland had to be slaughtered as unsafe to eat. Obviously, air pollution is never a local problem; it has a way of magnifying.

Solid Waste

Approximately 160 million tons of solid waste are generated in the United States each year—nearly four pounds per person per day. Most of this waste is burned, buried in the earth, or dumped in the ocean; less than 10 percent is recycled. Approximately 57 million tons of the solid waste produced each year are toxic or radioactive. Although it is clearly against the law to contaminate the environment with hazardous waste, the Environmental Protection Agency estimates that only 10 percent is disposed of properly. The severity of the problem can be appreciated when one considers that much of the waste can remain dangerous for up to a thousand years and that in many cases cleanup costs are prohibitive.

Depletion of Natural Resources

Natural resources can be classified in two ways: renewable and non-renewable. Resources such as trees, sunshine, and water are classified as renewable because they either are theoretically inexhaustible or with proper care can be replenished after use. Other resources such as coal, gas, and oil are classified as nonrenewable because they are neither inexhaustible nor replenishable—once they are used, they are gone. Energy can be produced from either renewable resources—such as water, wind, sunshine, and biomass—or from nonrenewable resources—such as coal, gas, oil, and nuclear fission.

Minerals are nonrenewable resources. Ominously, as a result of the need for various metals to support our technological society, most of the high-grade ore has already been used up. For example, the percentage of copper in mined ore has declined from 2.5 percent in 1906 to less than .5 percent today. Needless to say, it takes much more ore to produce a ton of copper today than it did in the past. It is a curious fact that some garbage dumps contain a higher percentage of metal than do active mines. Projections estimate that "by the year 2020, domestic oil supplies will be effectively depleted—by then the supply and quality of remaining oil will have become so low that other fuels will be used for most purposes" (Gever et al. 1986:55). Even worse, it is also estimated that by 2005 it will be pointless to continue exploring for oil and gas in the United States because more energy would be used in looking for them than they would eventually yield.

There are also dangers in the depletion of renewable resources. For instance, commercial fishers must travel farther (thus using more nonrenewable energy) and trawl longer to catch as many fish as in the past. They are also removing more immature fish each year, thus depleting the future stock of reproducing fish. There is also concern over the supply of trees, another renewable resource, which are now being harvested or removed for farmlands at a faster rate than new trees are being planted.

Overcrowding and Congestion

Part of the environmental problem cannot be objectively identified as easily as air or water pollution can. The overcrowding and congestion in densely populated urban areas are a dimension of the environmental problem that encompasses much of our daily life. The environment of the typical urban dweller is composed of more concrete than grass, more telephone wires and poles than trees, more skyscrapers than mountains, and more drainage gutters than babbling brooks. As a human-made environment, city life lacks natural beauty. As a line in a protest song goes, "We paved paradise to put up a parking lot."

Much of urban life is spent in a congested tangle of freeways, side streets, and alleys decorated by fire hydrants, power lines, stoplights, neon signs, fences, railings, and mailboxes. The few parks that do exist are likely to be overcrowded, so that privacy can be found only in one's house or apartment, which every year becomes more confining and more expensive.

Explanations of the Environmental Problem

At the simplest level, the environmental problem can be explained as the result of two interrelated factors: (1) population growth has made it necessary for larger concentrations of people to live in limited space; and (2) each year the technological revolution consumes more natural resources and spews out larger quantities of waste material than it did before. However, these are only contributory conditions. In and of themselves, they are not sufficient to explain why people choose to exploit the environment in destructive ways. Dorothy L. Sayers once said that a nation goes to war because its people have a bad philosophy of humanity. In a similar way, it could be argued that a nation has environmental problems because it has a bad philosophy of ecology. Sadly, one of the "philosophies" which have been held responsible for the present environmental crisis is Christianity.

Christianity as the Problem

In an essay entitled "The Historical Roots of Our Ecological Crisis," Lynn White proposed that "what people do about their ecology depends on what they think about themselves in relation to things around them." He further suggested that "human ecology is deeply conditioned by beliefs about our nature and destiny—that is, by religion" (1967:42). White is representative of a number of writers who have blamed an activist Western version of Christianity for our current environmental crisis. They argue that the Christian notion of a transcendent God who is removed from nature has allowed the exploitation of nature. Western science and technology have also grown out of Christian attitudes which see human beings as uniquely created in the image of God and, therefore, separate from and above nature. It follows that God is seen as allowing and even wanting humans to exploit nature for their own ends. Environmental problems are created when humans, seeing themselves as superior to nature, become contemptuous of it.

In most religions there is not such a sharp dichotomy between the supernatural world and nature. For instance, among some early Native American tribes, every spring, every stream, every mountain, and every tree was thought to have its own guardian spirit. Before cutting down a tree, altering a stream, or moving a stone, these spirits had to be placated. But when this pagan animism was displaced by Christianity, people began to exploit nature, to use her as they wanted without any regard for the ecological consequences.

Loren Wilkinson (1980, 1983), a Christian writer, agrees with White's contention that how people treat nature is dependent upon what they think of nature. Wilkinson argues that there is a direct relationship between what he calls "epistemology" (the way we think about nature) and technology (how we treat nature). As European settlers began to work their way west in America, Wilkinson believes that they adopted a "frontier epistemology." They viewed the virgin land as vast and wild, needing to be conquered and tamed. The cultivation of the Great Plains was seen as redeeming the fallen earth from its state of disuse. Animals that ran wild could be domesticated and employed for human purposes. Wild rivers that raged uncontrollably during spring floods could be dammed and thus provide energy for the growing population. The natural flow of rivers could even be altered by the creation of vast networks of canals and aqueducts to channel water to dry and thirsty agricultural lands.

I THINK FRANK HOLDS TO A FRONTIER EPISTEMOLOGY.

The frontier epistemology became questionable when Americans began to run out of virgin land. Nevertheless, when there was little frontier left to conquer, the natural resources were exploited even more intensely. The result is that nature itself, not having been replenished, is no longer the rich wilderness it once was and in fact is continuing to shrink. Some of the heaviest assaults on nature have come in Christian countries, because many Christians in the past did not give sufficient thought to the biblical view of nature.

The Technological Society

Another explanation of the environmental crisis centers on the nature of modern society. Within a mass, technologically oriented society, there is the tendency for individuals to become alienated from the natural environment. In such a society the only questions that count are technical ones like, "What is the most efficient way to do something?" and "How can we get the most for our money in the least amount of time?" The dominant factors in life are greed and speed. Thus, strip mining went unchallenged for years because it was the cheapest and fastest way to get at coal. Efficiency is not necessarily a bad value, except when greed and speed do not allow nontechnical questions to be asked; for example, What will the effect of efficiency be upon the natural environment?

In time, nature becomes subordinated to the artificiality of technological societies. We noted earlier (p. 132) that the primary problems of modern society are not only natural, but technological ones. At a certain point technology breeds new problems which can be solved only by further technical applications. Technique is responsible, for example, for polluted rivers and air, and the only conceivable solutions to these problems are technical. When the problems which progress creates cannot be solved through natural means, the movement away from nature has become irreversible (Ellul 1964).

Responses to the Environmental Problem

Some people continue to deny the existence of a serious environmental problem. They contend that the environmental problem is only a short-term condition that inevitably occurs in an advanced industrial society and that will be corrected if a free-market, capitalist economy is allowed to work itself out. Given that environmental problems are most severe where economic development has been given free rein, such a view is, in reality, a part of the problem.

Another response which seeks to deny the seriousness of the industrial assault upon the environment is the suggestion that curbing the rate of population growth will eliminate the environmental problem. The current size and density of the world's population are such, however, that this strategy can be taken seriously only as an effort to contain rather than solve the environmental crisis.

Yet another response to the environmental crisis seriously questions our current obsession with economic growth. Many people in technological societies argue that economic growth is necessary in order to maintain full employment and to take the edge off conflicts over the distribution of goods. If everyone's absolute share is increasing, then people are less likely to fight over relative shares. Others counter that the cost of an ever-increasing gross national product is the destruction of the environment. Instead of an ever-expanding economy, they advocate a steady-state economy as the solution to the environmental problem (Daly 1977).

In a steady-state economy there are a constant stock of physical wealth (capital) and a constant number of people. The central concept is the flow of income and consumption rather than the gross national product. It is argued that Americans have accepted the notion that if the gross national product increases, the standard of living must be going up. The proponents of a steady-state economy, however, point out two ways in which the gross national product can continue to rise without a corresponding increase in the standard of living. First, in our present economy, many a product is manufactured to be obsolete after a limited period of use in order that another product may be manufactured to take its place. So the gross national product increases; the standard of living does not. Ignored are the advantages of producing durable goods and later recycling them to be used again. Producing something to last twice as long would enable us to maintain the same standard of living without swelling the gross national product and destroying the environment in the process. Second, the costs involved in cleaning up the environmental mess caused by the ever-expanding output of goods are unjustifiably figured into the gross national product. For example, the one million dollars that may have to be spent to clean up a river or lake that has been polluted by a steel manufacturer is figured into the gross national product. Once again, there is no corresponding rise in the standard of living.

Although the logic behind the proposals for a steady-state economy is appealing, there is a major unsolved problem. What institutions will provide the control necessary to keep the stocks of wealth and number of people constant? The evidence to date seems to be that government control can move a society towards a steady-state economy, but only at the cost of sacrificing individual freedom.

A Christian Response to the Environmental Problem

A Christian response to the ecological crisis needs to begin with a biblically informed way of thinking about the environment. This means affirming that God intends for nature to be enjoyed and used by human beings, but rejecting the idea that nature exists solely to serve them. We shall consider two of Wilkinson's suggestions (1983) as to how the environment might be viewed—as a wilderness and as a garden.

Nature as a Wilderness: The Equality of All Things

According to those who view the environment as a wilderness, a better situation would emerge if fallen humanity would just leave nature to itself. For example, in arguing for a "Sabbath ecology," Richard Austin (1988) warns against a Sabbathless society in which land is never rested, debts are never canceled, slaves are never released, and all of life is viewed as a smoothly functioning machine. Whereas the frontier epistemology has virtually exhausted the land, a thoroughgoing "wilderness epistemology" would leave the land wild, but of little use to human beings. Some conservationists would deny any future development of wilderness areas and even convert some developed land back into wilderness. In the end, this view can lead to a religion that worships the earth and holds that nature itself is sacred and not to be tampered with. White (1967) suggests that the solution to the environmental crisis would be to go back to the Christianity of Francis of Assisi, who held to the equality of all creatures, including animals.

Many proponents of the wilderness epistemology see pantheism and Eastern mysticism as superior to Christianity. In pantheism, nature is protected because it is equated with God. Nature is similarly protected in Eastern religions, such as Zen Buddhism and Hinduism, which stress the unity of human beings with nature. Although the oneness-with-nature view is appealing, we know from Scripture that God created human beings separate and distinct from the rest of nature. Accordingly, we must reject the thinking of pantheism and Eastern mysticism on this score. As Francis Schaeffer (1970) pointed out, these religions in stressing oneness do not bring nature up to humankind, but rather bring humankind down to nature. No special dignity is ascribed to human beings in Eastern thought. Moreover, "far from raising nature to man's height, pantheism must push both man and nature down into a bog. Without categories, there is eventually no reason to distinguish bad nature from good nature. Pantheism leaves us with the Marquis de Sade's dictum, 'What is, is right' in morals and [humankind] becomes no more than grass" (p. 33).

We must make a similar judgment regarding the wilderness epistemology. Although we may intuitively find it appealing when compared to the frontier epistemology, it denies two Christian truths. First, the wilderness epistemology ignores the effect of the fall upon the environment. Genesis 3:17–18 states, "Cursed is the ground because of you; through painful toil you will eat of it all the days of your life. It will produce thorns and thistles for you, and you will eat the plants of the field" (NIV). In these verses we learn that the earth is to be at least in part a hostile environment; consequently, human beings cannot leave nature to go its own way, but must take an active role toward it in order to obtain needed food. Second, the wilderness epistemology, like pantheism and

Eastern religions, denies that although God creates humans as a part of nature, he also sets them apart from nature. Not only were Adam and Eve created in the image of God (Gen. 1:27), but God said to them:

> Rule over the fish of the sea and the birds of the air and over every living creature that moves on the ground. . . . I give you every seed-bearing plant on the face of the whole earth and every tree that has fruit with seed in it. They will be yours for food. And to all the beasts of the earth and all the birds of the air and all the creatures that move on the ground—everything that has the breath of life in it—I give every green plant for food. [vv. 28–30 NIV]

So then, in addition to being a separate creation, humans were given a special position and responsibility over nature.

It is true, of course, that some Christians use these same verses to justify the frontier epistemology. There is, then, some merit to the arguments which place the blame for the environmental problem at the feet of Christianity. In response we should point out that Christianity, like any belief system, is subject to a number of interpretations and applications. We must admit that nature has been wrongly exploited in the name of Christianity. But having admitted this, we must aggressively demonstrate that a truly responsible use and understanding of Scripture yields an alternative way of thinking about nature.

Nature as a Garden

At one extreme, thinking of nature as a frontier leads to the destruction of nature. At the other extreme, thinking of nature as a wilderness leaves nature as it is and of little utilitarian value to human beings. Can Christianity offer us a mediating position between these two extremes? Does biblical revelation give us any hints as to how we might use and enjoy nature without abusing it? Wilkinson proposes a "garden epistemology" under which the land is developed, but with due regard for its intrinsic value. Emphasis is placed on the relationship between human beings and the things of this world. It is recognized that we are interdependent with, and yet distinct from, nature. With this viewpoint, we go beyond the idea of taming and using nature for our own ends to a concern for what is best for nature, the resources which God has placed under our stewardship. A garden epistemology offers a balance between unrestrained development (the frontier epistemology) and unexcepted preservation (the wilderness epistemology).

An excellent introduction to this Christian view can be found in *Earthkeeping: Christian Stewardship of Natural Resources* (Wilkinson 1980). Nine months of intensive study at the Calvin Center for Christian Scholarship led seven scholars to the following principles which should be kept in mind as we think about our environment:

1. *God is Creator and Lord of the universe.* He is thus both utterly separated from it, as any maker is lord over his or her work, and he is utterly involved in it through Christ, the Incarnate Word, in whom all things are made, sustained, and redeemed.

2. *The creation, in all its intricacy and diversity, is good.* This goodness is not simply a declaration by God, but a recognition. And in the very independence of creation implied by that fact, we see the possibility that the goodness of creation might, in its freedom, come to be flawed.

3. *Through both their nature and their task, humans are made to share in the care and sustaining of creation.* Like the rest of creation, humans are made by God, and depend on creation for their sustenance as surely as beasts or trees. But unlike the rest of creation, they are made responsible to God. Thus they share in God's separateness from creation.

4. *The human relationship to God, to creation, and to other humans has become flawed.* Through the fall, it has become self-centered and destructive, a grotesque caricature of divine lordship. Instead of understanding their unique abilities as a means to love and obey God, honor other humans, and care for creation, humans have understood their dominion to be the occasion for increasing their own comfort and power at the expense of everything and everyone else.

5. *Both the model and the means for a restoration of the right human relationship to God, nature, and fellow humans are in Christ.* The Incarnation demonstrates the Creator's willingness to forsake what humans wrongly take to be the rights of lordship and dominion for the redemption of his creation.

6. *Redeemed humanity is directed to exercise dominion, stewardship, and justice, guided by the mind of Christ.* Redeemed humans are not to shun their powers of intellect, creativity, and technique. Rather, they are to use them for the wise and loving management of creation, developing the full potential of stone, beast, and human, and lifting all of that creation to share in their own "sonship" with Christ, the Creator. [Wilkinson 1980:257, emphasis added]

Understood as a garden, the environment must be tended. But nature requires more than responsible tending. The vast damage that has been done to the environment as a result of the frontier epistemology calls for a focused cleanup effort.

Tending the Garden: Redemptive Management

In chapter 3 we suggested that covenant is the basis of God's relationship with human beings and is meant to be the basis of all human relationships. Scripture tells us, however, that God established a covenant not only with Noah, but also with nature. We read in Genesis 9:9–10, "I now establish my covenant with you and with your descendants after you and with every living creature that was with you—the birds, the livestock and all the wild animals, all those that came out of the ark with you—every living creature on earth" (NIV). Evidence that God meant for human beings to establish their own covenantal relationship with nature is given in Leviticus 25:2–5:

> When you enter the land I am going to give you, the land itself must observe a sabbath to the LORD. For six years sow your fields, and for six years prune your vineyards and gather their crops. But in the seventh year the land is to have a sabbath of rest, a sabbath to the LORD. Do not sow your fields or prune your vineyards. Do not reap what grows of itself or harvest the grapes of your untended vines. The land is to have a year of rest. [NIV]

Further evidence that God desired that human beings maintain a covenant relationship with nature is found in the concept of the year of jubilee. Leviticus 25 tells us that each fiftieth year, the year of jubilee, all property acquired during the previous fifty years was to be returned to its original owners. God was making it known that the land could not be treated as a commodity which is indiscriminately bought and sold. Under the covenant care of the land, no one had the right to acquire vast amounts of property, as is the case in our modern materialistic economy.

The Bible also stipulates that humans are to rule over nature: "You made [man] ruler over the works of your hands; you put everything under his feet: all flocks and herds, and the beasts of the field, the birds of the air, and the fish of the sea, all that swim the paths of the seas" (Ps. 8:6–8 NIV). We agree with Fred Van Dyke (1985:44) that "the question is not 'Will humans rule nature?,' for we do rule nature. The question is rather 'How will we rule?'" Van Dyke suggests that we should aim to be servant-rulers and then describes what this entails:

1. Humans must exercise their responsibility to manage creation, which includes the use of technology.
2. Humans must manage from a perspective of intimate relationship with the creation. They are not to be estranged from their subjects (see the portrait of an ideal ruler in Deut. 17:15–20).
3. Humanity's primary goal in management is to meet the physical needs of the creation, enabling it to better fulfil its own "great commission" (Gen. 1). A secondary goal is to meet the needs of humanity. [p. 47]

The scriptural teaching about the relationship between human beings and nature leads to the metaphor of nature as a garden to be tended. Tending the garden does not mean dominating nature but assuming the role of a servant-ruler, which might be described as redemptive management. Just as humankind and nature both share in the consequences of the fall, so they both share in the hope of redemption. The apostle Paul expresses this truth in Romans 8:19–21: "The creation waits in eager expectation for the sons of God to be revealed. For the creation was subjected to frustration, not by its own choice, but by the will of the one who subjected it, in hope that the creation itself will be liberated from its bondage to decay and brought into the glorious freedom of the children of God" (NIV). It is the responsibility of humans, and especially of those who have experienced God's redemption, to work for the redemption of nature.

The prophet Isaiah vividly describes the harmonious relationship which will exist between redeemed humanity and redeemed nature in the new heaven and the new earth:

> The wolf will live with the lamb, the leopard will lie down with the goat, the calf and the lion and the yearling together; and a little child will lead them. The cow will feed with the bear, their young will lie down together, and the lion will eat straw like the ox. The infant will play near the hole of the cobra, and the young child put his hand into the viper's nest. They will neither harm nor destroy on all my holy mountain, for the earth will be full of the knowledge of the LORD as the waters cover the sea. [11:6–9 NIV]

Van Dyke (1985:48) summarizes how this redemption of creation is to be achieved:

> God can redeem creation, just as only God can ultimately redeem humanity. But we cooperate with God to the extent that we recognize [God's] purposes and work according to [God's] established ends. This frees us from captivity to the secular agenda and propels us toward distinctively Christian witness in the acts of stewardship. Indeed, Christians *must* assume leadership in the care of the environment. Regardless of the contributions of the Sierra Club, the Nature Conservancy, the Environmental Defense Fund, or any other secular organization, the Bible makes it brutally clear that there will be no *redeemed creation* if there is no *redeemed humanity.*

Before the Industrial Revolution nature was seen as inexhaustible and untamable. Today, however, we face an environmental crisis which has resulted from an aggressive exploitation of nature by means of modern technology. The whole world is in need of reviving. For this to be accomplished, Christians must be prepared to reject a theology of domination, move beyond a theology of stewardship, and embrace a theology of creation that includes the following points:

1. Creation has value because of its relationship to God rather than its utility for humanity.

2. Creation offers a trustworthiness and reliability that, while they are not to be idealized, express the presence of God's grace upholding the world.
3. God's work of redemption in Jesus Christ encompasses the whole of creation, and provides the grounds for mending the brokenness in the relationships of humanity to creation and both to God.
4. A fresh understanding of the Holy Spirit is central to the church's faith and witness in behalf of renewing the whole creation.
5. A trinitarian theology weaves together God's work of creating, redeeming, and sustaining the creation.
6. New models and pictures must be found that appropriately present the theological truth of God's relationship to the creation.
7. A theology of creation for our time must provide a new worldview, offering a fresh framework for reorienting science, technology, and politics. [Granberg-Michaelson 1990:12–14]

The Bible indicates clearly that God intends for human beings to be stewards, redemptive managers, servant-rulers, and caretakers of nature. Caretaking needs to start at the individual level, with each of us assuming stewardship responsibility for the resources God has lent us. Caretaking is also needed at the collective level, where families, churches, and communities can become involved in recycling, restoration projects, and cleanup campaigns. Given the severity of damage which has been done to our environment, however, responsible caretaking also requires that society as a whole make massive, coordinated commitments of time, energy, and money to begin the needed healing process. For we recognize that "at both a theological and a practical level, ecological threats and injustice are the inseparable parts of one whole. Neither can be pursued in isolation from the other, and the biblical vision of 'shalom' assumes such a wholistic integration" (Granberg-Michaelson 1990:14).

Topics for Review, Reflection, and Discussion

1. In the long run, what type of pollution will prove hardest to clean up?
2. Is there any truth to the statement that only wealthy countries have the luxury of being concerned with environmental problems?
3. How big a responsibility does our activist Western version of Christianity have for the current environmental crisis?
4. How has the dominance of greed and speed contributed to the problem?
5. Given equal technological development, is a capitalist or a socialist economy more likely to create environmental problems?
6. Is a steady-state economy capable of reducing environmental problems? Is it realistic?
7. What biblical evidence is there for thinking of nature as a frontier? a wilderness? a garden?

12

Poverty in the United States

From its beginning, America has had poor people, that is, people whose economic resources fall below an acceptable standard of living. Poverty has been determined in various ways in the past, both systematically and impressionistically. Currently the official poverty level is set by the Social Security Administration. On the basis of a finding by the Department of Agriculture that families of three or more persons spend on the average about one-third of their income on food, the poverty level is set at three times the cost of an economical food plan. Those families and individuals whose income does not reach this level are categorized as living in poverty. The poverty level varies according to the size and composition of families, and is revised each year to take into account changes in the consumer price index. In 1987 the poverty level was $9,056 for a family of three and $11,611 for a family of four. The level ranged from $5,778 for individuals to $23,105 for families of nine or more persons.

The Nature of the Concern

There are Americans who believe that the poverty level is set too high, for in comparison with many countries, those in America who are in poverty are rather well off. However, comparisons with other countries whose standard of living differs from that in America are irrelevant, for it is what Americans consider to be an adequate standard of living that counts. There are others who think that the poverty index is too low, for incomes at that level are inadequate to meet basic needs. While the official definition of poverty is necessarily arbitrary, most Americans agree that there are too many people in this country whose income is too low to provide sufficient food, livable housing (or any housing at all), adequate medical attention, proper child care, and other necessities of life. These conditions conflict with the American ideals of the worth of the individual, equality of opportunity, freedom of movement, and material, physical, and mental well-being. Evidence of concern is seen in governmental and private programs designed to reduce poverty.

General Programs to Reduce Poverty

One of the oldest of the major governmental programs that show concern about poverty is Aid to Families with Dependent Children (AFDC), which was established by the Social Security Act of 1935. This program provides cash payments to needy families, with eligibility and amounts of payment determined by each state. In 1988, twenty of the states provided AFDC benefits of less than two hundred dollars a month for a family of three; an additional eighteen states paid less than four hundred. In every state families with little or no income or assets, children under eighteen, and only one parent present are eligible for the program. In addition, almost one-half of the states help two-parent families if the father is out of work. The purpose of the program is to enable families to stay together rather than be forced to place their children with relatives or in foster homes.

Another federal program designed to help poor people who have special needs is Supplemental Security Income (SSI). This program was set up in 1972 as an amendment to the Social Security Act. Its purpose is to help bring up to a federally established minimum level the income of the disabled (e.g., the blind) and others who are unable to help themselves.

Individual churches and groups of churches also offer a wide range of programs to help the poor. One example is Jubilee Ministries, sponsored by the Church of the Saviour in Washington, D.C., which has as its goal the transformation of the spirit of the poor by improving the condition of their lives. "Key components of its network of independent services are housing, unemployment, health care, child and family development, and help for the elderly, the homeless, and the handicapped" (Hunger Project 1989:1). Another example is the ministries of Kum Bah Ya in Lynchburg, Virginia, where the Church of the Covenant has brought together more than forty churches to provide a number of different services to the poor of the community.

Programs to Combat Hunger and Malnutrition

Americans are concerned that in a country where farmers produce more than enough to feed the entire population and are actually paid to let land lie idle, there are millions who have too little to eat. It is difficult to determine just how many Americans are undernourished and hungry, but surveys have shown rather consistently that the number is in the range of twenty to twenty-five million. Among these is a large number of young children and single women who are pregnant.

Both governmental and private programs have been established to help feed the hungry. The most far-reaching is the federal food-stamp program. Begun by an executive order in 1961 and made into law in 1964, it has undergone several subsequent revisions. The Hunger Prevention Act of 1988, for instance, expanded the food-stamp program and required the Department of Agriculture to provide technical assistance to nonprofit groups which are helping to feed the poor. The federal government has several other programs to combat hunger, including providing breakfast and lunch for schoolchildren, and bringing meals to isolated elderly people. The Women's, Infants', and Children's Supplemental Feeding Program (WIC) provides nutritious foods to pregnant and postpartum women, infants, and children under the age of five. The WIC has been highly praised by such groups as the Physicians' Task Force on Hunger in America at the Harvard School of Public Health for having made a significant difference in the diets of poor children in America.

Many private organizations have set up food-distribution projects to help the hungry. Most of these are local in the sense that they serve people in a particular city or county. An example is City Harvest, which collects excess food from restaurants and suppliers and then distributes it to the hungry in New York City. Many churches throughout America have food banks and soup kitchens where the hungry can obtain food. There are also nationwide collection and distribution centers. Among these is the Society of St. Andrew, located in the small town of Big Island, Virginia. One of its ministries is the Potato Project, which salvages potatoes which would otherwise be dumped to rot. In two years of operation the society has distributed over nineteen million pounds of potatoes to hungry Americans in forty-four states and the District of Columbia. This has been done at a cost of three-and-a-half cents a pound. SHARE-USA is a self-help organization based in San Diego, California. It buys food from producers in bulk, which is then given to the poor in exchange for labor at the registration and distribution centers (churches, synagogues, and civic clubs donate the use of their facilities).*

Programs to Combat Inadequate Housing and Homelessness

A comfortable and safe home of one's own is a quintessential part of the American dream. Yet many poor people in our country have inade-

---

Hunger Action Forum is a highly informative monthly publication on hunger in America and ways to deal with it and other aspects of poverty. This publication is produced as a public service by The Hunger Project, P.O. Box 789, San Francisco, CA 94101. The authors are greatly indebted to this organization for its monthly report, on which we have relied extensively throughout this chapter.

quate housing or no housing at all. Without proper housing it is difficult to hold a family together. A home is much more than just shelter. It is a web of intimate relationships, a place where one belongs, is accepted, and receives love and understanding. While these ideals are by no means guaranteed even in the most elegant and comfortable housing, they are virtually impossible to achieve unless a family enjoys adequate housing.

The most tragic cases are those individuals and families unable to afford any kind of housing at all; they are forced to live on the streets, in parks, in abandoned buildings, and in public shelters. It is not possible to determine accurately the number of homeless, but estimates run from two to six million (Smith 1989).

Early expressions of concern came with legislation that created agencies to make low-income housing possible. In the Great Depression of the 1930s, the Public Works Administration cleared slums in a number of cities and built apartments for the poor. The Federal Housing Administration was created to promote home ownership, and the Public Housing Administration was set up to oversee the operation of public housing. In 1965 Congress passed the Housing and Urban Development Act, which consolidated government bureaus dealing with housing, established a Department of Housing and Urban Development (HUD), and instituted a rent-supplement program for low-income families in nonprofit housing built and serviced by private groups such as church organizations.

Most private groups concerned about inadequate housing and homelessness concentrate on the city or county in which they are located. Earlier we mentioned Jubilee Ministries of Washington, D.C. Its housing program began in 1973 when two apartment buildings which were occupied but in poor condition were acquired and renovated. The tenants with the help of volunteers donated fifty thousand hours of labor to bring the buildings up to standard. By the end of 1988 various churches, businesses, and foundations had helped Jubilee Ministries acquire seven more apartment buildings and provide 315 renovated apartments to low-income families.

A few organizations working to combat substandard housing are national and international in scope. One of these is Habitat for Humanity International, with headquarters at Americus, Georgia. According to one of its brochures, "Habitat for Humanity International is an ecumenical, grass-roots Christian ministry with the goal of eliminating poverty housing. Unwilling to accept the fact that millions of people live without adequate shelter, Habitat challenges individuals, churches, companies, foundations, and other organizations to join in partnership with the poor to change the conditions in which they live."

Another organization involved in making adequate housing available to the poor is the Association of Community Organizations for Reform

Now (ACORN). It points out that there are tens of thousands of abandoned houses in American cities, while there are millions of people desperately in need of adequate housing. In thirty cities across the country ACORN is helping over seventy-five thousand people who live in dilapidated houses or who have no housing at all. With the guidance of ACORN these low-income families petition local governments to turn over abandoned houses to them for a nominal fee; in exchange they promise to rebuild the houses and occupy them. ACORN raises its own money, and its clients do the rebuilding.

Programs to Combat Inadequate Medical Care

A third aspect of poverty about which Americans have expressed concern is in the area of medical care. The great majority of America's poor receive inadequate care or none at all. One of the consequences of inadequate medical care is a high infant-mortality rate. Although the United States is an affluent, highly developed nation with extensive medical services, it ranked only twentieth in the world in infant survival in 1988 (Haupt 1990:9). An inordinately high rate among the poor pushes up the rate for the United States as a whole. Deprived of medical care, the poor are likely to have premature babies with a low birth weight, one of the major determinants of death in the first weeks of life. Another consequence of inadequate medical care is that the poor are likely to be sick often and for long periods of time, and to need dental and eye care.

After many years of debate and defeated proposals, Congress created Medicare and Medicaid in 1965 as amendments to the Social Security Act. Medicare was set up to ensure medical care for all Americans over the age of sixty-five. Medicaid, on the other hand, was established as a welfare program for people who fall well below the poverty level. Those receiving AFDC and SSI benefits are eligible for Medicaid, as are those who have exhausted all of their monetary resources and assets. However, fewer than two out of five poor people were covered by Medicaid in 1988, down from 65 percent in 1978 (Ansberry 1988:1); more-stringent eligibility requirements were the cause of the decline.

One of the results of the strict regulations on eligibility for Medicaid is that many of the poor have been denied hospital treatment because they are unable to pay for care. In a 1988 report Clare Ansberry cited a number of instances in which, despite laws against the practice, patients have been rejected or sent to other hospitals purely for economic reasons. In a few of these cases, patients died because care was given too late. According to Ansberry, an estimated 250,000 people a year are turned away by hospitals which are unable to absorb the costs of free care. Even so, hospitals have had to provide an estimated seven billion dollars' worth of uncompensated care. Ansberry quoted the president of the American College of Emergency Physicians as saying, "On the one hand, we have a moral, ethical and legal obligation to see a patient. Nobody, on the other hand, has a moral or legal obligation to pay for that care" (1988:1).

In order to help with the unmet needs of the poor, many communities have established free clinics. For example, the Spanish Catholic Health Center in Washington, D.C., cares for those who have no way to pay for the services, not even Medicaid. Catholic Charities supports the staff that operates the clinic, and medical care is given by doctors, nurses, dentists, and pharmacists who donate their time on a regular basis. The need in Washington and throughout the rest of the country, however, is far greater than the free clinics can meet. Therefore, many of the indigent cannot obtain help; even where it is available, they do not know how to go about getting it.

The Dimensions of Poverty

How many Americans live in poverty? Has the proportion of people who are below the poverty level changed over the past twenty-five years? Do those who are poor differ significantly from the nonpoor in terms of age, sex, race, ethnic background, areas of residence, and personality traits? We need to answer these and related questions in order to throw light on what causes poverty, admittedly an exceedingly difficult task.

In 1987, according to the United States Census Bureau (1989), approximately thirty-three million people, or 13.5 percent of the American population, were living below the poverty level. In 1959, the first year in which such statistics were gathered, 22.4 percent of the population fell below the poverty level. By 1966 the rate had dropped to 14.7 percent; it reached its lowest point to date in 1973, when 11.1 percent were in poverty. By 1983 the rate had moved up to 15.2 percent, and since then has hovered between 13 and 14 percent.

Who are the poor? According to 1987 census data, a few categories of Americans are represented in disproportionately high numbers among those below the poverty level. First, the young are overrepresented, for 21.2 percent of those below sixteen years of age were in poverty, a percentage considerably above the 13.5 percent for the population as a whole. This means that more than one-fifth of our children were being reared in poor families in 1987, and unofficial estimates indicate that the proportion is increasing.

Blacks and Hispanics were also found to be below the poverty level in disproportionately high numbers—33.1 percent of blacks, 28.2 percent of Hispanics, but only 10.5 percent of whites were officially classified as poor. The difference by race and ethnic background was even greater for children under sixteen years of age. Of blacks in that age category 46.7 percent were in poverty; of Hispanics, 40.6 percent.

There has been a feminization of poverty as well. A major factor here is the large number of single-parent families headed by females. In 1987, 46.0 percent of such families lived below the poverty line. More than one-half of black and Hispanic families headed by women were impov crished. Teenage mothers were twice as likely as older mothers to be below the poverty line.

Further, high levels of poverty are found in rural areas and inner cities. In both cases over 18 percent of the residents were below the poverty level in 1986—a rate 50 percent higher than that of the entire urban population (O'Hare 1988:2). In the 1970s the future of rural America looked promising, with a population growing faster than that of urban areas and with an economic foundation that appeared to be solid. These conditions changed in the 1980s, and the rate of poverty in rural areas increased rapidly.

Another significant finding concerns the number of years of schooling completed. In 1987, of those adults over twenty-five with less than eight years of education, 25.4 percent were in poverty, while for those who had one or more years of college, the rate was only 3.7 percent.

While there have been no definitive studies on the subject, some observers claim that the poor, especially the persistently indigent and those in the "underclass" (a debatable term in itself), do differ in basic characteristics from those who are in the mainstream of society. Oscar Lewis, an anthropologist, originated the expression *culture of poverty* to denote a way of life that ensues when people are forced to adapt to poverty (1968). Individuals in such circumstances feel despair and hopelessness from realizing that they will most likely never achieve success in terms of the values and goals of the dominant society. As a consequence, they become resigned and passive; living only for the present moment, they have no inclination to defer gratification; a sense of fatalism and powerlessness lowers their aspirations. Some sociologists believe that these characteristics become embedded in the poor and are passed on from generation to generation; such traits, it is asserted, must be changed before the poor can be helped. Others believe that behavior and attitudes will change when opportunities present themselves. They contend that if good jobs at decent wages were made available, the poor would be able to adapt.

Explanations of Poverty

Poverty in the United States is a multifaceted, complex phenomenon. While it is officially defined in terms of a relatively low income, there are other aspects of poverty which are not entirely the consequence of having little income and few assets. Low income is intertwined with such complications as low educational achievement, inadequate or no housing, malnutrition, and poor health. Considering all these interrelated factors, simple explanations of poverty need to be viewed with great caution.

The Individualistic Approach

A number of Americans assume that in an open society like ours, everyone who wants to avoid poverty can do so; healthy adults who do not obtain and hold on to a job that keeps them above the poverty level have only themselves to blame. This explanation, which may be termed the individualistic approach to poverty, holds that the United States has become a meritocracy—people generally get what they deserve. The situation healthy poor adults find themselves in is purely and simply a consequence of their own individual character and actions. Underlying this approach is the assumption that those who work hard and are intelligent succeed, while those having undesirable personality traits and less than average intelligence do not.

Philip Green has criticized the individualistic approach as being an argument, consciously or not, for the maintenance of the status quo (1981:167). Green also asserts that insofar as the individualistic explanation is based on assumed genetic defects, it "perfectly expresses the drive of the hereditarian to make inegalitarian bricks out of genetic straw." Another criticism by social scientists is that the individualistic approach tends to be more of an evaluation than an explanation. No scientific studies of genetic differences between the poor and nonpoor have appeared. In any case, the undesirable personality traits attributed to the poor do not explain why a relatively large number of Americans have risen out of poverty, while others slip into it after having been successful by society's standards.

The Federal Welfare System as a Cause of Poverty

An explanation of poverty that is presently being given a considerable amount of attention is that the federal welfare system itself, as it now operates, produces poverty. One of the most articulate and influential advocates of this position is Charles Murray, whose book *Losing Ground: American Social Policy, 1950–1980*, blames federal welfare programs for removing incentives to work, rewarding nonwork, and creating dependency. He concludes, "We tried to provide more for the poor and produced more poor instead. We tried to remove the barriers to escape from poverty, and inadvertently built a trap" (1984:9).

Murray supports his condemnation of the federal welfare program by pointing out that while welfare expenditures quadrupled from 1968 to 1980, the percentage of poor people did not change significantly. He attributes this lack of progress to the disincentives he claims are built into the present system. Murray contends that it is not only impractical but morally wrong as well to cater to the least industrious and the least responsible among the poor. While the welfare system was set up with the best of intentions and was motivated by generosity and compassion, the system has been destructive nonetheless. Murray's thesis has been boosted in a number of ways. Free copies of his book have been widely distributed, and the *Reader's Digest* reviewed it in a highly approving way. Entitled "How Uncle Sam Robbed America's Poor" (Methvin 1985), the review concluded that the federal welfare system has done little but perpetuate human misery.

Murray's data and explanation have been heavily criticized, in part because of his unequivocal assertion that they establish a cause-effect relationship between receiving welfare and being below the poverty level. William O'Hare points out that a large proportion of the poor receive no welfare benefits—only 59 percent of the poor received any kind of welfare at all in 1985 (1987:5). Such facts indicate that welfare is neither a necessary nor sufficient condition of poverty. Murray does not explain why the 41 percent who do not receive welfare became poor. Critics further contend that Murray has not even established that receiving federal welfare benefits is a contributory condition.

Noting that between 1968 and 1980 there were increases in both the number of people receiving welfare and the number below the poverty line, Murray quickly concluded that a cause-effect relationship was at work. He ignored the fact that between 1964 and 1973 there were a rapid increase in welfare benefits and a reduction in the rate of people living in poverty—from 18 percent to 11.1 percent. To go beyond the time frame of Murray's study, his explanation cannot account for the increase in the poverty rate from 13 to 15 percent between 1980 and 1983, a period when welfare benefits were cut.

If welfare benefits create poverty, we would expect those states that have high welfare benefits to have high rates of poverty, but this is not the case. Murray believes that AFDC cash payments to single mothers encouraged out-of-wedlock births. If so, we would expect the rate of out-of-wedlock births to be high in those states where AFDC payments are high. But, again, this is not the case. Finally, Murray contends that welfare benefits contribute to an attitude of irresponsibility on the part of the recipient. But William J. Wilson (1987:78–79) cites research showing that women on welfare are significantly more likely to use contraceptives and less likely to become pregnant than are women who are not on welfare. These findings are the opposite of what Murray's hypothesis on the effects of receiving welfare leads us to expect.

Critics claim that Murray has failed to take various significant economic factors into account. For example, he ignores the increase in the unemployment rate from 1973 to 1975, and the fact that unemployment was almost twice as high in 1980 as it was in 1968. Surely, contend the critics, unemployment contributed to the poverty rate in 1980. Among Murray's counterarguments is that unemployment has risen among black youth precisely because of the seductions of welfare. He fails to note that single men are eligible for very little in welfare benefits. For example, even if stringent conditions are met, youth living alone are eligible only for food stamps. In 1982, this came to about sixty dollars a month, clearly an insufficient amount on which to live (Hume 1985:22).

Finally, another study covering approximately the same time period reports quite different findings. Begun in 1968 with a random sample of five thousand American families, the "Panel Study of Income Dynamics" is still being carried out by the Institute for Social Research at the University of Michigan. Interviewers return each year to follow up on these families, including those members who have left the household. This type of study is termed "longitudinal," for it obtains data from the same persons year after year. In contrast, Murray's study is "cross-sectional": it takes aggregate data from each year and compares them with data from other years. The advantage of the longitudinal study is that it shows whether it is always the same people who are classified as poor, or whether there is movement both out of and into poverty. Murray contends that welfare benefits lure people into poverty and trap them there. Cross-sectional data, however, cannot tell us whether those below the poverty level stay there. Longitudinal data can.

A summary of the Michigan study in the decade 1969–78 reports that a large turnover took place in the poverty category. Specifically, "only a little over one-half of the individuals living in poverty in one year are found to be poor in the next" (Duncan 1984:3). Further, while almost one-fourth of the population of the United States received benefits from welfare sources in the ten-year period covered, less than 3 percent remained in poverty throughout the entire decade. The welfare benefits typically helped families dig out of a crisis that came from the death or departure of the chief breadwinner, a debilitating illness, or some other misfortune. Instead of being enticed into poverty by welfare benefits and entrapped there, the great majority of those in the sample were helped by such benefits to lift themselves out of poverty.

Sociocultural Explanations of Poverty

Explanations that place the cause of poverty outside the individual and in societal structures are somewhat different for those who live in inner cities and those who live in rural areas, despite the fact that these two groups have nearly identical poverty rates that are well above the rate for the nation as a whole. For poverty in the inner city, especially among blacks, we shall rely heavily on the explanation given by William J. Wilson (1987). Wilson cites two main factors. One is the transformation caused by the exodus of professional, middle-class families, especially blacks, from inner-city neighborhoods, and the consequent concentration and social isolation of the poor. With the loss of the more successful families, it has been difficult to maintain churches, stores, adequate schools, good housing, and recreational facilities. On the other hand, with the isolation of the poor come increased incidences of crime, out-of-wedlock births, female-headed households, and welfare dependency.

A second factor, according to Wilson, is the changes in economic structure, including the increasing polarization into low-wage and high-wage sectors, technological innovations, the shift from manufacturing to service industries, and the relocation of the surviving manufacturing industries to the suburbs. Therefore, the greatest losses have occurred in jobs with low educational requirements, while job growth has been in the areas demanding skills and educational achievement. In Wilson's view, a serious mismatch has emerged between the low educational level of inner-city youth and the requirements of rapidly changing industries. Manufacturing and blue-collar jobs have been lost, while highly technical jobs have increased.

We noted earlier that in the 1970s the economic future of rural America seemed bright, but that the 1980s brought instead a rapid increase in rural poverty. William O'Hare, director of policy studies at the Population Reference Bureau, cites two major changes, one demographic and the other socioeconomic, that underlie the increase in rural poverty (1988). Migration out of rural areas has accelerated since 1980, and most of those leaving have been young, highly educated adults. O'Hare cites figures showing that almost one-third of those who left in 1986 and 1987 were from eighteen to twenty-four years old. More than one-half of the adults who moved away had at least one year of college; almost 27 percent had four years of college, a much higher educational level than that of those who have stayed.

In the economic sphere there have been losses not only in farming, but also in other rural industries such as timber, oil and gas, and mining. Unemployment has risen with the loss of these jobs, although some rural workers have been able to move into low-paying service jobs. In 1986, according to O'Hare, 62 percent of the rural adults who were poor held a job. Because they tend to be married rather than single parents, and are likely to be working, the rural poor are not eligible for welfare, even though their income falls below the poverty line. They do not receive AFDC, do not live in subsidized housing, and are not eligible for Medicaid or food stamps. From O'Hare's explanation it is clear that far-reaching demographic and socioeconomic changes, rather than welfare, are making rural people poor.

The sociocultural explanations provided by Wilson and O'Hare can logically account for a number of facts about poverty given earlier in this chapter. Obviously, they throw light on the high rates of poverty in inner cities and rural areas. The relatively large number of children who live in poverty is explained by the fact that single mothers in inner cities and rural couples are particularly vulnerable to impersonal economic forces. The feminization of poverty is directly related to the high unemployment rate of young males, especially blacks. Young men who are unemployed are not in a position to support a family. Hence the rise in the number of single-parent families headed by females.

Treatment and Prevention of Poverty

Just as poverty with its multifaceted and complex nature defies easy explanations, so too does it resist attempts at treatment and prevention. We also need to note that the explanations one accepts determine what kinds of treatment and prevention are relied upon. Unlike other chapters, this time we shall deal with treatment and prevention together.

The Individualistic Approach

The individualistic approach implies that certain kinds of education and training might reduce poverty. Assuming that in general one gets what one deserves, the advocates of this approach assert that such traits as laziness, unwillingness to defer gratification, and irresponsibility will have to be changed. Perhaps those who are mentally and emotionally unable to obtain and hold on to jobs will have to be given special care by the rest of society. As a rule, however, the advocates of this approach blame the poor for being poor and so do not offer solutions to poverty. They assume that it will be with us as long as there are people who will not take advantage of the opportunities offered by American society.

Eliminating Welfare Programs

Charles Murray is highly explicit as to what he would do to reduce and prevent poverty. His most sweeping proposal

> consists of scrapping the entire federal welfare and income-support structure for working-aged persons, including AFDC, Medicaid, Food Stamps, Unemployment Insurance, Worker's Compensation, subsidized housing, disability insurance, and the rest. It would leave the working-aged person with no recourse whatsoever except the job market, family members, friends, and public or private locally funded services. It is the Alexandrian solution: cut the knot, for there is no way to untie it. [1984:227–28]

Murray is convinced that once a poor person is no longer dependent on welfare, "status will accrue to being independent, and in fairly short order. Noneconomic rewards will again reinforce the economic rewards of being a good parent and provider" (p. 229). While Murray is emphatic about eliminating all welfare programs for persons of working age, it is not entirely clear how he would provide for the children of the poor, the elderly poor, and the disabled. He believes that a network of local services will be developed to take care of the poor who are unable to work, but he is not sure how such a network will be established.

Murray also advocates changes in education. He proposes that all families be provided with vouchers entitling them to send their children to any school to which they can gain admission. This, according to Murray, would have "immediate, unequivocal, dramatic results," for it would promote competition among schools, forcing them to be productive or to close. Furthermore, he would have students pass a test before entering a particular grade or class. And he would give teachers full authority to enforce order in the classroom and to teach only those who want to learn. In regard to minorities, Murray would make the nation color-blind, judging all people solely on their merits; racial and ethnic minorities would not be given special help to catch up. Murray contends that affirmative action, as it has been practiced, is more condescending than the old racism, has actually promoted poverty, and should therefore be abandoned.

Changing Social and Economic Structures

Those whose research we have especially relied upon in summarizing the sociocultural explanations of poverty, namely, the Institute for Social Research at the University of Michigan, Wilson, and O'Hare, believe that the federal government has a major role to play in treating and preventing poverty. They reject the sink-or-swim policy of the individualistic approach and Murray's suggestion to simply do away with federal involvement. While applauding the accomplishments of churches and other groups in feeding the hungry, providing adequate housing and health care to the poor, and giving remedial education to the illiterate and semiliterate, they contend that more far-reaching programs are required from American society as a whole. Such programs must deal with both short-term and long-term problems.

Reform of the welfare system

Researchers who believe that the federal government has a major role to play advocate that the welfare system be made more effective, both for the working poor and for the persistently poor who cannot work. They point to the finding in the Michigan study that while one-fourth of the American population may need welfare benefits at some time during the course of a decade, only 3 percent are completely welfare-dependent. Accordingly, the welfare system should differentiate between the temporarily poor and the persistently poor (the truly disadvantaged or underclass).

While the persistently poor make up only a small percentage of those

HOW CAN WE BE SURE THAT YOU ARE ONE OF THE
TRULY DISADVANTAGED?

below the poverty line, they pose a special problem. One-third of the persistently poor are elderly people who have little or no chance of improving their lot. The only way to help reduce the hardship these people face is to provide public funds. Most of the rest of the persistently poor are single mothers whose offspring not only increase the need for income, but also require so much attention that full-time work outside the home is virtually an impossibility. Even if child care were available, it is unlikely that single mothers could find jobs that would pay enough to lift them out of poverty. Many of these women have little education and limited job skills, and most of the jobs that are available pay very low wages. It is likely that these women and their children will continue to need direct public assistance.

The temporarily poor, that is, the working poor, pose a different kind of problem. As the Michigan study points out, a fundamental dilemma for the welfare system is that "it should provide assistance to those in need, assure an adequate standard of living, and encourage all who need assistance to seek it; but should not lead those confronting only temporary hardship to develop longer-term dependency" (Duncan 1984:89). The study found that the present welfare system does not give sufficient help to enable the temporarily poor and those who need job training to move out of poverty.

O'Hare insists that greater welfare benefits should be made available to the rural poor who work. Despite the fact that one-quarter of them held two or more jobs in 1986, they could not pull themselves out of poverty. O'Hare also suggests relief for the 43 percent of the rural poor who pay property tax. For on top of their property tax the poor in rural areas are more likely than those in urban areas to pay federal income tax, state income tax, and social security tax. Two things the federal government could do, according to O'Hare, are (1) gear the earned income credit to family size so that workers with large families could reduce their income tax, and (2) further increase the minimum wage.

Workfare

One of the welfare reforms currently being discussed by legislators is workfare. The idea is that able-bodied adults who receive welfare should do some kind of work in exchange for the benefits. Some legislators have proposed that those who do not find a job within a specified period of time be cut off from welfare. Both O'Hare and Wilson, however, point out that this is not a new idea; and, as in the past, it is dependent upon the availability of jobs which the poor are capable of filling. O'Hare cautions, "A recent analysis indicates that the kinds of jobs that most rural welfare recipients are likely to be qualified for are difficult to find" (1988:15). Wilson (1987:162) reminds us that wherever unemployment is high, the poor will have a difficult time competing for those jobs which are available. He contends that no amount of remedial education, training, or wage subsidy will induce employers to hire the poor rather than experienced workers who are presently unemployed.

Child care

Another step to help the poor is to improve child care. There is general agreement that more facilities for child care are needed, that strict standards must be established, and that day care should be made accessible to low-income families who cannot afford the three thousand dollars a year required for each child. A problem jeopardizing the various proposals that have been made at the federal level is that many legislators are unwilling to add to the federal budget while attempts are being made to reduce the national debt.

Medical care for the poor

Earlier in this chapter we mentioned that only about 40 percent of the poor qualify for Medicaid. In 1988, a total of thirty-seven million

Americans were without medical insurance, an increase of 25 percent since 1980. Over the past several years there have been a number of legislative proposals to make medical care available to all, regardless of ability to pay. At the state level, Massachusetts has passed legislation that will make the uninsured eligible for coverage in 1992. The unemployed, the self-employed, small businesses, and other workers and their dependents not now covered will be able to obtain health insurance from a pool funded in part by the state and in part by a surcharge which employers will pay for each employee. The assumption behind the Massachusetts plan is that all Americans are entitled to receive adequate medical care. Its backers would like to see something comparable instituted at the national level.

Equality of opportunity for all

Wilson has proposed a policy that he believes will implement what is termed "the principle of the equality of life chances" (1987:116–18). He calls for the creation of a macroeconomic policy that will increase the competitiveness of American goods on the international market by reducing the federal deficit and making the dollar stronger. To enable the labor force to take advantage of present and future job opportunities, he advocates such measures as on-the-job training and apprenticeships that will elevate skills. In addition, he would have the federal government provide both transitional work for those who cannot find employment in the current job market and the means to relocate to where jobs are. The innovative, and controversial, part of Wilson's proposals is that such training, retraining, transitional employment, and funds for relocating would be made available to all Americans, not just to the poor.

Wilson's proposals to make certain opportunities available to all are similar to what is presently happening in many western European democracies, which "provide families with an annual benefit per child regardless of the family's income, and regardless of whether the parents are living together or whether either or both are employed" (1987:152). He points out that we already do have some benefits that are available to all families: the standard deduction on income tax and the earned income credit. Wilson argues that his proposals have two basic advantages. First, they are not limited to racial minorities and the poor, but are available to all. This makes them more politically acceptable and avoids the social stigma that attaches to those programs that are available only to the disadvantaged. Second, the persistently poor would receive disproportionately high benefits because their economic alternatives are so limited.

Persons who have had experience with programs designed to aid the poor by restructuring the basic economic system and the labor market are well aware of how formidable a task lies ahead. Yet they are convinced that such restructuring is necessary if we are to make significant reductions in the poverty level.

A Christian Response to Poverty in the United States

Over the last fifty years numerous programs with the goal of eliminating poverty in the United States have been developed. Vast amounts of time, energy, and money have been spent to combat poverty. Perhaps the most ambitious program to date was the federal government's "war on poverty" in the 1960s. Unfortunately, as the statistics we have presented indicate, the war on poverty has not been won.

Because of the failure of governmental efforts to win this war, it became increasingly popular in the 1980s for political leaders to argue that it is pointless for the federal government to attempt to do something about poverty. Our evidence shows, however, that as the federal government proceeded to do less in the 1980s, there was a corresponding increase in poverty in the United States. Can a Christian perspective on poverty contribute anything that has not already been considered? Our starting point in attempting to answer this question will be to examine what the Bible says about poverty.

Poverty as Explained in the Bible

While the Bible has much to say about poverty, too often it is used selectively to support a preconceived position. The most blatant example of this is demonstrated in the misuse of Jesus' statement, "You have the poor among you always" (Mark 14:7 NEB), to argue that Christians should do nothing about poverty. Similarly, some Christians, on the basis of a few scattered biblical references to specific historical instances, go as far as to attribute all poverty to drunkenness and laziness.

But an examination of the whole of Scripture reveals that the major cause it gives for poverty is oppression. Tom Hanks notes that in correlating "the biblical vocabulary for oppression . . . with the vocabulary for the poor and poverty, we find that in 122 texts oppression is indicated as the cause of poverty. The Hebrew lexicon even indicates an overlapping of meaning in some cases, so some words for poor should be translated the 'oppressed-poor'" (1981:19). Consider also that much of the Bible is written from the perspective of people who are oppressed and suffer at the hands of unjust rulers. In fact, Hanks estimates that "90 percent of biblical history is written from the perspective of a small, weak, oppressed, poor people."

It is hard for those of us who live in a free and wealthy country to understand Scripture as speaking for the oppressed. But while we may be tempted to spiritualize biblical texts on the subject, we can learn much from Christians in poor countries who take such passages literally and personally. When those of us in economically comfortable situations are tempted to regard laziness as the reason for poverty, we would do well to remember Pharaoh's view of the children of Israel when they were his captives. To their complaint that they could not make bricks because they were given no straw, Pharaoh replied, "You are lazy, you are lazy" (Exod. 5:17 NEB). Israel's great exodus from Pharaoh's oppression is the supreme Old Testament example of God's taking the side of the oppressed poor and acting in no uncertain terms for their liberation (Exod. 3:7–10; 6:2–5).

According to the Bible, then, oppression is the prime reason for poverty, and liberation is the solution to the problem. But let the Bible speak for itself:

> The Lord works righteousness [liberation]
>   and justice for all the oppressed.
> He made known his ways to Moses,
>   his deeds to the people of Israel. [Ps. 103:6–7 NIV]

> Turn to me and be saved [liberated],
>   all you ends of the earth;
>   for I am God, and there is no other. [Isa. 45:22 NIV]

The preoccupation with justice and liberation of the poor is not limited to the Old Testament, however. The New Testament Christians clearly felt the oppression of the Roman government. And Jesus placed himself squarely on the side of the oppressed when he stood up in the synagogue at Nazareth and read the liberating words of Isaiah: "The spirit of the Lord . . . has sent me to announce good news to the poor, to proclaim release for prisoners and recovery of sight for the blind; to let the broken victims go free, to proclaim the year of the Lord's favour" (Luke 4:18–19 NEB).

To the extent that inequality and poverty exist, *shalom* is not present in society. There are two different ways in which we can work to achieve *shalom*. First, Christians can become personally involved in efforts to empower the poor in their community. Second, Christians can support organizations and movements that seek to change those social structures that produce poverty and preserve inequality.

Empowering the Poor: An Example of a Holistic Community Ministry

In the late 1950s John Perkins, a black man living in the Los Angeles area, had a good job that adequately supported his wife and five children. But he had never forgotten the abject poverty he had experienced growing up as an orphan in rural Mississippi. So in 1960 he moved his family of seven back to Mississippi to begin the Voice of Calvary, a holistic ministry to the rural poor. This ministry was holistic in the sense that it recognized and focused upon the basic needs of poor people: personal salvation and economic self-sufficiency.

The Voice of Calvary addressed all the needs of the community, probing, challenging, and attempting to change any social structure which functioned to keep poor people dependent upon the existing system. Among the ministry's activities were protest marches, economic boycotts, drives to register new voters, educational programs for both children and adults, the development of a cooperative thrift store and distribution center, and the operation of a health clinic. The Voice of Calvary ministry has been successful in both empowering poor individuals to rise out of poverty and changing unjust social structures which served to retard economic development. Perkins's attempts to empower the poor were not without personal costs, however, as he was beaten and tortured by the sheriff and state police, and his brother died in his arms from gunshot wounds inflicted by a deputy marshal.

After a successful twenty-year ministry in Mississippi, John Perkins returned to the Los Angeles area to see if his holistic model of ministry could also work in an urban setting. Perkins's ministry is already proving successful among the very urban poor whom scores of community, county, state, and federal antipoverty projects have been unable to help. What is the difference?

The key, we believe, is that Perkins's approach seeks to empower the poor by both changing them and changing the community structures which perpetuate dependence. Government and private agencies have poured billions of dollars into a multitude of poverty-relief programs through the years. Unfortunately, most of these programs have served merely to keep the poor dependent. While the agencies involved pay lip service to the goal of fostering self-sufficiency, there are several reasons why they fail to accomplish this aim: (1) they are impersonal bureaucratic organizations; (2) they restrict their efforts to the individual level; (3) the persons in charge of the programs do not reside in the communities they are trying to help; (4) the majority are entrenched bureaucrats whose jobs depend on the poor staying poor; and (5) there is no effort to address spiritual needs. As a result, the poor have realized very little economic good from the vast amounts of money which were supposed to help them out of poverty. John McKnight (1989:38) expresses a similar position when he states that "service systems build on people's deficiencies; communities on their capacities."

To see what a biblically based empowering ministry to the poor might look like, let us examine the philosophy behind Perkins's ministry. To begin with, Perkins stresses the need to change both individuals and social structures. At the individual level Perkins identifies three goals: (1) *effective evangelism*—winning the poor to a saving knowledge of Jesus Christ; (2) *spiritual growth*—helping them mature in their relationship with God; and (3) *leadership development*—training the gifted among them to minister to the spiritual and material needs of others. The core of Perkins's ministry at the community level consists of what he calls the "three Rs of development"—*relocation, reconciliation,* and *redistribution* (Perkins 1981).

First, to be a part of the economic development of a poor community, one must relocate within it. Perkins believes that relocation is the only way in which one can truly identify with the people of the targeted community. He rejects what he calls a "yo-yo" ministry—commuting back and forth between the middle-class area where one lives and the poor urban area where one attempts to minister. Failure to relocate is one of the greatest reasons why most urban ministries are less than successful.

The second important step in ministry to a community is reconciliation between all its members regardless of social class or racial differences. Since Christians have experienced reconciliation to Christ through his death, they are called upon to break down the walls of hostility that separate and keep persons from different social and cultural backgrounds from loving each other. As Jesus himself said, "A new command I give you: Love one another. As I have loved you, so you must love one another. By this all men will know that you are my disciples, if you love one another" (John 13:34 NIV).

The third R, redistribution, Perkins describes as following logically from the first two, relocation and reconciliation:

> Finally, being God's people relocated in a community of need as a group reconciled to Him and to one another, we need to devise a new plan that will insure a more equitable distribution of goods and services within our own fellowship and for the people who experience us in the community. By this process of *redistribution*, we must show the world that we are sharing the love of God not only in terms of a verbal testimony but also in the sharing of resources with our new family. [1981:28]

The relationship between God's grace, which is the basis for reconciliation, and the believer's response to the poor is richly developed in 2 Corinthians 8. In this passage Paul stresses the point that God's grace to us is to find expression in our grace to the poor. In commenting on this chapter Stephen Mott (1982:32) states, "God's grace flows into [believers] and emerges as their grace toward the poor. God's benevolent act does not merely 'inspire' the response, it actually creates the ability to respond—it is both the reason and the power for the response."

Redistribution is more complicated than merely taking from the rich and giving to the poor. Rather, redistribution entails altering the existing community structures which are responsible for inequality. Economic equality on the community level does not necessarily mean that everyone receives the same amount, but rather that everyone has equal opportunity to be fairly rewarded. This may mean offering special training, services, or financial support to persons from culturally and economically deprived backgrounds. Among the possibilities are tutoring programs, job training, workshops on how to buy the most food for one's money and how to prepare nutritious meals, and paying for the education of children whose parents cannot afford to send them to college.

In summary, a ministry to empower the poor affirms their dignity by helping them develop the strengths to become meaningful participants in and contributors to their community's social and economic system. Having studied many programs designed to help the poor, we believe that a program has a better chance to empower the poor if it is small and personal, focuses upon both community and individual needs, and views people as having spiritual as well as social, psychological, and economic needs. We further believe that local churches are very well suited to the task of empowering the poor in contemporary society. Such programs will work best if churches minister in depth to a limited number of people living in a well-defined area.

Restoring Shalom:
Changing Social Structures That Generate Inequality

As we move away from the community level to the broader societal level, it becomes increasingly hard to visualize workable models for empowering the poor. One of the reasons for this is that poverty is so interrelated with a number of other social problems. Most obviously, the problems of juvenile delinquency, crime, racial discrimination, alienation, family instability, alcoholism, and drug abuse are disproportionately concentrated among the urban poor. As we have pointed out in the chapters dealing with these problems, injustice is often a contributory factor.

What we must do is to restore *shalom* at the societal level. The psalmist describes *shalom* in a society ruled by a king: "For he will deliver the needy who cry out, the afflicted who have no one to help. He will take pity on the weak and the needy and save the needy from death. He will rescue them from oppression and violence, for precious is their blood in his sight" (Ps. 72:12–14 NIV). For those of us living in a democratic society, *shalom* means speaking out, taking stands, and pursuing collective action which will bring about just social structures.

Although the Bible speaks of oppression as the major cause of poverty, we do not think of ourselves as an oppressive people. By any measurement it is tempting to argue that the government of the United States is one of the least oppressive. Persons of all ethnic groups do experience as much freedom in the United States as in any other nation of the world. To make such a claim, however, is to ignore the oppressive way in which we treated minority groups like blacks and Indians in the past. Among

Western democracies, we hold the distinction of having been the last to abolish slavery. We alternatively offered the Indians treaties (which we broke at will) and robbed them of their land. This past oppression goes far to explain why a disproportionate number of blacks, Indians, and other minorities are among the underclass, the truly disadvantaged. Restoring *shalom* will mean breaking the cycle of poverty that holds so many of these people in a continuous state of despair.

As we pointed out in chapter 5, Christians must not let ideological reasons for opposing preferential treatment prevent them from taking positive steps that will effectively empower those caught in the cycle of poverty. We have already suggested how this might be done at the community level. At the wider societal level it means supporting private and governmental efforts to assist, train, and employ persons who think of themselves, and are thought of by others, as useless. As Mott (1982:202) states, "It is not governmental generosity which has created the incentive for recipients of welfare programs to remain dependent, but the timidity of government and the failure of a full-employment policy." To the extent that our society believes that there will always be some useless people, there is no *shalom*.

In a broken and sinful world there will, of course, be some people who, because of a multitude of interrelated circumstances, cannot be empowered to economic self-sufficiency. This is and has been the case in all societies. The scriptural teachings about our responsibility for the dependent poor are clear and unambiguous:

> If you lend money to one of my people among you who is needy, do not be like a moneylender; charge him no interest. If you take your neighbor's cloak as a pledge, return it to him by sunset, because his cloak is the only covering he has for his body. [Exod. 22:25–27]

> For six years you are to sow your fields and harvest the crops, but during the seventh year let the land lie unplowed and unused. Then the poor among your people may get food from it. [Exod. 23:10–11]

> When you reap the harvest of your land, do not reap to the very edges of your field or gather the gleanings of your harvest. . . . Leave them for the poor and the alien. [Lev. 19:9–10]

> If there is a poor man among your brothers in any of the towns of the land that the LORD your God is giving you, do not be hardhearted or tightfisted toward your poor brother. Rather be openhanded and freely lend him whatever he needs. [Deut. 15:7–8]

> There will always be poor people in the land. Therefore I command you to be openhanded toward your brothers and toward the poor and needy in your land. [Deut. 15:11]

Defend the cause of the weak and fatherless; maintain the rights of the poor and oppressed. Rescue the weak and needy; deliver them from the hand of the wicked. [Ps. 82:3–4]

He who oppresses the poor shows contempt for their Maker, but whoever is kind to the needy honors God. [Prov. 14:31]

A generous man will himself be blessed, for he shares his food with the poor. [Prov. 22:9]

He who gives to the poor will lack nothing, but he who closes his eyes to them receives many curses. [Prov. 28:27]

Jesus answered, "If you want to be perfect, go, sell your possessions and give to the poor, and you will have treasure in heaven." [Matt. 19:21]

Give proper recognition to those widows who are really in need. [1 Tim. 5:3]

Look after orphans and widows in their distress. [James 1:27 NIV]

The biblical writers recognize that there will always be poor people, even if all oppression were to be done away with. They also clearly communicate that God desires that no one be poor or needy. Taken together, the verses we have cited point out the believer's obligation to attend to the needs of people who are poor and cannot do anything about their plight.

A case can be made that the poor should ideally be cared for by small, personal social groups such as the family (1 Tim. 5:4) and the church (v. 16). The biblical thrust is overwhelmingly clear, however, that when care from these intimate groups is not available, it is the duty of the community and society to help the poor and needy. Application of the principle of *shalom* means that there will be a safety net to catch and support the needy of our society. The Christian ethic demands that the poor without family or friends should be cared for. When this takes place, there is *shalom*.

Topics for Review, Reflection, and Discussion

1. How have the demographics of the homeless population changed during the last ten years?

2. What is meant by the feminization of poverty? What factors have brought it about?

3. What is the main cause of poverty in the United States? Is it possible to explain poverty in terms of a single cause?

4. What does a large number of working poor indicate about the economic system of a society?

5. Compare the advantages of workfare and welfare. Does the concept of empowering play a role?

6. How is poverty explained in the Bible?

7. Is it realistic to think that most of the poor can be empowered to the point of economic self-sufficiency?

13

Poverty and World Hunger

Nature of the Concern

As we settle down in the comfort of our easy chair, we grab the remote control and begin to sample the evening's television fare. Switching from one station to another we come to a troubling picture: World Vision is presenting a special on the starving people in Ethiopia. We feel a sudden twinge of guilt, but quickly change the channel before the discomfort grows too great. Ah, the nine-o'clock movie is just beginning—this should allow us to relax.

Perhaps the greatest cause for concern here is our lack of concern about poverty and world hunger. Or perhaps the problem is not so much a lack of concern as it is the erratic nature of our concern. We live in an age of media events like Live-Aid, Farm-Aid, Hands across America, and We Are the World. We get swept up in a sudden outpouring of concern for the poor—a concern which dissipates as quickly as it arises. However well motivated, such bursts of concern for the poor are like trying to cure a serious illness with Band-Aids.

Our concern about poverty is usually directed towards the poor in our own country. Without minimizing the problem of poverty in the United States, it is noteworthy that if our definition of poverty were used in the rest of the world, over half of the world's population would be classified as poor. Accordingly, our concern for the world will focus less on poverty than on hunger—not having enough food to eat. According to a conservative estimate by the United Nations, one out of every eight people in the world is seriously or chronically malnourished; about one-quarter of all children under the age of six are malnourished. Each year more than 15 million people die of hunger-related causes. Furthermore, current trends suggest that the situation is not getting better, but worse. In the *Global 2000 Report to the President* (1982:1) it was projected that the number of hungry people in the world would increase from 500 million in 1977 to 1,300 million in the year 2000. Thus, in terms of human suffering, hunger may be the most serious social problem facing the world today.

Dimensions of the Problem

World hunger is concentrated in those areas of the world that are undergoing rapid population growth without a corresponding rise in the economy. Geographically, this includes large pockets of people living in Africa, Central and South America, and the Far East. People living in east central Africa have been especially hard hit in recent years, as severe drought has added to the already serious problem of population growth outpacing food production.

There is also evidence that the battle against hunger in the poorest countries is losing ground. Rather than becoming self-sufficient, these countries must go deeper and deeper in debt just to feed their people. The poor countries of the world now owe about one trillion dollars to the governments and private banks of the United States, England, France, Japan, and West Germany. Although the citizens of the poor countries did not personally contract these loans, they are being forced to pay as cuts are being made in education, health care, and food subsidies, thereby increasing hunger.

During the last fifty years, the greatest amount of urban growth has been occurring in the Two-Thirds World. In western Europe and North America rapid urbanization has been accompanied by a very high level of economic development. The even more rapid rate of urban growth in poorer countries is, in contrast, presently accompanied by a very low level of economic development. The poorest of the poor in most countries of the world live in squatter settlements (Hutter 1988:142–44). Not only are the people in these settlements economically poor, but they are also deprived of the social structures of rural village life. Urban poverty is accentuated by the fact that each flood, drought, or other disaster sends a new wave of poor people to urban areas, where the relief agencies are located.

Explaining Poverty and World Hunger

It is tempting to try to come up with one all-embracing explanation for poverty and world hunger. But attributing these problems to laziness, war, drought, overpopulation, lack of economic development, greed, or exploitation of the powerless by the powerful is too easy. Although each of these factors may contribute to poverty and hunger, none, when considered alone, offers an adequate explanation. There may indeed be some people who are poor because they are lazy, but most poor people work very hard. War certainly produces poverty by consuming, destroying, and diverting great quantities of resources, but poverty also exists in times of peace. Drought produces poverty by destroying the means of livelihood and raising food prices, yet poverty exists even where rainfall is abundant.

While no single explanation can adequately account for the problem of poverty and hunger, overpopulation, underdevelopment, and economic exploitation deserve special investigation. After considering these three explanations and corresponding solutions for poverty and hunger, we will offer a biblical perspective that seeks to evaluate and integrate these three separate approaches.

Overpopulation

Nearly two hundred years ago, Thomas Malthus, an English clergyman, foresaw today's problem of world hunger. He explained that while population grows geometrically (1, 2, 4, 8, 16, 32), food production increases only arithmetically (1, 2, 3, 4, 5, 6). The disproportion between population growth and food production makes drastic shortages of food inevitable. As Malthus looked into the future, he predicted widespread famine, disease, and war.

Malthus's predictions about population growth appear to be coming true. Prior to the agricultural revolution (ca. 5000 B.C.) population figures were fairly stable; a high birth rate was balanced by a high death rate. As agriculture developed and more food was produced, the world population slowly grew to about five hundred million in A.D. 1650. By 1900 the growth rate was up to 1 percent annually, and world population had doubled, reaching one billion. The population doubled to two billion by 1940, doubled again to four billion by 1975, added another billion in just eleven years (1986), and at the present rate of growth will add yet another billion by 1995. Thus, while it took the whole of human history to reach one billion persons in 1900, it will have taken just ninety-five more years to reach six billion (see figure 7). It has taken a bit longer for Malthus's gloomy predictions to come true only because he did not foresee the increases in food production made possible by modern agricultural technology.

Prior to the advent of modern medicine, population growth was low because the high death rate balanced out the high birth rate. But then nearly all economically developing societies went through a transitional stage of high population growth due to a lowering of the death rate and

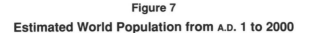

Figure 7
Estimated World Population from A.D. 1 to 2000

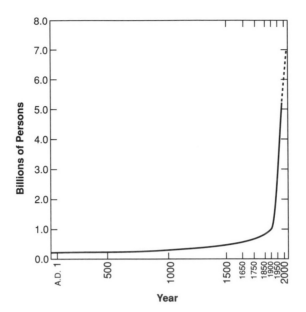

a continuing high birth rate. This transition in our own nation's history took place during the late 1800s and early 1900s. The population increased geometrically because medical technology greatly reduced the death rate, especially infant deaths, while the birth rate remained high. Then, as we moved into the twentieth century, family planning and birth-control techniques greatly reduced the birth rate. By 1970, the United States, along with most other technologically advanced societies, approached the stage of zero population growth, where the birth and death rates are equally low.

As a result, nearly all of the world's present population growth is taking place in the underdeveloped Two-Thirds World, countries that are trapped in the transitional stage of high birth rates and low death rates. The longer a country remains at this stage, the greater its population growth, and the greater the pressure placed upon its underdeveloped economy to provide more food for an exploding population. Malthus's prediction—that if a country does not check its population growth, nature will (in the form of famine, disease, or war)—is proving all too true at present. The great pockets of world hunger in Africa, Central and South America, and the Far East are characterized by famine, disease, and war.

Some, however, would argue that the world does not have a population problem, but merely the problem of how we can best use our resources and distribute food equitably. This argument pales, however, when we recognize that even if the present food supply could be evenly distributed and we could maximize the world's agricultural resources, the population explosion would still, in the end, result in the continuation of starvation conditions. The indisputable fact is that unless the current rate of population growth is reduced, the problem of world starvation will get worse.

Underdevelopment

Another proposed explanation of poverty and world hunger is the underdevelopment of the Two-Thirds World. One of the practical fruits of the scientific revolution in modern societies, it is pointed out, has been the harnessing of energy and consequent technological development. Traditional societies are at an economic disadvantage to the extent that they have not experienced a similar degree of technological development. They are agriculturally backward and unable to generate material wealth. Technological underdevelopment, then, lies at the root of poverty and hunger.

Development can be thought of as evolutionary—a series of small steps building on each other. Economic theorist Walt Rostow (1961), for instance, conceives of technological development as a five-stage progression: traditional agrarian society, preconditioning for takeoff, takeoff, drive to maturity, and high mass-consumption. In European and North American countries, this evolution in technological development began in the late 1600s and has continued over a three-hundred-year period. Unfortunately, underdeveloped countries today do not have the luxury of three hundred years in which to gradually absorb technological change. Exploding population growth, combined with the struggle to survive in the technologically based world economy, places great pressure upon underdeveloped countries to rapidly modernize.

Proponents of the theory that underdevelopment explains poverty and world hunger point out that by the standards of today's economically developed countries, most people throughout history lived in poverty. Therefore, to ask, "What is the cause of poverty?" is to ask the wrong question. It is argued that greater progress will be made towards eliminating poverty if we ask, "What is the cause of wealth?" The simple answer of technological development is offered as the universal solution for poverty.

Economic Exploitation and Dependence

Others argue against explaining poverty and world hunger in terms of underdevelopment. They point out that thirty to forty years of Western aid to and investment in the Two-Thirds World have not resulted in economic improvement. On the contrary, these contacts have led to a growing inequality. Through a process which began with colonization the Two-Thirds World has gradually come to be dependent upon the developed countries.

In his two-volume work, *The Modern World-System*, Immanuel Wallerstein (1976, 1980) argues that European nations began to make the poorer peoples of the world dependent on them in the sixteenth century. First, Europe plundered Latin America, Africa, and Asia for precious metals, spices, and slaves, destroying indigenous social organizations in the process. By the twentieth century this exploitation had intensified to the point that the poor countries found themselves completely dependent upon their earnings from the export of a few select products to the rich countries. In this process, called colonialism, natural tribal divisions were superseded by nation-states whose chief purpose was to benefit the European countries. These poorer states provided raw materials and cheap labor and, in turn, depended upon the developed countries for technological knowledge. According to the proponents of this theory, this economic arrangement lasted because of the vested interests of a minority of very rich people in the poor countries. While this minority prospered, the masses remained in poverty.

The Europeans placed constraints on development within the poor countries for economic reasons. To have allowed a colonial country which was rich in raw materials and resources to build factories to process those raw materials would have effectively eliminated its dependence upon the European nation. And so, during the 1700s, England tried to force the American colonies to ship cotton across the Atlantic Ocean so that it could be woven into cloth in England and then shipped back to America to be sold at a handsome profit. But while the American colonies gained their freedom from that unequal relationship, the revolution never came for many countries formed under colonialism. Although the vast majority of the world's poor countries became politically independent nation-states during the twentieth century, they continued to find themselves economically dependent upon the core capitalist countries.

Figure 8 presents a visual model of this system. The economy of the noncommunist world today centers in the United States, Canada, Japan, and central and northern Europe. The peripheral countries are the poor nations throughout the free world. The semiperipheral countries were at one time peripheral countries but now are candidates for core status; included among the semiperipheral countries are Mexico, South Korea, Taiwan, South Africa, and the Philippines. All of these countries are economically interdependent—but this interdependence is unequal, for the peripheral countries are far more dependent upon the core countries than the reverse. So while the era of colonialism is past, the functional dependence of poor countries upon rich countries continues to exist. The

Figure 8
Dependency in the World Economic System

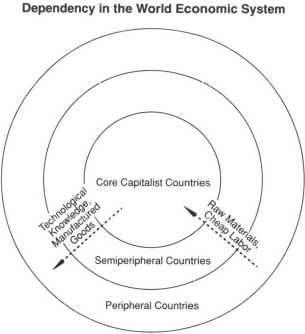

core countries have the capital, knowledge, and technology which generate more wealth, while the peripheral countries generally provide only raw materials and a vast pool of uneducated and unskilled cheap labor.

With the advancements in computer and electronic technology in the core countries, manufacturing has largely been taken over by semiperipheral countries. Thus, more clothing is now manufactured in countries like South Korea and Taiwan than in core countries. Other examples of heavy manufacturing which is moving from core to semiperipheral countries include the production of iron and steel and automobiles.

It would be wrong to assume that no one gets rich in semiperipheral and peripheral countries. On the contrary, the urban elite and landed families often amass extreme wealth, while the vast majority of the population remains in poverty. Ferdinand and Imelda Marcos, the former rulers of the Philippines, are a notorious example.

Multinational corporations based in the core countries work through the elite of the peripheral countries, offering them bribes or shares of the wealth to be generated. In return the elite make sure that their country's agriculture is devoted exclusively to a few cash crops intended for export. Thus, many Central American countries do not produce enough food for their own people because most of the good agricultural land is owned by a few rich families who are growing coffee, sugar, or bananas to be exported to the rich countries of the world. Whatever profits the multinational corporations do not take out of the poor countries are re-invested in ways that help only the few elite. One of the results of this growing inequality is that the small farmers in underdeveloped countries have been gradually squeezed off their land. Desperate pockets of poverty form as masses of landless poor vie for the few low-paying, unskilled jobs which are available.

Most proponents of the theory that poverty and world hunger are due to economic exploitation argue that the only way out of the dismal situation in which poor countries now find themselves is to break with the capitalist system in favor of socialism (a centrally planned economy). But this may be no solution at all. For it is possible to apply the theory of economic dependency to communist countries as well. The Soviet Union is the core socialist country, while most other communist countries have until recently occupied a place on the periphery. For decades the threat of military force kept even industrialized communist countries like Poland and East Germany in a state of dependency upon the Soviet Union. On the other hand, countries like Yugoslavia and China, which have long enjoyed a certain degree of autonomy from Soviet control, may gradually move towards becoming semiperipheral countries within the capitalist world economy. For example, consider the recent introduction of the Yugoslavian-built car, the Yugo, into the United States. It is obvious, then, from the inequality among the nations in the communist world that socialism is not the answer.

Various Approaches to Poverty and World Hunger

Just as there are no simple explanations of poverty and world hunger, so are there no simple solutions. We should be suspicious of those who offer a universal solution for the problem. In this section we shall find that the solutions most often offered reflect the major theories concerning what causes poverty and world hunger: overpopulation, underdevelopment, and economic exploitation and dependence.

During the early part of the twentieth century, as we saw earlier (pp. 42–43), a new gospel grew out of Christian liberalism. What came to be known as the social gospel (Rauschenbusch 1919) thought of evil as residing in social structures rather than in individuals. If sin is primarily structural rather than individual, it was argued, the primary aim of the Christian gospel should be to convert the evil social structures which corrupt individuals. There followed a polarization in the Christian community as to how to approach social issues. While fundamentalists devoted themselves exclusively to converting individuals and then waited for the new life in Christ to effect change from within, liberals sought to redeem humanity by eradicating social evils and then waiting for improvement in the lives and actions of individuals.

The intensity of the polarity between fundamentalists and liberals eventually cooled. The post–World War II years witnessed attempts at restoring the gospel to an integrated whole—proclaiming the good news that God seeks to liberate both the individual sinner from the bondage of sin and the poor and enslaved from the evils of oppressive social structures. Yet while the polarity within the Christian community has substantially subsided, there are two decisively different views as to how poverty and world hunger might best be conquered. Democratic capitalism is suggested by Christians who view underdevelopment as the major problem. Liberation theology is propounded by those who focus on economic exploitation. Before analyzing these views, however, we must look briefly at attempts to control poverty and world hunger strictly through population control.

Population Control

It can be argued that the simple solution to poverty and world hunger is to reduce the number of infants born into this world. However, this is easier said than done. For from the point of view of the poor, economic security is found not in limiting the number of children, but rather in producing many children and thereby assuring that one will be cared for when one is old.

Through the years many programs have tried to change the propensity of the poor to have large numbers of children; most have failed. The programs that have proven most effective in reducing population growth are not those that aim at changing attitudes, but rather those that use authoritarian means to change behavior directly. For example, population growth has been curtailed in China by passing laws forbidding the birth of a second child. Punishments for violation include fines, reductions in pay, denial of promotion, and even loss of one's job. In other countries, however, such authoritarian means have been less effective. The government of India, for example, has stopped the forced sterilization of women who have three children.

Population experts who would like to encourage the poor to produce fewer children face a dilemma. The accumulated evidence suggests that people begin to limit family size only after they experience some economic betterment or move to an urban area. Even in developed countries, the highest fertility rates are found among the people with the lowest income. As a result, the experts suggest that if programs to reduce poverty are to be effective, they should aim at improving economic conditions rather than limiting family size.

Democratic Capitalism

Proponents of the theory that poverty is due to underdevelopment argue that the problem can be reduced simply by propelling poor countries in the direction of democratic capitalism. They argue that wealth will inevitably develop in a society which has a democratic government and free-market economy. This is the official policy of the United States government and most other developed societies in their relations with poor countries. Thus they give aid in hopes that the poor countries will become developed. Douglas Kennard (1984:164–65) summarizes this view:

> In many agricultural programs, for example, it is assumed that rural peasants will adopt externally-introduced modern farming techniques when it is demonstrated that they can increase their yields and incomes as well as their knowledge. Consequently, as they abandon counter-productive cultural and superstitious practices, inequalities between rural and urban areas should decrease; in a like manner, as similar changes take place simultaneously, throughout societies of lesser-developed nations, inequalities between these and the more developed nations should be reduced. Practically speaking, this philosophy of change has been embodied in the agricultural development programs of the U.S. Agency for International Development (USAID) which have been patterned after the experience of modernized agriculture in the United States.

By harnessing machine technology, the economically developed countries of the world have generated wealth unmatched by all previous societies. Poverty and hunger exist in the Two-Thirds World, it is argued, because of the lack of economic development there. However, as modern science and technology have been introduced into underdeveloped countries, it has become increasingly evident that a variety of indigenous cultural factors are capable of retarding development. These factors include emphases on tradition rather than change, collectivism rather than individualism, family rather than voluntary associations, informality rather than formality, and passive acceptance of circumstance rather than active attempts to master one's environment. It is clear, then, that technological development cannot merely be deposited in another culture, for, if adopted, it may change that culture in unforeseen ways. Modernity entails more than adopting machine technology; it may also force a change in an entire way of life.

One of the main Christian advocates of democratic capitalism as the solution for poverty and world hunger is Michael Novak (1982, 1986). Novak believes that rather than asking, "What are the causes of poverty?" those concerned about poverty should ask, "What are the causes of wealth?" He believes that capitalism, more than any other economic system, is capable of producing unimaginable development and wealth. He relies heavily on Adam Smith's classic *Inquiry into the Nature and Causes of the Wealth of Nations* (1776), which argues that the essence of capitalism is not private property, markets, or exchanges, but an open spirit and ethic of development which liberates humankind from accepting poverty as willed by God.

Christian proponents of democratic capitalism, such as Novak, emphasize that it comports very well with the biblical doctrine of sin, encourages creativity, and promotes voluntary community. First, capitalism is an economic system which is created for sinners. While communism is a good economic system for saints, there are too few saints in the world to make it work. Capitalism, on the other hand, works because it takes human self-interest into account.

Further, when capitalism exists in a democratic environment, it prevents the accumulation of power in the hands of only a few individuals. In Novak's vision of the ideal system, the intellectual, political, and business communities check and balance each other. None of these groups gains power over the others; in fact, no group even trusts the others! While it may be possible for the three groups to cooperate at times, they must always closely watch one another. Thus, by recognizing the sinful nature of human beings, the leading forces in a capitalist democracy prevent the development of totalitarian social structures. A built-in weakness of collective economies, on the other hand, is their lack of realism about the basic nature of human beings.

Second, Novak argues that capitalism encourages creativity. This leads to invention and discovery, which in turn contribute to increased economic productivity. In a free market, people directly benefit when they create a better way of doing something. But socialist systems inhibit creativity—creative persons go unrewarded for their discoveries and inventiveness. Such societies seem ignorant of the fact that it is creativity and not natural resources that produces wealth. Resources are valuable only if human ingenuity finds a use for them. This can be illustrated by comparing the economic systems of Japan and Brazil. Japan is a prime example of a country in which democratic capitalism encourages creativity, which in turn has led to wealth, even though Japan has virtually no natural resources. While Brazil has many natural resources, it has been unable to translate those resources into wealth. The difference, it can be argued, is the creativity found within a free-market economy.

Third, a distinct mark of democratic capitalism, argues Novak, is the corporate bloc. While one's loyalty is tied to the family in traditional societies, in modern capitalism loyalty is placed in the voluntary community. Novak disagrees with the common wisdom that individualism is a problem in the United States. Instead, he believes that individualism is a problem in non-Western countries where people have difficulty transcending family loyalty. In capitalist societies, people are free to form associations based on common interest rather than kinship. This allows them to become members of many single-purpose communities composed of persons with whom they may have little else in common.

Perhaps the strongest support for the argument that democratic capitalism can overcome poverty more effectively than any other system is given in Peter Berger's *Capitalist Revolution: Fifty Propositions about Prosperity, Equality, and Liberty* (1986). Berger, a highly respected sociologist who identifies with the Christian tradition, examines the ability of both capitalist and socialist societies to generate material wealth, provide an equitable income for all, allow for upward mobility, ensure political liberty, and sustain economic development. The first of his fifty propositions asserts that "industrial capitalism has generated the greatest productive power in human history." Regarding income equity the sixth proposition states that "in Western societies (and in most societies elsewhere) technological modernization and economic growth, if they persist over time, first cause a sharp increase in income and wealth inequalities, then a sharp decline in these inequalities, and then a relatively stable plateau." As to capitalism's ability to help poor countries, Berger asserts that "the inclusion of a Third World country within the international capitalist system tends to favor its economic development."

But while Berger contends that capitalism is more able than socialism to provide political freedom, social openness, and economic growth, he also warns against the temptation to proclaim capitalism a Christian system. It is not! Capitalism should be regarded as a more or less useful framework for organizing economic activity rather than a Christian system of economics. Capitalism can be used to either develop or crush the best of human potential. Like any economic system, it needs to be infused with a Christian social ethic if it is to have any hope of leading to *shalom*—the state of peace, justice, and righteousness in society.

Liberation Theology

We now turn again to the theory that places the primary blame for poverty and world hunger upon social structures that prevent an equitable distribution of wealth. The advocates of this theory tend to suggest that socialism is the solution to poverty. In its more extreme form, what we have here is virtually a reformulation of Marxism. Christians who accept the theory that exploitation is the basic cause of poverty, however, tend to express its ideas in terms of liberation theology. Liberation theologians stress that the Bible's main explanation for poverty is the oppression of the poor and weak by the rich and powerful. Further, they often suggest that Christian behavior is more likely to be encouraged in an economic system that stresses cooperation rather than competition.

Since there is considerable variation in the extent to which liberation theologians choose to use biblical material in formulating their ideas, the content of liberation theology can vary greatly. Some evangelical Christians hold that liberation theology is merely an updated version of the old social gospel (see especially Nash 1984). The social gospel, as will be recalled from our discussion in chapter 3, proposed that sin is culturally transmitted and thus resides in social structures rather than in individuals. Some liberation theologians come close to this position. Others, however, assert that they are making a biblical corrective to an overly individualized, Western interpretation of scriptural teaching. Their theology places emphasis on the need to change both sinful individuals and sinful social structures. Most black liberation theology in the United States has this dual emphasis, although some within the Christian community argue that this movement stresses the need to change the social structure much more than the need for personal regeneration.

The most important architects of liberation theology have been South American Roman Catholic theologians. In his now classic book, *A Theology of Liberation* (1973), Gustavo Gutierrez contends that all theology should revolve around praxis. He argues that since the fourteenth century, theology has come to be thought of as rational knowledge; accordingly, the church has devoted her attention to formulating cognitive truths. Lost in this sterile, narrow concept of theology is any notion that theology entails bettering the world. In contrast, liberation theology is based upon praxis—the relationship between formulating truth and living out that truth in the world. Liberation theology, Gutierrez declares, emerges from the interplay between Christian belief and Christian practice.

The biblical roots of liberation theology make it more than merely a Christianized version of the theory that exploitation causes poverty. Because liberation theology takes sin into account, it calls for a spiritual revolution as well as a social revolution. Sin affects both individuals and social structures; thus there is a need for liberation at both levels. Gutierrez quotes Galatians 5:1, "For freedom Christ has set us free" (RSV), and then states that Paul refers here to liberation from sin—a selfish turning in upon ourselves and a refusal to love our neighbor. As a breach of friendship with God and others, sin is the ultimate cause of poverty, injustice, and oppression. In describing sin as the ultimate cause, Gutierrez is not downplaying the social structures which also contribute to these problems. What we must be especially careful to note here, however, is the fact that he does not ignore personal sin, for he states that "behind unjust social structures there is a personal or collective will responsible—a willingness to reject God and neighbor. . . . [Consequently,] a social transformation, no matter how radical it may be, does not automatically achieve the suppression of all evils" (1973:35).

Most of the confusion and controversy surrounding liberation theology stems from the multiple meanings of the term *liberation*. Gutierrez refers to three different levels of liberation: (1) political liberation—release from economic, social, and political oppression; (2) personal liberation—"Christ the Savior liberates man from sin"; and (3) historical liber-

ation—"man . . . assum[es] conscious responsibility for his own destiny" (p. 36). Gutierrez comments: "These three levels mutually affect
each other, but they are not the same. One is not present without the others, but they are distinct: they are all part of a single, all encompassing
salvific process, but they are to be found at different levels" (p. 176).

Most liberation theology is holistic, stressing that the gospel must pen-
etrate both individual hearts and social structures. Sin is not just an individual, private, or interior reality, necessitating only a spiritual redemption which does not challenge the order in which we live. Sin is also a
social, historical fact. It is the absence of brotherhood and love in relationships between people, a breach of friendship with God and with others that manifests itself in social injustice.

Thus, liberation theology can be a helpful corrective to the individualized, privatized, and materialistic brand of Christianity that has developed in our society. Two cautions must be raised, however. First, possibly because much of liberation theology has developed out of Roman
Catholicism, there is the danger that it may lead to the doctrine of justifi-

cation through works. Those who are working for liberation may come to be thought of as saved by this activity. Second, we must beware of the tendency in liberation theology to substitute a dichotomy of the oppressed and the oppressors for the traditional Christian dichotomy of the saved and the lost. These two dangers are related, and both have implications for the Christian view of salvation. Liberation theologians must be careful not to substitute sociological categories for theological categories. They must never lose sight of the fact that individuals must personally respond to the living God who offers salvation to all through faith.

An Evaluation of Capitalist and Socialist Economies

Proponents of the theory that underdevelopment is the cause of poverty see democratic capitalism (a free-market economy) as the solution. Proponents of the theory that economic exploitation is the cause of poverty see democratic socialism (a centrally planned economy) as the solution. In the current debate between the advocates of capitalism and socialism, unfair comparisons are often made. Both sides point to the negative effects of the other system. We shall try to avoid this trap as we examine how capitalist and socialist economies actually function in democratic societies.

Table 3 compares the strengths and limitations of capitalism and socialism. In general, free-market economies are better at generating wealth, while centrally planned economies are more successful in achieving financial equality and eliminating poverty and hunger. Free-market economies are self-coordinating and capable of taking care of themselves, but they lack the ability to make long-range decisions or to quickly reorient national priorities. On the other hand, the ability of centrally planned economies to regulate priorities is offset by their limiting of individual freedom of choice. While free-market economies provide greater opportunities and motivation for creativity and innovation, centrally planned societies provide greater economic security. Free-market economies result in greater diversification of ownership and economic power, although in reality many citizens are left out of the propertied class. Centrally planned economies are more able to ensure that all members of society share ownership and economic power, although in reality ownership by the state may not mean ownership by the people. While free-market economies encourage a consumerism which can lead to materialism, centrally planned economies, though not free from materialism, at least are not as driven by consumerism. It is interesting to note, however, that both the Soviet Union and China are trying to encourage consumerism as a way to economic growth.

It is unclear which system has the advantage over the other when it comes to control of production and consumption. Capitalists argue that

Table 3

The Strengths and Limitations of Capitalism and Socialism

	Capitalism (free market)	Socialism (centrally planned economy)
1. Capacity to generate wealth	Strength	Limitation
2. Self-governing coordination of economic production	Strength	Limitation
3. Diversification of ownership and economic power	Strength	Limitation
4. Allowance for freedom of choice	Strength	Limitation
5. Encouragement of creativity and innovation	Strength	Limitation
6. Equality of ownership and economic power	Potential strength	Potential strength
7. Meaningful participation by the individual in the economy	Limited strength	Limited strength
8. Consumer control of production and consumption	Limited strength	Limited strength
9. Achievement of financial equality	Limitation	Strength
10. Ability to make economic decisions on a long-range basis	Limitation	Strength
11. Ability to quickly reorient national priorities	Limitation	Strength
12. Elimination of poverty and hunger	Limitation	Strength
13. Freedom from materialism	Limitation	Potential limitation

consumers control production by selectively buying what they want. Socialists contend that this is an illusion, pointing out that capitalist producers utilize elaborate advertising to convince consumers to buy items they do not need or even want. Capitalists counter that although socialist economies claim to produce what people want, consumers actually have little choice and find that what is available is of poor quality.

Before we come to any conclusion about the ability of capitalist and socialist economies to address the problems of poverty and world hunger, two facts should be pointed out. First, contrary to the claims of Christians in both camps, neither economic system is inherently Christian. Each represents a way of handling the production, distribution, and consumption of material goods. Both have specific strengths and limitations, and are susceptible to sinful excesses. Neither represents the perfect system. If a society of perfect people existed, the emphasis on cooperation would probably move them in the direction of a centrally planned economy. But people are not perfect. Instead, they tend to behave in accordance with their own self-interests.

Second, there does not now exist, nor has there ever existed, a pure capitalist or socialist economic system. Neither seems capable of actualization in its pure form, regardless of what economic theories proclaim. All so-called socialist systems allow for some individual participation in market activity; all so-called capitalist systems involve a limited amount of government ownership and planning.

On balance, the problems of poverty and world hunger can probably best be overcome by an economic system which we would describe as *democratic capitalism with a heart*. While democratic capitalism comports with the basic nature of human beings, there is a need to build into this system checks against runaway greed and destructive competition. There is also a need to provide additional care and protection for the more dependent members of society since they, despite their weaknesses, are no less worthy than others in the sight of God.

A Christian Response

In the previous chapter we noted that the Bible views oppression as the main cause of poverty. When confronted with the biblical evidence, many of those who focus on underdevelopment argue that the biblical view is no longer relevant. Novak (1982, 1986), for example, argues that the biblical statements on the subject must be interpreted in light of the fact that, capitalism and the wealth it generates not having as yet come into operation, most people in Bible times lived just beyond the reach of poverty.

But while it is true that the application of machine technology has vastly improved the standard of living for many people in the world, the number of people living in poverty is greater today than it ever has been. The human heart has not changed since biblical times, and the assertion that economic oppression no longer exists simply ignores an enormous amount of evidence. A truly utopian social structure that would prevent humans from economically exploiting one another is not yet in place. Meanwhile, people are just as creative as ever in devising ways to achieve their own self-interests at the expense of others.

So then, the theory that exploitation causes poverty comports very well with the biblical explanation. Given opportunity, most people will exploit others. And now, modern technology enables the rich to take even more advantage of the poor. The cry of the prophet Amos is just as relevant today as it was to the original audience: "Hear this, you who trample upon the needy, and bring the poor of the land to an end . . . The LORD has sworn by the pride of Jacob: 'Surely I will never forget any of their deeds'" (Amos 8:4, 7 RSV).

The evidence accumulated by sociological research indicates that exploitation causes poverty. But this evidence does not rule out the fact that lack of economic development causes poverty. The latter explanation is also right; poor countries would be better off economically if they followed the lead of the more developed countries. However, a multitude of obstacles stand in the way. These obstacles include far more than "envy, intellectual poverty, lack of motivation and physical limitations," which one Christian writer naively suggests "are only the result of prior spiritual folly" (Middelmann 1987). We must ever bear in mind that some people are poor because they are powerless and thus are easy targets for economic exploitation.

As long as there are poor and hungry people in the world, there is no *shalom*. Yet feeding the hungry will not in and of itself bring about *shalom*. Rather, as we stressed in chapter 3, *shalom* will exist only when social structures allow poor people to rise out of their condition and feed themselves.

Another concept which was discussed in chapter 3, empowering, is also relevant here. It will be recalled that we defined empowering as an attempt to establish power in another person. As applied to the topic at hand, empowering means that the economically strong will assist the poor of the world to find ways in which they can become self-sufficient. The process will begin by helping the poor and powerless recognize their own strengths and potentials. Empowerers will then encourage, guide, and be willing to step back, so that the empowered learn by doing and not by depending. The economically powerful will respect the unique ways in which the empowered achieve economic competence, and will not try to control or enforce their own ways of doing and being. This means that economic powers like the United States and the Soviet Union will allow poor countries to develop in their own ways. The rich nations will not demand conformity to their ideology or deference to their vested interests.

Much empowering can be done simply through example, by demonstrating in action how to become economically self-sufficient. In some cases, however, it may be necessary for members of the body of Christ to practice economic *koinōnia*—the "sharing of one's possessions with other Christians." On the basis of his study of Scripture, Lindy Scott (1980:139–40) concludes:

> For the Christian who desires to affirm Jesus Christ as Lord, economic koinonia cannot be viewed as optional. The extent to which a person submits his or her finances to the Lord's control has a vital bearing on that individual's spiritual life. There can be no separation of the secular from the sacred, for Jesus Christ is Lord of both! Unless one pleads the cause of the afflicted and the needy, that person does not truly know Yahweh (Jer. 22:16)! The fruitfulness of prayer, considered by many to be strictly "spiritual," is either hindered or magnified by the neglect or practice of "material" sharing (Isa. 58; Prov. 21:13; 1 John 3:21–22). Economic koinonia

is a sacrifice which pleases God (Phil. 4:18; Heb. 13:16). Economic sharing, or the lack of it, will be reciprocated by God in the afterlife (Luke 16:25).

Given the complexity of the world economy, it is not easy for a Christian to know what to do about poverty and world hunger. God will call some of us to clothe the poor and feed the hungry. Others will be called to attempt to change the social structures which oppress the poor. Still others will be called to directly empower the poor. What Christians must not do is to do nothing. Our respective social and economic situations give each of us a unique opportunity for service to the poor.

Topics for Review, Reflection, and Discussion

1. What is the difference between being poor in a wealthy country and being poor in a poor country?

2. On balance, what is the major cause of worldwide poverty and hunger—overpopulation, underdevelopment, or economic exploitation and dependence?

3. Is it possible for worldwide economic development to keep up with the current rate of population growth?

4. Give examples of semiperipheral countries. How have these countries managed to improve their situation—by working at their own economic development or by escaping the exploitation of the core capitalist countries?

5. How convincing is Novak's argument that rather than asking, "What are the causes of poverty?" we should ask, "What are the causes of wealth?"

6. Which political-economic system is more consistent with the biblical ideals of freedom and justice—democratic capitalism or democratic socialism?

7. How cogent is the argument that because true communism was never really practiced in eastern Europe, the political-economic upheaval there should not be taken as evidence that capitalism is superior to communism?

14

Maintaining Peace in a Nuclear Age

Nature of the Concern

The problem of conflict, violence, and war is not new. It has, in fact, existed throughout human history. But since the Industrial Revolution, circumstances have changed. The application of modern technology to weapons and war makes possible a level of destruction undreamed of in the past. The weapons now stockpiled in the arsenals of industrial societies are capable of killing every man, woman, and child several times over and destroying virtually all life on earth Technological weaponry has made winnable war obsolete.

In addition to the potential cost of human life, the nuclear-arms race exacts an enormous economic cost. The billions of dollars spent on nuclear arms could be used to upgrade education, create jobs, improve roads and transportation, expand health care, assist the poor and needy, and make food available to starving people. To make matters worse, the increased spending for nuclear arms has come largely from money which the United States government has had to borrow. The annual deficit is roughly equal to the amount of money spent on the military buildup.

While the United States is involved in a race with the Soviet Union to build the strongest nuclear arsenal, it is losing the economic war with countries like Japan. Deficit spending couples with a sharp imbalance in trade with other countries. Americans have been importing much more than they have been exporting. Most economists agree that the deficit spending and imbalance in international trade cannot go on indefinitely without severely affecting our nation's economic health. Within the span

295

of ten years, the United States has gone from being the world's leading lender to being the leading borrower. Japan and oil-rich Near Eastern countries have bought vast amounts of American stock and real estate. During the last decade the Japanese yen has doubled in value against the dollar. It is a curious irony that while the United States is spending 7 percent of its national income on the military, Japan is spending 1 percent. The United States is, in reality, subsidizing Japan by providing military protection without allowing her to foot any part of the bill. The economic burden of the nuclear buildup is even heavier on the Soviet Union, which, with a gross national product only half that of the United States, spends an even larger proportion of its income on the military.

Some argue that military spending helps the economy because it provides needed jobs. In fact, nothing could be further from the truth. While every one billion dollars spent on the military creates sixteen thousand jobs, every one billion dollars invested in manufacturing creates thirty-five thousand jobs, and every one billion dollars spent in the service industries creates seventy-five thousand jobs.

Another cost of the nuclear-arms race is personal fear. When asked what they find most troubling about the world, a surprising number of children cite the prospect of a nuclear war. The fear of an atomic holocaust is an anxiety unique to our age.

Dimensions of the Problem

Although at least six countries have exploded atomic bombs and a number of others are thought to have nuclear weapons, the major producers and stockpilers of nuclear weapons are the United States and the Soviet Union. The United States and the Soviet Union possessed a total of 23,917 and 14,867 nuclear warheads respectively in 1983 (see table 4). It is difficult to illustrate the magnitude of destruction that these two countries are capable of inflicting on each other and the rest of the world. To begin, we shall compare the strategic capabilities of the two countries—"strategic" is the conventional term used to refer to a nation's capacity to deliver long-range nuclear warheads.

The Soviet Union has the advantage in land-based weapons, for it can deliver over twice as many nuclear warheads by intercontinental ballistic missiles as can the United States. The United States, however, has the advantage in sea-based weapons, for it can deliver over twice as many nuclear warheads by submarine-launched ballistic missiles as can the Soviet Union. The United States also has the advantage in the air, for it is capable of delivering over seven times the number of nuclear warheads by intercontinental bombers as can the Soviet Union. While the United States has the potential of obliterating 99,840 square miles of territory in the Soviet Union, the Soviet Union has the potential of obliterating 155,643 square miles of the United States. To gain an understanding of

Table 4

Number of Nuclear Warheads in 1983

	United States	Soviet Union
Strategic Nuclear Warheads (classified by delivery system)		
Intercontinental ballistic missiles	2,149	5,862
Submarine-launched ballistic missiles	4,800	1,865
Intercontinental bombers	2,626	345
Subtotal	9,575	8,072
Tactical Weapons (strategic-air-defense, antisubmarine, intermediate-range, and battlefield weapons)	14,342	6,795
Grand Total	23,917	14,867

Source: Coalition for a New Foreign and Military Policy, "U.S. and Soviet 'First-Strike' Capabilities" (Washington, D.C.: Coalition for a New Foreign and Military Policy, 1984).

the extent of this potential danger, consider that the central areas of America's thirty largest cities occupy only 6,000 square miles. The danger from nuclear fallout if the United States and the Soviet Union were to empty their arsenals would extend to 3,539,735 and 5,795,400 square miles respectively. By comparison it should be noted that the total land area of the United States, including Alaska and Hawaii, is only 3,600,000 square miles.

Even more horrendous is the potential damage that each country can inflict by using both its strategic and tactical nuclear weapons. Tactical nuclear weapons are designed more for defense and conventional warfare than for long-range delivery of warheads. The United States has the decided advantage in tactical weapons, possessing more than twice as many nuclear warheads as does the Soviet Union. By using all of their nuclear warheads, the United States and the Soviet Union have the potential of obliterating 213,655 and 241,470 square miles respectively. Such an attack by the United States would produce a lethal fallout area of 7,414,339 square miles, while a Soviet attack would produce a lethal fallout area of 8,894,250 square miles.

A nuclear war between the United States and the Soviet Union would also endanger and possibly destroy every other nation on the earth. Indiscriminate of national boundaries radioactive nuclear fallout would imperil all humans, animals, and vegetation. Clearly, the potential destructiveness of nuclear war dwarfs the potential destructiveness of all other social problems.

While both the United States and the Soviet Union could effectively

298 Analyses of Selected Social Problems

demolish the major urban areas of the other, neither side presently has the capability of delivering a first strike which would destroy the other's nuclear weapons. Although a Soviet first strike would kill millions of Americans and destroy many of our land-based strategic nuclear weapons, we would still have seventy-five hundred warheads on bombers in the air and submarines at sea, as well as thousands of tactical nuclear weapons in Europe. A first strike by the United States would be more damaging because the Soviets depend heavily on land-based missiles. The retaliatory strike by the Soviet Union would still be strong enough, however, to totally destroy life in the United States. Given this potentiality, some argue that each country is effectively deterring the other from attacking, and that reducing the number of weapons might actually be destabilizing.

Still another dimension was added in 1983 when President Ronald Reagan "challenged the nation's scientists and engineers to devise an 'impenetrable shield' of defense that would protect the American population against even the most massive nuclear attack by intercontinental ballistic missiles" (Managing a Delicate Balance 1987:2). With this, the Strategic Defense Initiative (SDI) was born. SDI, popularly known as "Star Wars," would entail a space-based system of lasers that would destroy attacking missiles. Proponents hail SDI for placing the emphasis on defense rather than offense and offering relative security from foreign nuclear attack.

Opponents of SDI argue that the program is technically infeasible and prohibitively expensive; if it were actually used, human survival would be doubtful. Others argue against SDI on the grounds that it will upset the delicate balance of power between the United States and the Soviet Union, and will result in the Soviets' developing their own strategic defense system, thus escalating nuclear warfare into space. Still others point out that any weapon capable of destroying an attacking intercontinental ballistic missile could also be used offensively to destroy targets on the ground with virtually no warning at all. Backers of SDI counter that "the proposed Strategic Defense Initiative has succeeded, if nothing else, in bringing the Soviets back to the negotiating table with serious intentions to seek major new arms control agreements" (Managing a Delicate Balance 1987:9). The future of SDI is still to be determined, both as a strategy to encourage the Soviets to negotiate and as a potential defense from nuclear attack.

Explanations of the Problem

There are several different reasons for the threat of nuclear war. On a purely practical level, there is the matter of technology. The threat of nuclear war came into existence in the middle of the twentieth century when the knowledge needed to produce such destructive weapons was developed. The application of modern technology to weapons of war has made possible a mass destruction of life and property which is completely beyond the capabilities of conventional weapons. But the ability to produce nuclear weapons is merely a necessary condition and not a sufficient condition of the nuclear-war threat.

Given the ability to produce nuclear warheads, we need to take a serious look at the motives human beings have for engaging in destructive conflicts. We shall list five motives which, when taken together, can help us understand why nuclear war is such a threat:

1. *Nationalism*, a fairly recent social invention, encourages a people to make decisions for themselves only, instead of for the good of the world as a whole. The complex technology and production systems which are needed to make nuclear weaponry would not be possible without the cohesion and strength of the modern nation-state.

2. *Differences in economic and political ideology* constitute the immediate reason why the United States and the Soviet Union are currently striving to gain dominance in nuclear weapons. To the rest of the world, the United States symbolizes the strengths of a capitalistic economy and a democratic government, and the Soviet Union symbolizes the strengths of a communist economy and centralized control. When one side feels frustrated in its attempts to demonstrate the superiority of its economic system, the temptation is to demonstrate superiority through force.

3. *Fear* (which stems from ignorance, lack of understanding, and mistrust) is a direct cause of the nuclear threat. Henry Kissinger likens the United States and the Soviet Union to two giants stumbling around a darkened room—they do not know nor understand each other. And we humans tend to fear and distrust those who are different from us and whom we do not know. Rather than seeking understanding, the typical human reaction is to try to gain power over those whom we fear.

4. A quest for *power*, which is related to the fear of others, is partly responsible for the nuclear buildup. Power is like an addiction that numbs people to their fear. And, of course, the ultimate power symbol in the contemporary world is nuclear weapons.

5. From a theological point of view, it can be argued that the underlying cause of the nuclear threat is *sin*. While this is true, explaining the nuclear threat as a result of sin runs the risk of oversimplifying the problem, for sin can take many forms. A subtle manifestation of sin that is easily overlooked is to see the threat of nuclear war as residing only in the enemy (the Soviet Union as the evil empire) while we view ourselves as sinless defenders of all that is good. A more obvious form of sin is materialism and greed, characteristics that are as prevalent in American society as in any other. Part of our motive for a strong nuclear arsenal may well be to defend the materialistic, rich life that we enjoy.

Although all nations strive to protect their own interests, and justifiably so, some are morally more responsible than others. For instance, an expansionistic regime may abuse weaker nations unless a powerful, morally responsible government steps in. The justification the United States has given for having forces and nuclear weapons in Europe is that the Soviet Union has in the past demonstrated its expansionist tendencies in actions in Poland, Hungary, Czechoslovakia, East Germany, and Afghanistan. The Christian community needs to be a strong voice in helping our government determine whether our current military presence in Europe and similar situations is a solution to a problem (e.g., the perceived Soviet threat) or is itself a part of the problem. Given the recent developments in eastern Europe, one possible course of action is to encourage our government to eliminate short-range nuclear missiles in Europe which are designed to reach only the countries of Poland, Czechoslovakia, Hungary, and Romania.

Various Approaches to the Problem

Although the focus in this chapter is on maintaining peace in the nuclear age, a Christian response to the issue of nuclear weapons must be based on a Christian view of the use of force, violence, or war to combat injustice. While there are a number of positions that Christians can take, most fall into one of three categories: pacifism, the just-war theory, and advocacy of holy war. As we proceed to describe each of these positions, it should be kept in mind that the goal of all three is the same—to achieve or to maintain peace and justice in the world.

Christian Positions on the Use of Force

Pacifism

It is a mistake to assume that pacifism amounts to doing nothing or taking the easy way out. On the contrary, it requires more courage to refrain from violence than to strike back at wrongdoing. Pacifism refuses to engage in violent acts and the taking of human life, even if those acts are intended to prevent greater violence. Before the church became institutionalized in the fourth century, pacifism was the predominant view taken by Christians, who found themselves a powerless minority. The appeal of pacifism can be seen in its simplicity and its apparent modeling after Christ, who took a moral stance against evil instead of trying to overcome it with physical force.

The major biblical text used in support of Christian pacifism is Matthew 5:38–44:

> You have heard that it was said, "Eye for eye, and tooth for tooth." But I tell you, Do not resist an evil person. If someone strikes you on the right cheek, turn to him the other also. And if someone wants to sue you and take your tunic, let him have your cloak as well. If someone forces you to

go one mile, go with him two miles. Give to the one who asks you, and do not turn away from the one who wants to borrow from you.

You have heard that it was said, "Love your neighbor and hate your enemy." But I tell you: Love your enemies and pray for those who persecute you. [NIV]

Pacifists maintain that they seek to model themselves after the entire life of Jesus. Their approach to evil is what has come to be known as nonviolent confrontation or passive resistance. They choose to engage in noncooperative (but still legal) behavior such as boycotts, sit-ins, and demonstrations, or in civil disobedience, which entails defying an evil law, government, or social structure. One advantage of nonviolent confrontation is that it operates outside of normal political channels, which are often dominated by self-interest.

The purpose of nonviolent resistance is to draw public attention to a moral position thought to be preferable to that of the Establishment. There is a reliance on moral persuasion instead of physical force as a means of bringing about desired change. To be effective, nonviolent resisters must be prepared to accept violence in the form of harassment, beatings, and jail terms. When officials in the Establishment meet nonviolent resistance with physical force, they run the risk of drawing attention to their own injustices. Mahatma Gandhi, who effectively used nonviolent resistance against Great Britain in winning political independence for India, stated that "passive resistance is an all-sided sword . . . it blesses him that uses it and him against whom it is used." Though he was not a Christian, Gandhi cited Jesus' admonition to turn the other cheek as one of the sources of his position.

The just-war theory

The just-war theory can be traced to Augustine, who argued that it is a Christian's duty to preserve order and to defend one's neighbor. The intent of this position is not to justify, but to limit and constrain the use of violence. Recognizing the destructiveness of war, advocates of the just-war theory severely restrict the conditions under which they admit violence to be morally justified. Paul Ramsey (1961) and Stephen Mott (1982) list six conditions, all of which must be satisfied if a war is to be deemed just:

1. *The cause must be just.* The motivating force behind the war cannot be greed, self-interest, pride, hatred, or revenge. The only acceptable cause is the pursuit of peace with justice.

2. *War must be the last resort.* Military conflict is justified only after all other means of obtaining justice have failed. War must always be seen as a sign of failure, a sign that human beings have failed to settle a dispute or to right an unjust social order in a more civilized way.

3. *The war must be fought by a lawful public authority.* War is justified

only when conducted by a recognized government. A major problem arises when the official state or government is the source of injustice, and thus needs to be brought down. In this case, the Calvinist tradition holds that sovereign power belongs to what it calls the "civil society"—"when a government exceeds its bounds and passes into tyranny, the authority to rule reverts to the people from whom it originates" (Mott 1982:109). "Lawful public authority" must be interpreted to mean that there is broad public support for the war effort. Governments that wage war against evil but do not enjoy broad public support—such as the United States' involvement in Vietnam during the 1960s—do not firmly fulfil this third condition.

4. *There must be a reasonable hope of victory.* If there is no hope of victory, then war is a futile and wasteful attempt to right injustice. It has been argued that one of the reasons Jesus did not encourage his followers to take a violent stance against the injustices of the day was that militant rebellion by a handful of Christians against the Roman occupation would have been futile.

5. *The probable good must outweigh the probable evil effect of the war effort.* It must be clear that what would ensue if the existing structure were allowed to continue unchecked is a greater evil than the potential destruction of lives and property from the war effort.

6. *The war must be rightly conducted.* This point questions the morality of winning at any cost and by implication places lethal force against civilians in the category of murder. While it may have been possible to avoid killing noncombatants when wars were fought with sticks and stones, swords, and bows and arrows, this is increasingly difficult given the impersonal, indiscriminate weapons of modern warfare. A bomb kills all persons in a geographical area, combatants and civilians alike. It is interesting to note that the Allied nations justified the saturation bombing of Germany during World War II on the grounds that in a technological society factory workers must be considered as much a part of the war effort as are soldiers. A further implication of the principle that war must be rightly conducted is that torture or the needless infliction of pain and suffering on the enemy is ruled out. This principle also eliminates terrorism as a legitimate means of bringing about social change, since its victims are, by definition, innocent. The dignity of human life must be maintained, even in times of war.

Those who hold to the just-war theory find scriptural basis in such Old Testament passages as Genesis 9:6 ("Whoever sheds the blood of man, by man shall his blood be shed") and Judges 6:16, where God reveals to Gideon how he is to handle Israel's oppressors: "I will be with you, and you will strike down all the Midianites together" (NIV). Less direct evidence for the just-war theory is found in the New Testament. Passages like Matthew 5:38–44, which seem to conflict with this position, are dealt with by arguing that Jesus is here teaching against the use of violent revenge. It is further argued that a consistent interpretation of these verses would prohibit every attempt to resist injustice, including all forms of nonviolent resistance. In response to those who contend that Jesus assumed and taught a pacifist position to his disciples, just-war theorists suggest that (1) Jesus' reluctance to use force does not necessarily mean that he disapproved of force in principle, and (2) Jesus taught his disciples not to fight not because violence is wrong, but because it would have led to a wrong end—prevention of his death.

In general, to justify their positions, pacifists tend to discount Old Testament teachings on the use of force, while just-war theorists tend to discount New Testament teachings on nonviolent responses to violence. Mott (1982:168) summarizes well the just-war position: "The claim of justice is prior to that of peace, because there can be no genuine peace without justice."

Advocacy of holy war

The third position which Christians take on the use of force can be seen as the just-war theory pushed to an extreme. The advocates of this third position are extreme in the sense that they are willing to resort to war as a means of preventing an evil social order from bringing about destruction. Examples of holy wars would be the Crusades that were waged by Western Christendom during the Middle Ages. These holy wars were justified on the grounds that God desired Christians to win back the Holy Land from Islamic control.

OF COURSE GOD IS ON OUR SIDE, HENRY; BESIDES, THIS IS NO TIME TO BRING UP THEOLOGICAL QUESTIONS.

Contemporary Christians who advocate what they consider to be holy wars tend to view the world in terms of sharp contrasts between good and evil. For example, some holy-war advocates think of God as being in favor of the United States against the Soviet Union, which they view as the evil empire. From a completely different ideological perspective, those who favor armed overthrow of the white racist regime in South Africa can also be classified as proponents of holy war. Thus, advocating holy war has less to do with one's ideological position than it does with certainty that God is on one's side in the fight against the evil intentions of others. Those who hold this view want to take the offensive against evil. Just-war theorists, on the other hand, think in terms of defense against evil.

Holy-war advocates find support for their position in a number of Old Testament passages in which God urges Israel to totally destroy the enemy and the enemy's property. We need cite only God's pledge to Israel as they anticipated entering the Promised Land: "But the LORD your God will deliver [the nations before you] over to you, throwing them into great confusion until they are destroyed. He will give their kings into your hand, and you will wipe out their names from under heaven. No one will be able to stand up against you; you will destroy them" (Deut. 7:23–24 NIV).

Deterrence: The Moral Defense for Nuclear Weapons

The United States presently has approximately twenty-five thousand nuclear warheads. How can this be justified? Three reasons are variously given for stockpiling a massive arsenal of nuclear weapons: a preemptive first strike, retaliation, and deterrence. A preemptive first strike means that the United States would hurl massive nuclear destruction on another country in order to prevent that country from doing the same to us. It should be obvious that such a use of nuclear weapons places a great burden of moral certainty upon the users. Such a tactic is sanctioned only by those who advocate holy war. Pacifists and just-war theorists see no justification whatsoever for making a preemptive first strike.

Some Christians argue that nuclear weapons should be used in retaliation for a nuclear attack by another country. The retaliation would be morally justified either as retribution and punishment for wrongdoing, or as an attempt to prevent further destruction at the hands of the hostile country. Both those who speak of preemptive first strikes and the proponents of deterrence, however, point out that it would be futile to attempt to retaliate for the purpose of preventing future damage after an initial nuclear attack. Thus, the primary reason for retaliation would be retribution for wrongdoing. Such retaliation, which would kill the innocent as well as those responsible for the initial aggression, is morally questionable.

The proponents of deterrence stress that the best way to assure that another country will never initiate a nuclear attack is to have the means to retaliate and to threaten to actually do so if attacked. The fact that we have a huge nuclear stockpile indicates that our policymakers believe that the other side poses an actual threat and would attack if they thought they could win. The bigger the stockpile of nuclear weapons and the greater the retaliatory damage they can inflict, the more effective the deterrence. Deterrence is the reason most often given by the United States government for stockpiling nuclear weapons.

Deterrence is tricky business, however, for it involves a certain amount of bluffing. For deterrence to be effective, an enemy country must be convinced that the United States will indeed retaliate if attacked. Deterrence can best be understood as a game in which the opponent is so intimidated, and becomes so convinced of being the inferior power, that the threat to retaliate will never have to be acted upon.

Two types of deterrence have emerged. *Conventional deterrence* refers to the ability to retaliate after suffering the enemy's worst possible nuclear attack. Conventional deterrence is already in place in the United States and the Soviet Union. Both countries could reduce their nuclear arsenal by more than half and still wipe out the other in retaliation for an attack.

Why the continued nuclear buildup, then, by both the United States and the Soviet Union? Continued nuclear buildup is needed, according to recent Pentagon theory, to achieve *extended deterrence*. The purpose of extended deterrence is to prevent conventional (nonnuclear) war. Because our conventional forces are outnumbered by the Soviets', the Pentagon contends we could not stop a nonnuclear attack without having to resort to strategic (long-range) nuclear weapons, which would involve much greater destruction than necessary. The solution, it is argued, is for us to be able to carry on a small, localized nuclear war without fear of nuclear counterattack by the enemy. To achieve this goal, we must develop a first-strike capability that would effectively disarm the Soviet Union in a single attack; that is to say, we must develop extended deterrence.

The question is whether the development of this first-strike capability is more likely to deter or cause nuclear war. For the United States to have extended deterrence would deny to the Soviet Union conventional deterrence. This would put the Soviets in a position where the combination of their nuclear weapons and fear, instead of discouraging them, might very well encourage them to strike first. A good argument can be made that those whom we ought to fear most are our own Pentagon theorists who are not satisfied with conventional deterrence, but who want instead to push towards extended deterrence. Their position cannot be supported on purely pragmatic grounds, to say nothing about the moral questionability of such nuclear buildup.

The Pentagon counters that they are only looking for a way to limit nuclear attacks to military targets, thus avoiding mutual assured destruction (MAD). It is reasoned that if the Soviets are convinced we are unwilling to risk MAD, and they feel their conventional forces can win, our conventional deterrence will not dissuade them from attacking, but extended deterrence might.

In arguing for a pacifist position, Donald Kraybill (1982:208–9) gives eight reasons why he thinks nuclear deterrence is contrary to Christian values of morality:

1. Deterrence is based on the manipulation and exploitation of fear.
2. While the threat of punishment for aggression does not necessarily belittle others, nuclear threats tend to degrade the opponent to subhuman levels by assuming that the enemy responds only to the promise of brutal violence.
3. Deterrence depends on a peculiar contradiction between terror and rationality.
4. Deterrence cultivates salvation by threat.
5. Deterrence blocks serious disarmament efforts because it requires a balance of bombs between the parties.
6. The most dangerous assumption behind deterrence is that nuclear weapons will never be used.
7. If deterrence fails, millions of ordinary Americans and Soviets who have had little or no responsibility for the war will be killed by the bombs.
8. Deterrence works only if the parties involved act as if they really would carry out their threat and thus imperil the whole world.

It is not only the enemy, but we ourselves, who are terrorized by our drive to achieve nuclear deterrence, for it is the nation that threatens to use nuclear weapons that also is the most likely target of a nuclear attack. Kraybill (1982:211) concludes that there are no moral or ethical grounds to "justify holding ourselves, our children, and other citizens of the world hostage to terror . . . [for it] vaporizes hope in young children and adults alike." It is ironic that in the contemporary world the greatest danger of being a victim of a nuclear holocaust is within those countries with the greatest number of nuclear warheads, while the safest place to be is in countries which have no capability for nuclear warfare.

A Christian Response: Seeking a Just Peace (Shalom)

The threat to peace in a nuclear society is a social problem which most directly disrupts *shalom*. As long as there are wars and rumors of wars, there is no *shalom*. As long as there are nuclear weapons and nuclear threats, there is no *shalom*. The good news that Christ offered was salvation for each person, and the promise of justice and peace. As an alternative to just war, then, we would propose that the Christian position regarding the threat of nuclear war be to seek a just peace.

God means for the church to be an active witness and an advocate for justice and peace on earth; the two must go together. The biblical concept of *shalom* means that there is no peace where there is injustice, and there is no justice where there is a lack of peace. The theme of a just peace "brings together the imperatives and promises of justice and peace. It addresses the whole of life—personal and social, spiritual and political, attitudinal and structural" (Thistlethwaite 1986:39).

While we believe that the concept of a just peace represents the biblical ideal of *shalom*, we realize that the Bible has not given us a blueprint for foreign policy. In seeking to apply biblical insights to foreign policy, Christians must resist the temptation to use Scripture selectively to support a predetermined position. It is true that in Scripture Yahweh is sometimes pictured as a holy warrior who demands the complete destruction of Israel's enemies, that Saul is chastened for not slaying all of the Amalekites (1 Sam. 15), that John the Baptist does not try to dissuade soldiers from military service (Luke 3:14), that Jesus said, "I have not come to bring peace, but a sword" (Matt. 10:34 RSV), and that Jesus used force to remove the moneychangers from the temple. But it is also true that this very same Jesus said, "Love your enemies . . . pray for those who abuse you" (Luke 6:27–28 RSV). The concept of *shalom*, rightly understood, provides a synthesis between these two positions.

Applying the concept of *shalom* to foreign policy means seeking a just peace in the world. It means seeking ways to reassure and even empower the enemy rather than threatening and controlling them through fear. It means realizing that the enemy's threat to resort to force and destruction may be motivated by fear and weakness. The ultimate solution to the nuclear-arms struggle will not be found by building bigger and more-powerful bombs, but by building bridges of understanding, and making both sides recognize their interdependence. Rather than striving to create two self-sufficient worlds, the two superpowers must seek security through a mutual empowering process.

Up to 1987, the United States and the Soviet Union steadily added to their nuclear arsenals, even though there have been at least twenty-five separate arms-reduction agreements since World War II. The signing of the nuclear-disarmament treaty in 1987 by President Ronald Reagan and General Secretary Mikhail Gorbachev may have signaled a hopeful change in the trend towards nuclear buildup. This treaty called for the elimination of the means of employing 859 American and 1,752 Soviet intermediate- and short-range missiles. It is hoped that the trust which has been generated between the two countries will lead to further reductions in nuclear arms. So far, there has been no reduction of the most devastating strategic nuclear warheads. Courage will be needed to take the step towards reducing these weapons as well.

Admittedly, self-interest has been the motive of both governments in seeking arms reduction. Indeed, we believe that any attempt at arms reduction will be successful only if it is seen to be in each country's own self-interest. However, what begins as self-interest can grow into interdependence, that is, mutual empowering. This means following arms reduction with trade agreements, social and cultural exchanges, and an opening up of both countries so that each can see the God-created common humanity in the other.

Some may have doubts that a nation can be called upon to act according to the same Christian principles as is an individual. Maybe a nation's foreign policy is by definition amoral. Given each government's responsibility to protect its own people, perhaps the most we can expect is a pragmatic and utilitarian ethic. Then, too, if our government is convinced that the Soviet Union poses a real threat, it would be acting irresponsibly if it did not prepare a counterthreat. These are legitimate doubts Christians may have in attempting to arrive at a morally responsible position regarding nuclear arms.

However, when it comes to the nuclear-weapons race, the United States has acted more out of fear than love. The apostle John has said, "There is no fear in love. But perfect love drives out fear" (1 John 4:18 NIV). Fear and self-interest have too often led us to identify the Soviets as the epitome of evil. In the past, this fear has been reinforced by some of our doomsday ideology, which identifies the Soviet Union as the antichrist who will not, and cannot, be budged from the goal of world dominance. Such pessimistic, deterministic thinking might well act as a self-fulfilling prophecy—the expectation that the Soviet Union will act aggressively may actually serve to encourage such behavior. We would do better if we regarded the vast changes which are currently taking place in the Soviet Union as evidence that atheistic communism is not the monolithic force which some pessimistic Christians portray it to be.

We could blow ourselves up in a nuclear holocaust tomorrow. Or Jesus may come tomorrow. As Christians we must not be apostles of darkness, doom, fear, and despair, but of light, faith, love, and hope. "About dates and times . . . you know perfectly well that the Day of the Lord comes like a thief in the night. . . . We, who belong to daylight, must keep sober, armed with faith and love for coat of mail, and the hope of salvation for helmet. For God has not destined us to the terrors of judgement, but to the full attainment of salvation through our Lord Jesus Christ" (1 Thess. 5:1–2, 8–9 NEB).

Topics for Review, Reflection, and Discussion

1. In what sense can it be said that modern weaponry has made winnable war obsolete?

2. Can the large amounts of money the United States spent on military buildup during the 1980s be justified on the grounds that what the Soviets had to spend in response has caused their economy to collapse?

3. Which position is most defensible—pacifism, the just-war theory, or advocacy of holy war?

4. Can an all-out nuclear war ever be justified in terms of the just-war theory?

5. Can deterrence work if a country is unwilling to follow through on its threats to use nuclear weapons?

6. Distinguish between conventional and extended deterrence. Is either morally defensible?

7. How can the concept of empowering be used to ease the world away from the threat of nuclear war?

Part 3

Conclusion

15

Paths to Christian Social Involvement and Change

We hope that the previous chapters have provided an understanding of the complexity of the causes and consequences of social problems. The reader may be feeling somewhat overwhelmed and even hopeless, wondering if any form of Christian involvement can help alleviate the situation. It has not been our purpose to overwhelm, but rather to provide a basis on which Christians can meaningfully participate in effective efforts to ameliorate social conditions.

As we pointed out in chapter 3, differences in theology lead Christians to adopt a variety of attitudes towards becoming socially involved. While some theologies lead to an individualistic approach to solving social problems, others lead to attempts to change social structures directly. Some theologies encourage Christians to take an active role by participating directly in the political process; others encourage believers to shy away from all political attempts to change society.

Strategies for Social Change

There are a number of paths that a Christian might follow to bring about desired social change. These paths differ in regard to the basic strategy adopted and the agent involved. Figure 9 represents an attempt to classify the various paths to social change.

313

Figure 9
The Various Paths to Social Change

Agent	Strategy			
	1. Evangelism	2. Meeting individual physical needs	3. Taking positions on social issues	4. Social action aimed at changing social structure
A. Individual Christian	1A Personal evangelism	2A Neighborliness	3A Statements by individuals regarding social issues	4A Social action by individuals
B. Local church or Christian community	1B Evangelistic meetings and Bible studies	2B Programs of the local church to meet the needs of congregational members and the community	3B Statements by the local church regarding social issues	4B Social action by the local church
C. Suprachurch structure (denominations, interdenominational groups)	1C Evangelism through mass media	2C Christian social-welfare agencies, orphanages, retirement homes	3C Statements by denominational and interdenominational organizations regarding social issues	4C Social action by denominational and interdenominational organizations

Evangelism as a Means of Social Change

The first path to social change is concentration upon preaching the gospel so that individuals may come to a saving knowledge of Jesus Christ. The assumption is that needed social change will follow as individuals in sufficient numbers are converted to Christ in a given community or society. Old-style fundamentalists identity with this strategy. Although the agent may vary—the individual Christian involved in personal evangelism, the local church holding evangelistic meetings, or interdenominational organizations utilizing the mass media for evangelism—the goal is still the same, the conversion of the individual nonbeliever to a saving faith in Jesus Christ.

The charge may be made that stressing the personal gospel to the exclusion of direct forms of social involvement is not really addressing the cause of social problems. The response on the part of old-style fundamentalists is that God does not call us to mix Christianity with politics. They might also respond that the heart must be changed first, for it is impossible to legislate change in people's hearts.

Meeting Individual Physical Needs

The second set of paths to social change involves meeting individual physical needs. We would hasten to say that most old-style fundamentalists also believe that Christians must actively be involved in meeting the physical needs of individuals. They take care, however, to stress that any focus upon meeting these needs must be secondary to the primary task of converting non-Christians.

In presenting our theology of social structures (chap. 3), we included a discussion of the biblical concept of neighborliness. One type of Christian social involvement is simply to be a good neighbor to another person in need (path 2A). The point of the parable of the good Samaritan is that Christians must be prepared to be neighborly to anyone—including the poorest and most despised persons in society, or even those whom we would be tempted to consider enemies. Christians are to draw no boundaries that would exclude them from meeting the needs of another person. Meeting the needs of another should be thought of as meeting the needs of Christ. As Jesus stated, "If anyone gives even a cup of cold water to one of these little ones because he is my disciple, I tell you the truth, he will certainly not lose his reward" (Matt. 10:42 NIV). One-on-one encounters in which we can meet the needs of another are a means towards social improvement in which all Christians can participate.

The physical needs of others can also be met within the context of a Christian community (path 2B). For example, all members of a local church can live out the ideal of *koinōnia* with each other. They will then become like family—brothers and sisters or parents and children to each other. As members of the body they will realize that "if one part suffers, every part suffers with it" (1 Cor. 12:26), that they should care for "those widows who are really in need" (1 Tim. 5:16), and that they should "look after orphans and widows in their distress" (James 1:27 NIV).

The Christian community must not, however, become so focused in upon its own needs that it fails to reach out to meet the needs of those outside the community. This emphasis on inclusive concern can be found in the concluding chapter of the writer of Hebrews: "Keep on loving each other as brothers. Do not forget to entertain strangers, for by so doing some people have entertained angels without knowing it. Remember those in prison as if you were their fellow prisoners, and those who are mistreated as if you yourselves were suffering" (Heb. 13:1–3 NIV). Caring for personal needs starts within the community, but this ministry is not complete until it finds expression in meeting the needs of persons who are outside of the Christian community.

Larger Christian groups, such as denominations or interdenominational organizations, also have programs to help meet social, material, and health needs (path 2C). Solutions to many social problems demand commitment of resources of a magnitude not usually available to a local church. Thus, retirement homes, orphanages, counseling agencies, and substance-abuse programs are best supported by the combined efforts of a number of local churches. Cooperation on the interdenominational level may also be the most effective way to influence governmental decisions on environmental issues and nuclear-weapons buildup.

Taking Positions on Social Issues

The third set of paths to social change involves taking positions on social issues. Although stopping short of engaging in direct action, persons and organizations making statements on social issues do hope that their pronouncements will help bring about desired change. Individuals who take positions not shared by their local church often seek identification with extrachurch organizations that are supportive of their cause.

In the 1950s and 1960s some local churches and denominations took a public stand in support of the blacks' struggle for civil rights. Other churches and denominations refused to take a stand, usually justifying their nonsupport by reasoning that the church should stay out of politics. Some of these denominations eventually offered supportive statements after blacks had won their major civil-rights victories. At the present time, a number of churches and denominations have issued statements in support of the black South Africans' struggle for justice. Others continue to refuse to take positions on social issues.

Along with taking public positions on the issues of the day, some Christians believe that they can be agents of desired social change by being an example of how God desires people to live in community. They maintain that the most biblical and effective way to change social structure is to be and act as a "called out people" (Mouw 1978). By their example they show how to live in community with others. Churches within the Anabaptist tradition have historically taken this approach to social change. Thus, while Anabaptist churches did not engage in direct political action to abolish slavery, they put their own safety on the line by supporting such movements as the underground railroad. John Yoder (1972:157), a major contemporary spokesperson for the Anabaptist tradition, contends that "the primary social structure through which the gospel works to change other structures is that of the Christian community."

Stephen Mott (1982:133) observes that "genuine Christian community contributes to social change in three ways. The first is through various forms of social action and service. The second is the impact its nonconforming life has on the surrounding community. Third and most important is the support it gives to the individual involved in mission." It is noteworthy that this observation appears in a chapter entitled "The Church as Counter-Community." For while it is true that many contemporary Anabaptist churches do advocate active participation in the political process, they also continue to emphasize that the church must be a called-out countercommunity. The power generated by visible countercommunities based upon the biblical norms of social relationships is precisely the force needed to change problem-plagued social structures.

Changing Social Structures

While it is possible to combat social problems by attempting to change individual hearts, providing for individual physical needs, and taking positions on issues, these problems continue to exist because of the unhealthy condition of social structures.* It is imperative to change those structures which contribute to social problems. Giving to the poor is a legitimate Christian response, but it is also necessary to create social structures that will empower the poor to help themselves. Providing help for drug addicts and alcoholics is a legitimate Christian response, but Christians must also work to change the social conditions that contribute to the problem of drug and alcohol abuse. Cleaning up a polluted environment is a legitimate Christian response to the ecological crisis, but Christians must also seek to change those structures that are responsible for polluting in the first place. Giving juvenile delinquents and criminals stiff penalties and attempting to rehabilitate them are legitimate

---

*For a biblically based discussion of the need for Christians to actively engage in attempts to change evil social structures see Robert Linthicum, *City of God: City of Satan* (Grand Rapids: Zondervan, 1990).

Christian responses to the increasing crime rate, but Christians must also work to change the social structures that have helped to make the crime rate in the United States one of the highest in the world.

Attempting to change social structures through direct action is, then, the fourth set of paths Christians can follow. A major issue facing Christian fellowships, churches, denominations, and interdenominational and parachurch organizations today concerns the legitimacy of this form of Christian involvement. It is our hope that the discussion of social problems in the previous chapters will lead the reader to the realization that Christians must be involved in changing social structures.

It is also our hope that Christian organizations will make sure their beliefs concerning the propriety of social involvement are consistent with their actions. Specifically, a Christian organization which takes the position that the church should never attempt to change the structures of society must always act accordingly. An organization is being inconsistent if it questions the propriety of another Christian group's lobbying against sexual discrimination and simultaneously lobbies for laws against abortion. In such cases, a little more introspection might result in less hostility between Christian organizations representing divergent political positions; a merging of efforts might even be possible. It appears to us that the Just Life movement, with its emphasis upon preserving life from the dangers of both the abortionist's knife and the nuclear bomb, is an encouraging sign that politically conservative Christians can unite in social action with politically liberal Christians. Should the conservative and liberal wings of the church ever combine their efforts, the effect upon the political decision-making process in the United States could be tremendous.

A Biblical Ethic for Social Change

There are a variety of ways in which Christians, either individually or collectively, can attempt to change unjust and harmful social structures. One of the first decisions Christians must make is whether to become involved in secular organizations with which they share a cause, or to work only within self-defined Christian organizations. The advantage of working within a Christian organization is the likelihood that its response to a social problem will be based upon biblical principles. This is the case, for example, with Charles Colson's prison ministries. In reality, it is probably appropriate for most socially concerned Christians to be involved in both secular and Christian organizations.

Another task Christians must perform is to set priorities in regard to the various strategies for accomplishing social change. An excellent discussion can be found in Mott's *Biblical Ethics and Social Change* (1982). In his analysis of what he calls "paths to justice," Mott begins with the contribution evangelism can make to social change—it satisfies "the personal need for healing in the center of our being" (p. 110). However, he quickly points out "the limits of evangelism for social change" (p. 112); "reliance upon individual change ignores the objective reality of social life and social evil" (p. 120). We agree with Mott that evangelism and social action are interdependent:

> The biblical concern is for the totality of creation. Therefore, in addition to utilizing the special gifts of the Spirit given to each of us, we are all to be active in witness and in working for justice. When the church neglects one part of this concern, the other part loses vitality and is endangered. Concern for inner personal commitment to God is part of the concern for the reconciliation of all creation. Political and social concern for the created world is motivated by God's grace within the individual. As servants of God, we must make both tasks our own if we would be true to either. [p. 127]

As Mott continues to formulate a biblical ethic for social change, he argues that in relating to the institutions of society the believer must balance three biblical commands: (1) Do not be conformed to this age (Rom. 12:2); (2) Be subordinate to every fundamental social institution (1 Pet. 2:13); and (3) Establish justice in the gate (Amos 5:15). Christians who desire to be faithful to all three biblical teachings will inevitably experience tension. As Mott states, "The command to submit reflects God's intention that the basic structures of society be instruments of good for his creation. The command to nonconformity is a recognition of the organization of social life in opposition to God. The command to establish justice places in the hands of God's servants the responsibility for recovering God's purposes for human society" (p. 143).

Mott's discussion of a biblical ethic for social change suggests a particular sequence that Christians need to follow as they attempt to change harmful and unjust social structures. First, Christians are obligated to work within the existing political and governmental system. In order for this effort to succeed, the political order must be a democracy which is fundamentally just. Responsive to the desires of its citizenry, such a system is capable of being reformed.

Second, Christians are obligated to seek social change through legal extragovernmental and extrapolitical means. When governments are fundamentally just, but unresponsive to citizens' needs, Christians, for the sake of justice, should resort to such measures as economic boycotts, peaceful marches, and orderly demonstrations in behalf of their cause. Examples of this type of social involvement are numerous. To bring pressure on the government to improve the conditions of migrant workers, Christians have boycotted grapes harvested by temporary immigrants specially contracted by the growers. Seeking to change federal laws, antiabortion groups have organized huge marches in Washington, D.C. Protesting against the dangers of nuclear war, other Christians have participated in demonstrations around production sites. The primary goal of such tactics is to call attention to the specific problem, in the hope that the government will be responsive and make the desired change.

Third, when legal efforts fail, Christians may resort to civil disobedience, an illegal though nonviolent method of attempting to bring about social change. This is the strategy for social change which fired the civil-rights movement in the United States when blacks were frustrated by the lack of government action prohibiting racial discrimination. More recently, persons have protested against the building of nuclear-power plants by blocking the entrances and thus risking arrest. By their very actions Christians who resort to civil disobedience are in effect declaring the existing governmental authority illegitimate and instead appealing to God's law as a higher power. Their goal is to draw attention to the harmfulness of an existing governmental law or practice, and to have it replaced by a law or practice more consistent with God's purposes.

Fourth, when all else fails, Christians may be called by God to engage in illegal violent means to bring about desired social change. They should do so, however, only as a last resort. We reiterate that in a democracy like the United States, changes in social structure can be brought about by the kinds of nonviolent means already discussed. However, in a society where there are no channels for peaceful change to secure human rights, Christians may feel impelled to use violence to overthrow the regime. Dietrich Bonhoeffer, for example, joined in the effort to overthrow Hitler through violence. Likewise, members of the French underground during World War II were convinced that violence was the only way of freeing their country from the brutal Nazi regime.

We suggest that the tenets of the just-war theory which we discussed earlier (pp. 301–2) are applicable in situations where Christians are tempted to seek to change harmful or unjust laws by participating in violent activity. Specifically, Christians should consider using force only if the cause is just, violence is a last resort and has a reasonable chance of success, the probable good outweighs the probable evil, and no injury will be done to innocent people. The reader will remember that another condition of just wars is that they are fought by lawful public authorities. While hardly acting as part of the existing public authority, Bonhoeffer and Christian members of the French underground clearly did not consider the Nazis a legitimate authority. In their view no lawful authority existed.

It must be pointed out that there are those who will under no circumstances condone the use of violence to change a society. In his insightful book, *Violence: Reflections from a Christian Perspective,* Jacques Ellul (1969) concludes that violence is wrong both on theological grounds because it harms fellow human beings who have been created in the image of God, and on practical grounds because the end result never justifies the violent means.

Some would make a distinction between doing violence to persons and doing violence to property. During the 1960s many Christians were opposed to the drafting of young men for participation in the Vietnam War. In response, some burned their draft cards, and others even burned the files at selective-service offices. More recently, some antiabortionists have sought to justify setting fire to abortion clinics on moral grounds.

As Christians choose to resort to more-extreme strategies, there is likely to be a corresponding decrease in the consensus hitherto enjoyed by churches and denominations. Therefore, it will be difficult to persuade a specific church or denomination to utilize, for example, civil disobedience as a means of pressuring the government to change abortion laws. Consequently, like-minded Christians may well become members of extra- or parachurch organizations that focus on a single cause. A curious phenomenon, however, is the formation and growth of certain churches on the basis of a common position on social issues. One example is local churches that have strongly identified with the Moral Majority movement.

An equally curious phenomenon has been the tendency for the boards of large mainline denominations to be marked by a liberal consensus on social issues which is not to be found among the laypersons who make up the denomination. Thus there often occurs a filtering-down process in which the local church, instead of originating social resolutions, simply approves of action taken by the minister-dominated hierarchy of the denomination. This decision-making process may explain why some members leave mainline churches for churches that are more theologically and politically conservative.

Those who view decision making in the church as a democratic procedure have problems with the methods used in mainline churches to come to positions on social involvement. On the other hand, those who accept a strong prophetic role for the clergy are more likely to justify these methods. There is support in the sociological literature for hierarchical decision-making. City, county, and state governments have a very poor record when it comes to combating racism and sexism. Significant reductions in racism and sexism came about only when the federal government began forcing local communities, counties, and states to comply with civil-rights laws. Racial prejudice declined only after discriminatory practices were outlawed. In chapter 5 we pointed out the importance of focusing our efforts upon racial discrimination rather than racial prejudice. In hindsight it now is clear that those denominations that dared to take prophetic stands and actions against racism in the 1950s and 1960s, even at the risk of losing members, were more faithful to biblical Christianity than were those that ignored the issue.

Holistic Social Involvement

Is one method of social involvement more biblical or more effective than another? We believe that an examination of the biblical material supports the legitimacy of each of the twelve paths to social change we have outlined. Christians who argue that only one method is biblical are

RALPH? OH, HE HASN'T FOUND HIS PATH TO CHRISTIAN SOCIAL INVOLVEMENT YET.

not being biblical themselves. We would do well to heed Mott's (1982:140) warning that "it is not for us to consult our personal predilections and pronounce which is the greatest, the primary, or the most powerful force for social change. Instead, we need a new boldness in affirming both Christian community and the tasks of the Christian in the world, and new creativity in carrying them out together. Both are given to us by God. Both flourish or fail together."

If each of the types of social involvement we have described is equally legitimate, someone might ask, "Does God desire that every individual believer, local church, denomination, and Christian organization follow every possible path, or can we bring honor to God by specializing?" As we pointed out in chapter 3, during the first half of the twentieth century Christianity in the United States became somewhat specialized. While the liberal wing of Christianity concentrated on changing sinful social structures, the conservative wing concentrated on changing sinful individuals. To argue that such a division represents a healthy church is like arguing that the temperature of a person with one foot in a bucket of ice and the other in a bucket of boiling water is, on average, very close to what it should be.

Such a bifurcation of kingdom work as prevailed earlier in this century is, we believe, a distortion of what God intends for the church to be. While each wing of the church was busy fulfilling its own sense of mission, it to a large extent was denying the legitimacy of the work of the other. It is important to keep in view Paul's analogy of the church as a living body, a unit made up of many parts (1 Cor. 12:12). The path each Christian takes towards social involvement will be complemented by the work of the other members of the body. As Paul writes:

> Now the body is not made up of one part but of many. If the foot should say, "Because I am not a hand, I do not belong to the body," it would not for that reason cease to be part of the body. . . . If the whole body were an eye, where would the sense of hearing be? If the whole body were an ear, where would the sense of smell be? But in fact God has arranged the parts in the body, every one of them, just as he wanted them to be. If they were all one part, where would the body be? As it is, there are many parts, but one body. [1 Cor. 12:14–20 NIV]

In verses 27 through 31 Paul uses the examples of apostles, prophets, teachers, and administrators to point out the importance and necessity of diversity and specialization in the Christian body.

Specialization in social involvement is, then, God's intent for individual believers, churches, and denominations. They must, however, always be aware of their functional interdependence with the other members of the body of Christ. The Salvation Army, for instance, which specializes in providing help for the poor and needy, functions interdependently with other denominations. Likewise, parachurch organizations like World Vision function interdependently with the body of Christ as a whole as they provide opportunities for Christians from many different denominations to help care for the poor and needy of the world. Charles Colson's parachurch organization allows a variety of Christians to become involved in prison ministries. An important point to bear in mind here is that sending a check to a Christian-oriented social ministry does not excuse us from becoming personally and directly involved in programs that aim at social improvements.

Holistic Christian ministry will incorporate many diverse paths to social change. The Christian organization that stresses revamping social structures, while ignoring the need for personal regeneration, is a distortion of what God intends the body of Christ to be. The Christian organization that stresses personal evangelism, but fails to see the need for changing social structures, is likewise perpetuating a distorted image of the true church.

Diversity and unity are not alternative options within the body of Christ; rather, the church is to be a unity of diverse parts. When a local church or Christian organization specializes in one type of social involvement, it needs to recognize its interdependence with the parts of Christ's kingdom that have other specialties. Rather than discrediting the paths to social change that they do not specialize in, churches need to find completeness by supporting and being supported by churches and parachurch organizations specializing in other forms of social involvement.

Topics for Review, Reflection, and Discussion

1. Is a church that is actively engaged in personal evangelism but not social action healthy? a church involved in social action but not evangelism?

2. When is it wise to mix Christianity with politics? When is it unwise?

3. What are the advantages and disadvantages of working exclusively within Christian organizations to combat social problems? of working within secular organizations?

4. Can you think of any examples in which Christians attempted to change harmful and unjust social structures without following a proper sequence—efforts within the system, legal extrapolitical activity, civil disobedience, violence? What were the results?

5. When is it right for a church to specialize in a given type of social involvement? When is it wrong?

Bibliography

Adorno, T., E. Frenkel-Brunswik, D. Levinson, and R. Sanford. 1950. *The authoritarian personality*. New York: Harper.

Allen, J. 1984. *Love and conflict: A covenantal model of Christian ethics.* Nashville: Abingdon.

Anderson, R. 1985. The gospel of the family. Fuller Theological Seminary. Unpublished manuscript.

Annis, H., and R. Smart. 1978. Arrests, readmissions and treatment following release from detoxication centers. *Journal of Studies on Alcohol* 39:1276–83.

Ansberry, C. 1988. Dumping the poor. *Wall Street Journal,* 29 November 1988, A-1, A-11.

Auletta, K. 1982. *The underclass.* New York: Random House.

Austin, R. 1988. *Hope for the land: Nature in the Bible.* Atlanta: John Knox.

Bacon, S. 1958. Alcoholics do not drink. *Annals of the American Academy of Political and Social Science* 315:55–64.

Bales, R. 1946. Cultural differences in rates of alcoholism. *Journal of Studies on Alcohol* 6:480–99.

Balswick, J. O., and J. K. Balswick. 1987. A theological basis for family relationships. *Journal of Psychology and Christianity* 6:37–49.

Balswick, J. O., and J. K. Balswick. 1989. *The family: A Christian perspective on the contemporary home.* Grand Rapids: Baker.

Balswick, J. O., and D. Ward. 1984. The church, the family, and issues of modernity. Consultation on a theology of the family. Seminar at Fuller Theological Seminary.

Banks, R. 1980. *Paul's idea of community.* Grand Rapids: Eerdmans.

Barnes, G. 1979. The alcoholic personality: A reanalysis of the literature. *Journal of Studies on Alcohol* 40:571–634.

Bartchy, S. 1984. Issues of power and a theology of the family. Consultation on a theology of the family. Seminar at Fuller Theological Seminary.

Beach, W. 1969. *Christian community and American society.* Philadelphia: Westminster.

Becker, H. 1953. Becoming a marihuana user. *American Journal of Sociology* 59:235–42.

Becker, H. 1970. *Campus power struggle.* Chicago: Aldine.

Bell, A., M. Weinberg, and S. Hammersmith. 1981. *Sexual preference: Its development in men and women.* Bloomington: Indiana University Press.

Bell, D. 1960. *The end of ideology.* New York: Free.

Bellah, R., R. Madsen, W. Sullivan, A. Swidler, and S. Tipton. 1985. *Habits of the heart: Individualism and commitment in American life.* Berkeley: University of California Press.

Berger, B., and P. Berger. 1983. *The war over the family.* Garden City, N.Y.: Doubleday.

Berger, P. 1967. *The sacred canopy.* Garden City, N.Y.: Doubleday.

Berger, P. 1986. *The capitalist revolution: Fifty propositions about prosperity, equality, and liberty.* New York: Basic.

Berger, P., B. Berger, and H. Kellner. 1973. *The homeless mind: Modernization and consciousness.* New York: Random House.

Billings, M. 1982. *Ideology and social psychology: Extremism, moderation and contradiction.* London: Blackwell.

Blum, R., et al. 1969. *Students and drugs.* San Francisco: Jossey-Bass.

Bonnie, R., and C. Whitebread. 1974. *The marihuana conviction: A history of marihuana prohibition in the United States.* Charlottesville: University of Virginia Press.

Booth, A., and J. Edwards. 1985. Age at marriage and marital instability. *Journal of Marriage and the Family* 47:67–75.

Brace, C. 1971. Introduction to Jensenism. In C. Brace, G. Gamble, and J. Bond, eds., *Race and intelligence,* 4–9. Washington, D.C.: American Anthropological Association.

Braithwaite, J. 1981. The myth of social class and criminality reconsidered. *American Sociological Review* 46:36–57.

Brecher, E. 1986. Drug laws and drug law enforcement: A review and evaluation based on 111 years of experience. *Drugs and Society* 1:1–27.

Brenner, J., R. Coles, and D. Meagher. 1970. *Drugs and youth: Medical, psychiatric, and legal facts.* New York: Liveright.

Bromley, D., and F. Britten. 1938. *Youth and sex.* New York: Harper.

Brown, H. 1984. What is liberation theology? In R. Nash, ed., *Liberation theology,* 3–15. Milford, Mich.: Mott Media.

Bureau of the Census. *See* U.S. Bureau of the Census.

Cahalan, D. 1970. *Problem drinkers.* San Francisco: Jossey-Bass.

Carson, R. 1962. *Silent spring.* Boston: Houghton Mifflin.

Cassens, J. 1970. *The Christian encounters drugs and drug abuse.* St. Louis: Concordia.

Chafetz, M. 1987. The third wave of prohibition is upon us. *Wall Street Journal,* 21 July 1987, 30.

Chalfant, P., and R. Beckley. 1977. Beguiling and betraying: The image of alcohol use in country music. *Journal of Studies on Alcohol* 38:1428–33.

Chalfant, P., R. Beckley, and C. Palmer. 1987. *Religion in contemporary society.* Palo Alto: Mayfield.

Christie, R., and M. Jahoda, eds. 1954. *Studies in the scope and method of the authoritarian personality.* New York: Free.

Cimons, M. 1990. U.S. 'lags behind' other nations in care of children, congressional report says. *Los Angeles Times,* 19 March 1990, A15.

Coalition for a New Foreign and Military Policy. 1984. U.S. and Soviet "first-strike" capabilities. Washington, D.C.: Coalition for a New Foreign and Military Policy.

Cochran, T. 1985. *The challenges to American values: Society, business, and religion.* New York: Oxford University Press.

Cohen, M. 1985. *Marijuana: Its effects on mind and body.* New York: Chelsea.

Conger, J., and W. Miller. 1966. *Personality, social class, and delinquency.* New York: Wiley.

Cotham, P., ed. 1979. *Christian social ethics.* Grand Rapids: Baker.

Cutter, C., and H. Cutter. 1987. Experience and change in Al-Anon family groups: Adult children of alcoholics. *Journal of Studies on Alcohol* 48:29–32.

Daly, H. 1977. *Steady-state economics.* San Francisco: Freeman.

Davis, J. 1985. *Evangelical ethics.* Phillipsburg, N.J.: Presbyterian and Reformed.

Dike, S. 1982. *Capital punishment in the United States*. Hackensack, N.J.: National Council on Crime and Delinquency.

DuBois, C. 1955. The dominant value profile of American culture. *American Anthropologist* 57:1232–39.

Duncan, G. 1984. *Years of poverty, years of plenty*. Ann Arbor: University of Michigan Press.

Ehrmann, W. 1959. *Premarital dating behavior*. New York: Holt, Rinehart.

Ellul, J. 1964. *The technological society*. New York: Random House.

Ellul, J. 1969. *Violence: Reflections from a Christian perspective*. New York: Seabury.

Ellul, J. 1976. *The ethics of freedom*. Grand Rapids: Eerdmans.

Ellul, J. 1984. *Money and power*. Downers Grove, Ill.: Inter-Varsity.

Farley, R. 1984. *Blacks and whites: Narrowing the gap?* Cambridge, Mass.: Harvard University Press.

Federal Bureau of Investigation. *See* U.S. Federal Bureau of Investigation.

Feiveson, H., and F. von Hippel. 1983. The freeze and the counterforce race. *Physics Today* 36:36–49.

Fenn, R. 1974. Toward a new sociology of religion. In P. McNamara, ed., *Religion American style*, 41–52. New York: Harper and Row.

Fields, C. 1987. Supreme Court upholds affirmative action plans in its first explicit ruling on voluntary goals. *Chronicle of Higher Education*, 1 April 1987, 1, 20.

Fingarette, H. 1988. *Heavy drinking: The myth of alcoholism as a disease*. Berkeley: University of California Press.

Forward, S., and J. Torres. 1986. *Men who hate women and the women who love them*. New York: Bantam.

Frazier, C., and J. Cochran. 1986. Official intervention, diversion from the juvenile justice system, and dynamics of human services work: Effects of a reform goal based on labeling theory. *Crime and Delinquency* 32 (April 1986): 157–76.

Frazier, E. 1986. *Barth and an evangelical feminist theology*. Ph.D. diss., Vanderbilt University.

Friedan, B. 1963. *The feminine mystique*. New York: Norton.

Fromm, E. 1941. *Escape from freedom*. New York: Holt, Rinehart and Winston.

Gallup, G., Jr. 1987a. Alcohol: Use and abuse in America. *Gallup Report* 265.

Gallup, G., Jr. 1987b. *Gallup Poll: Public opinion, 1987.* Wilmington, Del.: Scholarly Resources.

Gallup, G., Jr. 1988. *Gallup Poll: Public opinion, 1988.* Wilmington, Del.: Scholarly Resources.

Garfinkel, P. 1985. *In a man's world: Father, son, brother, friend and other roles men play.* New York: Norton.

Garrow, D. 1986. *Bearing the cross: Martin Luther King, Jr., and the Southern Leadership Conference.* New York: Morrow.

Gever, J., R. Kaufmann, D. Skole, and C. Vorosmarty. 1986. *Beyond oil: The threat to food and fuel in the coming decades.* Cambridge, Mass.: Ballinger.

Gilder, G. 1981. *Wealth and poverty.* New York: Basic.

Gillin, J. 1955. National and regional cultural values in the United States. *Social Forces* 34:107–13.

Glaser, D., B. Lander, and W. Abbott. 1971. Opiate addicted and non-addicted siblings in a slum area. *Social Problems* 13:510–21.

Glassner, B., and B. Berg. 1980. How Jews avoid alcohol problems. *American Sociological Review* 45:647–64.

Glassner, B., C. Carpenter, and B. Berg. 1986. Marihuana in the lives of adolescents. In G. Beschner and A. Friedman, eds., *Teen drug use,* 103–22. Lexington, Mass.: Heath.

Glazer, N. 1975. *Affirmative discrimination: Ethnic inequality and public policy.* New York: Basic.

Glick, P., and S. Lin. 1986. Recent changes in divorce and remarriage. *Journal of Marriage and the Family* 48:737–47.

Global 2000 Report to the President. 1982. Vol. 3. Washington, D.C.: Government Printing Office.

Glueck, S. 1956. Theory and fact in criminology. *British Journal of Delinquency* 7:92–109.

Glueck, S., and E. Glueck. 1950. *Unraveling juvenile delinquency.* Cambridge, Mass.: Harvard University Press.

Glueck, S., and E. Glueck. 1968. *Delinquents and nondelinquents in perspective.* Cambridge, Mass.: Harvard University Press.

Goddard, H. 1920. *Human efficiency and levels of intelligence.* Princeton, N.J.: Princeton University Press.

Gold, M. 1969. Juvenile delinquency as a symptom of alienation. *Journal of Social Issues* 25 (Spring 1969): 121–35.

Gomberg, E. 1985. Alcoholism: Psychological and psychosocial aspects.

In E. Gomberg, H. White, and J. Carpenter, eds., *Alcohol, science, and society revisited*, 186–204. Ann Arbor: University of Michigan Press.

Goodwin, D. 1985. Alcoholism and heredity: Update on the implacable fate. In E. Gomberg, H. White, and J. Carpenter, eds., *Alcohol, science, and society revisited*, 162–70. Ann Arbor: University of Michigan Press.

Gordis, E. 1987. Accessible and affordable health care for alcoholism and related problems: Strategy for cost containment. *Journal of Studies on Alcohol* 48:579–85.

Granberg-Michaelson, W. 1990. Reviving the whole earth. *Sojourners*, February-March 1990, 10–14.

Green, P. 1981. *The pursuit of inequality*. New York: Pantheon.

Grinspoon, L., and J. Bakalar. 1976. *Cocaine: A drug and its social evolution*. New York: Basic.

Gross, M. 1978. *The psychological society*. New York: Random House.

Grounds, V. 1987. Eschatology: Cutting the nerve of Christian social concern. *Evangelicals for Social Action Parley* 4.4.

Gutierrez, G. 1973. *A theology of liberation*. Maryknoll, N.Y.: Orbis.

Hancock, D. 1985. Alcohol and the church. In E. Gomberg, H. White, and J. Carpenter, eds., *Alcohol, science, and society revisited*, 355–70. Ann Arbor: University of Michigan Press.

Hanks, T. 1981. Why people are poor: What the Bible says. *Sojourners* 10:19–22.

Hart, A. 1988. Addicted to pleasure. *Christianity Today* 32 (9 Dec. 1988): 39–40.

Hart, H. 1987. The just shall live: Reformational reflections on public justice and racial attributes. *Christian Scholar's Review* 16:265–82.

Haupt, A. 1990. Preventing U.S. infant deaths. *Population Today* 18 (April 1990): 9.

Hayes, M. 1987. Alcoholism. In R. Harrison, ed., *Encyclopedia of biblical and Christian ethics*, 13. Nashville: Thomas Nelson.

Heitgerd, J., and R. Bursik, Jr. 1987. Extracommunity dynamics and the ecology of delinquency. *American Journal of Sociology* 92 (Jan. 1987): 775–87.

Hill, R. 1981. *Economic policies and black progress*. Washington, D.C.: National Urban League.

Hill, S. 1972. *Religion and the solid South*. Nashville: Abingdon.

Hilton, M., and W. Clark. 1987. Changes in American drinking patterns and problems, 1967–1984. *Journal of Studies on Alcohol* 48:515–22.

Hirschi, T., and M. Hindelang. 1977. Intelligence and delinquency: A revisionist review. *American Sociological Review* 42:571–87.

Hooton, E. 1939. *Crime and the man.* Cambridge, Mass.: Harvard University Press.

Horowitz, I., and W. Friedland. 1970. *The knowledge factory.* Chicago: Aldine.

Hughes, P. 1983. *Christian ethics in secular society.* Grand Rapids: Baker.

Hume, E. 1985. Provocative pages: A book attacking welfare system stirs furor in Washington. *Wall Street Journal,* 17 September 1985, 22.

Hunger Project. 1989. Jubilee Ministries. *Hunger Action Forum,* January 1989, 1.

Hunt, L., and C. Chambers. 1976. *The heroin epidemics.* New York: Halsted.

Hunter, J. 1983. *American evangelicalism: Conservative religion and the quandary of modernity.* New Brunswick, N.J.: Rutgers University Press.

Hutter, M. 1988. *The changing family: Comparative perspectives.* 2d ed. New York: Macmillan.

Jenkins, R., P. Heidemann, and J. Caputo. 1985. *No single cause: Juvenile delinquency and the search for effective treatment.* College Park, Md.: American Correctional Association.

Jensen, A. 1969. How much can we boost IQ and scholastic achievement? *Harvard Educational Review* 39:1–123.

Johanson, C. 1986. *Cocaine: A new epidemic.* New York: Chelsea.

Johnson, L. 1971. *The vantage point: Perspectives of the presidency, 1963–1969.* New York: Holt, Rinehart and Winston.

Keller, M. 1985a. Alcohol, science, and society: Hindsight and forecast. In E. Gomberg, H. White, and J. Carpenter, eds., *Alcohol, science, and society revisited,* 1–16. Ann Arbor: University of Michigan Press.

Keller, M. 1985b. On defining alcoholism: With comment on some other words. In E. Gomberg, H. White, and J. Carpenter, eds., *Alcohol, science, and society revisited,* 119–33. Ann Arbor: University of Michigan Press.

Kennard, D. 1984. A Christian critique of development perspectives: Modernization and dependency. *American Scientific Affiliation* 36:162–68.

Kinsey, A., et al. 1948. *Sexual behavior in the human male*. Philadelphia: Saunders.

Kinsey, A., et al. 1953. *Sexual behavior in the human female*. Philadelphia: Saunders.

Klein, M. 1971. *Street gangs and street workers*. Englewood Cliffs, N.J.: Prentice-Hall.

Kluckhohn, C. 1970. *Mirror for man*. New York: Fawcett World.

Knobelsdorff, K. 1987. Employee assistance programs help workers with drug and alcohol problems. *Christian Science Monitor*, 22 October 1987, 12:1.

Kraybill, D. 1980. Jesus and the stigmatized: A sociological analysis of the four Gospels. In C. DeSanto, C. Redekop, and W. Smith-Hinds, eds., *A reader in sociology: Christian perspectives*, 399–413. Scottdale, Pa.: Herald.

Kraybill, D. 1982. *Facing nuclear war*. Scottdale, Pa.: Herald.

Lab, S., and J. Whitehead. 1988. An analysis of juvenile correctional treatment. *Crime and Delinquency* 34 (Jan. 1988): 60–83.

Leerhsen, C. 1988. Alcohol and the family. *Newsweek*, 18 January 1988, 62–68.

Levy, M. 1967. *Modernization and the structure of societies*. Princeton, N.J.: Princeton University Press.

Lewis, C. S. 1970. The humanitarian theory of punishment. In *God in the dock: Essays on theology and ethics*, 287–300. Grand Rapids: Eerdmans.

Lewis, O. 1968. The culture of poverty. In D. Moynihan, ed., *On understanding poverty: Perspectives from the social sciences*, 187–200. New York: Basic.

Lewis, R., and G. Spanier, 1979. Theorizing about the quality and stability of marriage. In W. Burr, R. Hill, F. Nye, and I. Reiss, eds., *Contemporary theories about the family*, 1:268–94. New York: Free.

Lieber, C. 1985. Medical issues: The disease of alcoholism. In E. Gomberg, H. White, and J. Carpenter, eds., *Alcohol, science, and society revisited*, 233–61. Ann Arbor: University of Michigan Press.

Linsky, A., M. Straus, and J. Colby, Jr. 1985. Stressful events, stressful conditions, and alcohol-related problems in the United States: A partial test of Bales' theory. *Journal of Studies on Alcohol* 46:72–80.

Linsky, A., M. Straus, and J. Colby, Jr. 1986. Drinking norms and alcohol-related problems in the United States. *Journal of Studies on Alcohol* 47:384–93.

Linthicum, R. 1990. *City of God: City of Satan*. Grand Rapids: Zondervan.

Louria, D., T. Hensle, and J. Rose. 1970. Complications in heroin addiction. In O. Byrd, ed., *Medical readings on drug abuse*, 204–6. Reading, Mass.: Addison-Wesley.

McBride, N. 1988. "Zero tolerance": Zero effect? *Christian Science Monitor*, 23 August 1988, 3:3.

McGarrell, E., and T. Flanagan, eds. 1985. *Sourcebook of criminal justice statistics: 1984*. Washington, D.C.: Government Printing Office.

McGill, M. 1985. *The McGill report on male intimacy*. New York: Harper and Row.

Macklin, E. 1980. Nontraditional family forms: A decade of research. *Journal of Marriage and the Family* 42:905–22.

Macklin, E. 1987. Nontraditional family forms. In M. Sussman and S. Steinmetz, eds., *Handbook of marriage and the family*, 317–53. New York: Plenum.

McKnight, J. 1989. Why "servanthood" is bad. *The Other Side*, January-February 1989, 38–40.

McLean, S. 1984. The language of covenant and a theology of the family. Consultation on a theology of the family. Seminar at Fuller Theological Seminary.

Managing a Delicate Balance: Arms Control and the Strategic Defense Initiative. 1987. *Carnegie Quarterly* 32.1:1–9.

Marsden, G. 1980. *Fundamentalism and American culture*. New York: Oxford University Press.

Marx, G. 1967. Religion: Opiate or inspiration of civil rights militancy among Negroes? *American Sociological Review* 32:64–72.

Marx, K. 1964. *Economic and philosophical manuscripts of 1844*. Translated by M. Milligan II. New York: International.

Masserman, J. 1976. Alcoholism: Disease or dis-ease? *International Journal of Mental Health* 5:3–15.

Matsueda, R. 1988. The current status of differential association theory. *Crime and Delinquency* 34 (July 1988): 277–306.

Mayer, J. 1943. *Max Weber and German politics*. London: Faber and Faber.

Mead, M. 1935. *Sex and temperament in three primitive societies*. New York: Morrow.

Methvin, E. 1985. How Uncle Sam robbed America's poor. *Reader's Digest*, April 1985, 135–44.

Middelmann, U. 1987. A response to Stephen Mott. *Transformation* 4 (June-Dec. 1987): 36–40.

Moberg, D. 1972. *The great reversal.* Philadelphia: Lippincott.

Morland, J. K. 1969. Race awareness among American and Hong Kong Chinese children. *American Journal of Sociology* 75:360–74.

Morland, J. K., and C. Hwang. 1981. Racial/ethnic identity of preschool children: Comparing Taiwan, Hong Kong, and the United States. *Journal of Cross-cultural Psychology* 12:409–24.

Mott, S. 1982. *Biblical ethics and social change.* New York: Oxford University Press.

Mott, S. 1987. The Bible and economics: The contribution of the Bible to economic thought. *Transformation* 4 (June-Dec. 1987): 25–34.

Mouw, R. 1978. Toward a theology of social change. Paper presented at the Second IFACS Sociology Conference at Wheaton College.

Mouw, R. 1988. The life of bondage in the light of grace. *Christianity Today* 32 (9 Dec. 1988): 41–44.

Murray, Charles. 1984. *Losing ground: American social policy, 1950–1980.* New York: Basic.

Musto, D. 1986. Lessons of the first cocaine epidemic. *Wall Street Journal,* 11 June 1986.

Musto, D. 1987. *The American disease: Origins of narcotic control.* Rev. ed. New York: Oxford University Press.

Nash, R., ed. 1984. *Liberation theology.* Milford, Mich.: Mott Media.

National Council on Alcoholism. 1987. *Facts on alcoholism and alcohol-related problems.* Rev. ed. New York: National Council on Alcoholism.

National Institute of Mental Health. 1970. *Report on the XYY chromosomal abnormality.* Washington, D.C.: Government Printing Office.

National Institute on Drug Abuse. 1987a. *National household survey on drug abuse.* Rockville, Md.: U.S. Department of Health and Human Services.

National Institute on Drug Abuse. 1987b. *Drug abuse and drug abuse research.* Rockville, Md.: U.S. Department of Health and Human Services.

Niebuhr, H. R. 1951. *Christ and culture.* New York: Harper and Row.

Nilsen, M. 1987. Changing those things we can: A Christian approach to alcohol. *The Other Side* 23 (March 1987): 34–37.

Norwood, R. 1985. *Women who love too much.* New York: Simon and Schuster.

Novak, M. 1982. *The spirit of democratic capitalism.* New York: Simon and Schuster.

Novak, M. 1986. *Will it liberate? Questions about liberation theology.* Mahwah, N.J.: Paulist.

O'Hare, W. 1987. America's welfare population: Who gets what? *Population Trends and Public Policy* 13 (Sept. 1987). Washington, D.C.: Population Reference Bureau.

O'Hare, W. 1988. The rise of poverty in rural America. *Population Trends and Public Policy* 15 (July 1988). Washington, D.C.: Population Reference Bureau.

Osherson, S. 1986. *Finding our fathers: The unfinished business of manhood.* New York: Free.

Pandina, R. 1985. Effects of alcohol on psychological processes. In E. Gomberg, H. White, and J. Carpenter, eds., *Alcohol, science, and society revisited,* 38–62. Ann Arbor: University of Michigan Press.

Pattison, M. 1984. The church and the healing of families. Consultation on a theology of the family. Seminar at Fuller Theological Seminary.

Peele, S. 1986. The implications and limitations of genetic models of alcoholism and other addictions. *Journal of Studies on Alcohol* 47:63–73.

Perkins, J. 1976. *Let justice roll down.* Ventura, Calif.: Regal.

Perkins, J. 1981. *A call to wholistic ministry.* Arlington, Va.: Open-Door.

President's Commission on Law Enforcement and Administration of Justice. 1967. *The challenge of crime in a free society.* Washington, D.C.: Government Printing Office.

Price-Bonham, S., and J. O. Balswick. 1980. The noninstitutions: Divorce, desertion, and remarriage. *Journal of Marriage and the Family* 42:959–72.

Public Policy Report. 1984. Bread for the world. *Evangelicals for Social Action Newsletter* 1:1–2.

Public Policy Report. 1987. Public policy and the poor. *Evangelicals for Social Action Newsletter* 3:1–4.

Ramsey, P. 1961. *War and the Christian conscience: How shall modern war be conducted justly?* Durham, N.C.: Duke University Press.

Rauschenbusch, W. 1919. *A theology for the social gospel.* New York: Macmillan.

Reich, C. 1968. *The greening of America.* New York: Random House.

Reichart, S. 1969. A greater space in which to breathe: What art and drama tell us about alienation. *Journal of Social Issues* 25 (Spring 1969): 137–46.

Reiss, I. 1967. *The social context of premarital sexual permissiveness.* New York: Holt, Rinehart and Winston.

Reiss, I. 1971. *The family system in America.* New York: Holt, Rinehart and Winston.

Reiss, I. 1986. *Journey into sexuality: An exploratory voyage.* Englewood Cliffs, N.J.: Prentice-Hall.

Riesman, D. 1950. *The lonely crowd.* New Haven, Conn.: Yale University Press.

Roach, M. 1985. The biochemical and physiological effects of alcohol. In E. Gomberg, H. White, and J. Carpenter, eds., *Alcohol, science, and society revisited,* 17–37. Ann Arbor: University of Michigan Press.

Roe, A. 1945. Children of alcoholic parents raised in foster homes. In *Alcohol, science, and society,* 115–27. New Haven, Conn.: Quarterly Journal of Studies on Alcohol.

Rokeach, M. 1960. *The open and closed mind.* New York: Basic.

Rookmaaker, R. 1970. *Modern art and the death of a culture.* London: Inter-Varsity.

Rosenbaum, D. 1987. The theory and research behind neighborhood watch: Is it a sound fear and crime reduction strategy? *Crime and Delinquency* 33 (Jan. 1987): 103–34.

Rossi, A. 1984. Gender and parenthood. *American Sociological Review* 49:1–19.

Rostow, W. 1961. *The stages of economic growth: A non-communist manifesto.* New York: Cambridge University Press.

Rudy, D. 1986. *Becoming alcoholic: Alcoholics Anonymous and the reality of alcoholism.* Carbondale, Ill.: Southern Illinois University Press.

Sadoun, R., G. Lolli, and M. Silverman. 1965. *Drinking in French culture.* New Haven, Conn.: College and University.

Schaeffer, F. 1970. *Pollution and the death of man.* Wheaton, Ill.: Tyndale.

Schlafly, P. 1972. *The Phyllis Schlafly Report,* May 1972.

Schneider, A. 1984. Divesting status offenses from juvenile court jurisdiction. *Crime and Delinquency* 30 (Jan. 1984): 347–70.

Schuman, H., C. Steeh, and L. Bobo. 1985. *Racial attitudes in America: Trends and interpretations.* Cambridge, Mass.: Harvard University Press.

Scott, L. 1980. *Economic koinonia within the body of Christ.* Mexico City: Editorial Kyrios.

Seeman, M. 1957. On the meaning of alienation. In L. Coser and B. Rosenberg, eds., *Sociological theory,* 4th ed., 401–14. New York: Macmillan.

Seeman, M. 1959. On the meaning of alienation. *American Sociological Review* 24:783–91.

Shaw, C., and H. McKay. 1969. *Juvenile delinquency and urban areas.* Rev. ed. Chicago: University of Chicago Press.

Sheldon, W. 1949. *Varieties of delinquent youth.* New York: Harper.

Shoemaker, S. 1965. *Extraordinary living for ordinary men.* Grand Rapids: Zondervan.

Simpson, D. 1989. *The politics of compassion and transformation.* Athens, Ohio: Ohio University Press.

Simpson, G., and J. M. Yinger. 1985. *Racial and cultural minorities.* 5th ed. New York: Plenum.

Sinclair, A. 1966. *The better half: The emancipation of the American woman.* New York: Harper.

Slater, P. 1970. *The pursuit of loneliness.* Boston: Beacon.

Smedes, L. 1984. *Forgive and forget.* New York: Harper and Row.

Smelser, N. 1973. Processes of social change. In N. Smelser, ed., *Sociology: An introduction,* 2d ed., 709–61. New York: Wiley.

Smith, A. 1776. *An inquiry into the nature and causes of the wealth of nations.* Chicago: University of Chicago Press, 1977 reprint.

Smith, K. 1989. The homeless and "points of light." *Christian Science Monitor,* 31 May 1989, 18.

Snyder, C. 1958. *Alcohol and the Jews.* Carbondale, Ill.: Southern Illinois University Press.

Soviet Military Power, 1985. 1985. Washington, D.C.: Government Printing Office.

Spanier, G., and R. Margolis. 1979. Marital separation and extramarital sexual behavior. Paper presented to the International Academy of Sex Research, Prague, Czechoslovakia.

Stratton, R., A. Zeiner, and A. Paredes. 1978. Tribal affiliation and prevalence of alcohol problems. *Journal of Studies on Alcohol* 39:1166–77.

Straus, R. 1985. The social costs of alcohol. In E. Gomberg, H. White, and J. Carpenter, eds., *Alcohol, science, and society revisited*, 134–48. Ann Arbor: University of Michigan Press.

Stromsten, A. 1982. *Recovery: Stories of alcoholism and survival.* New Brunswick, N.J.: Rutgers Center of Alcohol Studies.

Struck, D. 1988. One law prevails in war on drugs: Supply and demand. *Baltimore Sun,* 1 May 1988, 1A–2A.

Sutherland, E., and D. Cressey. 1970. *Criminology.* 8th ed. Philadelphia: Lippincott.

Szinovacz, M. 1987. Family power: Relations and processes. In M. Sussman and S. Steinmetz, eds., *Handbook of marriage and the family,* 651–93. New York: Plenum.

Tarter, R., A. Alterman, and K. Edwards. 1985. Vulnerability to alcoholism in men: A behavior-genetic perspective. *Journal of Studies on Alcohol* 46:329–56.

Taylor, J., J. Helzer, and L. Robins. 1986. Moderate drinking in ex-alcoholics: Recent studies. *Journal of Studies on Alcohol* 47: 115–21.

Taylor, L. 1984. *Born to crime: The genetic causes of criminal behavior.* Westport, Conn.: Greenwood.

Terman, L. 1938. *Psychological factors in marital happiness.* New York: McGraw-Hill.

Thistlethwaite, S., ed. 1986. *A just peace church.* New York: Office for Church in Society, United Church of Christ.

Thomas, W., and D. Thomas. 1928. *The child in America.* New York: Knopf.

Thornberry, T., and M. Farnworth. 1982. Social correlates of criminal involvement: Further evidence on the relationship between social status and criminal behavior. *American Sociological Review* 47:505–18.

Ullman, A. 1958. Sociocultural backgrounds of alcoholism. *Annals of the American Academy of Political and Social Science* 315:48–54.

U.S. Bureau of the Census. 1987. *Statistical abstract of the United States, 1987.* Washington, D.C.: Government Printing Office.

U.S. Bureau of the Census. 1988. *Statistical abstract of the United States, 1988.* Washington, D.C.: Government Printing Office.

U.S. Bureau of the Census. 1989. *Statistical abstract of the United States, 1989.* Washington, D.C.: Government Printing Office.

U.S. Federal Bureau of Investigation. 1987. *Uniform crime reports—1986.* Washington, D.C.: Government Printing Office.

U.S. Federal Bureau of Investigation. 1988. *Uniform crime reports—1987.* Washington, D.C.: Government Printing Office.

U.S. House of Representatives, Select Committee on Crime. 1970. *Marihuana.* Washington, D.C.: Government Printing Office.

U.S. Law Week. 1988. Traynor v. Turnage, and McKelvey v. Turnage. Nos. 86–622 and 86–737. *Law Week* 56:4319–28.

Vaillant, G. 1983. *The natural history of alcoholism: Causes, patterns, and paths to recovery.* Cambridge, Mass.: Harvard University Press.

Van Dyke, F. 1985. Beyond Sand County: A biblical perspective on environmental ethics. *Journal of the American Scientific Affiliation* 37:40–48.

Vernon, G. 1962. *Sociology of religion.* New York: McGraw-Hill.

Vold, G., and T. Bernard. 1986. *Theoretical criminology.* 3d ed. New York: Oxford University Press.

vonKnorring, L., et al. 1987. Personality traits in subtypes of alcoholics. *Journal of Studies on Alcohol* 48: 523–27.

Walker, L. 1986. Resource managers and the environmental ethic. *Journal of the American Scientific Affiliation* 38:96–102.

Wallack, L., W. Breed, and J. Cruz. 1987. Alcohol on prime-time television. *Journal of Studies on Alcohol* 48:33–38.

Wallerstein, I. 1976, 1980. *The modern world-system.* Vols. 1–2. New York: Academic.

Walter, P. 1982. Our drinking dilemma. *The Lutheran,* 17 November 1982.

Weil, A., N. Zinberg, and J. Nelsen. 1968. Clinical and psychological effects of marihuana in man. *Science* 162:1234–42.

Weis, D., and J. Jurich. 1985. Size of community of residence as a predictor of attitudes toward extramarital sexual relations. *Journal of Marriage and the Family* 47:173–78.

Weitzman, L. 1985. *The divorce revolution: The unexpected social and economic consequences for women and children in America.* New York: Free.

Wexler, P. 1983. *Critical social psychology.* Boston: Routledge and Kegan Paul.

White, L., Jr. 1967. The historical roots of our ecological crisis. *Science* 155:1203–7.

Wilkinson, L., ed. 1980. *Earthkeeping: Christian stewardship of natural resources.* Grand Rapids: Eerdmans.

Wilkinson, L. 1983. Environmental epistemologies: A Christian response. Paper presented at the annual meeting of the American Scientific Affiliation, Newberg, Oregon.

Williams, J., and J. K. Morland. 1976. *Race, color, and the young child.* Chapel Hill: University of North Carolina Press.

Williams, R., Jr. 1970. *American society.* 3d ed. New York: Knopf.

Wilson, J. Q., and R. Herrnstein. 1985. *Crime and human nature.* New York: Simon and Schuster.

Wilson, W. 1980. *The declining significance of race.* 2d ed. Chicago: University of Chicago Press.

Wilson, W. 1987. *The truly disadvantaged: The inner city, the underclass, and public policy.* Chicago: University of Chicago Press.

Wolterstorff, N. 1983. *Until justice and peace embrace.* Grand Rapids: Eerdmans.

Wooldredge, J. 1988. Differentiating the effects of juvenile court sentences on eliminating recidivism. *Journal of Research in Crime and Delinquency* 25 (Aug. 1988): 264–300.

Yoder, J. 1972. *The original revolution.* Scottdale, Pa.: Herald.

Zackon, F. 1986. *Heroin: The street narcotic.* New York: Chelsea.

Zelditch, M. 1955. Role differentiation in the nuclear family: A comparative study. In T. Parsons and R. Bales, eds., *The family, socialization and interaction process,* 307–51. Glencoe, Ill.: Free.

Scripture Index

Genesis

1:27—145, 156, 246
1:28–30—246
1:29—231
2:24—56
2:25—54, 56, 180
3:17–18—245
6:8—51
6:18—49
6:22—49
9:6—302
9:9–10—248
9:16—50
15:18—49
17:7—49
17:9—49

Exodus

3:7–10—268
5:17—268
6:2–5—268
21:12–14—89
21:18–19—92
21:23–25—95
21:23–36—91
21:26—92
21:33–34—92
22:1—93
22:3—93
22:25–27—272
23:10–11—272

Leviticus

6:30—93
10:9—205
16:20—93

19:9–10—272
25:2–5—248
25:25–28—95

Numbers

6:3–20—205

Deuteronomy

7:23–24—304
11:26–28—50
15:7–8—272
15:11—272
17:15–20—248
22:22–24—90

Judges

6:16—302
13:4—205

1 Samuel

1:13–18—205
15—307

Psalms

8:6–8—248
72:12–14—271
82:3–4—273
103:6–7—268
107:39–41—95

Proverbs

14:31—273
20:1—205

21:13—292
22:9—273
23:29–35—205
28:27—273

Isaiah

5:22—205
11:6–8—61
11:6–9—249
28:7—205
45:22—268
58—292

Jeremiah

22:16—292

Ezekiel

44:21—205

Amos

5:15—319
8:4, 7—291

Matthew

5:21—96
5:23–24—93
5:38—90
5:38–44—300–01, 302
6:19–21—120
6:21—47, 158
8:5–13—119
10:34—307
10:42—315
11:19—119

Subject Index